PENGUIN BOOKS

THE LONG MARCH 1935

Dick Wilson was born in Epsom in 1928, graduated with first class honours from Oxford, and went on to the University of California at Berkeley. He worked in the Far East as an editor for ten years, and has been a journalist with the *Financial Times* and the *Guardian*. He now edits the *China Quarterly*, the journal published by the University of London. His previous publications include *A Quarter of Mankind* and *Asia Awakes*.

DICK WILSON

THE LONG MARCH 1935

*The Epic of Chinese Communism's
Survival*

PENGUIN BOOKS

Penguin Books Ltd, Harmondsworth, Middlesex, England
Penguin Books, 625 Madison Avenue, New York, New York 10022, U.S.A.
Penguin Books Australia Ltd, Ringwood, Victoria, Australia
Penguin Books Canada Ltd, 2801 John Street, Markham, Ontario, Canada L3R 1B4
Penguin Books (N.Z.) Ltd, 182–190 Wairau Road, Auckland 10, New Zealand

—

First published by Hamish Hamilton 1971
This revised edition published in Penguin Books 1977

—

Copyright © Dick Wilson, 1971, 1977
All rights reserved

—

Made and printed in Great Britain
by Hazell Watson & Viney Ltd,
Aylesbury, Bucks
Set in Linotype Juliana

To Sally

Contents

PART THREE *The Consequences*

APPENDICES

MAPS

Acknowledgements

TRIBUTE must first of all be paid to the late Edgar Snow and Jerome Ch'ên, the two pioneers in reconstructing the Long March, I am proud to regard both as friends, and have been greatly helped by them in writing this book.

I am also heavily indebted to many friends who assisted with translating from the Chinese and in locating documents and other material, especially to Frank Aller, Robert Tung, Lee Yip Lim, Dieter Heinzig, Smarlo Ma, Olof von Randow, M. H. Su and Kayser Sung. Trygve Lötveit was kind enough to let me see a typescript of his work on the Kiangsi Soviet before publication, and Huang Chen-hsia generously allowed me to see an advance chapter of the book *Communist China's High Command* by himself and William Whitson. Bill Brugger and David Wilson also made invaluable suggestions regarding source material.

My thanks also to the libraries of the School of Oriental and African Studies in London, the Union Research Institute and United States Consulate-General in Hong Kong and the University of Singapore for extending facilities to me.

Finally, I express my appreciation to Juminah binte Kamis for typing the book, and to Malcolm Gabriel and Francis Kee for drawing the maps.

Thanks are due to the following for permission to quote published material: the *China Quarterly* for Howard L. Boorman's 'Mao Tse-tung' (London, No. 16) and Jerome Ch'ên's 'Resolutions of the Tsunyi Conference' (London, No. 40); the Monthly Review Press, New York, for Agnes Smedley's *The Great Road*; the Oxford University Press for Jerome Ch'ên's *Mao and the Chinese Revolution*; Mr Edgar Snow for *Red Star Over China* and *The Battle for Asia*; Mrs Helen Foster Snow for *Red Dust: Autobio-*

graphies of Chinese Communists; Weidenfeld & Nicolson Ltd and McGraw-Hill Company Inc. for Samuel B. Griffith's *The Chinese People's Liberation Army*.

DICK WILSON

A word about Chinese names

To write a Chinese name in another language is an arbitrary business, since the Chinese script is ideographic, not phonetic – the writing expresses only the meaning and not the sound. Transliteration into English, therefore, is a matter of choosing which roman letters best convey the sound of the name as it would be spoken by a native of Peking.*

There are four principal systems of transliteration used in the West, the Wade-Giles (most common in Anglo-Saxon scholarship), the *pinyin* (which the Chinese government itself adopted in 1958 and its standard romanization system), the EFEO (Ecole Française de l'Extrême Orient) and the Lessing (the German system).

Thus the family name of China's late Prime Minister Chou En-lai (all Chinese names, of course, put the family name first and the given name – usually two names, hyphenated – last), is spelt Zhou in Peking's foreign-language publications, Chou in London, Tcheou in Paris and Dschou in Berlin. Mao Tse-tung's given name is Ze dong, Tse-tung, Tsé-toung and Tsö-tong, respectively. The province which Anglo-Saxons know as Kiangsi takes on, in

* This is different from the name as spoken by a Cantonese or a Szechuanese. Thus Chiang Chung-cheng has become immortalized to the West as Chiang Kai-shek, because that is how the characters of his name sound when read aloud by a native of Canton, headquarters of the Kuomintang movement in the years when Chiang first became famous. But normally foreigners take their sounds of Chinese names from the way they are spoken in Peking, centre of the language called *putunghua* – or Mandarin – which prevails across most of northern and parts of central China and which the Chinese are trying to make their national speech.

modern Chinese foreign-language publications (and, for instance, in the various editions of Nagel's excellent *Guide* to China), the form Jiang Xi.

The Wades-Giles and EFEO systems have the further refinement of using apostrophes to indicate a softening of a consonant. The sound p is rendered p', while the sound b is rendered p. Thus P'eng is pronounced Pung, while Peng is pronounced Bung, and similar rules apply to K'ang and Kang, T'eng and Teng. Accents are also used – Ch'en in Wade-Giles is Chen in *pinyin*, Ts'ön in EFEO, and Tjön in Lessing (and is pronounced identically in all four systems as Chun).

For the Anglo-Saxon man in the street these apostrophes and accents are meaningless, and their consistent use in the Wade-Giles system creates a scholastic barrier to understanding and sympathy. They are usually dropped, therefore, in newspapers, magazines, atlases, encyclopaedias and reference books.

An Anglo-Saxon author seeking a wide readership is thus placed in a dilemma. The pedantry of Wade-Giles and the total unfamiliarity of *pinyin* put both out of court, and the best compromise seems to be Wade-Giles without the 'frills' of accent or apostrophe. This is how the ninety-nine per cent of readers of this book who have not undertaken the formal study of the Chinese language will have read the well-known names in their papers and periodicals, and this seems the best way to present a story to them without putting them off. My apologies to the scholars. I have retained an accent or apostrophe only where a man uses it for his own name when writing in English – and thus positively requests us so to know him.

Introduction

ON 16 October 1934, about 100,000 Chinese Communist men and women set out on the most extraordinary march in human history. Abandoning their soviet base (as large as Belgium) in the south-central province of Kiangsi, they burst through the stranglehold of their enemy, Chiang Kai-shek's Nationalist or Kuomintang forces, and began a trek on foot which was to last for a whole year and take them 6,000 circuitous miles to the other end of China.

The leaders began the Long March divided and demoralized. The evacuation of the Kiangsi base could be viewed only as a defeat, owed in large part to the mistakes and bad judgement of the Chinese Communist Party leaders and their Russian and other European Marxist advisers. The exigencies of the March resolved this dissension; during its course Mao Tse-tung emerged as the most powerful leader, a position which, though it did not allow him always to have his own way, he never afterwards entirely forfeited.

The Long March led the Communists through eleven provinces, over raging rivers and snow-capped mountain ranges, through swamps and forests. They had to fight against Nationalist armies as well as the troops of provincial warlords, local bandits and hostile tribesmen. At one point where water was unknown they could survive only by drinking their own urine. Soon after they began their odyssey, the collapse of most of the other scattered Communist bases in various parts of China left on the shoulders of Mao and his colleagues on the Long March the burden of the survival of Communism in China. As Mao's men disappeared from view in the impenetrable interior of Western China, abutting on Tibet, many observers assumed that Chiang Kai-shek had won his civil war and that Communism was decisively beaten in China – possibly in Asia as a whole.

But when the ragged remnants of Mao's band approached Yenan, in the shadow of the Great Wall in Northern China, at the end of October 1935, the tide had unexpectedly turned. Mao's leadership, acting upon the discipline and dedication which the rigours of the Long March had forged, transformed the Communist movement into the driving force which succeeded, fourteen years later, in taking over the entire country and pushing the Nationalists into the sea. The Long March thus changed in character from a desperate retreat to a prelude of victory.

This extraordinary epic has become one of the great stories of the twentieth century. Edgar Snow, the American journalist, was one of the first to reach Mao's headquarters after the conclusion of the Long March, and to transmit to an astonished world, in his book *Red Star Over China*, some of its detail. 'Adventure, exploration, discovery, human courage and cowardice, ecstasy and triumph, suffering, sacrifice, and loyalty, and then through it all, like a flame, an undimmed ardour and undying hope and amazing revolutionary optimism of those thousands of youth who would not admit defeat either by man or nature or God or death – all this and more seemed embodied in the history of an odyssey unequalled in modern times.' [1]

This was the reaction of the first outsider to be told the story. But Snow was only the first to record the awe and admiration of a world which had supposed that such feats were things of the past. Field Marshal Lord Montgomery called the Long March 'an amazing feat of endurance'.[2] Simone de Beauvoir wrote the story of modern China with '*The Long March*' as a title, and it has become an image in every continent of the continuing possibilities of human endurance and determination.

General Samuel B. Griffith, the American military historian, described it as 'an even more majestic achievement' than the retreat of the 10,000 Greeks from Persia to the Black Sea four centuries before Christ: 'the Chinese Communists repeatedly tested and confirmed man's ability to undergo indescribable hardship, to overcome every challenge placed in his path by a nature determined to thwart him; to trumph over enemies equally determined to destroy him; and to reach his goal. Alike, Greeks and Chinese endured scorching heat, bitter cold, thirst and hunger. Alike, they climbed snow-covered mountains, ate roots, slept in the snow, marched and fought and marched again. Alike, they reconciled internal disputes that threatened to tear them apart. Alike, they survived.' [3] But Mao's Chinese marched 6,000 miles to Xenophon's Greeks' 2,000; they marched for a year, not merely four months; they were ten times more numerous than the Greeks; and their survival had infinitely more historical significance than Xenophon's companions'.

In China itself *Chang Cheng*, or the 25,000-Li * March, has become part of the mythology of modern Chinese nationalism and Communism. The official record shows that the 1 Army Corps, the vanguard of the First Front Army, covered 18,088 *li*, not 25,000, but the latter figure has become entrenched in the mythology. 18,000 *li* is still as far as from New York to San Francisco and back again.

'The Red Army fears not the trials of the Long March
And thinks nothing of a thousand mountains and rivers.' [4]

So Mao Tse-tung wrote in one of the poems which he composed during the Long March. One of the principal concerns of the political leadership in Peking today is to try to re-create, if only in part, the spirit and earnestness of this, the Chinese Communists' finest hour.

The Long March secured the survival, and therefore the eventual victory, of the Chinese Communist Party in the struggle which raged for almost thirty years between the Left and the Right for the privilege of occupying the Dragon throne in Peking and of presiding over the fateful process of modernizing this ancient nation. It also ensured that the Communist rulers of China in the 1950s, 1960s and 1970s would be profoundly influenced by the experience.

Their suspicious attitude towards the Soviet Union and their fierce independence of Moscow's tutelage; their distrust of the city as a modern institution and of urban life as a corrupting and

---

* One *li* equals almost one-third of a mile.

demoralizing force; the unity, discipline and secrecy which characterized the conduct of their party's affairs and their government's operations for so long; their idealism and simplicity, and their preference for the guerrilla ethic over the values of the technocrat; the long ascendancy of Mao Tse-tung over the Chinese Communist Party and in so many sectors of the world Communist movement as a whole – all these either have their roots in the Long March, or else were so crystallized and refined during those twelve months that the stamp of the Long March is indelibly marked on them.

As General Griffith remarks in his book on the Chinese People's Liberation Army: 'The Long March placed its peculiar and irrevocable mark on the Party and the Red Army. The experience of incredible trials surmounted and dangers overcome confirmed the positions of the leaders who shared them. Ever since those days, days when each man repeatedly faced an ultimate test in one form or another, the "Long Marchers" have until recently practically monopolized top positions in the hierarchies of the Party and its army. From this trial emerged a group of tested leaders, supremely confident of their ability to shape the destiny of their Party and their country. And from it, too, sprang an indoctrinated army endowed with a rich experience, convinced of the righteousness of its cause and equipped with a dynamic doctrine of guerrilla and mobile war.' [5]

In a sense the power struggle which broke out in Peking at the time of the Great Proletarian Cultural Revolution in 1966–9 represented conflict over the continuing relevance of the Long March experience in governing the China of the 1960s and 1970s.

It is curious that an event so stirring in its heroism and so crucial for world history has been relatively neglected by writers and scholars. Edgar Snow's *Red Star Over China* is still regarded by many as the authoritative book on the Long March, although it is now forty years old and devotes only one of its twelve parts to the Long March as such. In any case his account was based entirely on what one group of participants chose to tell him at the time. Since then a certain amount of other testimony has been recorded, notably by participants in the Long March who later left the Communist movement, and some documents have been published and other details come to light which enable a more comprehensive account to be put together.

The records of the Communists themselves are fragmentary. Their 'historian' of the Long March, Hsu Meng-chiu, told the English correspondent Nym Wales afterwards: 'We lost nearly all of our official documents in the Grasslands and in crossing rivers. Many carriers were drowned, being hampered by the dispatch cases. We also burned many documents that could not be conveniently carried. Now we have scarcely any historical records.' [6] What documents there were risked being doctored or suppressed because of the political tensions within the Party and the world Communist movement. The resolutions of the extremely important Politburo meeting at Tsunyi, in the middle of the Long March, were not made generally available until they were 'discovered' thirty-five years later by a non-Communist historian in an early, and soon re-edited, Chinese language version of Chairman Mao's selected works.[7]

Much weight has therefore to be put on the memory of the men involved, and this is only too human. General Peng Teh-huai was once explaining to Robert Payne, another of the small band of Western visitors to Yenan in the years after the Long March, the way a certain defensive breakthrough in one of the Kuomintang encirclement campaigns in Kweichow had been planned, when he paused suddenly. He had made a mistake: the battle he was describing was a quite different one which had occurred in Szechuan several hundred miles away. 'There were so very many battles,' he reflected. 'Now, when I look back, it seems to be one enormous battle going on forever.' [8]

Payne found the experience a common one. 'So it was,' he wrote, 'with all the commanders; they remembered small details and forgot the decisive events, and most of all they remembered the marshes and the snows, the strange landscape on the edge of Tibet where Lin Piao nearly perished and Mao was sick. . .' Mao himself, once asked by a former teacher of his what was the oddest thing they encountered on the March, replied after a moment's thought: 'I suppose it was the fish. We came to places where so few people had been before that if you waded into the river, the fish would leap into your hands.' [9]

Scholars have tended to be inhibited from collecting and evaluating material on the Long March because of the difficulty of the subject matter and the controversial nature of the evidence available. As an American writer has aptly put it, this whole period of Chinese Communist history is 'the journalist's delight and the scholar's nightmare'.[10] Since 1935 there has been a gradual process of 'tidying up' history on the part of the Chinese Communists, whose interest lies in portraying the Long March as a fully successful result of flawless decision-making on the part of the present leadership. Those aspects of events on the Long March which put the leadership in anything other than a fully heroic light have been systematically omitted from the official histories and accounts. On the other hand, the materials collected by the Nationalists, which are available to scholars in Taiwan and, through microfilm, in many of the centres of learning in America and elsewhere, show exactly the opposite bias, tending to portray every Communist as a brutal animal, and every Nationalist as a saint.

The thorough study of this, as of any other phase of modern Chinese history, requires a full familiarity with the Chinese language, the Chinese tradition and Chinese history. Chinese scholars themselves are obviously best equipped in these respects, but they have been reluctant to write of the Long March because it is impossible to treat it truthfully without doing damage to the official propaganda and mythology of both the Communists and the Nationalists. The Chinese scholar who is willing to offend both régimes is still a very rare bird indeed, and even those Chinese who have settled down in the West have so far preferred to tackle less controversial topics. Jerome Ch'ên, the celebrated historian at York University in Toronto, is an outstanding exception to whom all students of the Long March are enormously indebted.

If the Communists had in fact been defeated by the Nationalist Armies in 1934, what difference would this have made to the Japanese occupation of China and to the unfolding of the Japanese military operation that led first to Pearl Harbour and ultimately to Hiroshima? The survival of Communism as the result of the Long March ensured that the civil war in China continued for another decade to divide China in the face of its Japanese enemy.

Yet the Communists proved to be the tougher resistance fighters during the periods when they were co-operating with the Nationalists against Japanese aggression. Who can say what would have happened?

Maybe the Japanese would have been deterred from taking China's weakness so much for granted. Conceivably the ambitions which led to Pearl Harbour might have been checked at an earlier stage. America might never have become so involved with Asia as she did by consequence of having to defeat Japanese imperialism. There might have been no Pacific war in the early 1940s, no Korean war, no Vietnam war. China might have emerged under Nationalist leadership as a power on the Asian and world scene comparable, perhaps, with the India of Nehru.

Chiang Kai-shek would never have been so close to the Russians as the Chinese Communists were in the 1950s, but nor would he have been so obsessively hostile to them as Mao Tse-tung was during the 1960s. The Asian scene would today appear very different had those few thousand soldiers tramping about the wastelands of Tibet failed to survive their epic. Without modern Chinese Communism, the whole history of world Communism would have been vastly different. The Russian leadership of world Marxism would have remained unchallenged for a much longer period, and the breakdown of monolithic Communism delayed.

All these are among the tantalizing 'if's' of history. Speculation along such lines is inevitably subjective and can be misleading. But of one thing there can be no doubt. The Nationalist Party, the Kuomintang, did not in the end carry conviction as a movement capable of preparing China for modernization. Chiang himself was an extremely able man, but he was unable – his subsequent success in the infinitely less challenging conditions of Taiwan notwithstanding – to instil into his lieutenants and followers the discipline and idealism which a revolution needs and which the Communists under Mao Tse-tung acquired.

In the 1930s the whole world of China seemed on the threshold of disaster. A millennial culture which for long periods of history had been measurably in advance of other civilizations in Europe and the Mediterranean, but which was unhappily undergoing a phase of decadence and breakdown when it met the full dynamic force of modern European imperialism, China had taken the first serious step towards modernization by deposing in 1912 the Manchu imperial system. But the Kuomintang, first under Sun Yat-sen and later under Chiang, proved unable to control the political forces released by the establishment of the Chinese Republic. Provincial warlords ruled unchecked and beyond the control of the Central Government. Policies of social and economic reform could not be implemented comprehensively or fully by the Nationalist Government. China under Chiang was still a prey to foreign intervention and influence.

In the late 1960s Mao too found that the political forces which had been unleashed in China were beyond the control of a single political authority in Peking. But at least during the first two decades of Communist rule in China, from 1949 to 1969, a number of basic steps were taken on the path to becoming a modern society. A sense of national pride and self-respect was created, a self-confidence *vis-à-vis* the foreigner and foreign countries; the inequalities and inefficiencies of absentee landlordism were removed; some of the basic infrastructure for industrial and economic development was built up; reforms in education, in public health and in family relationships were set irresistibly in train.

China might henceforth gradually break down into smaller political units comparable in size and population to the nation-states of Europe, but the process by which 800 million Chinese were brought into the twentieth century and came to terms with the widened horizons which the industrial and scientific revolutions of Europe have brought to the world, would continue irrevocably.

The Long March epitomizes the new spirit which the Communists for a time brought to contemporary Chinese life, and which they hope will be transmitted to future generations of Chinese. Let there be no mistake: the March cannot be whitewashed as a victory, nor can its official Communist Party image be accepted. Luck and help from outside – whether intended or not – played as big a role in the Chinese Communists' ultimate success as their own strategy on the March. But whatever its consequences, and whatever use is made of it by propagandists in the future, the Long March remains an unparalleled human story of sheer dogged grit and determination. Edgar Snow says [11] that Hannibal's march over the Alps 'looked like a holiday excursion beside it', and whatever the political mileage which the heirs to the Long March will make of it, the pure bravado of the collective and individual feats of this great army in 1934–5 must claim respect and admiration from every generation and from every quarter of the globe.

PART ONE

The Context

Chapter 1

The Tradition of Peasant Uprising

THE central figure in Chinese history, and even in the Chinese politics of today, is the peasant, who still accounts for more than eighty per cent of the Chinese population. In the rhythmic pattern of China's millennial history, peasant revolt has regularly played a leading role, and the Long March must first of all be understood as the turning-point of the most recent and most overwhelming – though not necessarily the last – of the peasant rebellions which have changed Chinese history.

A period of prosperity under a strong and energetic ruler was usually followed by a period of economic recession and court intrigues under weaker rulers. A period of anarchy would then ensue during which the country became divided among contending factions or even thrown open to foreign invasion or popular uprisings. Eventually a new leader would emerge, sometimes a general, sometimes a scholar, to restore order, establish his personal authority and found a new dynasty. The whole process would then be repeated.

This 'cycle of Cathay' has been played out over a vast, sprawling land relatively undeveloped and with a predominantly peasant population. Even under good conditions central government of a society larger, in terms of both area and population, than the whole of Europe, was difficult. When the standard of administration deteriorated, ruling China as a single entity became virtually impossible.

Popular discontent and peasant unrest usually stemmed from the heavy demands of the tax collector, compulsory military service and the forced labour or *corvée*, which most Emperors eventually imposed on their subjects. The first of these peasant uprisings to attain fame was that of the 'Red Eyebrows', which began in Shantung province in the year A.D. 18. The Emperor Wang Mang had instituted, after usurping the throne, a series of radical reforms which seemed on the surface to meet with popular support. He became known to some as 'China's first socialist' for his land reform and other policies.

In fact these measures were designed to curb the power of the nobles rather than to improve the lot of the peasants. Some reforms were never implemented, others were improperly administered. And when the mounting cost of fighting wars against the 'barbarians' on the land borders of China made it necessary not only to suspend the reforms but also to disrupt the economy, the 'Red Eyebrows' took to the field against the Emperor.

Bands of revolutionaries, with their eyebrows painted red as a badge of their revolt, marched on the capital, killing landlords and government officials on the route. Many of the Emperor's soldiers dispatched to suppress the rebels joined them instead. Eventually a prince of the royal family which Wang Mang had deposed reasserted control, and put an end to the chaos in A.D. 25.

Many of the features of the Red Eyebrows revolt were repeated in later revolutions. Popular economic grievances, the farmers' hunger for land, the conflicting role of the army (which often had strong peasant and regional sympathies), the distinguishing 'badge' – all had their counterparts even in the Communist Revolution of our century.

The next popular revolt was that of the 'Yellow Turbans' which erupted in A.D. 184 and brought about the collapse of the eastern Han Dynasty. They added a new feature to the pattern, namely the profession by the revolution's leaders of a particular religion or set of ideological beliefs, in this case a popular version of the Chinese philosophy of Taoism. This revolt lasted twenty years and ended with the division of China into three separate kingdoms.

China was later reunited under the Sui Dynasty in 589, and this was succeeded in turn by the Tang Dynasty which introduced a new land law aiming at the equal distribution of farmland and the protection of peasants from the loss of their property. But the recurring cycle rolled on and popular discontent came to a head after a disastrous famine in Chekiang province in 860. In this case the peasant and the scholar who jointly led the rebellion failed to bring it to victory. A period of anarchy and disorder followed until the Sung Dynasty was established in 960, followed by the Mongol conquest in 1280.

The Mongols in turn were overthrown by a peasant who became successively a monk and then the first Emperor of a new Ming Dynasty. This founder of the Ming, Chu Yuan-chang, began his reign with revolutionary legislation, redistributing land and compiling new land registers. But the laws became progressively badly administered, the original austerity of Chu's court gradually gave way to a revival of imperial splendour, palace intrigue and factional squabbling came to the forefront, and foreign wars, together with the need to defend the coasts against Japanese piracy, drained funds from the treasury.

Peasant uprisings marred the final years of the Ming Dynasty, combined with invasions by the Manchus to the north of China and by the activities of secret societies. These had always been a feature of Chinese life, and they frequently took on an important role during times of economic difficulty or political oppression. But peasant leaders, often supported by scholars who had failed to gain high positions at the court, found difficulty in establishing themselves and building an enduring state system. The Manchus captured Peking in 1644, and the cycle began again.

The Manchu or Ching Dynasty was in the beginning one of the most brilliant in China's long history: under the Emperor Chien Lung, at the end of the eighteenth century, China became one of the glories of the world and the object of envy and admiration in the Europe of Voltaire and Diderot. But gradually the need to fight military campaigns against the Mongols, Tibetans and other 'barbarians' from Central Asia together with the extravagance of the court, made it necessary for the peasant to be fleeced. There was a sharp rise in the numbers of population at this time, without any corresponding rise in production. There were several popular insurrections during the eighteenth and early nineteenth centuries, in some of which such secret societies as the 'White Lotus' and the 'Society of Heaven's Law' were involved. But the most serious of these was the Taiping uprising.

The leader of the Taiping or 'Great Peace' rebellion was an

unsuccessful scholar who came from a poor peasant family in Kwangtung province and who in his early years had come under Christian missionary influence. In the 1840s he established a new religious movement based on the ideal of a 'Heavenly Kingdom', and this provided the ideology for the rebellion.

The Taipings were ahead of their time in many respects. In the areas which they ruled and within their own ranks, they divided land in fair shares, they practised the communal distribution of food and clothing to some extent, and they were totally opposed to taking opium, drinking wine, smoking tobacco or continuing the age-old custom of binding women's feet. Instead they preached the new gospel of female emancipation and the right of a widow to remarry. The Taipings renounced all ties with homes and property, and they built up strong followings in the countryside, by-passing, like the Communists a century later, the large centres of urban resistance.

'The land of the world must be tilled in common by the people of the world,' said one of the Taiping texts. 'When we have an insufficiency here, the people must be moved there, and *vice versa*, so that plenty in one place may relieve famine in another. All the world must enjoy the happiness given by God the Heavenly Father, and land, food, clothing and money must be held and used in common, so that there is no inequality anywhere, and nobody lacks food or warmth.'[1]

At one point the Taipings held sway over much of the southern half of China, and in 1853 they set up their capital at Nanking. But they lacked trained administrators and failed to provide any systematic organization of the countryside which they ruled. Furthermore, they repelled many educated Chinese by their fanatical beliefs, their uncouth manners and their adherence to a foreign faith.

Their growing arrogance and belief in a divine mission also alienated the Western powers which by then had become firmly entrenched in Shanghai, Canton and other treaty ports. Although many of the Westerners in China had initially favoured the Taiping movement as showing some signs of a more modern outlook on life, in the end they came to the aid of the imperial government and helped to suppress the rebellion. A certain Captain Charles

Gordon of the Royal Engineers played an important role in the final defeat of the Taiping forces.[2]

The Taipings uncannily foreshadowed the Communists a century later. They faced the same dilemmas. In 1852 the Taipings could have marched north from Wuhan to unseat the Manchu Emperor, but instead their generals were tempted by the opulent city of Nanking and they lost their strategic opportunity. In Nanking the ordinary rank and file had to undergo spartan austerity, but the leaders themselves rode in palanquins, kept harems and pursued other extravagances. Eventually they quarrelled among themselves and thus made the imperial counter-attack possible. All these mistakes were avoided by the Communists during and after the Long March, and Mao and his comrades were constantly aware of the lessons of history.

Many decades later Chu Teh, the Communist general whose tactics ensured the survival of the Communists during the military campaigns of the Long March, recalled how, as a boy, he had listened to the tales of an 'old weaver', an itinerant artisan who had fought in the Taiping Army.[3] When Chu's Red Army reached the remote gorges of the Tatu River on the borders of Tibet in the course of its Long March, it came upon some of the Taiping spears and used them in subsequent battles on the Long March. Some of the rules of military discipline for which the Communist Red Army became famous in the 1930s were borrowed from the Taiping model. Even the name of the Chinese Communist Party – Kung-chan-tang, or 'Sharing Wealth Party' – is a conscious echo of the Taiping slogan, 'The Wealth Must be Shared'.

Finally, the Boxer rebellion at the very end of the nineteenth century, though unsuccessful, spelled the doom of the last Ching Dynasty which ultimately fell to the republican revolutionaries in 1911–12. The Boxer revolt had no ideological foundation, but erupted in Shantung province in 1898 as a secret society movement whose members practised boxing and sword fighting.

The rebellion reflected the miserable conditions of this region of China at that time, which were exacerbated by the effects of China's forced trade with the West and by some of the worst floods and famines in Chinese history.

The Boxers began as both anti-Manchu and anti-foreign but

the famous Empress Dowager Tzu Hsi succeeded in blunting the anti-imperial force of the rebellion, which then became exclusively nationalistic and anti-foreign. It thus reached its peak in 1900 in the famous siege of the foreign legations in Peking, a blockade which was raised only by a strong international force sent from Europe.

The Boxer rebellion failed, but the Boxers were really the founders of modern Chinese nationalism. Their revolt had a continuing and growing influence on Chinese opinion, and it greatly strengthened the position of the radical revolutionary groups under Sun Yat-sen, the founder of the Nationalist Party or *Kuomintang*. The Boxer rebellion was the curtain-raiser for the revolution of 1911–12 which overthrew the Manchu Dynasty.[4]

This brief review of Chinese history brings out what Jerome Ch'ên, the non-communist biographer of Mao Tse-tung, calls 'the traditional pattern of peasant revolt, a protracted military struggle from one or several base areas with the poor peasants as the main supporters'.[5] Mao and many of his colleagues in the Communist leadership on the Long March were profoundly influenced by the heroes of previous peasant wars.[6] Mao makes a number of references in his works and speeches, for example, to Li Kuei, who led a peasant rising towards the end of the northern Sung Dynasty and whose exploits were described in the famous Chinese novel *The Water Margin*, which has been translated by Pearl Buck under the title *All Men Are Brothers*,[7] and which was one of the few books carried and read by Mao throughout the Long March.

By the time the Communists were fighting for supremacy in China, the situation of the Chinese peasant was as bad as it had been during many of the previous revolutions. The average size of a Chinese farm was about 3.3 acres from which an adult farmer could earn perhaps sixty-five *yuan* (or US $16) a year. The landlord usually took half of this, and the balance was hardly enough for the tenant's livelihood and that of his family. He was obliged to borrow from moneylenders to tide over the slack season, and to pay interest of thirty per cent or more a year.[8]

There was a steady decline going on in the 1920s in the area of farmland under cultivation and also in the degree of owner-farming. In 1918 it was estimated that about thirty per cent of the farm population were tenants, but a decade later the proportion was thought to have risen to more than half. R. H. Tawney, the famous British economist, in his book *Land And Labour In China*,[9] concluded that in the province of Hunan as many as eighty per cent of the rural population were tenants, and that in Kwangtung and Fukien the ratio was two-thirds. Similar results were found in a League of Nations survey [10] published in 1934. These poor tenant farmers were harassed, as in previous centuries, by extortionate taxation on the part of both the central government and the provincial or regional warlords, and by the *corvée*.

Conditions were clearly ripe for a further instalment of the cycle and the ability to mobilize and exploit peasant grievances proved to be the saving factor in Chinese Communist strategy. Mao Tse-tung declared: 'The peasants' fight for land is the basic feature of the anti-imperialist and anti-feudal struggle in China. ... The Chinese bourgeois–democratic revolution is in essence a peasant revolution ... the basic task of the Chinese proletariat in the bourgeois–democratic revolution is therefore to give leadership to the peasants' struggle.' [11]

Mao thus committed what Benjamin Schwartz, the pioneer American historian of Chinese Communism, called 'heresy in act never made explicit in theory'.[12] His principal contribution to Communist theory was contained in his famous theory of contradictions, which asserts that in semi-feudal, semi-colonial countries such as China, a revolutionary Leninist Party could successfully carry out revolution and remain Marxist without relying on the proletariat.[13] Jerome Ch'ên has described Mao's military strategy, the essential ingredient in the formula which turned the Long March from a rout into a preparation for victory, as 'a union ... of Marxism–Leninism and the Chinese traditional pattern of peasant revolts'.[14]

Chapter 2

The Kuomintang

WHEN the Manchu Dynasty was toppled in 1912, and China was proclaimed for the first time a Republic, the political organization which appeared most ready to take the lead in giving an ancient state the modern administration it now required was the Kuomintang – which means, literally, the People's Party, but is usually translated in Western languages as the Nationalist Party. The Kuomintang became at first the leading party, as distinct from the various personal factions and military cliques which were also involved, in the drama to decide China's political direction during the twentieth century. Only after the Long March and the war with Japan in the late 1930s and early 1940s did the Communists finally supplant the Kuomintang as the most powerful political organization in the country, and the Kuomintang was the Communist's principal enemy during most of its career. It was the almost successful drive by the Kuomintang to destroy the Communist power bases in the Chinese countryside which led to the Long March itself in 1934.

The origins of the Kuomintang go back to 1894, when a successful 27-year-old doctor named Sun Yat-sen threw up his practice and entered into full-time revolutionary politics. With a few relatives and friends he formed the *Hsingchunghui*, or Society for the Regeneration of China, which aimed at the overthrow of the ineffectual Manchus. Sun, a Cantonese intellectual of unusual stamp, had been trained – in Canton and Hong Kong – by American and British medical professors, and he was well aware of the far-reaching changes which would have to be instigated if China was to regain her parity with the Western powers and catch up with Western science and Western social progress. His group was financed by overseas Chinese merchants from Hong Kong, Malaya and other parts of South-East Asia who were also impressed by the gap between the thrusting Western imperialists and the weak, spineless China of the Manchu Empire.

Sun preached the famous Three Principles – of Nationalism, to supersede the narrow provincial and clan loyalties of the Chinese; Democracy, to carry into national life the self-governing processes prevalent in the villages; and Economic Development, to improve the material standards of the ordinary man's life. Personally incorrupt, Sun died a poor and disappointed man, his gifts being better for revolution than for the administrative aspects of national reconstruction. 'His strength,' wrote an American historian with intimate knowledge of the Chinese republican revolution, 'was that of the iconoclast, not that of a constructive statesman.'[1] Idealistic and impetuous, Sun overestimated the popular appeal of revolution and failed to build up a real power base for his organization.

His group tried repeatedly to achieve a *coup d'état* against the Emperor, but without success, so that Sun himself was obliged to leave the country and visit Europe. During the Boxer rebellion his followers launched an attack on the government in Kwangtung province, but it proved abortive. In 1905 the group was reorganized in Tokyo as the *Tungmenghui*, or Alliance Society, attracting many of the Chinese who were studying military science in Japan (one of them was Chiang Kai-shek).

When the 1911–12 Revolution started, Sun was in America, and he could not reach China until it was already two months old. His group, now called 'Komingtang', or 'Revolutionary Party', was in the forefront of the fighting and Sun was elected provisional President of the new rebel government. But there were many other groups and individuals who joined the anti-Manchu bandwagon and owed nothing to Sun Yat-sen or his friends. One of these was the former commander of the imperial army, Yuan Shih-kai, a northern aristocrat who had fallen foul of the Manchu royal family and who openly talked of the need for a 'limited monarchy' and other reforms. Sun renamed his Party 'Kuomintang', since the revolution was achieved and national unity was now the urgent priority, and in order to maintain a united front among the anti-Manchu forces he voluntarily surrendered the Presidency to Yuan.

But Yuan intended to dominate the alliance, and the various reformers found that they nursed very different notions of the way in which Chinese affairs should be run. The tension flared up very quickly when Yuan decided to have himself declared Emperor, and he was soon struck down by rival strong men from the north. By 1917 Peking was under the control of a band of northern war-lords in league with (and financed by) Japan, while Sun Yat-sen sat in Canton as generalissimo of the southern provinces. China was divided. But Sun proved no more successful in the south than in the nation at large. He could not persuade the southern generals to follow his orders, and in 1921 one of them seized power in Kwangtung province. Sun had to seek help from any quarter – from the various northern warlords as well as foreign powers.

It was at this stage that a genuinely friendly hand from outside could have earned Chinese gratitude. But most of the foreign powers were still distrusted by Chinese intellectuals. Although the infant Chinese Republic had declared war on Germany in 1917, the Allied victors at Versailles proceeded to award the former German concessions in Shantung province to Japan instead of re-storing them to China. This was a blatant derogation from Presi-dent Wilson's famous Fourteen Points, the fifth of which had declared that the people's wishes should be as decisive as govern-ment interests in achieving a fair and just solution of colonial claims arising out of the First World War. It was followed by the West's rebuff of its own Asian ally, Japan, which had asked for a declaration of universal racial equality to be written into the new League of Nations. These two betrayals of Wilsonian idealism at the Peace Conference destroyed the West's popularity in China.

The new Russian régime, by contrast, projected a more sym-pathetic image. Themselves in revolt against the Western capital-ist establishment, the Russian Communists had promised to renegotiate the unequal treaties which the Tsars had 'imposed' on China and were the first European government to give up special privileges and concessions on Chinese soil. Besides, Lenin's radical programme struck a chord in the minds of Sun and other would-be reformers who sought for dramatic change in China. Lenin had praised Sun Yat-sen's programme as early as 1912, and in 1920 Voitinsky, representing the Communist International, called on Sun in Shanghai.

The approach proved rewarding, and in 1922, when the warlord Chen Chiung-ming expelled the Kuomintang from Canton, the newly-formed Chinese Communist Party, protégé of the Russians, agreed to make an alliance with Sun. A few months later Adolf Joffe, another Comintern emissary, signed a joint declaration with Sun agreeing, among other things, that Communism and soviets were not suited to Chinese conditions and that the old nineteenth-century territorial treaties could be renegotiated. Sun was probably repeating the words of one of the Comintern envoys when, justifying his Soviet honeymoon to his own right wing, he observed that 'the experienced leaders of the Soviet Union are interested in working with *our* party and not with the inexperienced students of the Communist Party'.[2]

Sun now began to reorganize his party and its army along soviet lines. Chiang Kai-shek, one of his young officers, was sent to Moscow for military studies, and Mikhail Markovitch Gruzenberg, known as Borodin, was dispatched by the Russians to help Sun at home. The First Congress of the Kuomintang in January 1924 officially reinterpreted the Three Principles to include equalization of land-holding, state control of industry and various social reforms. Later that year Borodin and Vassily Blücher (known as Galen), another Comintern envoy, set up the Kuomintang Whampoa Military Academy where Sun's army was henceforth to be trained.

The symbol of this period, now known as the First United Front between the Chinese Communists and the Kuomintang, was the well-known fact that Chiang Kai-shek was its Commandant and Chou En-lai the Deputy Head of its Political Department. Many of the generals on both sides who fought each other so bitterly on the Long March and afterwards were graduates of this strange institution.

But Sun died, a disappointed man, in 1925, and a tussle for the succession broke out within the Kuomintang. Without Sun the left-inclined and the right-inclined of his followers found it increasingly difficult to get along. Borodin found himself in a peculiarly difficult dilemma, wanting to retain both the military strength and the leftist potential of this unwieldy organization. Early in 1926 he threw his support to a faction which included Chiang Kai-shek and which seized military control of Canton with some trade union support and the help of the Whampoa cadets.

A few weeks later, while Borodin was away, Chiang struck out again, this time on his own. He took personal command of Canton, disbanding and dismissing some of the left-wingers who had helped him up the ladder only weeks before. The position of the Communists in the Kuomintang was much weakened, and yet Borodin came back and accepted this *coup*, still hoping that Chiang could be nudged into the right direction when the real need came. Chiang, after all, continued to talk the language of world revolution and to use Communist phraseology.

Under its forceful new leader the Kuomintang now debated anew the long-cherished dream of marching north to defeat the provincial warlords and reunite China under a central Republican administration. The Russians encouraged the project, as did some of the Chinese Communists. Louis Fischer correctly described the emotional background to this expedition when he wrote that it was as if the two streams in Chinese republican politics, left and right, were saying to each other: 'Gentlemen, we know we must fight one another. But we need a wider arena. Let us delay the day of reckoning and meanwhile go forward to a common goal.'[3] So the ideological rivals marched against their common foe, the regional warlord of no particular ideology.

The Northern Expedition of 1926 resulted in the capture of Wuhan and a number of other cities in central China. The Communists were presented with new fields of opportunity for mass organization and indoctrination among the peasants and townsmen, which they exploited to the full. But Chiang gained enormous prestige, which gave him more leverage in his relationship with the Comintern. He lost little time in disposing of his erstwhile leftist allies, who had helped him to power but whose patriotism he doubted and whose radicalism he disliked. At the end of March he entered Shanghai on a gunboat and on 12 April his men systematically annihilated the Communist organization in the city. It was the year in which he become a convert to Christianity and consolidated his position in Chinese public life by marrying Mayling Soong, the beautiful daughter of one of the richest families in China.

The systematic massacre of Communists and their sympathizers in Shanghai decisively established Chiang as the strong man of the Kuomintang. Born in 1887, and thus six years senior to Mao, Chiang Chung-cheng (Kai-shek is the Cantonese form of his courtesy name) was a man of action whose personal integrity was undisputed but whose judgement of character was poor.[4] He built up around him a group of lieutenants too many of whom were corrupt, sycophantic and incompetent. On the eve of his final expulsion from the Chinese mainland by the Communists it was reliably estimated that private Chinese cash deposits in American banks reached US $2,000,000,000.[5]

But that was later. At the time of the Long March, Chiang was still a hero in the eyes of many Chinese and foreigners as well. Few could have guessed that he was to meet his match in Mao Tse-tung, or that Communism was to prove stronger than the democratic republicanism of the Kuomintang.

Chapter 3

The Chinese Communist Party

MARXISM at first made little impact on Chinese intellectuals.
Not until 1917 did Lenin prove that this particular philosophy
could serve as a blueprint for the kind of revolution which the
Japanese had already produced, in the Meiji Restoration of 1868,
and for which Chinese reformist circles desperately longed. This
was not entirely surprising, since Marx had expected capitalism
to break at its most developed point in the industrialized West
and he had little to say about the 'backward nations' of Asia.
'Pre-Leninist Marxism,' Professor Benjamin Schwartz of Harvard
observes, 'had no message immediately relevant to the situation
in which the Chinese intelligentsia found themselves.' [1]

But two leading Peking intellectuals were excited by the
October Revolution in Russia. Chen Tu-hsiu, who had rested a
radical programme of reforms on the twin pillars of 'democracy
and science', and Li Ta-chao, who had sought a resurgence of
Chinese civilization through some mystical act of national identification with the new Western-initiated course of world history,
were by 1918–19 thoroughly disillusioned with the 1911–12
Revolution in China.

The Kuomintang had failed to rise to the challenge of the
infant Republic. 'The false signboard "Chinese Republic" has been
hanging for eight years now,' complained Chen, 'but it is still
the old medicine which is being sold.' The Bolsheviks presented
a more dramatic and forceful version of the Western model which
Chen and Li had sought vaguely to follow. Li started a society
for the study of Marxism at Peking University in 1918, accepting
the messianism of the Russian Revolution but not yet its doctrinal base.

The revelation of the West's overt racialism at the Versailles

38

Peace Treaty, which sparked off the Chinese student demonstrations known as the May Fourth Movement, enhanced the attraction of Marxism–Leninism, especially as Lenin unfolded his theory of imperialism and promised to hand back the Asian territories seized by the Tsars over two centuries of Russian aggrandizement. The concept of Asian backwardness being the product of international finance capital led by the wealthy European and American corporations was tailor-made for the intellectuals of Peking and Shanghai at this moment. Marxism–Leninism offered not only a recipe for China's modernization but, perhaps even more important, an heroic role for China in the great new drama of world history.

Indeed, it can be argued that Marxism, unlike anarchism, Fabianism and some of the other Western philosophies with which Chinese intellectuals of the period were flirting, corresponded with important elements of the old Confucian tradition and was thus more acceptable to men who, though rebelling against certain manifestations of that tradition, were still its products. The élitist assumption, for example, that state power in the proper hands could lead man to the good society needed no introduction in China. The justification of authoritarianism and organizational discipline in the name of a higher morality was well-known in Chinese civilization.

In 1920 labour groups were formed in Peking and Shanghai,[2] embracing not only Marxists but rebels of many other colours as well, and the Communist International sent Gregory Voitinsky to China as its representative – the first of a succession of Western and Indian Communists whose part in the tangled story of the movement in China is still so controversial. Groups of activists were thrown up in Canton, Changsha (under Mao Tse-Tung) and other cities, and some of the Chinese students abroad, in France and Japan, joined local Marxist organizations. A circle of the students in Paris, including Chou En-lai, Li Li-san, Chen Yi and Teng Hsiao-ping, set up a Young China Communist Party at the beginning of 1921.

All this activity was finally brought under one roof, so to speak, at the first founding Congress of the Chinese Communist Party held in Shanghai in July 1921. Twelve delegates, including

Chang Kuo-tao and Mao Tse-tung (but not Chen Tu-hsiu or Li Ta-chao, nor Chou En-lai or Li Li-san, both in Paris, nor Liu Shao-chi, then in Moscow) met in a girls' school in the French Concession of the city, later adjourning, when the attentions of the police were aroused, to a boat on the waters of Niehpu lake. They represented fifty-seven Chinese Marxists organized in six groups scattered about the country, together with one in Japan.[3] In the new organization Chen Tu-hsiu, though absent from the Congress, was appointed Secretary-General of the Party and Chairman of its Central Committee.

But the Chinese Communist Party was only a party in name. It had no mass organization, and its founders were more familiar with the blackboard and the lecture-room than with the factory floor or the soap-box. They must have seemed a very long-term bet indeed from the vantage-point of Moscow, and the Russian Communists found Sun Yat-sen's Kuomintang, the full heir to China's anti-monarchical revolutionary nationalism, with nine years of history behind it, and boasting at least an army and an apparatus on the ground, a more likely broker for the hoped-for marriage between China and Communism.

The word from Moscow in the 1920s was a harsh one for the Chinese comrades to accept. As Karl Radek put it in a reply to a Chinese delegate at a Comintern Congress in 1922: 'When our Chinese comrade told us here, "We have struck deep roots in China," I must tell him, "Esteemed Comrade, it is a good thing to feel confident of one's strength when one starts to work. Nevertheless, things have to be seen as they are." The comrades working at Canton and Shanghai have failed to associate themselves with the working masses . . . Many of our comrades out there locked themselves up in their studies and studied Marx and Lenin as they had once studied Confucius . . . You must understand, comrades, that neither the question of socialism nor of the Soviet republic are now the order of the day . . . The immediate task: (1) To organize the young working class. (2) To regulate its relations with the revolutionary bourgeoisie elements in order to organize the struggle against the European and Asiatic imperialism.'[4]

Thus the battle opened which was to persist right through to the present day, between the interests of world Communism as seen from Moscow and the interests of the Chinese revolution as viewed from China. Lenin's insistence on courting the Kuomintang in order to loosen the West's hold on the 'backward areas' of Asia almost split the infant Chinese Communist Party, to the majority of whose members the Kuomintang was the epitome of all that was worst in China's incipient bourgeois and capitalist class.

In the summer of 1922 Maring, the Dutch Comintern agent, proposed to the Chinese Party a formal alliance or united front with the Kuomintang with the goal of transforming it into a proletarian movement. Sun had insisted, in his talks with Comintern emissaries, that the Chinese Communists should be absorbed into his own party, and the Russians were willing to pay that price. By waving the big Russian stick, Maring got his way with a reluctant Chinese Communist Party Central Committee.

But, as one of the Chinese Communist chroniclers puts it, 'while the Party Central Committee respected the motion of the Internationale, most of the comrades had only approved a democratic revolutionary united front and were quite doubtful about entering the Kuomintang'.[5] Chen Tu-hsiu and his colleagues regarded their proposed 'ally' as too narrowly nationalistic, too reliant on military force, and too prone to temporize with the reactionary elements in its own ranks. The eventual uneasy compromise was that the Communists would enrol in the Kuomintang as individuals, but that the Communist Party would maintain its separate existence.

This so-called 'first united front' between the rival groups contending for power in China lasted for four years. It was subject to constant strain and provocation on both sides, especially from the Kuomintang's far right and the Communists' far left. But there were some factors to support it. The bloody suppression by a northern warlord of a previously powerful railway workers' union in 1923 was a shock to the Communists, some of whom felt that the Kremlin might have been correct in viewing the strength of the Chinese proletariat as flimsy. The Kuomintang was at this time a fairly loose-knit organization and membership was not too demanding on the Communists.

The leftward developments within the Kuomintang in 1924–5

– the Whampoa academy, the dispatch of officers to Moscow for training, the more radical interpretation of the Three Principles – were the work of Borodin, not of Chen or the other Chinese comrades, but they proved that the alliance was not entirely unfruitful from the latter's point of view. Furthermore, the Chinese Communist Party was able to pursue its goal of organizing mass support under the Kuomintang umbrella – and retained control of this organization after the united front collapsed.

After Chiang's Shanghai massacre in April 1927, the Communists clung for a time to the left-wing faction of the Kuomintang, which finally splintered off from Chiang's faction as a result of it. But in three months even that survival of the united front collapsed. The question of land redistribution was a fatal stumbling-block. Chen Tu-hsiu became the scapegoat for the failure of the united front, and the leadership of the Chinese Communist Party passed to Chu Chiu-pai, a bookish man with none of Chen's prestige or political following. The First Civil War, of 1927–35, broke out.

For the rest of 1927 the Chinese Communists struggled energetically but vainly for a revolutionary tide which would sweep them to power and enable them, in Schwartz's phrase, 'to beat down the iron wall of proletarian indifference'.[6] The new leadership, with Comintern approval, adopted a 'putschist' programme of urban and rural uprisings. The Party would at last go out and fight the Kuomintang, proclaim the agrarian revolution, rouse the people against their oppressors and sweep the reactionaries out of the cities.

Mao Tse-tung and others with regional followings were instructed to organize Autumn Harvest rebellions, at a time when the peasants would be particularly hostile to the levies traditionally made on the harvest by landlords, moneylenders and tax collectors. A military rising was planned at Nanchang, and the Red Armies under Ho Lung, Yeh Ting and other Communist guerrilla chieftains were then to march triumphantly on Canton to establish a new revolutionary government.[7]

But things turned out differently. The urban proletariat had been profoundly discouraged by the 'White Terror' of the Kuomintang against labour organizations, Communists and their sympathizers. The extravagant hopes of quick success which the Kremlin had inspired in the days of the united front, followed by the repeated disasters of the Kuomintang purges in Shanghai and elsewhere at the beginning of 1927, fatally reduced the political interest of the Chinese factory worker in the Communist cause.

Nanchang fell to the Red Army, but only for a few days, and the cream of the Communist forces was destroyed on the road to Canton. After the final defeat at Swatow, Ho Lung fled to Shanghai, Chou En-lai had to escape by boat to Hong Kong (whence, sick with malaria, he went to Moscow), while Chu Teh assembled the scattered remnants of the revolutionary arm in northern Kwangtung. Mao's peasant armies failed to take Changsha, the Hunanese provincial capital, because of military inexperience and lack of popular support. He himself was captured,[8] and he had to bribe his way out of captivity before regaining contact with his men and leading them to lick their wounds in the remote and almost inaccessible mountains of Chingkangshan, on the border of Hunan and Kiangsi – where Chu Teh later joined him.

Meanwhile Stalin urgently needed a victory in China for his own (Fifteenth) Party Congress in Moscow, and his Comintern envoys, the Georgian Besso Lominadze and the German Heinz Neumann, were told to organize an uprising in Canton. This was achieved on 11 December 1927, and for three days Stalin had his Canton Commune. But then Kuomintang forces, aided by British gunboats from Hong Kong, retook the city and the Chinese Communists were left in almost total disarray.[9]

Trotsky called the putschist policy of 1927 an act of lunacy: 'At the end of 1927,' he wrote, 'Stalin's faction, frightened by the consequences of its own mistakes, tried to make up at one stroke what it had failed to do over a number of years. Thus the Canton revolt was organized. The leaders continued to labour under the assumption that the revolution was still on the increase. In reality the revolutionary tide had already been replaced by a downward movement. The heroism of the foremost workers of Canton could not prevent the disaster caused by the adventurous spirit of its leaders. The Canton revolt was drowned in blood. The Second Chinese Revolution was definitely crushed. ... Early in 1928, when the Chinese Revolution was at a low point, the Ninth Plenary Session of the Executive Committee of the Communist International proclaimed a course toward an armed uprising in China. The result of this lunacy was the further defeat of the workers, the liquidation of the best revolutionaries, the disintegration of the party, and demoralization in the workers' ranks.'[10]

Towards the end of 1927 the Comintern authorized the setting up of soviet * areas in China. One of the first was the Hailufeng Soviet Republic formed in Kwangtung province in November by Peng Pai, the renowned Communist peasant organizer in the south. But even this had collapsed by March of 1928, in spite of gaining the local farmers' support by dividing land and burning title deeds.[11] By then Chu Chiu-pai had been unseated in the Chinese Communist Party leadership and rebuked for his errors (he retired to Moscow under the name of Strakhov). Li Li-san now staked his claim to the highest position, strongly backed by Chou En-lai. Mao had already been expelled from the Politburo because of his mishandling of the Autumn Harvest uprising.

The Chinese Communist Party met in Moscow in the summer of 1928 to consider the débâcle. The leaders were more or less evenly divided between those, like Chang Kuo-tao, who felt that the defeats of the past year should inspire caution and consolidation, and the more optimistic who believed that if the crest of that wave had eluded them, there was nevertheless another wave in sight which could be ridden all the more surely because of the lessons of the previous one. It was this latter viewpoint, expounded most eloquently by Li Li-san and Chou En-lai, which seemed on balance to prevail in spite of Russian reservations.

The new line was to encourage soviet areas and to seek 'initial victory in one or several provinces'. The activities of Mao and Chu Teh in Chingkangshan were thus given a certain endorsement by the Party. The precarious pockets of resistance which these two, along with Ho Lung and other guerrilla generals in the southern interior, had created were, after all, the only positive accomplishments of the Communist movement at this time, and it was hardly politic to maintain their disgrace.

---

* A soviet, of course, was a piece of territory administered and governed by representatives of the Chinese Communist Party.

But Li Li-san and Chou En-lai returned to China in 1929 determined to build up the urban proletarian base which would be needed for the ultimate Communist victory. Li's team in the new Politburo was one that had won its spurs in the labour organizations of the cities. Mao and his crude peasant forces might be temporarily saving the day, but there was no intention on the part of the Kremlin, the Comintern or the Chinese Communist Party Central Committee to give the leadership of Chinese Communism over to such unorthodox hands.

The trouble was that the proletariat was still unwilling to rise to the occasion. As a Chinese Communist Party circular lamented at the end of 1928: 'Unfortunately ... our party units in the cities have been pulverized and isolated. Nowhere in China can we find one solid, industrial cell. ...' [12] There were a number of strikes, to be sure. In Shanghai alone there were more than a hundred during 1928. But most of these were led by the 'Yellow Unions' of the Kuomintang, and they aimed at better wages and shorter hours of work rather than the overthrow of the Kuomintang régime.

Li's disappointments in the cities only increased his resentment of the Maoist heresy, and he inveighed against the peasant mentality of those who doubted the wisdom of staking all on an urban insurrection. The peasantry, he roundly declared, 'is petty bourgeois and cannot have correct ideas regarding socialism; ... its conservatism is particularly strong and ... it lacks organizational ability. Only a proletarian mentality can lead us on to the correct revolutionary road.' [13] If the Party accepted Mao's view that the countryside must be taken before the towns, 'our hair will be white before the revolution is victorious'.[14]

But the soviet areas gained in strength and prestige during 1929 without either the Kremlin or its Chinese Party colleagues being able to do anything about it. The forces of Mao and Chu steadily extended the territory under their control, and the Mao–Chu group began to go by the name of the 'Real Power Faction'. The remoteness of Moscow from all this was graphically underlined by its publication early in 1930 of an obituary of Mao, who was said to have fallen a victim of consumption,[15] and by the remark of Stalin at the Russian Party Congress that summer: 'It is said that a Soviet Government has already been created there ! * I think that if this is true, there is nothing surprising in it.' [16]

The Li Li-san leadership now made its call for a nation-wide revolt. It was Li's dream that the world-wide rising against imperialistic capitalism, then in the throes of the great Depression, would begin in China, its weakest link. Declaring that the Chinese revolution might be 'the final decisive class war of the world',[17] the Central Committee in June 1930 instructed the Red Armies to integrate themselves under Mao's and Chu's command, to leave their rural bases and to launch attacks on a number of near-by industrial cities, notably Wuhan and Changsha.

Chu Teh explained afterwards that he knew the strategy was wrong : 'Mao and I sensed this, but lacked sufficient information to reject the plan; and we were practically alone in our misgivings.' [18] There was no mood of doubt, however, in the poem which Mao composed just before his men marched on Nanchang :

> June : the peerless troops attack
>   the corrupt and villainous,
> Seeking to bind the cockatrice
>   with a rope a myriad ells in length.
> On the far side of the Kan River
>   a patch of ground has turned red,
> Thanks to the wing
>   under the command of Huang Kung-lueh.
>
> The million elated workers and peasants
> Roll up Kiangsi like a mat
>   and thrust straight on to Liang Hu.
> The heartening Internationale,
>   like a hurricane,
> Whirls down on me from heaven.[19]

The Red Armies lost the day, however. Peng Teh-huai's Fifth Red Army managed to occupy Changsha, but only for a few days. His small arms were no match for the heavy artillery, light aircraft and gunboats of the Kuomintang. Mao and Chu openly re-

---

*i.e., in the Chinese interior.

pudiated the Li Li-san line, withdrew their troops and reorganized at Kian in Kiangsi, determined to rebuild the rural base from which they believed they could, over the longer term, erode the power of the Kuomintang.

Early in 1931 Li Li-san paid the price of failure and was replaced by a new group in the higher circles of the Party, the so-called Returned Student Faction or Twenty-eight Bolsheviks, young men who had trained at the Sun Yat-sen University in Moscow and then returned to China in 1930 with its Rector, Pavel Mif, the man now named to represent the Comintern in China at this awkward juncture. Led by Chen Shao-yu and Chin Pang-hsien (better known by their pseudonyms, Wang Ming and Po Ku respectively), this clique of Russian protégés quickly made themselves unpopular.

'These fellows,' commented one disgruntled Party veteran, 'were all young students who, needless to say, had made no contribution whatsoever to the revolution. While we were carrying on the revolution they were still suckling at their mothers' breasts. ... These men who were infants in terms of their revolutionary background were now sent back to be the leaders of the Chinese Revolution!' [20] Mao rudely called them 'three-year-old babies'.[21] But they were not entirely stupid, and Shanti Swarup, the Indian sinologist, has argued that one of them (Chang Wen-tien, also known as Lo Fu) was not only a considerable theorist but even provided Mao with some of his intellectual framework for the confusing social scene of China in the 1930s.[22]

At a Central Committee meeting in January 1931 Chou En-lai and other colleagues of Li Li-san abjectly confessed their policy errors, and the Twenty-eight Bolsheviks were foisted on the Party by Mif. Li had already fled to Moscow where he also recanted. The Comintern was back in control of the Chinese Party, but not of its most powerful arm in the soviet areas. Party morale among city and labour union circles was by now thoroughly undermined by the bewildering shifts in the Comintern line on China, the yawning gulf between Russian advice and Chinese reality and the imposition of the young Bolshevik upstarts as Party leaders. The Party thus threw away its last chance of retaining any significant following among the urban proletariat.

The Wang Ming leadership proceeded, almost suicidally, to alienate the Shanghai trade union leaders at the same time as it campaigned against the 'rightist deviationism' of Mao.[23] The result was to make inevitable the transfer of the effective leadership of the Chinese Communist movement from the Party headquarters in Shanghai to the distant villages of the hinterland where Mao Tse-tung and Chu Teh were grooming their rustic rebel armies.

Chapter 4

Mao and Chu, the March Commanders

WHO were these twin stars of the guerrilla galaxy who now came to the rescue of a dying Party? What bound them together into the famous Mao–Chu duo, enabling them to out-manoeuvre Party rivals and Kuomintang enemies alike – and finally to wheel the vanguard of their movement through the trials and tribulations of the Long March to ultimate victory?

Mao Tse-tung was born in the small Hunanese village of Shao-shan on 26 December 1893.[1] His parents were poor peasants who gradually raised themselves, through hard work and shrewd judgement, to the point where they employed labourers and carried on a certain amount of petty trade. Ultimately they farmed about three acres, sold their neighbours' grain to the urban merchants, and lent their savings to others less fortunate – at high rates of interest.

Mao started work on the farm at the age of five, but two years later his father sent him to a tutor to be taught reading and writing; as the eldest son he should be able to keep the farm's accounts and write letters. The boy became immersed in the new world of books thus opened up to him, especially the romantic historical novels which described the Chinese counterparts of Robin Hood and Hereward the Wake – *The Romance of the Three Kingdoms* and *The Water Margin*, full of heroic tales of popular bandits challenging the effete and corrupt court.

After five years of Confucian classics at his village primary school, Mao was summoned back to work full-time on the farm and its expanding accounts. He began to quarrel with his stern father, giving away money to beggars when times were bad and helping poor farmers to get their harvest in before the rain when his hands were needed at home.

But he yearned for his schoolbooks and insisted eventually on enrolling first at a more modern local higher primary school and then, at 18, at a Middle School in Changsha, the provincial capital. Here he came to sense for the first time the currents of politics and read his first newspaper, a publication of Sun Yat-sen's group which so fired the young man that he wrote an article (the first of a famous line) advocating a republic with Sun as President, and displayed it on the school wall. The anti-Manchu movement was gaining ground at this time, and the once subversive writings of such reformist intellectuals as Kang Yu-wei and Liang Chi-chao were all the rage. Mao was particularly excited by the lives of George Washington, Napoleon, Peter the Great and Abraham Lincoln.

During the 1911–12 Revolution against the Manchu dynasty Mao shaved off his queue* (an act of open defiance against the régime, which compelled all adult men to conform to this Man-churian hairstyle), left school and joined one of the rebel armies in Hunan. But once the Republic was proclaimed he left to continue his studies in Changsha, devouring Chinese translations of Adam Smith, Darwin, J. S. Mill, Spencer, Montesquieu, Rousseau, Tolstoy and a host of other Western writers. Friedrich Paulsen's A System of Ethics cast an exceptionally strong spell on the 20-year-old Mao. He also studied the radical newspapers put out by the intellectuals of Shanghai and Peking, including Chen Tu-hsiu and others who later embraced Communism. He kept copious notes of everything he read. A library to him, he said himself, was like a vegetable garden to an ox.

'At this time,' he later told Edgar Snow, 'my mind was a curious mixture of ideas of liberalism, democratic reformism, and utopian socialism. I had somewhat vague passions about "nineteenth-century democracy", utopianism and old-fashioned liberalism, and I was definitely anti-militarist and anti-imperialist.' [2]

In 1918 Mao went to Peking to help organize the students who now began to go to France under the 'work-study' scheme. One of his former teachers from Changsha who was lecturing there se-

---

* He displayed characteristic ruthlessness, yet equity, by forcibly shearing off the queues, or pigtails, of ten other students who had vowed to follow suit but took fright at the last moment.

cured a modest job for him as library assistant at Peking University. Mao had to keep the register of library users, and set out and replace the newspapers which the students asked. for. His salary was eight *yuan* – about US $2 – a month, and he shared a tiny bedroom with seven other Hunanese students : 'I used to have to warn people on each side of me when I wanted to turn over.' [3]

The job was menial, but the librarian was Li Ta-chao, the man who did perhaps more than anyone else to establish Marxism in China. When Mao arrived in Peking, Li was acclaiming the October Revolution in Russia. Mao's attempts to converse with the intellectual lions of Peking in the precincts of the library were often rebuffed (Hu Shih, one of the most renowned, refused to talk to him when he learnt that the young man was a mere library assistant), but he joined Li's 'Marxist Study Group' and became also a disciple of Chen Tu-hsiu, the other pioneer of Chinese Marxism. At that time Chen was still advocating parliamentary democracy, and Li's Marxism was more an enthusiasm than an understanding conviction.

The following year Mao went back to Changsha and organized a student strike during the May Fourth Movement protesting against Versailles. By 1920, after reading the *Communist Manifesto*, Kautsky's *Class Struggle* and Kirkupp's *History of Socialism* (all in Chinese translation), he regarded himself as a Marxist both in theory and in action. He led the Hunanese delegation to the founding congress of the Chinese Communist Party in July 1921. A few months later he married his old teacher's daughter, whom he had courted in Peking.

Mao's sense of nationalism, his concern for the restoration of China's self-respect, was formed very early in his career. At a football match between his own school in Changsha and a rival establishment of American origin,* Mao cheered his side on with the shout: 'Beat the slaves of foreigners.' [4] In 1923 he remarked sarcastically in an article : 'If one of our foreign masters farts, it's a lovely perfume.' [5]

He played a considerable role in the first period of collaboration between the Kuomintang and the Chinese Communist Party in

---

* The Yale-in-China preparatory school.

1923–4, so much so that his colleagues criticized him for being too subservient to the Kuomintang's interests.[6] In fact it would be fairer to say that he recognized the value of the Kuomintang for China's national resurgence before Stalin, the Comintern and most of their Chinese protégés did – just as later he was the first to see when the time was right to break with the Kuomintang.[7] He retired again to Hunan in order to avoid the opprobrium of being too friendly with the 'patriotic merchants' and other bourgeois but anti-foreign, anti-imperialist elements in the rival organization.

It was then that Mao discovered – against all the indications of Marxist theory and the *idées fixes* of his intellectual friends – the latent revolutionary dynamism of the peasantry. He found the farmers of his province genuinely stirred by the foreign oppression of the Japanese, British and French in the Treaty Ports, and he threw himself into organizing peasant associations. But he continued to use the Kuomintang apparatus more than the Communist Party's as a vehicle for his work, being Principal of its Peasant Movement Training Institute. He supported Chiang Kai-shek's Northern Expedition, and Stuart Schram sees in these links 'a common bond of nationalism' [8] between the two men who ultimately became such rivals.

Soon afterwards, in 1927, he conducted his famous investigation into the peasant movement in Hunan, the Report of which constituted one of his major contributions to Chinese Communism. The revolutionary energy which he observed in the Hunanese countryside led him to predict that:

'In a very short time, several hundred million peasants in China's central, southern and northern provinces will rise like a tornado or tempest – a force so extraordinarily swift and violent that no power, however great, will be able to suppress it. They will break through all the trammels that now bind them and push forward along the road to liberation.' [9]

This Report has been described by Benjamin Schwartz as 'almost completely bare of Marxist trappings', and as 'simply a blunt and passionate plea that the peasant associations be given complete freedom of action'. Another American sinologist concludes that the Hunan Report, 'as the work of a vigorous young Communist unhampered by deep knowledge of Marxist theory, reflected doctrinal immaturity rather than political heresy'.[10] Mao estimated that the peasants were contributing around seventy per cent to the success of the Chinese revolution, while the urban workers and the military could be given credit for only thirty per cent between them.

By this time Mao was losing favour with the Communist Party leadership. He was tarred with the brush of those of his early patrons in the Party who advocated policies which in Moscow were identified with Trotsky, and which later were damned as heretical.[11] His obsession with the peasantry disturbed the urban intellectuals who dominated Party debates. Mao's programme for confiscating landlords' land in Hunan was far to the left of both the Comintern and the Chinese Party line, and Li Li-san accused him of representing 'localism and conservatism of peasant consciousness'. He had already been expelled from the Party's Central Committee once, and then, at the end of 1927, he was again thrust into the wilderness and disgraced for almost a year.

But Mao was now ensconced in Chingkangshan, beginning to build up the power base from which he would later challenge the Party leadership and take control himself.

The paintings of the hagiographers of the 1960s show Mao at this period as a Christ-like figure aglow with intelligence and feeling. Indeed, a copy by an Indian artist of such a portrait hung in one of the offices of the Vatican for some time in the late 1960s before its true derivation was realized – after which it was hurriedly removed. Some of the early photographs do in fact suggest a quiet intensity which can lend to an otherwise undistinguished face a certain beauty.

The aspect which struck all who mixed with Mao was his stillness. In any group he was the one who abjured gestures or dramatic attitudes, compelling attention by the consuming force which he seemed to contain. A lifetime of chain smoking stained his fingers and blackened his teeth. But when Edgar Snow came face to face with him at Pao An in 1936, a year after the Long March, he found 'a gaunt, rather Lincolnesque figure, above average height for a Chinese, somewhat stooped, with a head of thick black hair grown very long, and with large searching eyes, a high-bridged nose and prominent cheek-bones'.[12]

Some years later Robert Payne saw him at a play put on by the Red Army in Yenan:

'There was the heavy, leonine head, with blue-black hair, very thick, muscular shoulders, a long, smooth forehead, the spectacles glinting and the hands braced against the knees. One can tell more about a man from the way he enjoys drama than from observing him elsewhere. What was strange was that he was wholly feminine, reflected all the gestures of the actors, pursed his lips when they were roaring with anger, and gently waved his arms when the firecrackers exploded; and he glowed with the wildest joy when the armies of stage peasants, in beautiful embroidered costumes, at last overthrew their feudal lords in still more beautifully embroidered costumes. It was medieval morality, and Mao enjoyed its medieval gusto.' [13]

Agnes Smedley found Mao effeminate and faintly repellent when she first met him. But she wrote, 'the sinister quality I had at first felt so strongly in him proved to be a spiritual isolation. As Chu Teh was loved, Mao Tse-tung was respected. The few who came to know him best had affection for him, but his spirit dwelt within himself, isolating him.' [14]

In his personal habits Mao was slipshod, uncaring for his appearance. Even after 1949 he often appeared with cascading socks, frayed cuffs and baggy trousers. With splendid unselfconsciousness he once took his trousers off to lie down more comfortably during a conversation between Edgar Snow and Lin Piao, and on another occasion Snow noticed him 'absent-mindedly turn down the belt of his trousers and search for some guests'. Snow commented: 'His nonchalant habits fitted with his complete indifference to personal appearance.' [15] Even when he moved from his cramped quarters in the Yenan caves to the Small Palace of the Fragrant Concubine on the shores of Peking's North Lake, he continued to live simply, almost frugally, his only extravagance being a private swimming pool. [16]

But there was no false modesty when it came to using his name for political purposes. The cult of Chairman Mao can be traced back to 1942, as he finally consolidated his hold over the Party, and in 1945 he actually wrote an anonymous article urging his compatriots to follow Mao's way. [17] That was the year in which the Party Constitution enshrined The Thought of Mao Tse-tung as necessary 'to guide the entire work' of the Chinese Communist Party.

He was always a late riser and a late sleeper, preferring to work at night and rest during the day. Gunther Stein described the conclusion of a lengthy interview with the words: 'At three in the morning, when I finally got up to go, with a bad conscience, aching limbs and burning eyes, he was still as fresh and animated and systematic in his talk as in the afternoon.' [18]

His bodyguard gave the following account of Mao's writing the famous essay *On Protracted War* in 1938. For the first two days he did not sleep at all, working continuously by the light of a pair of candles and sometimes overlooking his meals. His only overt act of refreshment was an occasional mop of the face with a hot flannel. By the fifth day he was perceptibly thinner and his eyes shot with blood, yet he still ignored food and went on writing. On the seventh day he was so engrossed that he failed to notice that the fire was burning a hole in his right shoe. Suddenly he jumped to his feet in pain, burst into laughter and asked, 'How did that happen?' He then drank a little wine and resumed work. The following day he developed a headache, lost his appetite and could not sleep. The doctor diagnosed fatigue but Mao plodded on until the essay was finished on the ninth day.[19]

There was never a less abashed bookworm than Mao. Snow records that when he was interviewing Mao every night on the Chinese Communist Party's history, a visitor once brought a batch of new philosophy books along. Snow was asked to postpone his appointment while Mao 'consumed those books in three or four nights of intensive reading during which he seemed oblivious of everything else'.[20]

Mao's poetry is widely admired. Jerome Ch'ên comments: 'No doubt Mao's status as a poet has been enhanced by his eminence as a political figure; nevertheless his poetic abilities, although they are uneven, are of no mean order and would have ensured him a place in contemporary Chinese literature independent of his preeminent position in the political sphere.' [21]

But his claims to be an original philosopher are somewhat forced. The keynote of his writings is his great belief in the power of the will. 'There is only unproductive thought, there are no unproductive regions,' he declared. 'There are only poor methods of cultivating the land, there is no such thing as poor land. Provided only that people manifest in full measure their subjective capacities for action, it is possible to modify natural conditions.' He was idealistic enough to be driven, in Schram's phrase, by an 'unquenchable desire to harmonize the two conflicting imperatives of "conscious action" by individuals and impeccable social discipline',[22] and hence the contradiction which persisted to the end of his régime and which convulsed the nation in the Cultural Revolution of 1966–9, because he wanted people to accept his ideas voluntarily without being willing to stand aside and watch them make mistakes if they rejected his lead.

His calm exterior hid the turbulent romantic side of his personality. By his own account, 'my parents had married me when I was fourteen to a girl of twenty, but I have never lived with her – and never subsequently did. I did not consider her my wife . . .'[23] In 1921, when he was 28, he married Yang Kai-hui, his beloved ethics teacher's daughter. Snow says that their match 'was celebrated as an "ideal romance" among radical youths in Hunan. It seems to have begun as a trial marriage . . .'[24] But Yang was executed by the Kuomintang when the Red Armies left Changsha in 1930. A quarter of a century later Mao penned his most famous love poem, 'The Immortals', dedicated to the widow of an old friend and co-revolutionary who had fallen in battle against the Kuomintang in the 1930s. Yang, the name of Mao's wife, means 'poplar', and Liu, the name of his dead friend, means 'willow'.

> My proud poplar is lost to me,
>   and to you your willow;
> Poplar and willow
>   soar to the highest heaven.
> When they asked Wu Kang*
>   what he had to give them
> He presented them
>   with cassia wine.

---

* Wu Kang, because he sought immortality – whose secret was supposed to be in the possession of the goddess of the moon – was con-

The lonely goddess
    who dwells in the moon
Spreads her wide sleeves
    to dance for these good souls
    in the boundless sky.
Suddenly word comes
    of the Tiger's* defeat on earth,
And they break into tears
    that fall as torrential rain.[25]

Soon after Yang's death Mao took another bride, Ho Tzu-chen.[26] A girl almost half his age, Ho was a forceful character said to have taken command in the field: she nevertheless bore Mao five children during the nine years they spent together. After the Long March (on which she accompanied Mao despite her pregnancy) she was sent to Russia for medical treatment, and Mao fell in love with Chiang Ching – then known as Lan-ping ('Blue Apple'), a seductive Shanghai film star whose leftist sympathies had brought her to Yenan.

Mao's colleagues and admirers were shocked by his abandonment of the faithful fighter Ho, but Mao insisted on divorcing her. It was said that the Chinese Communist Party Central Committee finally gave a grudging consent to the new match only on condition that Chiang Ching shunned the public stage and kept to her place in Mao's household – unlike her predecessor and the other Politburo wives, who all had positions and public responsibilities in various Party organizations.[27] This was a grievance which burst out in 1966, when Chiang Ching emerged briefly as a political figure in her own right during the Great Proletarian Cultural Revolution – and betrayed her resentment of those who had condemned her in the Yenan days to thirty years of isolation and unwanted privacy.

Mao had been stirred very early in his career by the inequity of

---

demned in the Chinese legend to cut down the cassia tree on the moon, but it became whole again as soon as his axe had done its work. The legend is similar to that of Sisyphus, who trapped the Greek god of death.

* i.e. Chiang Kai-shek's.

women's status in China. At 26, moved by the suicide of a young girl forced by her parents to marry, against her will, he issued nine articles in a single fortnight denouncing the restraints on individual liberty imposed by the old traditions and hailing 'the great wave of the freedom to love'.[28]

Mao's full personality has eluded the biographers. Edgar Snow has set out the brief autobiography as it was told him in 1936, but we now know that this picture was distorted in a number of respects to serve Mao's immediate purposes at that time.[29] Subsequently two scholars have attempted to piece the story together. Stuart Schram's Mao Tse-tung is the most comprehensive account, Jerome Ch'ên's Mao and the Chinese Revolution,* though it ends in 1949, the most sure-footed. But somehow the whole man escapes all his portraitists, and only tantalizing glimpses come through.

Of his indispensability to the Communist victory in China, however, there is no doubt. 'No one else,' says Robert Payne, 'possessed the peculiar talents he had : the patience, the foresight, the astonishing capacity to learn thoroughly from his mistakes, the knowledge of military science, and the capacity to think in broad, strenuous outlines . . . He was not simply a political figure : he was the novelist whose novel had become suddenly true, or the poet whose words have suddenly become people.' [30]

Jerome Ch'ên concludes : 'Under this learned, resolute, experienced, ruthless and sensitive man, the Chinese Communist Party attained unity, strength, and eventually complete victory. No one else in the entire Communist movement in China can claim a greater share of the merit for their success.' Above all, Mao was, in Howard L. Boorman's phrase, the 'cultural domesticator of Communism' in China.[31]

But Mao Tse-tung would never have been able to survive his years in the wilderness, nor impose his will upon a divided and directionless Party, without the help of his famous colleague Chu Teh. When Chu joined Mao in the mountains of Chingkangshan in 1928, they recognized each other as complementary, and a

---

* Supplemented by his Mao, in the Great Lives Observed series. Robert Payne's Mao Tse-tung, though more readable than the others, is undocumented and not consistently reliable.

partnership was forged which apparently lasted through the Long March until the days when the Communist Party's struggle for power could be taken for granted. One has to say 'apparently', because there is evidence of tension between these two men all along. Such tension is normal in any close relationship, however, and the collaboration was more important than the friction.

Like Mao, Chu Teh came from a poor peasant family. He was born on 12 December 1886, in Szechuan Province, in the southwest of China.[32] His name means 'Red Virtue'. His childhood and youth were spent, again like Mao's, in gradually and painfully breaking away from the traditional mould of his family, to join some of the reform groups which were laying the foundation for the Republican Revolution of 1911–12. In 1909 he enrolled at the Yunnan Military Academy, where, again like Mao, he read with enthusiasm the lives of great men like George Washington, the liberal political thought of the West, and the tracts of Kang Yu-wei, the Chinese reformer. He joined the secret Republican organization *Tungmenhui*, which was an intellectual and political version of the *Ko Lao Hui*, the nationwide secret society which he also subsequently joined by drinking a blood oath in an isolated hill temple. The young Chu led a movement to abolish capital punishment in the Yunnan Military Academy.

In 1911–12 he was involved in the fighting which took place in his province over the fall of the Manchu Dynasty and the establishment of the Republic, complicated by the ambitions of the local warlords. In 1915 he first heard of Chen Tu-hsiu and his 'New Tide' movement for mass education, democracy and science at Peking University, and was greatly attracted. But soon he was appointed by the local warlord to be Garrison Commander in the city of Luchow, and here he began to sink back into the feudalistic way of life, enjoying his power and using it to promote his relatives.

Two of his brothers, whom he had encouraged to take military positions, were killed in action, and his old-fashioned parents, who despised the life of a soldier, were profoundly shocked. This was the time when Chu, like so many other Chinese of that generation trapped by their circumstances, began to take opium. He felt himself directly responsible for his younger brothers' death, and even felt himself partly to blame for his father's subsequent death.

In 1922 Chu was forced out by his enemies and had to escape across the River of Golden Sands and the Tatu River, with the help of his secret society contacts, to his home province of Szechuan. This was the same route by which he was destined to lead the Communist armies on the Long March thirteen years later.* According to his autobiography as told to Agnes Smedley, he smoked his last pipe of opium at this point and began on a local herb cure which caused him insomnia. It was here also that he saw for the last time his wife and son, who were murdered by warlords several years afterwards.

For he did not stay in Szechuan, but made his way to Shanghai on a Yangtze River steamer, a very confused man. Smedley describes his activities at this point as the 'gropings of a man, once a poor peasant, who had tasted power and prestige and at least some of the flesh pots of life.' [33] Edgar Snow was told that he spent a whole month sailing down the Yangtze River to Shanghai on a British steamer, and that no opium was available on board : his cure from the addiction was protracted and painful.[34] On arrival at Shanghai he took a rickshaw to the French Hospital and asked the doctors to cure his insomnia. He stayed there for a week, during which he read every newspaper he could lay his hands on and decided to join the Communist Party.

In Shanghai Chu was appalled at the misery of the poor industrial workers, and he began to meet some of the leaders of the modern movement. Sun Yat-sen invited him to go back to Yunnan to reorganize his army there in the Republican cause, but Chu refused because he regarded alliances with warlords as a squirrel cage; he said that he would rather go abroad and learn about Communism, which had been successful in Russia. But Chen Tu-hsiu, the Communist Party Secretary-General, rebuffed Chu's approaches, reminding him that Communist Party membership required a good deal of study and application. 'One of my feet remained in the old order and the other could find no place in the new,' Chu complained.[35]

In September he sailed on the French liner Algiers to Singapore,

---

* It was in Robert S. Elegant's phrase, a 'one-act rehearsal for the Long March': China's Red Leaders (London, Bodley Head, 1952), p. 76.

India, Africa and Marseilles, to join the Chinese students who were searching for the secrets of modernization in Paris and other Western cities. He became a popular member of these groups, although, at thirty-six, he was old enough to be a father to some of them. One of his first acts was to take the train to Berlin to see Chou En-lai, who arranged for him at last to join the Communist Party – but secretly so that he might still take a place in the Kuomintang organization when he returned to China. Chu devoured Berlin systematically as he did the other European cities which he visited, listening to Beethoven, attending the opera, touring the factories, palaces and museums.

In 1923 he joined the Political Science faculty at Göttingen University, but his German was very poor and his formal studies did not progress well. In the summer of 1926 he was arrested by the German police and expelled, sailing to Leningrad with three trunks full of books, maps and notes. He returned to Shanghai, resumed his Kuomintang connections in Szechuan Province – and began, for the first time, to read the articles of Mao Tse-tung.

At the end of 1926 Chu Teh was appointed as the Kuomintang Garrison Commander and Police Commissioner at Nanchang, and it was here that his opportunity to serve the Communist cause presented itself. A few months later he met secretly with Chou En-lai, Li Li-san, Ho Lung and – their first historic meeting – Mao Tse-tung.[36] This was the conference at which the Nanchang Rising, in which armed peasants and workers were to begin the agrarian revolution, was planned. Chu, as the Garrison Commander, attempted to put the other senior Kuomintang officers off their guard by throwing a dinner and *mahjong* party, but they sensed trouble and left before the party had got into full swing. The rising had to be brought forward by a few hours.

Chu then took command of the revolt,[37] and led the vanguard of the Red Armies to Canton, where the new Revolutionary Government was to be proclaimed. But his troops were cut to pieces by Chiang Kai-shek's at Swatow, and Chu had to lead his few surviving men to the southern part of Hunan, overcoming the doubting Thomases who thought it more politic to disband. Only 900 men remained with him, but they renamed themselves the Workers' and Peasants' Revolutionary Army, with Chu as their

Commander-in-Chief, Chen Yi as Political Commissar, and Lin Piao as one of the five detachment commanders.

Within weeks of this retreat, Chu learned that Mao, in similar disarray, had rallied his few remaining loyal followers in Chingkangshan, the mountainous area that lies between Hunan and Kiangsi. By April he had joined Mao in Chingkangshan, and the famous partnership began. Chu almost immediately saw in Mao the political mentor for whom he had sought so long, a man whose political ideas and judgement he could trust and follow for the rest of his life. He was the first of the military leaders of the Communist movement to recognize the need completely to subordinate the army to political direction, and so these two men encouraged and complemented each other at a time when either, deprived of the other's support, might well have fallen into relative oblivion along with the many other inadequate leaders of the Chinese Communist Party.[33]

If Mao provided the political genius, which ensured the maximum support from the people in the area where the Communists were campaigning, and which managed to get the prima donnas of the Red Army and the Central Committee to work together with the minimum of destructive friction, it was Chu who succeeded in winning the actual battles against the Kuomintang. As Robert Payne puts it, 'The theory, as he relates the battles, seems to be pure Mao; the practice, the knowledge of the possible, the way in which forces can be grouped together for maximum effectiveness, seems to come from Chu Teh.'[39]

Chu was a man of immense resourcefulness. He once saved his life after being captured by pretending to be a cook. 'Don't shoot me,' he shouted, 'I'm only the cook. Don't shoot a man who can cook for you!'[40] At this time he had a price of $250,000 in silver placed on his head by Chiang Kai-shek. His tough exterior disguised a deep sense of humility which often irritated Mao, and which Agnes Smedley guessed was due 'not only to his poor peasant origin and his peasant's respect for men of culture and learning but perhaps also ... to an unconscious sense of guilt rooted in the years he had spent as a militarist'.[41]

Like Mao, he was a much-married man. His first wife, the daughter of a progressive intellectual, died within a few years of the wedding. His second wife was also the daughter of a scholar, and his third was a writer who was subsequently tortured and beheaded by Kuomintang officers, who mounted her head on a pole in Changsha to deter Communist sympathizers. Chu's fourth wife, Kang Ke-ching, was a peasant girl who accompanied Chu on the Long March and made her name as one of the toughest of the small band of women who survived it.

As a jovial, simple – if somewhat guilt-ridden – soldier, Chu did not shine in the later years of the Chinese Communist Party story.[42] It was noticed at Yenan, after the Long March, that he adopted a more elaborate wardrobe than most of the Communist leaders, and his role in the Chinese People's Republic after 1949 seemed to be that of an old hero worthy of affection but not to be given any responsibility. It was said in well-informed circles in Peking even before the Cultural Revolution began in 1966 that Chu had commissioned a Chinese writer to compose his biography, and that Mao – or Mao's group – refused to allow it to be published, presumably because it might have suggested that not every single victory on the Long March and at other moments of the Communist struggle was due to the genius of the Chairman. A criticism in a secret 1961 army bulletin of the 'erroneous influence' of a Comrade 'XX' has been linked by one commentator with Chu Teh.[43]

Some of this tension came into the open after 1966 when all the leaders came under criticism in war-posters and Red Guard newspapers. It was said at this time, in radical publications circulating within China which called Chu Teh an 'ambitious warlord', that Chu had challenged Mao's advice at the important Tsunyi conference during the Long March; that he, with others, had wanted to lead the Red Armies to fight against the Japanese immediately after their arrival in Shensi after the Long March (thus opposing Mao's view that it was wiser to wait and recuperate); and that he had disagreed with Mao on a number of other occasions.[44] It has even been suggested that Chu deliberately deserted Mao in the middle of the Long March to follow his fellow-Szechuanese in the Fourth Front Army under Mao's rival in the Communist guerrilla hierarchy, Chang Kuo-tao.[45]

Some possible confirmation of these charges might be read into the fact that Chu Teh's autobiography as told to Agnes Smedley reveals almost nothing about the period 1931–4; either Chu was still, in 1937, confused over the right line to take about the complex intra-Party struggles of those years, or he preferred to play down parts of the story which it might be impolitic to have publicized.[46]

Chen Yi, one of Chu Teh's protégés (and later China's ebullient and notoriously indiscreet Foreign Minister), was said to have confided once that Chu always bore a grudge against Mao for mishandling their guerrilla campaign in Hunan in August 1928.[47] One of the features of the Kutien conference of the Red Army in December 1929–January 1930 was said to be the defection of Lin Piao, another of Chu Teh's protégés, to Mao's side in the debate between the two leaders.[48] A year later the Futien mutiny in the Red Army was said to have been accompanied by slogans supporting Chu Teh and Peng Teh-huai against Mao.[49] Chu and Peng enjoyed a ready popularity with their men, whereas Mao was sometimes standoffish and gave the appearance of being conceited. Chu was no doubt confused some of the time as far as politics were concerned, and perhaps his adherence to the Maoist line diminished with the length of time since his last briefing session. But he did support Mao at the Tsunyi Conference in January 1935, and Mao has reportedly commended him for resisting the move at the Ningtu Red Army Conference in August 1932 (at which Mao was deposed from the chairmanship of the Military Commission) to expel Mao from the Party.[50] The subtleties of the Mao-Chu relationship are among the chief mysteries and fascinations of the Long March.

But these elements of dissension, and possibly of mutual envy, were to come out only later. At this time, in 1928, six years before the Long March began, each of the two men apparently recognized in the other the partner which he needed. Chu had found at last an intellectual who could make sense of the confusing conditions of China at that time and yet could also understand the peasant mentality, a combination almost unique in the Communist leadership. Mao, for his part, found a brilliant military tactician, a quick-thinking general who had the intelligence to see that fighting was worthless if it were not linked to some specific and well-conceived political objective. For the next seven years these two men fought side by side, if not always in perfect harmony, to secure the survival of the Communist idea and the ultimate victory of the Chinese Communist Party.

Chapter 5

Chingkangshan and the Kiangsi Soviet

CHINGKANGSHAN is a great wild outcrop of forested mountain, about 150 miles in circumference, on the borderline between the provinces of Hunan and Kiangsi. Its volcanic peaks are foggy most of the year and its woods of pine, spruce and bamboo are full of wolves, boars, even leopards and tigers. For centuries Chingkangshan was a final and impregnable retreat of bandits, and the only inhabitants were a few hundred descendants of bandits divided into five villages. But in October 1927 Mao Tse-tung arrived with the dispirited remnant of his Communist forces and ensured its fame for a different reason. The Autumn Harvest Uprising had failed, Mao himself had been taken by the Kuomintang and forced to buy his way out of captivity, and the Chinese Communist cause was about to die what seemed to many observers its last death in the overthrow of the short-lived Canton Commune. Yet Chingkangshan was to be the turning-point of the entire story.

For it was here that the Communist leaders were obliged to come fully to terms with the reality – as distinct from the niceties of Marxist analysis – of the Chinese scene. Even as he began the ascent to the mountain, Mao had to break one of the Chinese Communist Party rules in order to survive. He had to strike up an alliance with the bandit chieftains of the areas, Wang Tso and Yuan Wen-tsai. He had only 1,000 men, and it was essential to have the 600 bandit forces—not to mention their 120 rifles – on his side rather than against him.[1]

He justified this by necessity, but he also argued that these unorthodox allies were among those *éléments déclassés* (the others being soldiers, robbers, beggars and prostitutes) who could make excellent revolutionary fighters if given the right leadership. Besides, the bandits belonged to the *Ko Lao Hui*, the secret society

66

which had played such a valued part in the 1911–12 Revolution.[2] But the Central Committee (which had already expelled him for his failure and insubordination at Changsha,[3] though he did not learn of this till the following spring) bitterly attacked his romantic liaison with the bandits in defiance of all Marxist-Leninist principle.

In the spring of 1928, Chu Teh's army of 900, with Chen Yi and Lin Piao, arrived in Chingkangshan, with orders from the Central Committee to correct Mao's errors and bring him to heel, so to speak. But the reunited Red Armies were immediately attacked by Kuomintang forces, and repulsed them without difficulty. Elated by this success, the leaders held a formal conference at Maoping, where they agreed to set up a new revolutionary base and to integrate and reorganize their forces into a new Fourth Red Army with Chu as Commander-in-Chief and Mao as Political Commissar.

The new army was to be an egalitarian one in such matters as pay and rations, and it was to follow Mao's Three Rules of Discipline (obey orders, don't take anything from workers or peasants, and hand in everything taken from local landlords and gentry) and Eight Additional Rules (put back the doors you use for bed-boards, replace the straw borrowed for bedding, speak politely, pay fairly for what you buy, return everything you borrow, pay for anything you damage, don't bathe in the sight of women, and don't search the pockets of captives).[4] As for its tactics against the vastly superior and better-armed enemy, they were summed up in the quatrain that was to become the most famous expression of the principles of guerrilla warfare from Cuba to Vietnam, Angola to Bengal:

> If the enemy advances, we retreat.
> If the enemy halts and encamps, we harass.
> If the enemy seeks to avoid battle, we attack.
> If the enemy retreats, we pursue.

Mao's crystallized experience on how to organize an army made sense to Chu and his colleagues. Mao and Chu also agreed on their agrarian policy. All land was to be confiscated without compensation and distributed to the poor peasants – who would be armed and trained to defend it. Landlords were to be overthrown and executed, although the so-called intermediate classes, the middle and rich peasants and the petty merchants (men like Mao's own father) were to be treated with reasonable moderation and restraint so as not excessively to antagonize vocal sections of the rural community. The idea was to extend the area of the soviet by a series of waves.[5]

Later in 1928 the Party Central Committee in Shanghai confirmed this land policy, but ordered the ownership to be retained in the soviet Government's hands. By this time, however, Mao had developed second thoughts. Reporting on agrarian policy to a second conference at Maoping at the end of 1928, Mao explained that crude collectivization was counter-productive. 'The peasants did not respond well . . .,' as one soviet official put it. 'Their demand was for land of their own which each family could cultivate for itself. . . .'[6]

Mao felt that only landlords' land should be confiscated, that this should be vested in peasant ownership and that sale of land should be permitted afterwards. But all this was regarded in Shanghai as unnecessarily lenient to the rich peasants, who were notoriously conservative and acquisitive. Mao was not yet powerful enough to carry Chu with him in challenging the Central Committee's authority, and his 'rich peasant line' was dropped.

The Chu–Mao duumvirate was now added to by Peng Teh-huai, another Hunanese Communist peasant leader who had joined the army at 16 in the early days of the Republic, rose to command a regiment in the Northern Expedition of 1926, and subsequently rebelled against the Kuomintang.* He brought the 1,000 survivors of his Fifth Red Army to Chingkangshan in November 1928.[7]

Chu and Mao now felt strong enough to swoop down into

---

* Peng's people were rich peasants, and at the age of nine he was condemned to death by his family for kicking his grandmother's pot of opium off the stove. An uncle interceded and he was allowed to leave home instead. Snow described him as 'open, forthright, and undeviating in his manner and speech, quick in his movements, full of laughter and wit . . . physically very active, an excellent rider and a man of endurance . . . a non-smoker and a teetotaller' (Red Star Over China, pp. 265 and 267–8).

Kiangsi and Fukien and begin to extend the soviet area, though they temporarily lost Chingkangshan to the Kuomintang in the process. A new central revolutionary base was formed, centred on the town of Juiching, comprising parts of Kiangsi, Fukien and Hunan. Others were being formed meanwhile in other parts of China – Ho Lung's in Hupei–Hunan, Chang Kuo-tao's in Oyuwan, Teng Hsiao-ping's at the Left River and a dozen more. But the Kiangsi soviet of Mao and Chu was the biggest and most successful.

Mao himself had a dangerous bout of malaria at this point. One of his soldiers managed to pass through enemy lines to bring back quinine from Shanghai (though on a second similar mission he was caught and executed), and Doctor Nelson Fu, the Christian convert from the British Baptist Mission who headed the Red Army Medical Corps, was able to save Mao.[8]

Gradually Mao built up his power base in the soviet. He sought to purge the Red Army of its miscreants (those who succumbed to gambling, opium-smoking and personal gain) and to stiffen its discipline and its subordination to the Party. He began to see that the most likely way of conquering China was by slowly extending the soviet areas, by relying on guerrilla warfare and by avoiding the big cities until the last. But this depended on gaining – and keeping – peasant support, and this in turn meant a flexible and sophisticated approach to land redistribution.

During these early years in Chingkangshan and Kiangsi Mao moved away from the fairly doctrinaire line, common among the Party leaders then, of aggressive social revolution in the countryside (complete confiscation and thorough redistribution) to a more restrained position which saw the need to woo the intermediate pieces in the rural game of chess – the rich peasants and smaller landlords – away from the Kuomintang and the real aristocratic power-holders, the gentry.

It was an excellent plan to go all out for peasant revolution if a quick success were envisaged. But if it was really going to be a long slow haul, then better to take on only one enemy at a time. It was enough at this stage to keep the rich peasants out of the soviet Government apparatus, while allowing them their share of land to farm as they wanted. But this, in the eyes of the Shanghai

Party leaders, was rightist deviationism and opportunism of the first order.

Generals always prefer to take cities, for their plunder and supplies, and the official Party line, under Li Li-san, of making another shot at urban revolt, was attractive. Mao remained in a minority on this question.[9] But the disastrous failure of the attack on Changsha and Nanchang in September 1930 led many to pay more respect to his views. Mao had understood the military situation better than the Central Committee did, and he was gradually gaining supporters in the Party and in the Red Armies.

He hastened the process by his swift and ruthless suppression at the end of 1930 of a mutiny among his soldiers at Futien. He had ordered the arrest of more than 4,000 men on suspicion of belonging to a secret Kuomintang organization, of favouring rich peasants and of generally disobeying his orders. But an officer named Liu Ti rebelled, freed the prisoners and overthrew the local provincial soviet Government. About a hundred of Mao's followers were killed and it is said that Chu Teh's wife was captured by the mutineers, who denounced Mao as a 'Party emperor'.[10] The suppression of the Futien mutiny cemented Mao's reputation as a tough and forceful leader – and also got him into trouble with the Politburo. In August 1931 he was replaced by Chou En-lai as political commissar of the First Front Army, and in October Wang Chia-hsiang replaced him as Director of the General Political Department of the Red Army. It was afterwards rumoured that Chen Yi had been Mao's chief hatchet man at Futien, and that Chen's excessive bloodthirstiness in carrying out the assignment had caused the Politburo to decide to leave him behind when the Long March began.[11]

The Kiangsi soviet now began to undergo a series of five encirclement campaigns by the Kuomintang forces. The first, in December 1930–January 1931, was ineffectual. The Communists captured their first radio sets as a result of it. The second, in the spring of 1931, was equally unsuccessful, and the Red Armies took 20,000 prisoners and rifles. The third campaign that summer was led by Chiang Kai-shek in person, with forces ten times bigger than the Red Armies. Luckily for the Chinese Communist Party, the Japanese occupation of Manchuria caused the Kuomintang to call off the campaign.

At the end of 1931, two Kuomintang brigades surrendered to General Chu Teh, who thus acquired 20,000 rifles, several hundred machine guns, more than a hundred pieces of artillery and many radios. The Red Armies now boasted 200,000 men and 150,000 rifles, and they held sway over twenty-one counties embracing a population of two and a half million people.

Mao's leading position in all this was confirmed at the First All-China Soviet Congress held at Juiching in November 1931. The Mao–Chu partnership had repulsed three encirclement campaigns by the Kuomintang, rooted out enemy agents within the Red Armies, executed the Futien rebels, consolidated its faction's power in the Kiangsi–Fukien area, managed the election of delegates from that area to the Congress, and provided the Party (at a time when Comintern funds were scanty) with its chief source of revenue from the soviet area taxes.

The Chinese Communist Party Central Committee leaders who came to Juiching (Chou En-lai slipped out of Shanghai disguised as a clergyman with a long beard and a black robe)[12] did not entirely approve of Mao, and they had sufficient power in the Party organization to turn him aside, had they wished. Yet Mao was elected Chairman of the Central Executive Committee of the All-China Soviet Government, with its seat at Juiching. The Wang Ming group still controlled the Politburo, but henceforth people spoke of Mao *Chu-hsi* (Chairman Mao) instead of the old Mao *Wei-yuan* (Commissioner Mao). Hsiang Ying and Chang Kuo-tao were his Vice-chairmen.

The best explanation of this is that offered by Trygve Lötveit in a recently published study : 'The Party leaders did not want to ignore the machinery which Mao had built up in the Central Soviet Area. As a group they possessed an expertise in handling the theories of Lenin and Stalin, and they had some experience of underground activity from their base in Shanghai, but they had not yet sufficient confidence in their ability to deal with the administrative tasks of the new republic which was to be built up under unfamiliar circumstances in the Chinese hinterland. They therefore wanted, not to replace, but to make use of Mao and his supporters who were experienced in organizational work in the soviet areas.' [13]

Chou En-lai stayed behind in Juiching after the Congress, and became the new field commander, as it were, of the Communist base. For the first time Mao now faced an experienced and sophisticated rival in his own backyard – and not until the Long March was the rivalry to be patched up. Chou was a completely different type of man from the others on the Politburo. As he himself later confessed, 'I am an intellectual with a feudalistic background. I had had little contact with the peasant-worker masses because I had taken no part in the economic process of production. My revolutionary career started abroad, with very limited knowledge about it obtained from books only.'

Chou had been born into a Mandarin family of Chekiang province in 1898. Unlike the other Communist leaders, he never lost an opportunity of paying his respects to his family, visiting its shrines and maintaining contact with its members. He once told a public audience that his mother's grave was in enemy-occupied territory : 'How I wish I could just go back there once to clear the weeds on her grave – the least a prodigal son who has given his life to revolution and to his country could do for his mother.' On another occasion he said in a dinner speech, choked with emotion : 'It has been thirty-eight years since I last saw my old home. The poplars in front of my mother's grave must have grown very tall by now.' Yet he resolutely refused to save his brother's father-in-law, a rich and unrepentant landlord, from the fury of the peasants after 1949.[14]

At school he was a leader in everything, and even took a woman's part, with great success, in a school play. He went on to Japan and France to pursue his studies and his political interests, which were radical from the start. In Paris, where he lived in Billancourt near the Renault factory, he was leader of the students (including Chen Yi and Teng Hsiao-ping) who founded the Communist group there in 1920–21. In Berlin he also organized a Chinese Communist Youth Corps, into which he had inducted Chu Teh, among others. Many of his junior colleagues of those days in Europe were now in positions of high responsibility in the soviet area under Mao.

Chou's dexterity in resolving factional squabbles among the overseas students, his unflagging charm and expert diplomacy, stood him in good stead in his subsequent career in China. One of his colleagues in Paris later reminisced: 'Chou En-lai is rather weak in his mastery of political theories, but he can summarize my ideas and re-present them much better than I can. We depended on him to prepare all our public statements, either orally or in writing, because once he handled them they were sure to be accepted by all groups involved.' [15]

Back in China, in 1924, he became a leading figure in the Whampoa Military Academy, where he served under Chiang Kai-shek and taught Lin Piao, and quickly gained acceptance as a leading figure on the Chinese political scene – together with his wife, Teng Ying-chao, a Communist whose political ability and loyalty to Chou were unquestioned, and who was one of the women to undertake the Long March. Their only child had been stillborn during the troubles of 1927.[16]

Chou was in Shanghai personally leading labour revolts when Chiang ordered the massacre of Communists in April 1927. Soon after his escape from the city he was elected to the Chinese Communist Party Central Committee and to the Party Secretary-Generalship. Thereafter he remained one of the top three in the Party hierarchy through all its changes, thus gaining a reputation for time-serving which is not deserved. He was simply more skilful than the others in sensing political currents, assessing factional realities and handling personal relations. His aristocratic graces, albeit worn with deep humility, earned him occasional envy or dislike in the Party, but his dedication to the cause of Communism was never doubted. It was said – by outsiders – that he was forever the faithful lieutenant and could never aspire to be the supreme leader of a proletarian-peasant movement.

Yet eventually he became the Prime Minister, Foreign Minister and chief fixer of the Communist Government, and the best-known of its members in the eyes of the outside world. Suave and persuasive, he became for many, Chinese and non-Chinese alike, the embodiment of Chinese Communism, especially of its intellectual and artistic promise. Even in 1966–70, when much of this earlier promise had been abandoned, he still managed to swim with the main, life-saving currents of internal Chinese politics and from that position to salvage as much as possible of Chinese national unity, economic development and intellectual life. During the Cultural Revolution he saved the administrative structure of the country from collapse, prevented the extreme radical faction of the Maoists from seizing power, curbed the over-zealous campaigns of the anarchistic Red Guards, and kept the army from benefiting too much from the chaos.

But all that lay far ahead as Chou grimly prepared in Juiching in 1932 for the next stage of the Chinese Communist revolution and his three-year tussle with Mao Tse-tung. Chou had no position in the soviet Government, but he was a leading member of its Central Executive Committee and he was the most senior Politburo member present in Juiching – taking precedence over Mao. Inevitably tension grew between the two men.

The immediate issue was a military one. In June 1932 the Kuomintang, momentarily recovered from the shock of the Japanese attack on Manchuria and Shanghai, launched its Fourth Encirclement campaign, with 150,000 troops under Ho Ying-chin and Chen Cheng (who eventually became Vice-President of Taiwan). The campaign lasted for eight months, with a truce in the middle by tacit mutual consent.

Chou wanted positional warfare to be used in fighting the enemy and holding the base, though he was willing to employ the famous guerrilla 'lure' tactic behind enemy lines. His preference was for a highly centralized army defending a fixed base. This ran completely counter to the principles of guerrilla warfare developed by Mao Tse-tung for a situation where your enemy is stronger and better-equipped but where the peasantry support you. Chou, however, felt that the Red Army had at last come of age and no longer needed herding by a personalized leadership into small bands of hit-and-run guerrillas.[17]

In August 1932, at the Ningtu Conference, Chou forced Mao off the Military Committee of the Party's Central Bureau for Soviet Areas (which in Party ranking was superior to the soviet Government itself) – and a few months later, in May 1933, Chou actually took over Mao's position as Chief Political Commissar of the Red Armies. Mao in any case fell ill again and was hospitalized under Doctor Nelson Fu's care for four months. The Ningtu Conference represented the nadir of Mao's fortunes and following in Kiangsi. According to one source who was in the soviet area at the time, Mao's views at this meeting were opposed by Chou En-lai, Chu Teh, Peng Teh-huai, Liu Po-cheng, Chen Yi and Jen Pi-shih as well as by Chang Wen-tien and the others of the Twenty-eight Bolsheviks faction.[18]

After the Long March Mao denounced these views as 'the theories and practices of hotheads and ignoramuses', and as too slavishly dependent on Russian military textbooks: 'Those comrades who vigorously opposed "guerrilla-ism" argued along the following lines. It was wrong to lure the enemy in deep because we had to abandon so much territory. Although battles had been won in this way, was not the situation different now? Moreover, was it not better to defeat the enemy without abandoning territory? And was it not better still to defeat the enemy in his own areas, or on the borders between his area and ours? The old practices had had nothing "regular" about them and were methods used only by guerrillas. Now our own state had been established and our Red Army had become a regular army. Our fight against Chiang Kai-shek had become a war between two states, between two great armies. History should not repeat itself, and everything pertaining to "guerrilla-ism" should be totally discarded. The new principles were "completely Marxist", while the old had been created by guerrilla units in the mountains, and there was no Marxism in the mountains.

'The new principles were the antithesis of the old. They were: "Pit one against ten, pit ten against a hundred, fight bravely and determinedly, and exploit victories by hot pursuit"; "Attack on all fronts"; "Seize key cities"; and "Strike with two 'fists' in two directions at the same time". When the enemy attacked, the methods of dealing with him were: "Engage the enemy outside the gates", "Gain mastery by striking first", "Don't let our pots and pans be smashed", "Don't give up an inch of territory" and "Divide the forces into six routes". The war was "the decisive battle between the road of revolution and the road of colonialism", a war of short swift thrusts, blockhouse warfare, war of attrition, "protracted war". There was, further, the policy of maintaining a great rear area and an absolutely centralized command. Finally there was a large-scale "house-moving". And anyone who did not accept these things was to be punished, labelled an opportunist, and so on and so forth.

'Without a doubt these theories and practices were all wrong. They were nothing but subjectivism. Under favourable circumstances this subjectivism manifested itself in petty-bourgeois revolutionary fanaticism and impetuosity, but in times of adversity, as the situation worsened, it changed successively into desperate recklessness, conservatism and flightism. They were the theories and practices of hotheads and ignoramuses; they did not have the slightest flavour of Marxism about them; indeed they were anti-Marxist.' [19]

The rebuff at Ningtu was never forgotten: thirty-four years later Mao reminisced at a Cultural Revolution meeting that, 'at the Ningtu conference, Lo Fu wanted to expel me but Chou En-lai and Chu Teh objected'.[20]

But the difference went much deeper than military strategy. Mao and Chu Teh had declared war on Japan in April 1932 in the name of the soviet Government, and Mao now advocated a coalition with the Kuomintang and another united front in the face of Japanese aggression. The Chinese Communist Party failed, however, to endorse this line. Under the influence of the Comintern it attached more importance to capitalism (which hardly existed in China) than to feudalism or imperialism (which, as Mao saw, were the central issues). The Central Committee was urban-oriented and romanticized the proletariat, while Mao based everything on the peasants. The debate was well summarized in Chou En-lai's stinging public rebuke to Mao and his followers in 1932:

'All those who regard the seizure of one or several entire provinces as not an immediate but a distant goal; all those who are sceptical about occupying metropolitan centres and prefer to lead the soviet régime and the Red Army toward remote areas; all those who are hesitant about a positive outward expansion of Communism to enable the Red Army to utilize its full potential, who prefer to tie the hands of our armed comrades with such assignments as propaganda in the villages and raising funds for the army, forgetting that the principal mission of the Red Army is to destroy our enemy through combat; all those who still linger in a past stage for which a gradual expansion of military action and a defensive and conservative strategy were proper and who are consequently unwilling to move swiftly to deal a fatal blow to the enemy in the non-Communist area; all those who neglect the urgent need to support and respond to Red Army action all over the country in order to distract the enemy, are committing a serious error of rightist-opportunism.' [21]

In fact the Red Armies under Chou were able to repel the Kuomintang attacks, the fourth and penultimate in the series of encirclement campaigns, and Mao's criticisms tended to go unregarded or dismissed as obsolete romanticism. His attachment to the rules of warfare set out in Sun Tzu's Art of War and other Chinese classics, and his disdain for modern technical innovations were mocked as 'insisting on substituting a medieval copper clock for a modern timepiece'.[22] Only in the following year, when the euphoria of this success was evaporated by the intensity of the final encirclement campaign, did Mao's consistent advocacy of guerrilla tactics begin to regain favour among the generals.

Early in 1933 Chou was reinforced in Juiching by many of the remaining members of the Politburo who could no longer safely stay in Shanghai. Wang Ming himself retired instead to the U.S.S.R.,[23] but Po Ku now took command in Juiching, with the Comintern military adviser, Otto Braun (a German), known as Li Teh, at his elbow. Li Teh had been smuggled up from Canton under some matting in a small river junk.[24]

The Politburo ordered a general mobilization in the soviet area, an expansion of the Red Armies to a million men, a fresh campaign to take cities, and a new peasant policy of executing landlords, attacking rich peasants and screwing higher taxes out of the countryside in order to finance the new offensive. To Mao it seemed like collective suicide. But those who supported him were systematically criticized, demoted and purged in the Central Committee's drive against the 'ultra-cautious guerrilla-ism' of Lo Ming, one of Mao's men who openly opposed the 'Bolshevik forward and offensive line'. The purge involved Mao's own brother, his secretary and such Maoists as Teng Hsiao-ping, Tan Chen-lin, Teng Tzu-hui, Lu Ting-yi, Ku Pai, Hsieh Wei-chun, Hsiao Chin-kuang and Ho Shu-heng.[25] Mao's political power base was drastically weakened.

But Chiang Kai-shek changed all these plans by returning in August to take command of the Fifth Encirclement Campaign, even more highly organized and equipped than its predecessors. The military pretensions of Chou En-lai, Po Ku and Li Teh were put to the test in defence instead of the ambitious expansion plans they had announced, and on the outcome would depend the fate not only of the intra-Party leadership struggle but even of the Party itself.

Chapter 6

The Decision to March

THE fifth encirclement which began in August 1933 was a formidable operation. Chiang Kai-shek had almost a million men at his disposal, backed up by an air force of 400 aeroplanes and an immense arsenal. He had just secured a fifty million dollar wheat loan from the Reconstruction Finance Corporation, and he had the moral support of all the Western powers.

Von Seeckt and Von Falkenhausen, his two German military advisers, had devised a remorseless gradual throttling of the troublesome Communist base. A tight economic blockade was imposed on the soviet area, which was known to be desperately short of salt and dependent for cloth, kerosene, medical supplies and many other items of trade with the neighbouring non-soviet districts.[1] 'Fiery walls' of scorched earth were thrown about the Communists, and narrowing circles of concrete blockhouses, dubbed 'tortoises' by the Red Armies, and linked by barbed wire fences, were constructed to hem them in. New roads were built to open up the area to Chiang's motorized units. All these preparations were noted with apprehension in Juiching. Guerrilla-ism, as Chu Teh later explained, is 'useless in block-house operations'.[2]

Chiang's seventy-five divisions pushed forward in four columns and the two armies see-sawed for two or three months. But the clash was interrupted by an event that was to throw both sides into orgies of recrimination. The Kuomintang soldiers of the Nineteeth Route Army who had defended Shanghai against Japanese invasion in 1932 were now stationed in Fukien Province, where they formed the east wall of the Fifth Encirclement. But they were disgruntled at Chiang's policy of pacifying the Chinese interior before turning to deal with the Japanese, even though they had themselves fought against the Communists in the past. In October

79

1933 their generals rebelled against the Kuomintang and declared a 'People's Government', which professed a certain degree of left-wing policy and sent an envoy to Juiching to discuss possible co-operation against Chiang and the Japanese.

The Nineteenth Route generals were renowned for their anti-Japanese militancy, but had not hitherto been noted for any socialist leaning. Mao, according to one version of this story, urged caution in responding to their approach, but Chou suggested immediate talks and two Communist emissaries were sent back to Foochow. A Preliminary Agreement to resist the two common enemies was signed on 26 October. It was understood that certain concessions would be made to the Communist cause in Fukien by way of freedom of speech and assembly, a guaranteed right by labour to strike and so forth. But the Fukien rebels paid only lip service to this programme, and the Communists were thus in a quandary how to proceed, not wanting to get mixed up with a group of reactionaries desperately seeking to save themselves by insincere promises.

Meanwhile Chiang suspended operations on the other fronts and sent his crack 88th Division south to close the gap which the mutiny had left on the Chekiang–Fukien border. The rebels could not resist the superior and better-transported main Kuomintang forces without Communist help. Chou En-lai and Po Ku felt that the Red Armies should go to the aid of the rebels by keeping Kuomintang troops engaged elsewhere. But according to Kung Chu, the Communist general who later defected, Mao still wanted proof of good faith from the Fukien rebels before helping them.[3] Denying any genuine revolutionary element in the Fukien revolt, he told the Second National Soviet Congress in Juiching on 27 January 1934 that 'the appearance of the People's Revolutionary Government [in Fukien] represents a new mode of deceiving the people applied by a part of the reactionary ruling class in order to save their destiny from death'.[4] Whatever the final decision – and this is obscure – Communist help, if it came at all, came too late to save the Nineteenth Route Army.

Subsequently the Chinese Communist Party was criticized in Moscow for losing an opportunity to embarrass the Kuomintang and perhaps spoil its offensive. By that time the Comintern was plugging the line of united front with bourgeois nationalist groups against Japanese imperialism. The Chinese Central Committee accepted a degree of blame, but the question was still a sensitive and controversial one in 1936, when Pavel Mif, the Comintern patron of Po Ku and Wang Ming, offered the opinion that it had been a 'serious mistake' to place so narrow an interpretation on the Preliminary Agreement.

When Edgar Snow interviewed Mao in 1936 he was told that 'we could have successfully co-operated with Fukien, but due to the advice of Li Teh ... and the advisory group in Shanghai we withdrew instead'.[5] The Wang Ming leadership, and its European advisers, were made the official scapegoats for the affair. Probably, as William F. Dorrill has suggested [6] in a recent article examining this Fukien Revolt incident, Mao by then needed an explanation for the defeat of the Red Army in Kiangsi in 1934, one that would enable the Party to build up a new invincible image and to assure those warlords whose cooperation it was then (in 1936) seeking of its *bona fides* in proposing a united front.

But on this, as on so many other incidents just before and during the Long March, we have insufficient testimony to be quite sure of what really happened during the debates of the Party leadership. There is some evidence which suggests that Mao was more sympathetic towards the Fukien rebels whereas the Politburo was more haughty and sceptical. Certainly Mao was more aware of the potential of harnessing anti-Japanese feeling, even temporarily in the Communist cause, and the Fukien incident provided a classic example of this. But the balance of power was so delicately poised in Juiching at this time that discrepancies between thought and speech, between private word and public writing, are only to be expected.

During this lull in the Fifth Encirclement campaign, in January 1934, the Communists staged their Second All-China Soviet Congress. This time the Twenty-eight Bolsheviks under Po Ku probably secured a majority on the seventeen-man Praesidium which led the Central Executive Committee of the soviet Government and had the power to elect its Chairman. The Politburo apparatus had had a year in which to infiltrate Mao's carefully constructed power base, and it had not scrupled to resort to crude Stalinist terror tactics – a fact that later made Mao's brand of leadership, which wrapped an iron hand of certitude in a velvet glove of endless intellectual persuasion,* seem more palatable.

Before 1934 the Central Committee was critical of Mao's alleged excessive terror tactics in dealing with opposition. Subsequently, as Po Ku's faction consolidated itself in the Kiangsi soviet, it justified an even fiercer Red terror in which guilt did not have to be proved by legal process before execution. Probably, as Trygve Lötveit concludes in his study of this period,[7] the Committee was using anything at first to take a dig at Mao, who in the early years of the soviet was very likely sufficiently unsure of his ground to dispense with legal niceties. In 1934, when Mao had developed a judicial machine which he could reasonably trust, but when the newly-arrived Po Ku smelt a Kuomintang agent under every bed, the positions were reversed. It would be an over-simplification to see in these differences of approach to Party discipline merely the contrast between one leader, basically kind, and another, fundamentally cruel.

Po Ku and his faction were clever – or insecure – enough to have Mao re-elected at the January 1934 Congress as Chairman of the soviet Government. But this meant little. Chang Wen-tien (Lo Fu), another Bolshevik, was made Chairman of the Council of People's Commissars, and acted as a strong Prime Minister to Mao's figurehead Chairman.[8]

In August, according to Kung Chu,[9] Mao was actually expelled (for the third time) from the Central Committee, excluded from Party meetings and placed under a form of house arrest at Yutu, by order from Moscow – because of his independent action over the Fukien incident, according to one source, but more likely because of Mao's general opposition to the Politburo line of Po Ku and Chou En-lai.

Meanwhile the Fifth Encirclement was resumed by an impatient Chiang, and this time there was nothing to distract him from his objective. Mao and Chu Teh advocated that the Red Army should break through the ever-tightening Kuomintang circle, split into

---

* Save where force was necessary to answer force, as in the Futien mutiny.

small units and fight guerrilla campaigns in the areas to the north and east of the enemy lines where there were no blockhouses. Li Teh rejected this advice, insisting that the base must be defended in the same way as it was being attacked – by trenches, block-houses and positional combat. Besides, the abandonment of the soviet area and its population would destroy the Communists' credibility as a rival régime to the Kuomintang.

When one of the participants was later asked by Edgar Snow how Li Teh, who spoke no Chinese and whose Russian had to be interpreted by the Russian-trained Po Ku, was able to get his way on tactics, the reply was: 'He was very confident and very authoritative. He pounded his fist on the table. He told Mao and others, that they knew nothing about military matters; they should heed him . . . He had the prestige of the world Communist supporters behind him.' [10]

In April 1934 the final proof came of the misguided defensive posture of the Communists. They were shatteringly defeated at the battle of Kuangchang, on the Fukien-Kiangsi border, leaving 4,000 dead in the field and taking 20,000 wounded away with them. The main Red Army force was now crippled, and the gateway to Juiching, the soviet capital, lay open to the Kuomintang troops. The Communists' desertion rate began to soar, and an army news-paper admitted that desertion had become 'an enemy even more fearful than Chiang Kai-shek'. Soldiers used to commit suicide by pointing their rifles to their throats and pressing the trigger with their toes.[11]

By June only a few counties were left in Communist hands, and it became a clear-cut question of either breaking out or else sitting down to await annihilation. One Red group broke out in July under Fang Chih-min (who was suffering excruciating pain from piles) and Fu Yu, combining the Seventh and Tenth Armies under the name of 'Anti-Japanese Advance Detachment'. The soviet government, under Mao's signature, declared that if this detach-ment found armed forces ready to join with the Communists in fighting against Japanese aggression, the rest of the Red Armies would follow 'to unite with all armed forces in China for a com-mon struggle.'[12] The vanguard headed for southern Anhwei and actually reached the Yangtze River at Wuhu, near Nanking, thus tying down Kuomintang troops as the main Red force set out on the Long March. But the enemy pushed it back to Kiangsi and Fang was captured (and later beheaded, after being exhibited in various places in a bamboo cage). A small part of the force survived.[13]

In August another large group of 10,000 men, the VI Army Corps under Jen Pi-shih, Wang Chen and Hsiao Ke, marched through the Kuomintang lines to north-eastern Kweichow where it linked up with Ho Lung's Third Army at Nanyaochieh near Tungjen in October and formed, jointly with it, a new Second Front Army controlling a Hunan–Hupei–Szechuan–Kweichow soviet base (and diverting Kuomintang forces in Hunan to the northern part of that province to allow Chu Teh's main force to pass through its southern districts).

A third break-out was that of Cheng Tse-hua's Twenty-fifth Army, which marched through the Hupei–Hunan–Anhwei border region to Shensi. Later all three of these forays were explained as advance diversionary columns designed to throw the Kuomintang off the scent of the main Red force and allow the key First Front Army (comprising the I Army Corps under Chu Teh and Mao, and the III Army Corps under Peng Teh-huai) to complete its preparations for the Long March.

Hsingkuo fell to the Kuomintang in September, leaving only six Red counties. Mao lay ill with malaria at Yutu, with a temperature running as high as a hundred and five degrees, under Doctor Nelson Fu's ministrations.[14]

In mid-September a statement by Hsiang Ying, one of the Central Committee members, hinted at an abandonment of the base,[15] and Chang Wen-tien made the prospect explicit in an article in the Party-organ, Red Flag, on 1 October. The leaders had reluctantly come to the view that a break-out was inevitable, though even then Li Teh and Po Ku insisted that the First Front Army should march as one unit rather than splitting as Mao had suggested. Chou En-lai, Po Ku, Li Teh and Mao met on the night of 2 October and agreed to evacuate the base. It was, in the words of the historian C. P. FitzGerald, 'a resolute, desperate venture, which at best only promised some hope of survival and from which few can have hoped to snatch victory'.[16]

But Li Teh organized the operation, and Mao's only supporter on the Revolutionary Military Council – Chu Teh, its Chairman – had been replaced by Chou En-lai on the eve of the evacuation order. Mao at this time was pale and huge-eyed with fever, and the balance of power within the leadership could be surmised from the fact that many of Mao's followers (including Chen Yi, Tan Chen-lin, Hsiao Hua and Teng Tzu-hui) were left behind with the rear-guard along with other opponents of the Bolshevik clique. The evacuation was conducted in great secrecy, and Mao afterwards criticized the failure to tell the commanders what was afoot.[17]

The immediate goal was to reach Ho Lung's Second Front Army base in north-western Hunan. When Kuomintang troops blocked the path to this destination, the First Front Army sought to cross Kweichow to unite with Hsu Hsiang-chien's troops in north Szechuan. After the Tsunyi Conference in January 1935 the immediate task was defined as 'to found a new Soviet in the vast territories of Yunnan, Kweichow and Szechuan',[18] and only after Szechuan proved too strongly defended did the March set Shensi province in north China as its goal.

When Robert Payne later asked Mao about this, he replied : 'If you mean, did we have any exact plans, the answer is that we had none. We intended to break out of the encirclement and join up with the other·soviets. Beyond that, there was only a very deliber-ate desire to put ourselves in a position where we could fight the Japanese.' [19] Mao told André Malraux in 1965 : 'in the north we found the possibility of contact with Russia, the certainty of not being surrounded'.[20]

Indeed, Mao subsequently insisted that the Long March had been, in his eyes, 'entirely unnecessary',[21] since with better generalship the Fifth Encirclement could have been defeated and a new rural base established near Shanghai. But in view of the heavily outnumbered plight of the Communists in 1934 this seems more of a pious hope and an *a posteriori* self-justification than a realistic assessment.

So in the first few days of October the battered survivors of the five Kuomintang offensives packed their rucksacks and loaded their mules for what appeared to be an ignominious retreat through enemy lines towards a vague and seemingly hopeless salvation. The much-vaunted Kiangsi soviet, the pride of the international Communist movement and the main hope of the Chinese Communist Party, had completely vanished. Would its like ever be seen again? Many who braced themselves for that fateful march of October 1934 must have thought it unlikely.

PART TWO

The March

Chapter 7

Daily Life on the March

MOST of the wounded, who now numbered about 20,000, had to be left behind in the care of villagers, and a force of some 6,000 fit soldiers was assigned to stay in Kiangsi as a rearguard. Chen Yi was named military commander, Hsiang Ying the Political Commissar and Kung Chu* the Chief-of-Staff of this detachment. Observers noted that a large number of Mao's supporters were appointed to it – presumably reflecting Po Ku's and Chou En-lai's dislike of his criticisms. Many of those who stayed behind were captured and killed – including Mao's younger brother Mao Tse-tan.

Chu Teh explained afterwards: 'We left many of our ablest military, political and mass leaders behind. One was the chairman of the All-China Federation of Labour, who was captured and beheaded by the Kuomintang seven months later. Ho Shu-heng, Commissar of Justice, and Chu Chiu-pai, former Secretary of the Party and now Commissar of Education, were also left behind because Ho was in his middle sixties, while Chu was slowly dying of tuberculosis. Chu Chiu-pai had been one of the leaders of the cultural renaissance and a member of the Central Committee of the Kuomintang under Sun Yat-sen's leadership. Ho and Chu were to be smuggled to Shanghai. Eight months later they were captured by the Kuomintang and beheaded at Lungyen, together with a number of women leaders.

'We also left behind about 20,000 of our wounded, scattered in

---

* Kung had already become disenchanted with the C.C.P.'s new (May 1934) tough line against the rich peasants and with the growing subservience of the Po Ku leadership to Comintern dictation. He deserted from the Red Army in December 1934 and wrote a memoir, *The Red Army and I*, which is an important source for the period.

mountain hospitals. After recovering, these men left the hospital and reported for duty. Maimed men were given money, sent to their homes, and allotted a pension of $50 a year. These pensions were paid out so long as our comrades in Kiangsi had money.' [1]

After several weeks the enemy occupied the chief base areas, but the rearguard enabled the main force to get out of the Kuomintang trap, and various remnants of it were later gathered into Chen Yi's New Fourth Army in 1937.

Hsiang Ying told his story to Edgar Snow in 1938: 'We decided to decentralize our remaining forces, breaking them up into small partisan bands of several hundred men each, scattered over an extensive territory. In these new formations we gave up all attempts to defend a base. We confined our operations to swift attacks on small enemy detachments, which we could take by surprise. By these methods we were able to maintain ourselves, though with the complete lack of any fixed base of operations our material condition became very serious.

'By the end of 1936 our forces were confronted with desperate odds. The enemy gave us no rest. We had some kind of skirmish at least once a week. New tactics deprived us of fighting with advantage or even on equal terms. At times we believed our Western armies had entirely perished. At night we dared not sleep in towns or villages for fear of surprise attack. We had to make our beds in the forests of the mountains. For nearly two years I never undressed at night, but slept with even my shoes on. So did most of our men. In that time I wore the same cotton uniform, which became ragged and faded and patched.

'We never had enough to eat. Had it not been for the help of the people we would have starved. Many of our smaller units, cut off by Nanking troops, were saved by the farmers, who hid their rifles. The farmers gladly shared with us what rice they had. Our farmers' unions continued to function secretly, bringing us news of enemy movements and offering us refuge. The farmers hated the thought of the landlords returning and to them our defeat meant return of the landlord system. Soon the enemy began wholesale arrests of our peasants and burned and destroyed our friendly villages.

'We lost all contact with the outside. We were like wild men, living and fighting by instinct. Many of our best commanders were killed, or died of disease. We had no medicines and no hospitals. Our ammunition ran very low. Many of our guns became useless; we had no arsenal and could not repair them. We could not even make bullets, and practised extreme economy with those we had. Sometimes the farmers would smuggle in a little ammunition for us. But the blockade made this more and more difficult.

'At times we retired into the uninhabited forests. We learned the trails of Fukien and Kiangsi foot by foot. We knew every corner of the mountains. We learned to fast with nothing to eat for four or five days. And yet we became strong and agile as savages. Some of our look-outs practically lived in trees. Our young men could go up and down mountains with incredible speed. Many times the encirclement brought the Nanking troops within a few miles of our forces. But our knowledge of the country, and the peasants' help, always enabled us to attack and break through at the correct points, or elude the enemy entirely.

'We did not even hear news of the Sian Incident of December 1936, until weeks after it happened. It did not alter our conditions in the least. After Sian, Nanking was able to turn some of its best forces to the task of destroying us. We felt only a brief interruption in the attacks from the end of 1936 until April 1937. That spring Nanking mobilized over thirty divisions for a final annihilation of all traces of the Red Army in south-east China. In the last offensive over 250,000 men surrounded the Wu Ling Mountains, in a circle with a diameter of two to three hundred li.

'The anti-Red forces narrowed the circle around us. The enemy built many new roads, blockhouses and fortifications. They depopulated many villages, burned them, and carried off all stocks of grain. They burned down thousands of trees on the mountains, and tried to trap us. Many of our scouts and couriers were captured.

'Late in 1937, we still had no direct instructions from the main Red Army, and no information of Chu Teh and Mao Tse-tung. One of our couriers finally returned, however, with the full report of the Sian Incident, and of the end of civil war in the north-west. We promptly issued a manifesto addressed to the Government and the attacking armies, reiterated our support for the united front, and demanded a cessation of war. We affirmed our willingness to subscribe to the Communist declaration issued in Yenan of March 15.'[2]

Eventually a truce was struck, but the fighting resumed a year or two later.

Meanwhile the main force of the First Front Army that assembled near Yutu on 15 and 16 October to challenge the innermost line of Kuomintang blockhouses on the Anyuan–Hsinfeng–Kanchow road comprised some 85,000* regular soldiers and 15,000 officials of the soviet Government and Party (Hsu Meng-chiu says 120,000–130,000, but that must include partisans and guerrillas). The factories and military arsenal were stripped and most of the hardware and equipment buried, the rest being strapped on to the backs of mules and donkeys. Sewing machines, printing presses, heavy weapons, banknotes, gold bullion, silver dollars and thousands of documents were in the cavalcade. Mao Tse-min,[3] the middle of the three Mao brothers, was in charge of this equipment and treasure, which held down the speed of the columns. 'Mules, horses and luggage ... crowded the narrow paths,' wrote Liu Po-cheng afterwards. 'Consequently, we could cover only one valley a night and we were very tired. Since the enemy used highways and marched at a great speed, we could not shake him off.' The transport column used sometimes to lag behind by ten days' march, and in heavy rain could take five hours to complete one mile. 'Some base plates were so heavy they had to be carried by a dozen hefty young fellows. Every time we climbed a slope, forded a river or edged along some narrow precipitous paths, it took us an hour to cover half a li ...'[4]

Currency notes for the soviet area as well as those issued by the Kuomintang Government were carried in order to pay the Red Army's way in poor areas, and the Mexican silver dollars which were then still an acceptable international currency in the Far East were certainly included in the Marchers' resources. According to one report the Communists paid $250,000 in this currency to

---

* A defector later estimated only 70,000 combat soldiers, 9,000 'working staffers' and 5,000 civilian conscripts and horse grooms to make 84,000: *Issues and Studies* (Taipei), Vol. 4, No. 4, January 1968, p. 39. Li Teh (Otto Braun) says 45,000 soldiers and 15,000 non-combat men (*Horizont*, East Berlin, No. 31, 1969).

the Kwangtung provincial command of the Kuomintang to pass through their lines unmolested. There was at least one case where another Communist column was replenished with 'four coolie loads of silver' in the form of ransom for two foreign missionaries taken prisoner en route.[5]

These two, Alfred Bosshardt and Arnolis Hayman, were captured by the forces of Hsiao Ke on the way from the Kiangsi base to Kweichow to join Ho Lung's army, and accused of espionage (in other words, giving information about Communist movements to the Kuomintang authorities). Bosshardt, a young Swiss, helped Hsiao to read a French map of the province. But on trying to escape he was sentenced to eighteen months' imprisonment by the military court, and had to serve the term out on the March. 'I've been in the line of the procession,' he recalled much later, 'when a message has been sent back from the head saying, "Such and such prisoner cannot walk any more. Shall we release the prisoner?" And a message would go back, "No. He must be killed." And then the guards would say, "Let me do it! Let me do it!" Simply no feeling at all – it was like killing a chicken.'[6] Bosshardt was nevertheless impressed by the relative restraint and constructiveness of the Communists. When Edgar Snow was told about this in Shensi a year later the Communists added with pride that they gave him his travelling expenses to Kunming, the nearest city, when he was finally released,[7] but Bosshardt did not mention this when he recalled the incident thirty years later in retirement in Manchester.

In these and other respects the retreating Communists behaved – at least in the early stages of the Long March – like a provisional government on the road.

'Each man,' said the chief artillery engineer afterwards, 'carried five pounds of ration rice and each had a shoulder pole from which hung either two small boxes of ammunition or hand grenades, or big kerosene cans filled with our most essential machinery and tools. Each pack contained a blanket or quilt, one quilted winter uniform, and three pairs of strong cloth shoes with thick rope soles tipped and heeled with metal.

'The people also gave us presents of dried vegetables, peppers, or such things. Each man had a drinking cup, a pair of chopsticks thrust into his puttees, and a needle and thread caught on the underside of the peak of his cap. All men wore big sun–rain hats made of two thin layers of bamboo with oiled paper between, and many had paper umbrellas stuck in their packs. Each man carried a rifle . . .

'Everyone going on the Long March was dressed and equipped the same. Everyone was armed.'[8]

Bosshardt recalled that the soldiers in his column had no leather shoes, only cloth sandals, shreds of twisted cloth bound on to the bare foot with string or straw. In the rain they would dissolve in a day, and so fresh sandals had to be plaited whenever there was a halt. Soldiers would weep in pain after a long stage of marching. The only European to undergo the entire March – Otto Braun or Li Teh – took size eleven shoes and could never get new ones big enough.[9]

The sick and some of the leaders were able to ride on horseback, but there were very few horses and most of the men had to walk the entire way. Peng Teh-huai, commanding the I Army Corps in the vanguard, walked most of the route, frequently giving his horse to others in need of it, and Chu Teh 'rode only half the time', according to his wife, 'and walked the other half'. One of the participants explained later that 'Mao had to ride because he was sick, and he had one bodyguard.' Mao's horse was in fact his favourite dun-coloured steed, captured at Changting at the end of 1928 from a Kuomintang general who directed the battle from a sedan-chair![10] Dr Nelson Fu was the only man privileged, for obvious reasons, to conserve his strength by being carried on a chair, although another account explains that Chou En-lai, having stayed awake in the night to confer with Mao and Chu and listen to the radio receiver in order to plan for the following day, was carried by stretcher when the next day's march began, 'which gave him the only chance for a rest'. The same account adds that all the leaders had to do farm work during the March, with the exceptions of Mao and Chou.[11]

Mao followed the style described by his batman a few years earlier, during the Kiangsi campaigns: 'He had only the simplest of belongings. Two cotton and wool mixture blankets, a sheet, two of the ordinary uniform jackets and trousers, a sweater, a patched umbrella, an enamel mug which served as his rice bowl, and a grey brief-case with nine pockets. On the march he used to carry the brief-case himself, and the umbrella, and I made a roll of the rest of the things. When we made camp I used to make up his bed with the blankets and sheet. He used the rest of his belongings as a pillow.' [12]

For the Long March itself Mao discarded his brief-case, but had acquired a proper enamel food container, a three-decker. He was still recovering from malaria when the journey started, and was described by one of his men as 'thin and emaciated'.[13] Later he took to his feet, except for a period of relapse when he had to be carried on a stretcher. In addition to this attentive orderly-cum-bodyguard, Chen Chang-feng, who was than about 20 years old, Mao's needs were looked after by a male nurse, Chung Fu-chang, and a secretary, Huang Yu-fang.[14] Chen used to prepare boiled water for him at each stop along the way.

Among the marchers were thirty-five women, the wives of the highest Government and Party officials. The rest of the women and all the children, including two of Mao's, had to be left behind. 'My new wife remained behind,' Wang Cheng explains. 'Of course, she didn't want to . . . , but I was political commissar of the army and if my wife had gone on the Long March, all the other wives would have insisted upon going, and that would have caused great trouble . . .'[15] Too young to go on the March, the children were placed out with peasant families and all trace was lost of them. Despite careful and prolonged searches by the People's Liberation Army fifteen years later after the area was recaptured, none of these children was found. Mao's wife, Ho Tzu-chen, was several months pregnant when the March began, and was wounded in a low-flying bomber attack in Kweichow in the early stages of the March. It was said that she had twenty pieces of shrapnel in her body, yet she survived the ordeal and bore Mao yet another child in 1937 before going to Russia for medical treatment.[16] Ho Lung's wife also gave birth on the March, and the Swiss missionary Bosshardt sewed clothes for the baby.[17]

Mao offered the opinion afterwards that the women had been more courageous than the men.[18] The most outstanding example, by common consent, was Kang Ke-ching, the wife of Chu Teh. She took her own weapons and knapsack on the March and was even said on one or two occasions to have carried a wounded soldier on her back.[19] Chu, she explained, had an orderly to attend to his meals and clothes, and in any case 'he did not like the idea of women devoting themselves only to domestic affairs'. She had no time even to wash her own clothes on the March. 'I always carried three or four rifles to encourage the others.' Kang first took command in 1934 when visiting a village on Party work. 'By chance,' she afterwards explained, 'we met the enemy and had to grab our guns and fight. I was temporarily elected commander by the 300 men there. I was the only woman. We fought for two hours; then the enemy retreated. I don't know whether I killed anyone or not – I couldn't see the results of my shooting – but I am a very good marksman. I must say this was a happy day for me.' This formidable person refers to two women commanders on the March, herself and the sister of Ho Lung, who died in battle.[20]

Tsai Chang, wife of Li Fu-chun, and Teng Ying-chao, Chou En-lai's wife, were two famous women Communists on the Long March, both ill with tuberculosis during much of it, and Li Teh, the German, brought his 'Chinese wife' from Kiangsi along with him. Other leaders who brought their wives included Chang Wen-tien, Teng Fa, Po Ku, Yeh Chien-ying and Yang Shang-kun. Chang Kuo-tao's Fourth Front Army boasted an independent regiment of women, 2,000-strong.[21]

A hostile source says that Chou En-lai was annoyed by Li Teh's need for female companionship after his arrival in Kiangsi, and adds that the latter was so enormous in physique that 'small and thin women' could not put up with him. Eventually a stout girl called Hsiao agreed to marry the German – but she deserted during the Long March. According to the same source, Li Teh had a huge appetite, wanting half a catty of pork or beef, four eggs, half a catty of vegetables and some soup in one meal. He insisted on bread rather than rice, so the Central Committee found a baker for him. He smoked and drank a lot, and a courier was sent from Kiangsi to Hong Kong to obtain good quality tobacco and wine for him. He would never march, and either rode a horse along the route or else, if it were a long stretch, would be carried on a wooden litter by four carriers. But how distorted this portrait is, and how much of it, if true, survived on the Long March, is a matter of conjecture. It sounds overpainted.[22]*

If babies were left behind, the army had its own 'toddlers', or Young Vanguards of 11 or 12 years old. Snow described conversations with some of these 'little red devils': one of the 12-year-olds, a short but solidly built boy, was known as 'Little Ball' because although he ran like a tiger cub he would keep tripping over. These lads were the orderlies, buglers, mess-waiters, water carriers, nurses, secretaries and messengers of the army.[23]

Snow, who knew China well, described the Red Army soldiers he saw in Shensi the year after their Long March as 'perhaps the first consciously happy group of Chinese proletarians I had seen'. Unlike most Chinese armies, they were not carefully segregated according to provincial origin, but mixed. 'Their different provincial backgrounds and dialects did not seem to divide them, but became the subject of constant good-natured raillery.' They used to sing at the slightest pretext, and had a vast repertoire of propaganda and folk songs. Some regiments had propaganda units, one of which 'set up posts along the route of march, beating gongs and drums and singing songs to encourage the fighters'. But there were many moments on the March when no one could raise a tune to his lips.[24]

An official history gives the proportion of peasants in the Red Army in April 1934, just before the March, as sixty-eight per cent: proletarian workers accounted for thirty per cent. Most of the soldiers were under 23 years old, the exact breakdown by age being given as one per cent below 16 years, fifty-three per cent between 16 and 23 years, forty-four per cent between 24 and 40 years and four per cent over 40. Some twenty-eight per cent of the army were Communist Party members, and another seventeen per cent were Youth League members.[25]

---

* Otto Braun, alias Li Teh, has written his own account of the Long March: his testimony, though politically suspect as published in East Germany at the height of the anti-Maoist campaign in Eastern Europe, is most valuable because he was the only foreigner to participate. Braun, 'Von Schanghai bis Jaenen', *Horizont* (East Berlin), 1969, Nos. 23-32 (weekly): see Dieter Heinzig in *The China Quarterly*, No. 42, April 1970, p. 131.

The level of discipline was high. When Snow was on the road with the Red Army in Shensi in 1936 he recorded that 'When we passed wild apricot trees on the hills there was an abrupt dispersal until everyone had filled his pockets, and somebody always brought me back a handful... But when we passed private orchards, nobody touched the fruit in them, and the grain and vegetables we ate in the villages were paid for in full.' [26] Sometimes the rules of discipline were perplexing. In Ho Lung's column the Swiss missionary Bosshardt noted that when they sheltered one day in a grove of pomelo (that delicious cross between a grapefruit and an orange) beside themselves with hunger, they did not touch the fruit because no one could be sure whether the trees belonged to a peasant or a landlord. In the end a woman came out and began to sell them ! [27]

The rule was that the property of the rich – the landlords and the local officials – in the areas where the Red Army went could be confiscated, but only by order of the confiscation department of the Finance Commission, not by any company commander or corporal; and only the appointed officers of this department were empowered to distribute such goods. The Marchers were generally hungry, but every now and again there was a feast – of ham in Yunnan, or ducks in Kweichow. 'When we captured great warehouses of salt, every man in our ranks filled his pockets, and ate it, like sugar.' [28] The worst stretch for food was the Grasslands of Chinghai.

Smoking became a luxury on the Long March, and Mao especially missed his cigarettes. 'During the Long March,' Snow observes, 'Mao and Li Teh had carried on original botanical research by testing out various kinds of leaves as tobacco substitutes.' There is one account of the Marchers' exchanging opium for cigarettes and salt with enemy soldiers on the route. [29]

The practice was to sleep, if possible, on the removable doorboards of the village where they were, rehanging them next morning. Mao, says his batman, slept in a hammock. [30]

The marching was often strenuous beyond belief. The Ho Lung forces once marched for twenty-seven consecutive days without a single rest day, and twice they marched right through the night as well as through the preceding and following days, with only short halts: on one day they covered fifty miles.[31] Bosshardt remembers that on nights when torches were forbidden in case they were seen by the enemy, each soldier in Ho Lung's army marched with his hand on the shoulder of the man in front of him.

According to the official record, the main force of the First Front Army averaged almost one skirmish each day on the Long March, and had fifteen whole days of major pitched battle. They made 235 day marches and eighteen night marches, with a hundred days of halt (sometimes fighting) in between. But fifty-six of those days of halt were taken all at once in north-west Szechuan, and if the other forty-four are averaged out over the 6,000-mile route they mean one whole day's halt for every 114 miles.

The average daily coverage was thus seventeen miles over the whole year, or twenty-six miles if the eight-week recuperation in Szechuan is left out of the account. Commander Tso Chuan told Snow also that they crossed eighteen mountain ranges, five of them permanently snow-capped, twenty-four rivers and twelve provinces, and that they took sixty-two cities and towns along the route as well as breaking through the enveloping armies of no fewer than ten different provincial warlords.[32]

Dr Nelson Fu (Fu Lien-chang) observed afterwards that, 'A great many of our people now have heart trouble from the Long March, and others have nervous troubles from the strain. ... Just after the Long March we had numerous cases of ulceration of the feet and legs because of bad conditions, wounds and general anaemia. Because of the blockade I could buy only one thousand dollars' worth of medical supplies and equipment in preparation for the Long March. ... For one tin of alcohol costing seven dollars we have had to pay forty dollars to the merchants who smuggle it in.' Dr Fu explained that malaria and dysentery were the chief scourges in Kiangsi, Kwangtung and Hunan; dysentery, typhoid and influenza in Szechuan, Kansu and Shensi; mountain sickness, indigestion, typhoid and trachoma in Sikang; and thyroid trouble for lack of iodine in Yunnan.

Cholera, meningitis and syphilis were prevalent also in Shensi, but 'So far, only ten of our soldiers have become infected with syphilis, as we are very strict on this matter. About ninety per cent of our soldiers are sexually inexperienced. We have no

problem of immorality as the men are too tired and too busy. . . .'
Lo Ping-hui, who commanded the rearguard in the March, fell un-
conscious for two hours with dysentery after capturing the city of
Tienchuan by the Tatu River, and Mao Tse-tung, Chou En-lai
and other leaders were extremely ill with malaria, tuberculosis
and other diseases at various times on the Long March.[33]

The General Headquarters group when it left Kiangsi consisted
of a regiment of the Red Army University under Yeh Chien-
ying, the G.H.Q. itself with the Revolutionary Military Council
and the Chinese Communist Party Central Committee, the
soviet Government, the Chinese Communist Party functionaries
and those of the Young Communist League and the Anti-Imperialist League, and the Supply Department – including the
arsenal, the mint, the printers with their presses, the tailors with
their sewing machines, the Sanitary Department with its doctors
and nurses and 480 stretcher-bearers.[34] It was preceded by Lin
Piao's I Army Corps and Peng Teh-huai's III Army Corps in the
vanguard and protected on the right by the IX Army Corps, on
the left by the VII Army Corps and in the rear by the V Army
Corps. No wonder that the Marchers, in Snow's phrase, 'often
made a solid serpentine of fifty miles or more curling over the
hills'.[35]

Chapter 8

Breaking Out of the Circle

'Around five o'clock in the evening [of 16 October],' Mao's batman records, 'Mao and about twenty others left Yutu by the North Gate, and then turned to the left towards the river, which was all yellow, roaring and foaming, as though calling on the armies to advance. Soon the sun set and the gusts of bitter wind chilled us. The Chairman wore a grey cloth uniform and an eight-cornered military cap, with no overcoat. He walked with enormous strides along the riverbanks.' [1] The March had begun.

The diversionary detachment, the performance of the rearguard and the secrecy of the operation duly misled the Kuomintang intelligence, and the enemy did not become fully aware of the comprehensiveness and destination of the breakout until four weeks later. A newspaper report dated 8 November 1934, based on Kuomintang information, remarked that 'The Communists in Kiangsi, after their recent defeats by Government troops, are proving exceptionally stubborn and it may be some months before they are entirely dislodged.' [2]

The soviet base was ringed by the four armies of Generals Chiang Ting-wen to the east, Chen Chi-tang to the south, Ho Chien to the west and Kuo Chu-tung to the north.[3] The pressure came from the east and the north, and it was these two armies which prised the Communists out of their stronghold. The Red Army at first moved south-west towards the line held by the politically less reliable Kwangtung provincial troops, and the Kwangtungese retreated before them back to their own province. Five days later the Red Army passed through the first enemy defence line near Hsinfeng after some skirmishing.

The assembly movement in the few days preceding the 16th had been so swift, so quiet and unobtrusive, that the enemy was

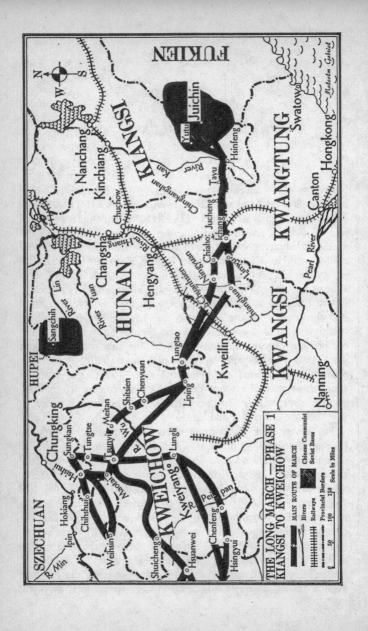

THE LONG MARCH — PHASE 1
KIANGSI TO KWEICHOW

MAIN ROUTE OF MARCH
Rivers
Railways
Provincial Borders

Chinese Communist
Soviet Bases

0   50   100   150   Scale in Miles

FUKIEN

KIANGSI

Nanchang
Kinchiang
Chuchow
Kan River
Juichin
Yutu
Hsinfeng
Tayu
Jucheng
Chiaho
Chingkangshan

HUNAN

Changsha
Hsiang River
Hengyang
River Yuan
Sangchih
Lin
River

Chuanhsien
Ninghsien
Chiahol
Kwangchang

Tungtao

Kweilin

KWANGSI

Nanning

KWANGTUNG

Swatow
Canton
Hongkong
Pearl River

Liping
Chenyuan
Shihsien
Wu
Meitan
Tsunyi
Lungli
KWEICHOW
Kweiyang
Pei pan
Chenfeng
Hsingyi
Hsuanwei
Shuicheng
Weihsin
Maotai
Hsishui
Tungtse
Sungkan
Chungking
Chihshui
Hokiang
Ipin
R. Min

SZECHUAN
HUPEI

Malcolm Gabriel

caught off-guard – besides being put off by heavy rain and clouds hiding the moon at night. The Communists went only by night at first to avoid detection, but soon had to speed things up to shake off the enemy, and there was one seventy-two-hour stretch during which they alternated four hours on the road (at three and one-third miles per hour) and four hours' rest throughout.[4]

The Communists now divided into two groups which crossed the Hsinfeng River by the Wangmu and Kupo ferries respectively. One group struck north-west, crossed the Chang River between Nankang and Tayu and cut across the Kanchou–Nanhsiung road to occupy Chengkuo, north of Jenhua in Kwangtung province, on 5 November. It then cut through the second line of Kuomintang blockhouses which extended from Kweitung to Jucheng on the Chingkangshan mountains of the Hunan–Kiangsi border, where Mao and Chu had first established their base almost seven years before. It reached Chengkou, and descended westwards into Ichang, crossing the third line of enemy defence along the Canton–Wuhan railway, and arriving at Linwu. Meanwhile the second group of Communists had taken a more southerly route through northernmost Kwangtung province in order to confuse the enemy. The two groups were reunited at Linwu in southern Hunan on 16 November.[5]

Relieved of some of their printing presses and other useless encumbrances which they had shed on the mountains, the Communists now spread out in south Hunan to Chiaho, Ningyuan and Lanshan. The enemy was bewildered, supposing that the Red Army would strike north for Chungyang and Changsha. Ho Chien, the enemy commander, therefore sent forces under Liu Chien-hsu and Hseuh Yueh to the Linglu–Tungan region, slightly to the north of the Red Army, to cut it off. Enemy troops under Chou Hun-yuan and Li Yun-chieh were stealthily pursuing from the rear, hoping to surround the Reds near the Hsiao River.

But the Red Army split into two again, one section proceeding westwards by a northerly route, capturing Taohsien, the other taking the southern route via Chianghua and Yungming in order to confuse the Kwangsi provincial troops. They reunited across the provincial border in Chuanchou (or Chuanhsien) in Kwangsi, having eluded their pursuers and crossed first the Hsiao River and then the Hsiang River, which was the fourth and last line of the Kuomintang blockade. The Red Army had broken out of the circle.

'Once in enemy territory,' as the Chief Engineer at G.H.Q. explained it to Agnes Smedley, 'we often marched at night to avoid air raids. Night marching is wonderful if there is a moon and a gentle wind blowing. When no enemy troops were near, whole companies would sing and others would answer. If it was a black night and the enemy far away, we made torches from pine branches or frayed bamboo, and then it was truly beautiful. When at the foot of a mountain we could look up and see a long column of lights coiling like a fiery dragon up the mountain side. From the summit we could look in both directions and see miles of torches moving forward like a wave of fire. A rosy glow hung over the whole route of march. . . .

'When hard-pressed by superior enemy forces, we marched in the daytime, and at such times the bombers pounded us. We would scatter and lie down; get up and march, then scatter and lie down again, hour after hour. Our dead and wounded were many and our medical workers had a very hard time. The peasants always helped us and offered to take our sick, our wounded and exhausted. Each man left behind was given some money, ammunition and his rifle and told to organize and lead the peasants in partisan warfare as soon as he recovered. Sometimes one or two companies would become separated from our main forces during battle but they merely retreated into the mountains and developed partisan areas.'[6]

As with so many incidents on the Long March, there is some mystery about the surprising success of the Red Army in escaping relatively easily through these cordons of hostile troops. Chiang Kai-shek and the military leaders of the officially pro-Kuomintang provincial forces of Kwangtung and Kwangsi were not on the best of terms, and these latter formed the weak side of his trap. According to some writers [7] they allowed the Communists to pass through the north-west corner of their domain unmolested, in order to avoid a large-scale battle there which would draw Chiang's own army and thus give him a chance to assert his authority over them.[8]

Another version is that Chiang Kai-shek hoped the Hunanese forces of Hsueh Yueh would push the Communists into Kwangsi where the Kwangsi troops and the Red Army would destroy each other, allowing him to step in. But instead the Kwangsi troops, like the Kwangtung forces earlier, merely withdrew before the advancing Reds, allowing them to cross the Hsiang River.[9]

The Red Army may thus have been saved by the long-standing yearning for autonomy on the part of the non-Mandarin-speaking southern and south-western provinces – a yearning that was no whit abated when their own turn came to assert central control over south China fifteen years later. They may also, as we have seen, have sugared the pill with Mexican dollars.[10]

There is also conflicting evidence as to the severity of the final battle to cross the Hsiang River, as Jerome Ch'ên has set out in a recent article.[11] Liu Po-cheng described it as an engagement which lasted a week and cost the Red Army 'half its men'. Miu Chu-huang, the Chinese Communist historian, also terms it a fierce battle, and Hsu Meng-chiu (like Liu Po-cheng, an eyewitness) told Nym Wales it was a five-day fight. Ch'ên states roundly in his *Mao and the Chinese Revolution* that the battle of the Hsiang River 'cost nearly 50,000 men'.[12]

Hsueh Yueh's account implies that the crossing of the Hsiang River was not difficult,[13] and Anthony Garavente, in his study of this section of the Long March, concludes that the Red Army reached Tsunyi in January 1935 with its numbers 'fairly well preserved' because it had avoided major encounters. When the Maoists turned the tables on the leadership of Li Teh, Chou En-lai and Po Ku at the Tsunyi Conference five weeks later no mention was made of any military disaster at the Hsiang River. Braun states categorically there were 'no devastating losses in the first phase of the March', despite 'all assertions to the contrary made by Chinese historians'.[14]

As Jerome Ch'ên remarks, it is curious that the loss of over half the Red Army was not thought worthy of inclusion in the indictment of its leadership at that time. But perhaps it would have been tactless of Mao to have harped on the numerical losses, and he might needlessly have alienated some of the generals involved if he had made an issue of it. For the time being it seems better, in the light of this contradictory testimony, to regard the Hsiang River as the site of the first substantial battle of the Long March, one which was theoretically won by the Communists but only for a price which could not be paid again. Liu Po-cheng's memory may have exaggerated the casualties of this particular engagement, as distinct from those of the entire period from Yutu in October to Tsunyi in January, but some losses there must surely have been.

It was here at the Hsiang River that the real nature of the challenge they were undertaking struck home to the Communist leaders. The army had to fight in two parallel columns to allow the heavily-laden non-combatants of Party and Government to proceed safely in the corridor between them. Many of the casualties were to be accounted for by this burden. As Mao's successful resolution at the subsequent Tsunyi conference put it, 'there were the elephantine columns of the Military Commission and the rear organizations of each army corps to add to the logistic and operational difficulties and to turn all combat units into covering units'.[15]

And yet, after all the bloodshed of that fierce battle, the Communists reached the other side of the river and struck north-west into Hunan again only to find, contrary to their confident expectation, an enemy force five or six times bigger than themselves standing between them and their goal – Ho Lung's soviet base at Sangchih in north-western Hunan. Chiang Kai-shek had tumbled to their strategy and sent several divisions to reinforce the area west of the river. Hunanese provincial troops were massively deployed along the line Huitung–Tsinghsien–Suining–Chengpu, preventing access to the north of the province. The encirclement was broken, but the Red Army was still on the run without a clear goal in view.

Chapter 9

The Kweichow Campaigns

THE First Front Army now had to change direction. Instead of heading north across Hunan to the Sangchih soviet area, 250 miles away, it was obliged to fall back on the next nearest (or next least distant) surviving base, that of Chang Kuo-tao in northern Szechuan. A senior general on the Long March, Liu Po-cheng, afterwards attributed the new strategy to Mao Tse-tung. In his account, resentment against the Po Ku military leadership reached a peak during the battle of the Hsiang River, and 'at this critical stage ... Mao Tse-tung came forward with a plan which saved the Red Army. He proposed to give up the attempt to join the Second and Sixth Army Groups [at Sangchih], and proposed that the Central Red Army wheel towards Kweichow where the enemy was weak. ... Mao Tse-tung's proposal won the support of most comrades. ... Mao Tse-tung's firm demand for a change of policy saved the remaining 30,000 Red Army men from extermination.' [1] The Szechuan base lay beyond Sangchih and was twice as far. The only way to reach it was by circling round the Kuomintang forces in Hunan and Szechuan provinces to find a path through the sparsely-defended province of Kweichow and across the lower Yangtze river. So the tattered and depleted Red Army struck north-west to begin a great arc intended to bring it to the haven of Pachou, Chang Kuo-tao's new capital in the mountains of the Szechuan–Shenshi border. Little did they realize the arc was to be stretched into a nightmarish half-circle.

Chang Kuo-tao and Hsu Hsiang-chien had been respectively the political commissar and military commander of the Fourth Front Army, which comprised in its origin the troops of the so-called Oyuwan* soviet area in the mountainous country between

---

* The name is a Chinese abbreviation for the three provinces on which this soviet area impinged – Hupeh, Honan and Anhwei.

Wuhan and Nanking. In 1931, when the Chinese Communist Party Central Committee was obliged to leave Shanghai, it could have been expected to choose the Oyuwan base as its new *pied-à-terre*, since it was larger and more strategically placed in the Yangtze region (relatively near to Shanghai, Nanking and Wuhan, the important industrial centres and railheads) than the Kiangsi soviet 400 miles further south. The Oyuwan leaders were also more loyal to the Central Committee. But it was precisely for this reason that it was thought necessary to send most of the big guns of the Politburo south to bring the increasingly recalcitrant Mao to heel.

At its height in the early months of 1932 the Oyuwan base boasted an army of 60,000, a post office, a mint, textile mills and farming co-operatives. But its very location, a few days' march from the industrial and communication complex of Wuhan, enensured a constancy of Kuomintang military attack and economic blockade, under the direction of Von Seeckt. At the end of 1932 the Fourth Front Army was obliged to abandon the base just as the First Front Army had to in Kiangsi almost two years later. Hsu Hai-tung (later destined to receive Mao and the First Front Army in Shensi after the Long March) was left behind to command the rearguard, while the main force of the Fourth marched westwards through the Hupeh–Honan border country and across southern Shensi to a hilly part of eastern Szechuan, where it established in the spring of 1933 a new soviet base with a capital at Pachou.[2]

Fortunately for it the Szechuan provincial warlords were then busy feuding with one another, and the Kuomintang's efforts to bolster the provincial defence against the Fourth Front Red Army were diluted by the fact that the Second Front Army under Ho Lung was making forays from Sangchih into the south-eastern districts of Szechuan, so that the Szechuanese warlords were threatened on two fronts. It was towards this more promising situation that the First Front Army now moved.

After the Hsiang River the First Front Army had to negotiate the difficult roads across the Yuehcheng or Hsiyen mountain range, known locally in the Kwangsi speech as 'Old Mountain' or Laoshan. One of the soldiers recalled this passage:

'Our most bitter trials came when we had to pass along narrow and dangerous mountain paths, through narrow passes, across narrow bridges, or swim icy streams. At such times our advance troops slowed down and the rear ones would take one step forward and stand for ten. We could not move forward and we could not sit down to rest. Some men fell asleep as they stood.

'At other times we marched through storms with a fierce wind and rain whipping our bodies. Under such circumstances we would not use our torches and the paths were slippery and dangerous. Sometimes we covered only a few li at night, and, soaked through, had to bivouac in the open.

'There was Laoshan (Old Mountain) on the Kwangsi border where we went up a mountain so steep that I could see the sole of the man ahead of me. Steps had been carved out of the stone face of the mountain, they were as high as a man's waist. Political workers went up and down the columns encouraging our struggling men and helping the sick and wounded ... News came down the line that our advance columns were facing a sheer cliff and that there was no way of getting the horses up. After a time came the order to sleep where we were and continue climbing at daybreak.

'The path was no more than two feet wide at any point and even if one succeeded in lying down he could not turn over without rolling down the mountainside. There were great jutting boulders everywhere and even the path was covered with sharp stones.

'Since there was nothing else to do, I folded my blanket, placed it beneath me, and tried to curl up on the path. I was so weary that I fell asleep. Some time during the night the cold awoke me. I wrapped the blanket about me and tried to roll myself up in a little round ball, but I still could not sleep. I lay and watched the twinkling stars in the sky. They looked like jade stones on a black curtain. The black peaks towering around me were like menacing giants. We seemed to be at the bottom of a well.

'Up and down the path I saw many small fires lit by men also awakened by the cold. They were sitting around and talking in low voices. Apart from their faint voices the silence was so great that I could hear it. It was sometimes near, sometimes far away, sometimes loud and sometimes faint, and at other times like spring silkworms eating mulberry leaves. I listened intently and it sounded like a complaining mountain spring, then like the distant murmur of the ocean. . . .

'Next morning my group finally reached the sheer cliff that had stopped us the night before. It was Leikungyai (Thunder God Rock), a solid cliff of stone jutting into the sky at about a ninety degree angle. Stone steps no more than a foot wide had been carved up its face, and up this we had to go without anything to hold on to. Horses with broken legs lay about the foot of the cliff.

'Our medical units suffered the most because the sick and wounded had to get off the stretchers and either crawl or be pushed, dragged, or carried up. The women comrades of the Medical Corps ceaselessly comforted and helped the men in their care . . .

'Old Mountain was the most difficult mountain we had climbed so far.'[3]

After scaling Laoshan, the 'Old Mountain', the gallant First Army now began to cross Kweichow province in a north-westerly direction towards Szechuan, fighting against the troops of the Kweichow warlords. Tungtao was taken and the Kweichow border crossed in the middle of December. It took the town of Liping in westernmost Hunan on the 14th and halted there while the Politburo leaders conferred. Little is written about this hurried meeting, at which the growing tension between the Po Ku leadership and the Maoists presumably dominated, but where Mao may have regained a *de facto* seat on the Central Committee. It was decided to continue to Tsunyi, the northernmost city of Kweichow and the last before dropping down into the famous red basin, the rice-bowl of Szechuan. A military briefing by Lin Piao and Nieh Jung-chen of the I Army Corps at this time declared that 'the current strategic policy of the army is first to proceed to northern Kwei-chow, then take by surprise Tsunyi and Tungtse, organize the masses and open up a new base for resisting the Japanese'.[4]

To throw the formidable army of Hsueh Yueh off the scent, one Red column made a feint at Kweiyang, the capital of Kweichow province, and Hsueh Yueh duly sped west to relieve the city while the Communists went in a more northerly direction, pushing the weak Kweichow provincial troops of Hou Chih-tan before them.

They crossed the Chingshui River and reached the Chenyuan–Shitsien area, from which it looked as if they would forge north-east to join Ho Lung at Sangchih, less than 200 miles away. Instead, the main force continued north-west towards the Wu River ferries. Afterwards Mao Tse-tung was to question why the opportunity to strike northwards into north-west Hunan was let slip.[5]

Lo Ping-hui, commanding the rearguard, describes how a larger enemy force could be thrown off the scent in these Kweichow campaigns. 'When we are surrounded on three sides, we make a frontal attack and then leave one small heroic force to hold the position while the main body of troops retreats quickly and goes around to the enemy rear. Then when the White [enemy] lines converge they have nothing in the bag except a small force, and stand looking foolishly at each other. Of course, this requires the greatest spirit of sacrifice from the small Red force which has to hold the position. ...' On another occasion in Kweichow when they were outnumbered, this general put a company on each of two conspicuous mountain tops and told them to walk about in circles displaying themselves to look as if they were a large force, distracting the enemy while three other Red companies attacked in the rear. 'We held this position for two days,' Lo recalls, 'long enough to save our main forces elsewhere – and the foolish Kuomintang officers sent messages, which we intercepted, saying that they had "bottled up the main Red Army!" The mountain was thickly wooded. As all my men stayed in the open spaces in order to be visible, the reconnoitring airplanes thought we were a force too huge to hide under the trees. ... The whole campaign,' he adds, was 'like a monkey playing with a cow in a narrow alley.'[6]

The continued westward march involved entering the Wumeng mountain range, a great thrust of high ground criss-crossed by gorges which projects from Yunnan province into western Kweichow and southern Szechuan. And it meant crossing Kweichow's biggest river, the Wu. When the advance guards of the First Front Army reached the south-east bank of the Wu River, on New Year's Eve according to one account, they found a stream which was at least 250 yards wide, full of submerged rocks and flowing at a speed of between five and six feet a second.[7] Cliffs overhung it on each side, so that from mid-stream the sun was never visible.

There was a ferry crossing, approached on each side by a tortuous three-mile path down the cliff-side, but the three enemy regiments which guarded the crossing had sunk the two ferry boats on their own side of the river. They had also built trenches and fortifications on the north-west bank. The Kuomintang forces which were pursuing the Red Army lay only twenty miles behind it.

The 2nd Division of the I Army Corps tried to force the river that same night. Its sappers hastily built 'centipede' rafts of bamboo and also a bridge to be pulled across once the crossing was captured. A small detachment of strong swimmers * was picked from the ranks of the 2nd Division 4th Regiment – ten of them, in one account, eighteen or twenty or twenty-two in others – to swim across at nightfall and destroy the enemy's warning system. Stripped to the waist and armed with Mauser automatic pistols, they plunged into the icy water as soon as it was dark. Heavy cannon fire covered their passage successfully, but the current was too swift for them to pull the ropes for the bridge across. A bamboo raft was launched to take the ropes instead, but it was sunk in mid-stream by enemy fire. The swimmers, their presence on the other side made useless, returned : one of them died of cold and exhaustion.

Next day the Communists worked furiously to build more double-decker rafts for a second attempt on the following night. After dark two raftloads set out with instructions to signal their arrival on the other side with their electric torches. The first raft was carried nearly three-quarters of a mile downstream before regaining the friendly bank. The second, manned by Captain Mao Chen-hua and four soldiers, armed with a light machine-gun and two carbines, neither signalled nor returned. A third raft had to turn back because of the fierce current.

After this second set-back, the Communist Commander decided to cross by day so that the rafts could be poled successfully over the current. Soon after dawn lightly-armed rafts were despatched under cover of artillery. When they had about fifty yards to go

---

* Lo Ping-hui, the rearguard commander, notes that 'most of the Red Army men cannot swim, as they are from inland regions' (Wales, *Red Dust*, p. 128).

they heard machine-gun fire from the other side – but aimed at the enemy, not at their own boats. It was Captain Mao Chen-hua's detachment, which had landed on the other side, climbed up the bank, heard the sounds of machinery above their heads and found themselves at the feet of the enemy position. Afraid of giving themselves away by flashing their torches, they lit a match as a signal to their colleagues waiting on the south-east bank, but of course it was not seen. So they stayed put all night, and when at first light they saw the Red rafts coming they surprised the Kuomintang with machine-gun fire which effectively covered the final stretch of their crossing.

Enemy reinforcements came at this precise moment, while further raftloads of Communists joined the battle. A Kuomintang counter-attack down the steep river-bank almost succeeded when it was distracted by unexpected fire from the flank. A Red detachment had climbed an almost sheer cliff just to the left of the ferry crossing and was able to shake the enemy off balance at the critical moment. The Kuomintang fled, and the rest of the First Front Army crossed the Wu River on the 'skin' boats used by the Miao tribesmen of that region and on the bamboo rafts. It was now possible to advance on Tsunyi and draw up a plan to cross the mighty Yangtze River itself.

The 4th Regiment having forced the river, the 6th Regiment under Colonel Chu Shui-chiu and Political Commissar Wang Chi-cheng was instructed by Liu Ya-lou (Political Commissar of the 2nd Division) to march to Tsunyi and take it by storm.[8] Chu and Wang studied the map and planned their strategy on horseback. The Kweichow provincial forces at Tsunyi numbered 3,000 to the 4th Regiment's 1,000. In heavy rain the Communists captured an entire enemy battalion by a pincer attack on a village ten miles out of Tsunyi. No one escaped to warn the city. And this allowed Tsunyi to be taken by a stratagem as old as the hills on which it stands.

'So, as it were,' wrote Commissar Wang afterwards,* 'we lopped

---

* This is the first of a number of occasions in this book where long-ish eyewitness passages from books or articles published in Communist China are quoted, in spite of their detectable propagandist note. In the absence of any alternative kind of first-hand description, the only other courses of action open to the historian are to omit such

off the feelers of the enemy at Tsunyi. Or rather, we turned them into our feelers. From among the prisoners we picked a company commander, a platoon leader and about a dozen soldiers who came of poor families, and asked them at length about the enemy's defences at Tsunyi.

'I began by asking their names, their places of birth and what their families were. They were sort of awestruck as they stood up one by one, held themselves rigid, clicked to attention and answered my questions in a most respectful manner. The company commander must have cast such former airs of self-importance as he had had to the winds, for when he spoke he stuttered and did not even dare look me in the face.

'Seeing that they were still scared and suspicious, I began to explain our policy towards prisoners-of-war. I told them that our Red Army belonged to the workers and peasants, and that our aim was to overthrow the warlords and landlords so that the poor might lead a better life. Realizing how little they knew, I went on to explain why there was no equality between the rich and the poor and why we wanted to overthrow the warlords and landlords. Finally I said to them, "Now think it over and tell me this : what did you enlist for? Who benefited?"

'That must have brought home to them the truth of my words, for some of them began to dab their eyes and others hung their heads in silence. One of them said, "We are poor people. We enlisted because we were starving." Two others took off their military caps with the Kuomintang emblem on them, threw them to

---

material altogether or else to summarize it in his own words (which might be even more misleading). I have usually preferred to quote, believing that the propagandist additions to the tale are so patent that no discerning reader could miss them, that the true heroism is so readily distinguishable from the false that the reader can be left to judge for himself. These passages also convey something of the political or ideological climate in which the Red Army worked, and which even more strongly affects what may or may not be written about such recent history in Maoist China. I do not mean to suggest that each detail of such accounts can be taken literally, only that they help, if judiciously digested, to convey an impressionistic picture of what the Long March was like.

the ground and stamped on them, shouting angrily: "We've been tricked! We aren't going to die for the warlords and landlords!"

'When I saw that they were beginning to see things in their true light, I told them that we were going to attack Tsunyi that very day and that we would amply reward anyone who told us the enemy positions in the city in detail. That brought the enemy company commander to his feet at once. After making a bow he said: "Sir, we've been treated so well by the Red Army, and we beg for a chance to give to you our services!" Then he went on to describe every detail of the enemy's defence works at Tsunyi, drawing a map as he did so. He also told us the actual strength of the garrison.

' "Can I trust your words?" I asked him, with a meaning glance at the other captives.

' "Every word of it!" said the company commander cringingly. "If I've said a single false word, you can cut off my head right now!" The other captives, who seemed to have come to an awakening too, nodded to confirm the truth of their company commander's protestations.

'When the talks ended we gave each of them three silver dollars. At that time we were rather hard up and had little money to spare. But we always did the right thing by our prisoners-of-war. Clutching the silver dollars, they could hardly conceal their gratitude. "Our officers," they said, "told us you were all horrible, red-nosed, blue-eyed creatures [9] who indulged in orgies of killing and burning down houses. They frightened us by saying that if we fell into your hands, you'd gouge out our eyeballs and disembowel us! We never imagined you were such nice people. Why, you've actually saved our lives."

'An idea suddenly occurred to me. Now that we knew everything about the enemy in Tsunyi and that no one had escaped from the village, why shouldn't we disguise ourselves as enemy troops, make use of the captives to trick the garrison and win an easy victory? I had a word with the regimental commander and he readily agreed ...

'The main actors in this "farce" were Comrade Tseng Pao-tang, commander of the 1st Battalion, the men of the 3rd Company, the Scout Platoon and the thirty or so regimental buglers.

They were to dress up as enemy troops. The captives I'd talked to were to go with them as guides. The rest of the regiment were to follow and launch an all-out attack if our plan fell through.

'About 9 p.m. we set out in pouring rain. It was pitch-dark and extremely slippery on the road, so we kept stumbling all over the place, getting covered with mud and looking more like clay figurines than men. We all got our new straw shoes stuck in the mud and could not for love or money get them out again. We hated parting with them, but we should have held up our advance if we'd insisted on recovering them, so we were forced to leave them behind – those straw shoes we held so dear, which we had worn crossing countless mountains and rivers. We tramped on barefooted; and it was no joke with all the pebbles, puddles and brambles.

'After more than two hours' quick going the heavy downpour finally subsided – there was only an occasional sprinkling. Soon through the darkness we saw a light in mid-air. Our captives whispered to us that we were approaching the city, and that the light was the lamp in one of the gate towers. We immediately started kicking up a din, put on a spurt towards the city wall, behaving as if we were running helter-skelter from some enemy in hot pursuit.

' "Who goes there?" an angry voice challenged us from the gate-tower and we heard someone click his rifle-bolt.

' "Friends. Your own men!" our captives calmly replied in the local dialect.

' "What unit?"

'This time our captive company commander made his answer as we had arranged beforehand.

' "The battalion stationed on the city outskirts," he whined. "Today the Communist bandits surrounded us. We lost the village – battalion commander killed. We're First Company. I'm in command – what's left of us. The bandits are after us. Open up. Let us in!"

' "What's the name of your battalion commander?' someone asked.

'The company commander answered without the least hesitation. There was a moment's silence – evidently the enemy soldiers on the gate-tower were not prepared for all this. We could hear them muttering to each other. Of course we had no intention of giving them time to consider the situation carefully, so we organized another "attack". We broke into an uproar, yelling at the top of our voice: "Come on, open up! Come on, open up! The bandits'll be on us any minute!"

' "Stop clamouring!" someone shouted down. It was evidently an officer, and we could hear from his voice that he was still annoyed at being woken up.

'So we had to "obey" the officer's orders, and stopped clamouring. Suddenly we were caught in the glare of flashlights from the gate-tower — they were making another check on us. But the flashlights couldn't, of course, show them who we actually were. As far as the soldiers on the gate-tower could see, we really were "their own men", in Kuomintang military caps, so they said: "All right, wait a moment and don't fuss. We'll open for you."

'We could hardly keep from laughing. Silently we fixed bayonets, held our rifles at the ready and waited anxiously for them to open the gate to welcome "their own men".

'First we heard the bolts of the city gate being pulled back, and then the creak of the high, thick gate itself being opened. In a scared voice an enemy soldier asked one of our scouts: "Are the Communist bandits across the Wukiang? They are pretty fast, aren't they?"

' "They are that!" answered our scout. "And now they've entered Tsunyi! Listen, you! We're the Workers' and Peasants' Red Army of China!"

'With which our scouts pointed their rifles at the heads of the two enemy soldiers. They promptly surrendered their weapons, gave a wail and sank to the ground like two coils of noodles.

'So without firing a shot our men rushed through the "breach" like a flood. They set about cutting the telegraph wires and putting the enemy soldiers on the gate-tower out of action. The thirty buglers who were in the van of the attack sounded the charge as our soldiers streaked into the city like lightning. Before long, the whole place was seething: the blare of the bugles mixed with the chattering of machine guns and rifles stirred the hearts of everyone who heard them. Everywhere we could hear the shouting of our brave soldiers as they pounced upon the enemy and the cries of the enemy trying to escape. We took the greater part of the garrison prisoner – many of them had just tumbled out of bed and hardly had time to put any clothes on. Only a few managed to escape through the north gate. That was a sight – the way they ran for their lives leaving all they had behind them.' [10]

So Tsunyi was 'liberated' from the notorious Kweichow warlord Hou Chih-tan, and the Red Armies gained the offensive. Three separate groups – Chang Kuo-tao to the north, Mao and Chou to the south and Ho Lung in between – were now threatening to encircle Szechuan province. For a short while, and for the first time in many years, the Communists were fighting on exterior lines with the initiative in their own hands. They could afford a brief lull in the fighting, and Mao was now ready to make his bid for party leadership.

Chapter 10

Second Thoughts at Tsunyi

WHEN they occupied Tsunyi in early January 1935,[1] the Party and the Red Army leaders could at last sit down to consider their dilemma without being pressed by the enemy. Chu Teh recalls that he had time to address a mass meeting there on 15 January in memory of Karl Liebknecht and Rosa Luxemburg.[2] The First Front Army spent in fact twelve days[3] in the city, resting, recruiting – and recriminating. An enlarged meeting of the Politburo of the Party Central Committee was immediately convened, against some resistance by the Po Ku leadership, which presumably sensed the current of hostility and argued that another meeting so soon after Liping was unnecessary.[4] As it turned out, this was the most important Politburo meeting in the Party's entire history, for it dramatically reversed Party policy and reshuffled its leadership in favour of Mao Tse-tung, the man who remained thereafter its dominating personality and who led it into power fifteen years later.

The Tsunyi Resolutions adopted on 8 January 1935 constitute the most important document to be produced in the Long March, and it is therefore necessary to set out the essential parts of them at length. The full text first appeared in a Chinese edition of Mao Tse-tung's *Selected Works* published in 1948 in the *Chin-Chi-Lu-Yu* Anti-Japanese Base Area, where a military Communist soviet-type administration was conducted by a group of officers at that time apparently loyal to Mao – notably Peng Teh-huai, Liu Po-cheng, Teng Hsiao-ping and Po I-po.[5] But this edition did not circulate widely and only one copy of it is apparently known outside China or has been seen inside China by any foreign scholar. The document was omitted from all other editions of Mao's *Selected Works*.

In 1957 it reappeared in manuscript form in Volume Three of *Chung-kuo Ko-ming-shih Tsan-kao Tzu-liao* (Reference Material on the History of the Chinese Revolution), a compilation of Chinese People's University historians in Peking, though no foreign scholars noted it at the time. A summary of the Resolutions was, however, published in the original Chinese edition of Ho Kan-chih's book *History of the Modern Chinese Revolution* in 1957.

But the English edition of Ho's standard official history, published three years later, dropped even this condensed version of the Tsunyi Resolutions, and the world had to wait until 1969 for the mystery to be cleared up. In that year Dr Jerome Ch'ên published in the *China Quarterly* in London a full translation of the Resolutions, based on the University manuscript to which he had gained access – precisely how, he does not reveal. Such are the frustrations, and the thrills, of successful detection, that bestrew the path of the contemporary sinologist.

The Resolutions adopted at the Tsunyi Conference of the Politburo on 8 January 1935 are entitled 'Summing up the Campaign against the Enemy's Punitive Encirclement Drive'. They open uncompromisingly with the statement: 'Having listened to Comrade XX's survey of the Fifth Encirclement and Comrade XXX's supplementary report, the enlarged conference of the Politburo regards Comrade XX's survey as fundamentally incorrect.'

Dr Ch'ên surmises that Comrade XX is Po Ku, the senior Party leader at the time the conference opened, and the man who, as Chairman of the Military Commission, would undoubtedly have been the first to make a general report at the conference. With less certainty Ch'ên suggests that Comrade XXX may be Wang Chia-hsiang, a Deputy Chairman of the Military Commission, and the scholar Chi-hsi Hu's argument that he is Chou En-lai is more convincing.[6]

The Fourteen Resolutions successfully pressed upon the Politburo by Mao Tse-tung at Tsunyi are fully set out in the *China Quarterly*. Here it is enough to summarize them briefly and to quote some of the more interesting passages. They are concerned principally to condemn the policy followed till then by the Politburo under Po Ku's leadership and by the Military Commission, especially by Li Teh, the German.

Po Ku is accused of defeatism in the face of the Fifth Encirclement Campaign by the Kuomintang, of underestimating Red morale and overestimating the enemy's strength. The Maoist version of the Red Army's strategic dilemma was that: 'At the present stage of the Chinese civil war, when we do not yet have the support of urban proletarian uprisings and mutinies of the white army units; when our Red Army is still very small; when our soviets constitute only a tiny portion of China; when we do not yet have aeroplanes, artillery and other sophisticated weapons; when we are still fighting on interior lines; and when the enemy are still attacking and surrounding us, our strategic line has to be one of decisive battles for defence. ... We must not engage the enemy in a decisive battle in which we have no confidence to win because we have neither discovered nor created the enemy's weakness. We eshould use our secondary forces, e.g. guerrilla units, armed masses, independent battalions and regiments, and a part of the main forces of the Red Army, to confuse or bait the enemy.

'We must check the enemy with mobile warfare while our main forces should retreat to a suitable distance or transfer themselves to the enemy's flank or rear. They should be secretly assembled, awaiting a favourable opportunity to strike at the enemy. Fighting on interior lines, the Red Army's retreat and hiding can tire the enemy out and cause him to feel conceited and relaxed, thereby inducing him to make mistakes and expose his weaknesses. ...

'We should wait until he has advanced to a suitable distance before surrounding and annihilating him, this is to lure the enemy to penetrate deeply into our territory. For victory, we must not refuse to give up some parts of the soviet territory and even to withdraw temporarily our main forces out of the soviet.'

The famous slogan of Po Ku, 'Not an inch of soviet territory to be lost', was 'politically a correct slogan'. But to apply it mechanically to military operations was 'a total mistake'. The Po Ku policy of 'pure defence' had meant disposing the Communist forces so that they could resist attack from all directions, which meant not being strong enough to resist anywhere and enabling the enemy to destroy the Red units one by one. The Maoist Resolutions cited the lost battles of Hsunkou, Tuantsun, Chienning and Wenfeng as examples of this error.

Another mistake was to neglect mobile warfare, the one thing in which the Red Army was especially skilled (and Mao was careful to cite Comintern telegrams, on this as on other issues, to support his argument). The battles just mentioned, as well as those of Chiang-chuntien and Hufang, had presented opportunities for this kind of tactic, and so did the mutiny of the Nineteenth Route Army in Fukien. But fear of the Kuomintang blockhouses and the theory of 'short, swift thrusts' advocated by 'Comrade Hua Fu' had caused these chances to be let slip.

This is the first reference to 'Comrade Hua Fu', whom Dr Jerome Ch'ên identifies as Chou En-lai but whom two other scholars, Warren Kuo and Chi-hsi Hu, more plausibly identify as Otto Braun or Li Teh, the German. Articles by Hua Fu advocating the 'short, swift thrust' (*tuan-tsu tu-chi*) had begun to appear in the Kiangsi press as early as April 1934, with the observation that the enemy was no longer being lured far from blockhouses and that ways of forcing him into more mobile fighting must be found. Chen Jan (Warren Kuo's informant) positively identifies Hua Fu as Li Teh, and the articles are said to smell of having been translated from a foreign language (i.e. German). It should be noted that the 'short, swift thrust' of Hua Fu sounds identical, at least, on the surface, with the 'short attack' so highly praised after the Long March and attributed then, in Edgar Snow's account, to Lin Piao, Mao Tse-tung's disciple. Chi-hsi Hu, whose discussion of this point seems particularly convincing, comments that the differences between Mao and Li Teh thus narrow down, where fundamentals are concerned, to the question whether the soviet base at Kiangsi should be defended or evacuated.[7]

The leadership hitherto was taken to task at Tsunyi for having lost perspective on the Communist Revolution in China. 'It must be realized,' Resolution 9 declared, 'that the civil war in China is not a short, but a long, protracted war.' When things went well, as in the first four Encirclement Campaigns and even in the Fifth up to the battle of Guangchang, the Red Army should take the offensive. But when things began to go badly, as in the later stages of the Fifth Encirclement, 'we may temporarily retreat in order to preserve our strength'.

Proper training and rest for the Red Army were also neglected, and losses of men should have been kept to the minimum. 'We must know that only by preserving our personnel can we preserve our soviet. The soviet could not exist without a strong Red Army. With a strong Red Army, the soviet territories temporarily lost can be recovered in the end. Furthermore, new soviet territories can be acquired only by relying on the Red Army.'

One of the most controversial charges made in these Tsunyi Resolutions against the Po Ku leadership was, of course, that of mishandling the Nineteenth Route Army mutiny in Fukien, which Mao Tse-tung now described as 'the crux' of the question of exploiting divisions within the enemy's ranks during the Fifth Encirclement. Po Ku and his colleagues were condemned for failing to follow up the truce concluded with the Fukien rebels and for 'justifying this with empty leftist words'. A 'golden opportunity' was lost – although the evidence that Mao and his group realized this at the time is, as we have already seen, ambiguous.

Once the Fifth Encirclement began to show signs of success the Communists should, according to Resolution 11 at Tsunyi, have quickly planned their retreat – from May rather than August. This dilatoriness led to bewilderment and unnecessary losses when the evacuation of the base was eventually carried out. Otto Braun in particular was criticized: 'In Comrade Hua Fu's mind, our breakthrough of the siege was essentially a flight in panic, a sort of house-removal operation, not a resolute fighting operation. There was inadequate briefing of Party workers and officers, so that morale dropped. If better military decisions had been taken, Mao now argued, 'the central soviet could have been saved, the Fifth Encirclement could have been broken, a base area in Hunan could have been established and the strength of the Red Army could have been largely preserved'. One hardly knows which to regard as more exaggerated, the alleged faults of Po Ku and Li Teh or the extreme claims of Mao Tse-tung.

Two specific examples of military rigidity were cited in this Resolution: the fact that the Red Army, when it reached the

Hunan–Kweichow border, was 'mechanically ordered to advance towards the areas under the control of the II and VI Army Corps'; and the fact that when it arrived at the Wu River it was told to mop up small groups of the Kweichow provincial army and bandits instead of counter-attacking against Chiang Kai-shek's pursuing troops on the Szechuan–Kweichow border.

All these mistakes were labelled as 'right opportunism', and their perpetrators were rebuked for dictatorial tendencies. Li Teh under his pseudonym of Hua Fu, 'monopolized all the work of the Military Commission' and thus made a mockery of its collective leadership. Differing views were unheeded or suppressed. The Party leaders as a whole had spent too much energy on recruitment and supplies and had left Po Ku, Chou En-lai and Li Teh too free a hand on strategy and tactics.

Po Ku himself understandably bore the brunt of the Maoist onslaught. He was specially named for omitting to correct Chou's 'mistaken way of conducting the war', for failing to admit his own mistakes and for refusing to accept the criticism of the 'overwhelming majority' of the enlarged Politburo Conference. Chou trimmed his sails to the new wind, but not Po Ku.

The next step was to correct all these mistakes, to 'found a new soviet in the vast territories of Yunnan, Kweichow and Szechwan, to recover our lost soviets', and to carry all this forward to eventual national triumph. The loss of the central soviet was 'merely a setback in the soviet revolutionary movement as a whole'. The final paragraph of the Tsunyi Resolutions speaks for itself in summing up the bitter dispiritment which many of the Long Marchers must have felt at that moment, as well as the brave face which Mao alone seemed able to put on their situation:

'The enlarged conference of the Politburo points out that the mistakes in the Party's military leadership in the past were only a partial mistake in the general line of the Party, which was not enough to cause pessimism and despair. The Party has bravely exposed its own mistakes. It has educated itself through them and learnt how to lead the revolutionary war more efficiently towards victory. After the exposure of mistakes, the Party, instead of being weakened, actually becomes stronger.'

Chapter 11

The Politburo Reshuffle

THE story of how Mao Tse-tung, who had left the Kiangsi soviet in semi-disgrace, persuaded a majority of his colleagues to vote for his draft resolutions at Tsunyi remains one of the most fascinating and controversial aspects of the Long March. There is little in the records or the memoirs of the participants to shed light on this apparent turn about in allegiances, and the affair has to be reconstructed as if it belonged to pre-history.

The Politburo was not, of course, present in Tsunyi in its entirety. Wang Ming, its titular leader, was in Moscow, Hsiang Ying had remained behind in the rearguard in Kiangsi, and Liu Shao-chi had almost certainly gone to the 'white' areas to organize resistance against the Kuomintang there. According to Hans Heinrich Wetzel, the former German Communist, Liu left for Shanghai on the eve of the March with a false passport identifying him as Chao Kang-ming, a professor of history from Yunnan.[1] If the list of Politburo members at this time compiled by Hatano Kenichi, the Japanese scholar, is accepted,[2] this would leave only eight members at Tsunyi, as follows: Chang Wen-tien, Chou En-lai, Chu Teh, Liang Po-tai, Mao Tse-tung, Po Ku, Wang Chia-hsiang and Wu Liang-ping.

A majority of these eight probably counted themselves members of the Twenty-eight Bolsheviks or International faction loyal to Wang Ming and the Comintern, namely Chang, Liang, Po Ku, Wang Chia-hsiang and Wu.[3] Furthermore, Chou En-lai and Chu Teh had, in the period immediately preceding the Tsunyi Conference, been supporting the International faction. Strictly speaking, therefore, Mao was a lone voice of dissent on the Politburo. But the meeting was not confined to these eight. It was, in the classic device of Communist Parties modelled on Lenin's, an 'enlarged' conference comprising, according to the few sources available, at least eighteen or nineteen people and even as many as thirty-five to forty.[4] The additional participants were the senior military officers of the various constituent forces of the Red Army. The Communists found themselves, after all, in the middle of a protracted military operation and military affairs were the dominating question on the Politburo's agenda. What more natural than to invite those who knew best the military situation and the morale of the officers and men?

The leading military men at the conference must certainly have included Liu Po-cheng, Lin Piao, Nieh Jung-chen, Peng Teh-huai, Yang Shang-kun, Yeh Chien-ying and Li Teh, the German. Dr Jerome Ch'ên has argued that it seems 'questionable' whether a foreigner would have been allowed to attend. But there were precedents for Comintern representatives from Europe attending high-level meetings of the Chinese Communist Party, beginning with Maring, the Dutchman, at the founding First Congress. A Red Guard publication in 1967 condemned one Wu Hsiu-chuan for having, *inter alia*, acted as Li Teh's interpreter at the Tsunyi Conference where he made both a report and a speech, and now Otto Braun himself has claimed attendance. (One wonders, incidentally, if Chu Teh was able to converse at a simple level with Braun in his native language.)[5]

Others who probably attended were Teng Hsiao-ping[6] (a Central Committee member and editor of *Hung-hsing*, or *Red Star*, the Red Army publication), Teng Fa (the Chief of Political Security), Teng Tai-yuan (a former Political Commissar of the 3rd Army Corps), Chen Yun,[7] Ho Ke-chuan (*alias* Kai Feng, Political Commissar of the VIII Army Corps),[8] Lo Mai (*alias* Li Wei-han), Li Fu-chun, Wang Shou-tao and Tung Pi-wu. If Liu Shao-chi had been with the Marchers at Tsunyi, then he would undoubtedly have attended, but he was almost certainly absent. One source says that Liang Po-tai had been sent off to the 'white' areas before Tsunyi, and that Wang Chia-hsiang was absent from the debate because of his serious abdominal injury (he went through the entire March with numerous fragments of shrapnel inside him, but if he could survive those 6,000 miles on the road he could also perhaps have been carried into the conference room to vote).[9]

Mao thus won the day, but only by bringing the generals into the meeting. His majority at Tsunyi would have been impossible without the support of the senior army spokesmen – Lin Piao, Nieh Jung-chen and Peng Teh-huai. The same pattern was followed in 1965–6, when Mao again called in the army to defeat his Party rivals. But at least in 1935 there was the justification that the immediate problem faced by the Party was primarily a military one, namely how to escape from Chiang Kai-shek's superior forces.

The fact that his victory at Tsunyi was a military rather than a political one is extremely important in view of the common assumption that Mao's leadership in the Party became firmly established on this occasion. As Dr Jerome Ch'ên has pointed out, Mao's *Selected Works* were never published at Yenan in the Shensi soviet area, where the Chinese Communist Party had its headquarters after the Long March, until 1948, whereas editions of the book were distributed before then in other soviet areas controlled by the Red Army.[10] This would certainly suggest that Mao had more support in military than in civilian Party circles (these circles overlapped, of course, to some extent, but the distinction between them is nevertheless a political reality). Ch'ên even goes so far as to doubt whether Mao gained Party leadership at all at Tsunyi, citing Japanese Communist sources for the view that he acquired only military power at that meeting.[11]

In support of this argument, Ch'ên raises three questions:

(1) 'It is not clear whether the eighteen participants in the conference represented the majority required to elect a new chairman of the Politburo legitimately.' Ch'ên also points out that Mao could not have been elected Chairman of the Central Committee, because that post was not created until the Party's Seventh Congress in 1945. The Politburo in any case did not have power under the Party's Constitution to elect a new Central Committee Chairman, being itself elected by the much larger Central Committee. So, Ch'ên suggests that, at most, Mao might have been named Chairman of the Politburo (and Heinzig suggests of the Politburo Standing Committee, not of the Politburo itself). In the exigencies of the Long March the legal niceties of the Party Constitution were no doubt viewed flexibly, as they were on other occasions in

the C.C.P.'s history. No one in the Party, as far as is known, has yet raised questions about the legitimacy of the Tsunyi meeting or its decisions. It seems rather academic, therefore, to debate the legality of the proceedings, at least in the absence of further information from Party archives. Snow offers the view that Mao's formal election to the chairmanship of both the Politburo and the Central Committee took place at Lochuan in August 1937, and implies that the Tsunyi meeting somewhat informally transferred authority from the General Secretary to Mao as the chairman of the (disintegrated) soviet Government and of the Revolutionary Military Council. But others believe that Lochuan was a Politburo, not a Central Committee conference, and that the post of Central Committee Chairman was unknown at that date.[12]

(2) 'Chang Kuo-tao's defiance of Mao at the Lianghokou and Maoerhkai conferences of the Politburo might imply that Mao did not have the authority to coerce Chang.' Ch'en also cites Chang's statement to Wang Chien-min [13] that Mao only became Chairman of the Government, not the leader of the Party, at Tsunyi. If this means Chairman of the soviet Government, Mao had been holding that post since 1931, although it is conceivable that he was dropped from it just before the Long March began. But the meeting we are discussing was of the Politburo, not of the soviet Government, which had become defunct on the March. Since Chang became the principal Party rival of Mao's after the Tsunyi Conference, it seems unwise to rely on his views on this particular matter. His defiance at Maoerhkai, after the two Red Armies had joined forces on the Long March, is better explained on political than on legal grounds.

(3) 'The Party machine continued to show disagreement with Mao before and after the Rectification Campaign of 1942-4.' This is the most weighty of Ch'en's three reservations about Tsunyi. But it may confirm merely that Mao's ascendancy on this occasion was the result of a rushed, two-day patching of quarrels in the heat of the Kuomintang chase and with purely military considerations uppermost. What more natural than that the Party machine should wait for confirmation of the new leadership once the military crisis was over and the missing Politburo members were available again? And at Yenan, Mao had to begin his real fight to

consolidate the temporary advantage he had won over his rivals at Tsunyi. In the polemical language of a Radio Moscow broadcast in 1968, 'Mao Tse-tung himself merely became a member of the central leadership at Tsunyi but did not occupy a supreme post in the Party. It was long afterwards that he succeeded in usurping the leading position....' [14]

How, then, did Mao gain military support for his candidacy, whether temporary or permanent, as Party leader at Tsunyi? The two strongest groups in the Party in the initial stages of the Long March were the International faction and the Whampoa cadet faction. But each of these had become somewhat demoralized by the necessity to abandon the Kiangsi base, the severe losses en route to Tsunyi and the continuing uncertainty over the destination of the retreating Red Army.

The Internationals enjoyed two advantages; they had the backing of the international Communist movement (which to a Chinese revolutionary of that day, aware of the material and technological superiority of Europe over China, must have carried considerable weight), and they were adept at Marxist theoretical analysis.

On the March, however, where foreign friends were impotent to help and where the fallibility of their advice became only too obvious, it was possible for Mao to subvert this prestige and mock the Internationals as mere copy-ists, following a false foreign star instead of searching out China's own. Besides, Mao's Marxist theory was improving since his embarrassing earlier attempts of the late 1920s. As things went progressively wrong for the Communists during 1934, Mao was perhaps able to insinuate in Party circles the idea that the Russian-trained comrades were not consistently brilliant at theory either.

But, most important of all, the Internationals laboured under one crucial disadvantage: they had virtually no military experience. Po Ku confessed to Edgar Snow that he had never fought a single battle before he arrived in the Kiangsi soviet as acting Party leader in China at the end of 1932. [15] The Internationals were altogether less seasoned in the field. Po Ku was fifteen years junior to Mao – 27 years old at Tsunyi, to Mao's 42 – and was probably less able to live down the aura of failure that was inevitably building up around his group by the end of 1934. The further the Communists retreated into the rural interior, the more the urbanized Internationals were out of their element.

All this has assumed the cohesion of the Internationals as a conscious sub-group in the Party leadership. In the absence of the kind of running gossip which accompanies every turn of Western politics, commentators on Chinese Communist affairs tend to seize on common experiences and background as signs of political collaboration, forgetting that while these factors often *explain* an alliance between two or more politicians they very rarely *dictate* one, or not for long.

When Pavel Mif escorted his Chinese students home in 1930 and pushed them into the front line of the Chinese Party leadership, they naturally stuck together and supported one another. But no group in Chinese politics has ever discovered the secret of immunity from factionalism and they have all in the end splintered into smaller units. There is no reason to believe that every one of the Twenty-eight Bolsheviks, merely because they shared the experience of having trained in Russia, remained fully loyal to Wang Ming and Po Ku throughout the decade in which Mao battled with those two rivals. Divisive personal, regional and intellectual factors were also at work, and it could well be that the solidarity of the Internationals has been exaggerated.

Wu Liang-ping, for example, was apparently sufficiently close to Mao in 1936 to act as his interpreter (when necessary) with Edgar Snow, and he told Snow, whether truthfully or not one cannot say, that he had been a supporter of Mao since the Kiangsi soviet.[16] And Chang Wen-tien evidently led a small group of his own within the International faction which had supported Mao on certain issues, notably land distribution, during the Kiangsi period.[17] Indeed there is one view that Po Ku was already losing power before the Long March and that Chang had become compromise Secretary-General in January 1934, at the Central Committee's Fifth Plenum.[18] Mao's political survival in 1933 is attributed by an Indian sinologist [19] to the partial support of Chang, who was afterwards praised by Mao for having 'played a useful part at Tsunyi'.[20]

The same point can be made even more strongly about the second grouping in the Party leadership, the so-called Whampoa Cadets who tended to gravitate around Chou En-lai, sometime Deputy Political Director of the Whampoa Military Academy. Chen Tu-hsiu, the veteran Party leader, once referred scathingly to 'Chou En-lai's Whampoa clique in the soviet areas'.[21] Yeh Chien-ying, Hsiao Chin-kuang, Pan Tzu-li, Li Ta, Chen Keng, Hsu Hsi-chen and Chou I-chun have all been mentioned as adherents of this group.[22] But the most famous product of the Whampoa Academy, Lin Piao, had aligned himself with Mao Tse-tung well before the Long March, and his group had less to hold it together than the Internationals did.

There is danger in making analogies across such cultural frontiers, but one would surely question the validity of discussing alignments within the Republican Party of the United States on the basis of whether the individuals concerned were returned Rhodes Scholars from Oxford or had graced the various campuses of the University of California. Moscow and Whampoa were more important alma maters for the Chinese Communist, because his experience there was more binding, more dangerous, more conspicuous, but it was still only one of many experiences and was not as decisive or as permanent as some of the sinologists would have us believe.

In any event, whatever loyalty the Whampoa Cadets may have forged to Chou En-lai in the earlier years, his patent inferiority to Chu Teh as a military leader must have eroded the solidarity of this group during 1931–4. Chou himself played an ambiguous role at Tsunyi, as he so often did at moments of crisis in his own life and in the Party's dramatic history.

Mao's own band of supporters was far less impressive than Po Ku's or Chou's. One group of them, including his brother Mao Tse-min, Hsieh Chueh-tsai, Hsu Teh-li, Li Fo-chun, Tsai Chang and Lin Po-chu, were relatively minor figures from the Hunan provincial Party branches.[23] Another informant lists Teng Hsiao-ping, Ku Pai and Hsieh Wei-chun as leaders of a 'Kiangsi faction' favourable to Mao,[24] while Lin Piao and Tan Chen-lin had been trusted lieutenants of Mao since Chingkangshan days. The men who were purged during the Lo Ming campaign in Kiangsi could also presumably be reckoned as loyal to Mao, and these included

Teng Tzu-hui, Ho Shu-heng and Lu Ting-yi.[25] But some of these had stayed with the rearguard in Kiangsi. Chu Teh's position was more complicated. He had collaborated closely with Mao, more than anyone else in the Red Army had done, and yet when the big guns of the Central Committee began to appear in Kiangsi he was readily disoriented and had voted against Mao at such important conferences as the one at Ningtu.

To a large extent these groups revolved around personalities – Po Ku's, Chou En-lai's, Mao Tse-tung's. The charismatic aspect of their operation was probably the single most important element in the equation which was struck at Tsunyi.

But many senior cadres and army officers remained aloof or relatively uncommitted to these factions. There were, for instance, a number of older military officers who had graduated, not from Whampoa but from other academies, and who had become progressively disenchanted with the Internationals' leadership in the field of battle and with the advice of Li Teh, the Internationals' 'foreign expert'. This almost certainly sums up Chu Teh's attitude by the time the Red Army had reached Tsunyi, and it was probably shared by such commanders as Peng Teh-huai, Liu Po-cheng, Lo Jung-huan, Lo Ping-hui, Tan Chen and Teng Tai-yuan. Li Teh now tells us that both Peng and Liu were non-committal about Mao's leadership at Tsunyi and a Kuomintang historian describes Liu's attitude at this conference as gradually changing from anti-Mao to pro-Mao, thus weighing the balance in Mao's favour.[26]

These men were not, perhaps, fanatical adherents to either of the competing ideological lines preached by Po Ku or Mao. They were primarily soldiers, not totally apolitical since every Communist commander had a certain minimum of political motivation for his participation in the Red Army movement, but still concerned more with the actualities of social injustice than with philosophical theories. They probably supported Mao at Tsunyi because he held out the promise of more military realism in the testing months that lay ahead, not because they had been either converted to his political views or become disillusioned with those of Chou En-lai or Po Ku.

Liu Po-cheng, for example, the Szechuanese who lost an eye on the March and earned the nickname Liu Tu-yen (Dead-eyed Liu), was the first Chinese Communist general to have been thoroughly trained in Moscow, where he spent three years at the Red Army Academy. He had helped Chu Teh in the Nanchang Uprising, owed his next step in his career to Chou En-lai, and presumably he felt some bonds with the other Russian-trained leaders, in other words the Twenty-eight Bolsheviks. As the bold tactician on Chu Teh's staff his military rating stood as high as Lin Piao's or Peng Teh-huai's, and yet his political position within the Party debates was probably neutral.

The balance of power within the Communists on the Long March at the beginning of their epic was probably more delicate than earlier observers had supposed, and it may not have needed very many individual changes of vote within the senior thirty or forty leaders present to have tipped the scales in Mao's favour. By the same token, his new power after Tsunyi was not as total or as solid as many used to believe. Snow puts the matter precisely: 'Mao now held the mandate of the Red Army and the Party to lead them *on the Long March*.' And, as a German sinologist adds, 'After Tsunyi Mao took advantage of the critical military position which made his opponents co-operate with him, and tried to win them over to his side.' [27]

If a macro-historical approach were needed to fill out this all too inadequate micro-historical reconstruction of the Politburo reshuffle at Tsunyi, three broad generalizations would be found acceptable to most students of this period. In the first place, Mao's promotion represented the upsurge, after fourteen years of foreign direction of the C.C.P., of the indigenous Chinese Communists – those who had never been abroad, or who had remained relatively untouched by their visits overseas, and who viewed Communism primarily as a solution to urgent Chinese problems rather than as a leading combatant in a world war of philosophies. As Jerome Ch'ên puts it, Mao's triumph at Tsunyi was 'a victory of the rural soviet over the urban Party Centre, of a man who had spent all his life among the peasants and the lower orders of society over those who were well-versed in doctrines, Eastern and Western'. [28] Specifically, he was able to exploit the general exasperation with the bull-headed authoritarianism of the German Li Teh. By not criticizing the leadership of Chou En-lai by name, Mao enabled his former superior to dissociate himself from Li Teh and one Chinese scholar believes that 'a tacit agreement between Mao and Chou at Tsunyi is quite plausible'.[28]

Secondly, Mao owed his success to his more tactful handling of the Red Army commanders and more sympathetic understanding of their problems. The deserters since leaving Kiangsi were Chou's new recruits, not the old hands of the Mao–Chu army.

Finally, Mao offered the style of leadership that was needed by the Chinese Communists in 1935, a style that could grip the emotions as well as the intellect, that could identify, and plausibly exaggerate, the few elements of hope in an otherwise bleak prospect. Like Churchill after Dunkirk, Mao was a good man to have at the head of the column when things looked really hopeless. Like Churchill, he knew the secret of appealing to the deepest instincts of his countrymen and arousing their will to resist, to endure, to go on against all the odds. Like Churchill, he led his men to victory – and was afterwards, in the different style of Chinese politics but just as hurtfully, rebuffed because his ideas about running his country in peacetime could not command a majority.

Some glimpse into Mao's leadership appeal is given by Edgar Snow who, after his second visit to the Communist headquarters in Shenshi after the Long March, commented :

'Mao's political intelligence explains his command of the Communist Party, but not the real affection in which he is held by the men of the army and the country people. In speaking, he has a way of presenting a most complicated subject so that even the uneducated man can seem to understand it. He is full of homely idioms and instances; he never talks above the heads of his audience but he never talks down to them either. There is a real flow of intimacy between him and the people; he always seems to be in contact. . . .

'Mao can rarely speak long without making a homely wisecrack or an epigram and he seems to maintain his leadership by winning all the arguments. He is very well read and an accomplished dialectician in debate. He has an interesting technique. He seldom makes a frontal attack against opposition. He delivers a blow here, another there, he outflanks his opponents' case, he breaks down its defences one by one, until gradually he has it completely encompassed and it falls apart before a last witticism, or a telling stroke of logic. He likes people and their laughter and is at home in any group. He has a lively imagination. I remember once seeing him laugh till he wept when somebody described to him a comedy he had seen in Shanghai. It was an American movie – Charlie Chaplin in *Modern Times*.' [29]

The only indication of the order of business at the Tsunyi Conference comes from Hsiao San (also known as Emil Hsiao or Emi Siao), the childhood friend of Mao.[30] Though he was not a participant, his account probably derives from official Party sources, even from Mao himself, and may therefore be considered with interest as well as with reserve. Hsiao says that Mao spoke first on the political and military mistakes of the Politburo in the preceding months. Chu Teh spoke next, criticizing both the Politburo and Li Teh, though many sources name Peng Teh-huai as the chief critic of military tactics. Po Ku then defended his position, surveying the revolutionary movement since 1931 and emphasizing the C.C.P.'s failure to appreciate the significance of constructing an anti-imperialist united front. This, as Dr Jerome Ch'ên puts it, must have appeared as 'a veiled criticism of the narrowness of Mao's peasant movement'.[31]

Chou En-lai was the fourth speaker, in Hsiao's account, making a clean breast of the strategic errors of the Politburo and himself. Hsiao says that Chou actually moved that Mao be given the leadership of the Red Army while he, Chou, retired from the Military Commission. By this move Po Ku, Chang Wen-tien and the others of the International faction had no choice but to accept Chou's proposal.

The outcome was that Mao was elected Chairman of the Revolutionary Military Council, in place of Chou, and the Council was reorganized. Yeh Chien-ying, Chou's colleague and supporter, was replaced as Chief of Staff by Liu Po-cheng. Teng Fa, head of the security police, was dropped from the Council and not replaced. Li Teh's executive powers of directing military operations were annulled and the Council took over. Chu Teh as Commander-in-Chief and Wang Chia-hsiang as Political Commissar continued to serve on the Council as before, and Chou remained a member.[32]

The leadership of the First Front Army was now as follows:

Commander-in-Chief: Chu Teh
Chief-of-Staff: Liu Po-cheng
    I Army Corps
Commander: Lin Piao
Political Commissar: Nieh Jung-chen
Chief-of-Staff: Tso Chuan
    III Army Corps
Commander: Peng Teh-huai
Political Commissar: Yang Shang-kun
    V Army Corps
Commander: Tung Chen-tang
    IX Army Corps
Commander: Lo Ping-hui

The Politburo was similarly reshuffled, Mao becoming Chairman (a post which had not previously existed) and Po Ku being replaced by Chang Wen-tien as Secretary-General. It is just possible that Chang had already occupied this post since the beginning of 1934, and that Po Ku's commanding position within the Internationals had been waning for the whole of that year.[33] Swarup, the Indian scholar of this period, even argues that the formula by which Chou En-lai and Chang Wen-tien set aside Po Ku in favour of Mao – and of Party harmony in the soviet areas – may have been reached in principle before the March, so that Tsunyi was 'no more than an act of registration for a development which was being gradually transformed into a reality'.[34]

Chang was one of the senior Twenty-eight Bolsheviks, and there is nothing to suggest that he was converted to Maoism at Tsunyi. Mao recalled later that it was Chang Wen-tien who had wanted to expel Mao from the Party at the Ningtu conference in August 1932, when Mao's fortunes were at their lowest ebb. But Mao went on to admit that Chang had played a 'useful role' at the Tsunyi Conference, and that 'it was impossible then without them [i.e without the Twenty-eight Bolsheviks]. But Lo Fu [Chang's pseudonym] was stubborn'.[35]

Probably the Internationals sought to minimize their losses at Tsunyi in the hope of making a comeback once the military crisis was over and Russian influence was available again. Po Ku was obstinate by temperament and as the titular head of the International faction he obviously had to go. But the others might well have reckoned that their best response to the generals' revolt and to Mao's challenge at Tsunyi was to bide their time. Rue suggests that 'some members of the former ruling clique were persuaded. At least they were willing to give Mao and Chu a chance to try their generalship – perhaps secretly hoping that they too would fail.' [36]

The issues at Tsunyi and the arguments are evident from the summary of, and excerpts from, the successful Resolutions of Mao in the previous chapter. The Resolutions do, of course, exaggerate the position of Po Ku, Li Teh and Chou En-lai, who had never completely abandoned guerrilla fighting in favour of positional warfare but had been forced to some extent into the latter by the circumstances of the Fifth Encirclement. Thus Chou had written in February 1934 that 'naturally, we must in the main fight mobile operations. However, we often witness nowadays that rencontres and mobile operations rapidly develop into positional engagements.' [37] The Kuomintang blockhouses had necessarily obliged the Communists to undertake a certain amount of positional fighting. Besides, the dispatch of guerrillas to fight behind the enemy's lines carried dangers of its own, as the defection to the other side of one such detachment, under Kung Ho-chung, in July 1934, had illustrated.[38] Po Ku commented; 'Unless they are under firm proletarian leadership, guerrilla activities are inevitably unco-ordinated and disorganized . . . and lead to the tendency to kill and burn indiscriminately.' [39]

Similarly the Maoists' criticism of the Po Ku leadership's failure to exploit the Fukien Mutiny of the Nineteenth Route Army is over-stretched. It is doubtful if Mao could have handled the affair any better in view of the political demands of the Fukien government for a united front between the Kuomintang and the Communists to fight Japan. There is in any case evidence, as we have seen, that Mao himself had strong reservations at the time about the wisdom of doing business with the Fukien rebels.

It would seem from the Maoist Resolutions themselves, therefore, that the Internationals had plenty of ammunition with which to defend their record and puncture the arguments of their opponents. But the mood was decisively against them, and the Communists preferred, for the time being at least, to place their destinies in the hands of the one man who still looked as if he could salvage something from what must have appeared a more and more calamitous expedition.

In fact, as an American scholar has written, Tsunyi in retrospect 'is the point at which the mass flight of the Red Armies was stemmed and the Long March began: when Chu Teh's superb generalship and Mao Tse-tung's political acumen united to turn victory into defeat'.[40]

Chapter 12

A Feint in Yunnan

THE military character of the Long March altered after Tsunyi. For one thing the ranks were thinned down to about a half of the 100,000 who set out from Kiangsi. Edgar Snow was told in Paoan in 1936 that the Marchers' numbers 'were reduced by about one-third by the time they reached the border of Kweichow province' in mid-December, and Chou En-lai volunteered the further estimate that 45,000 of the 90,000 combatants who had left Kiangsi had been 'lost' 'by the time the Red Army crossed the Chinsha River [or Yangtze] into Szechuan' on 1 May 1935.[1] Another estimate of the Marchers' strength on entering Tsunyi is only 30,000.[2] The opportunity was taken in Tsunyi to recruit several thousand, perhaps 20,000, new soldiers, mostly Kweichownese, Szechuanese and Yunnanese.[3]

Mao's aim now was apparently to strike into Szechuan and set up a new soviet area there in collaboration with the Fourth Front Army already established under Chang Kuo-tao and Hsu Hsiang-chien in the north of that province. His Resolutions at Tsunyi had cited as the immediate task the establishment of a new base area in the Szechuan–Kweichow–Yunnan region.

There were sound reasons for such a strategy. These three provinces were outside the direct control of the Kuomintang government at Nanking, and so the Communists' most dedicated and persistent enemy, Chiang Kai-shek, was unable to deal with them as effectively as he could, for example, in Kiangsi. Wang Chia-lieh ruled as the virtually independent warlord of Kweichow, while no fewer than seven warlords, each with their own territory and following, divided Szechuan between them. Liu Wen-hui, whom the Kuomintang had originally supported when he controlled the Chengtu half of the 'Red Basin', was still of some consequence, but the strongest warlord in Szechuan in 1935 was the provincial

Governor, Liu Hsiang, whose troops were strongly entrenched along the Yangtze River from Chungking, the capital, to Wahsien in the north-east.

Civil war had never ceased in Szechuan since the revolution in 1911, and one author lists a total of 478 military conflicts in this province in the two decades that followed it.[4] In conditions of such political instability, with the local population over-taxed and oppressed by the competing armies, the Communists could operate with maximum effectiveness. The chances of the various warlords' sinking their differences for a concerted military campaign against the Red Army seemed remote.

The Fourth Front Army base in the north had reached its high-water mark by January 1935, with some 80,000 – perhaps even 100,000 – men holding a perimeter that stretched, on its southern flank, from Paoning on the Chialing River to Suiting on the Chu River. Meanwhile, the Communist Second Front Army under Ho Lung and Hsiao Ke, based on Sangchih in the north-western tip of Hunan province and another pocket of mountain terrain in north-east Kweichow (ironically, only 150 miles from Tsunyi, but with hostile forces in between), was using the corridor of the Yiu Shui River and its tributaries in Szechuan and Hupei as a 'Ho Lung trail' linking the two strongholds. Ho Lung did not co-ordinate his movements with those of the Fourth Front Army, but his presence in the south-east tip of Szechuan and occasional forays into the Tangtang and Wu River areas reinforced the Communist threat to Szechuan.

Clearly the prospects in Szechuan outshone those in Shensi, where Liu Chih-tan and Kao Kang at this time boasted fewer than 10,000 Red soldiers, where the 'opposition', in the shape of the pro-Kuomintang Yang Hu-cheng, was in effective control of most of the province and where the material resources of the country-side were so poor. Hsu Teh-li told Edgar Snow in 1936 that north Shensi was 'culturally one of the darkest places on earth', and its population 'very backward indeed'. Chou En-lai added the comment that 'In Kiangsi and Fukien people brought bundles with them when they joined the Red Army; here [in Shenshi] they do not even bring chopsticks, they are utterly destitute.'[5] By contrast Szechuan was rich in both foodstuffs and minerals. And no doubt those two Szechuanese at the head of the Red Army, Chu Teh and Liu Po-cheng, added their voice to the choice of Szechuan as the next Communist base.

But Mao's problem was how to get across the heavily defended Yangtze River. 'The fate of the nation,' called Chiang Kai-shek at this point, 'and of the party * depends on bottling up the Reds south of the Yangtze.' Determined both to wipe out the Communists and to establish control over the wayward south-western provinces, Chiang had already moved to stiffen the discipline of the Szechuan warlords' troops. In the previous August (of 1934) he had pursuaded Liu Hsiang to accept two hundred Kuomintang military advisers, together with financial help from Nanking. On 12 January 1935, while the Red Army was still in Tsunyi, the Kuomintang General Ho Kuo-kuang arrived in Chungking with a group of senior officers to implement this agreement, and soon they took measures to improve the organization and fighting power of the Szechuan provincial army.

Meanwhile Kuomintang troops from Shensi province under the command of General Hu Tsung-nan began to strike at the Fourth Front Army of Chang Kuo-tao and Hsu Hsiang-chien in northern Szechuan. In about the middle of January Hsu had to suspend operations on his southern front in order to secure his rear. In this way the Szechuanese provincials, under the professional leadership of veteran Kuomintang officers, were freed to pose a serious obstacle to Mao's plans for crossing the Yangtze in the southern districts of Szechuan.

The first sally made by the First Front Army through the terraced fields yellow with rape blossoms was at Hokiang, where the River Yangtze makes a southward bend bringing it to a mere ten miles or so from the Kweichow border. While the main body of the Communists was recuperating at Tsunyi, a forward detachment of the Red Army moved northwards from the city to take the Loushan Pass (Loushankuan) and Tungtzu. On the Kweichow–Szechuan border, at Sungkan, they inflicted a defeat on the Szechuanese provincial troops. According to Chu Li-fu's account,[6] the Red Army, assembled in the countryside between Tsunyi, Meitan and Suiyang (in other words, to the north and east of

___
* The Kuomintang.

Tsunyi), now threw up fortifications to resist its pursuers, as if a more or less permanent occupation of the area were envisaged.

The Kweichow provincial armies of Wang Chia-lieh and Yu Kuo-tsai were pressing northwards towards Tsunyi to punish and evict the Reds. Hsueh Yueh and Lui Chien-hsu had crossed the Yangtze at the head of the Hunan army in pursuit of their quarry; the Szechuanese provincial army was advancing from Chikiang and Chengting and now divided to strike at Szunan, Fengchuan and Tungtzu; and even the Kwangsi provincial forces were closing in for the kill, having reached Kweiting, about a hundred miles south of Tsunyi.[7] The trap was tightening.

But as before, in the Fifth Kuomintang Encirclement of the previous year in Kiangsi, one sector of the circle was frail. In this case the weak link was the Szechuanese provincial soldiers on the western line of the Communist position. On the night of 16 January the workers at the arsenal in Chihshui, the Kweichow border town on the river of that name which flowed thirty miles downstream into the mighty Yangtze at Hokiang, staged a revolt. With the help of some of the poorer inhabitants they attacked the troops on guard. In consequence the Kweichownese provincial soldiers stationed there, putting discretion before valour, abandoned the town. When the vanguard of the Red Army reached Chihshui, having marched from Sungkan, Wenshui and Tashui, it was greeted by workers and local radicals waving banners.[8]

Other Communist units had meanwhile occupied Jenhuai and Maotai and even penetrated into the Szechuanese border areas near Kulin and Yungming. Maotai is, of course, the site where the famous rice wine of that name is produced; Chinese all over the world will toast their friends in Maotai wine rather as Britons would call for Scotch or Frenchmen for champagne. The distillery at Maotai housed no fewer than a hundred large earthenware vessels, each holding twenty *piculs* of wine and all full to the brim. The story that became legendary among the Long Marchers was that the first Communist soldiers to enter the distillery thought that the white liquid in the vats was for bathing, and they promptly soaked their tired and punished feet in the wine. Li Teh, the German, according to one description, was one of the first to hear of the 'find', and he and his colleagues 'became quite drunk' on the liquor, which is renowned for its strength and high alcohol content. 'By the time the last units had passed through Maotai,' says this chronicler, 'there was not a drop of the "foot water" left.' [9]

The First Front Army crossed the Chihshui River into Szechuan province on 26 January, according to most accounts. Liu Hsiang, the master of Szechuan, now acting with the stiffening of the Kuomintang officers, sent two brigades of his troops under Chang An-ping and Fan Shih-chieh to repel the Reds at Chihshui and Yungming. Another group was ordered to reinforce the defences along the banks of the Yangtze and hold the Wanyi–Kikiang area on the southern side of the river. Some of the units below the river were pulled back to secure the strategic Kuanyi bridge. Meanwhile the wealthy families of Chikiang and the known anti-Communist leaders in Chungking quietly left town in case the Communists succeeded in their push to the north. Mao's troops did indeed fan out into the little southern pocket of Szechuan which is contained in the curve of the Chihshui River, even occupying Weihsin (or Tsahsi) on the Yunan border.[10]

But they found the approaches to the Yangtze too heavily defended and so they unexpectedly backtracked, recrossing the Chinshui in mid-February and recapturing the Loushan Pass after a final successful battle with Wang Chia-lieh's Kweichow army. It was this tactic which Mao afterwards complained was resisted in the field by Lin Piao, who ignored the unusual order for four days. His men retook Tsunyi on 27 February, having wasted about five weeks in the fruitless attempt to cross the Yangtze. They also defeated the Kwangsi provincial forces, two divisions of them, under Wu Chi-wei near Tsunyi: the remnants, squeezed in a pincer attack between Peng Teh-huai's III Army Corps and Lin Piao's I Army Corps, scuttled to safety over the Wu River.

Tsai Shun-li, Political Director of the 142nd Regiment, described this engagement: 'Comrade Mao Tse-tung directed the encirclement of the enemy in a hundred-square-kilometre mountain area. In close encounter, our fighters charged into the enemy ranks, cutting them down with broadswords and hand grenades. Frightened in this hand-to-hand fighting, the enemy troops fled south. Most of them were wiped out. The rest trampled upon one another and many were injured or killed. A small number rushed across the Wuchiang River and hastily destroyed the pontoon bridge, leaving about a thousand of their own men stranded on the north bank to be captured by the Red Army. Twenty regiments were wiped out. This was the first major victory of the Long March.' [11] The Communists thus re-established their control of north–central Kweichow province and gained another spell of respite from enemy attack. Mao, elated by the Tsunyi Conference, celebrated the valour of the Red Army in recapturing the Loushan Pass in a poem of that name:

> Cold blows the west wind,
> Far off in the frosty air
>   the wild geese call
>   in the morning moonlight.
> In the morning moonlight
> Horses' hoofs ring out sharply
> And the bugle's note
>   is muted.
>
> Do not say
>   that the pass is defended with iron.
> This very day
>   at one step
>   we shall cross over it.
> We shall cross over it.
> The hills are blue like the sea,
> And the dying sun is like blood. [12]

But now came another bitter blow to Mao's hopes. Hsu Hsiang-chien's Fourth Front Army succeeded in repelling the Shensi Kuomintang troops which had attacked from the north, but promptly ran into tougher opposition from the Szechuanese provincial troops under their new officers from Nanking. It therefore abandoned its base in the fork of the Chialing and Chu Rivers in northern Szechuan and headed west for the safer, if less hospitable, wilds of the mountains leading to Tibet. After dealing fairly easily en route with the army of the local warlord, Tien Tsung-yao, the Fourth Army reached Sungpan in the far north of the province. Here it could be of no assistance whatsoever in helping Mao's men across the Yangtze.

When the news came on the Communists' primitive radio, it must have caused heavy disappointment. The flight of the Fourth enabled Liu Hsiang to marshal all his forces for the Kweichow border – and the Hunanese troops under Hsueh Yueh, by now known as the single most determined pursuer of the Long Marchers, were regrouping also for a renewed attack. Chang Kuo-tao, the Political Commissar of the Fourth Front Army, was henceforth labelled as a 'flightist' in Mao's book.

During March the First Army made a second entry into Szechuan, crossing the Chihshui River for the third time on 16 March. This was intended to mislead the Kuomintang into moving forces to the Yangtze in Szechuan again. But the Reds then turned about, recrossed the Chihshui for the fourth and final time and made a forced march south. These four operations across the Chihshui river formed the basis forty years later for a sharp criticism in the official Peking press of Lin Piao and Peng Teh-huai, who allegedly had 'worked in collusion to oppose Chairman Mao's concept of mobile warfare and were severely criticized by Chairman Mao'.[13] On 31 March 1935 the Red Army crossed the Wu River for the last time, three months after that first fateful crossing, and headed towards Kweiyang, the Kweichow capital. What were Mao's and Chu Teh's intentions now? Did they envisage a soviet area in Yunnan, where Kuomintang resistance would be negligible? Did they intend to strike for the Yangtze again further downstream where it takes, in Chinese, the new name of Chinsha – River of Golden Sand? Or would they march into Kwangsi, even into Kwangtung, to try their luck there?

No one on the Kuomintang side could tell. Many of the Communist rank and file themselves, most probably, could only guess. The Chinsha was a formidable obstacle, falling from a height above sea level of some 8,200 feet at Paan or Batang on the Szechuan–Tibet border to less than 900 feet at Yipin, where it enters the Red Basin to become the Yangtze. From beginning to end, from the headwater in Chinghai to Yipin, the Chinsha River falls by an average of about eighteen feet per mile. Its current is swift and navigation is treacherous. Up to Chiaochia there are many boats plying, but beyond this point the crossings become infrequent and none of them boasts more than ten or a dozen boats. For a force the size of the First Front Army, such a crossing would take many days and court disaster from an enemy which outnumbered it.

Above Lungchieh (or Yungjen), the great ferry at the junction of the Yalung and Chinsha Rivers which has been the chief crossing point, for millennia, of traders and travellers, passage can only be chanced by the 'skin boats' of the local tribesmen. The current would smash a wooden boat to pieces before it was halfway over. A Red Army crossing would have to be somewhere between Chiaochia and Lungchieh, and the Kuomintang had ample time to prepare the dozen or more possible ferry sites and render them impassable.[14]

As April opened the Communists drove south to envelop Kweiyang. They captured a car on one of the roads, containing valuable military maps of Yunnan, and this may have decided the issue. Chiang Kai-shek flew to Kweiyang to assume personal command of its defence, and some of the Red Army units feigned attacks on Wengan and Huangping to the east of Kweiyang. Mao sent a force to surround Lungli, just beyond the capital, and Chiang ordered Yunnan troops to come to the rescue. With Yunnan thus exposed, the Red Army suddenly changed direction yet again and headed south-west towards Yunnan, untroubled by the enemy forces which had been deployed elsewhere.

It was during this campaign that press reports spoke of the death of Chu Teh. Agnes Smedley showed one of them to him afterwards. It read: 'It is now revealed that Chu Teh was killed during a battle at Chutoushan [Pig Head Mountain] in the Tsatsu area. Chu was leading his column of troops in an effort to reach Kweiyang.... His body has not been encoffined.... It is wrapped in red silk and carried by his close followers. ... Chu had been suffering from a serious wound before he met his death.... His close followers in the Red Army offer sacrifices before the red silk-wrapped body at close intervals when they have a chance to take a brief rest in their escape for life.... It is now confirmed that the Red Army consists of no more than 10,000 men.'

Agnes Smedley reports: 'A contemptuous smile formed about General Chu's lips as he read this report which, incidentally, was about the tenth time he had been reported killed.' [15]

Chu was nearing his home country. 'In a Kuomintang newspaper at the time,' Agnes Smedley notes, 'General Chu found a news item about his second wife, Yu-chen, and son. Kuomintang militarists had fallen upon his wife's home in Nanshi and destroyed everything. Chu Teh's son, a student of nineteen, the report laconically remarked, had escaped but was being "hunted down". General Chu waited in the hope that his son would make his way to the Red Army. He never heard of his wife or son again. There was no doubt in his mind but that they were killed by the Kuomintang.'[16]

The Communists passed through Huishui, Changshun and Tzeyun, and then crossed the Peipan River, over a bridge constructed by their own engineers, to Chengfeng, Anlung and Hingyi. Here they entered Yunnan by crossing the Pan River, and divided into two columns. Both columns began to turn northwards again, or rather north-west. The main one made for Malung, Chanyi, Suntien and Sungming, appearing to see Kunming, the capital of the province, as its next destination. The smaller column, however, went up towards the Chinsha River in the general direction of Kiaokia, taking Hsuanwei and Hweitse.

Once more the Communists made a successful feint, this time at the Yunnan capital of Kunming (or Yunnanfu), which drew the enemy's attention away from their real objective. In the account of Chu Teh, as told to Agnes Smedley:

'By April, enemy armies were concentrated in north, east, and south Kweichow. The Yunnan Army had also moved into the south, leaving the western route into Yunnan province open. Unable to shake off such heavy enemy forces, on May 1 the Red Army suddenly drove westward through northern Yunnan over mountainous territory well known to General Chu from the past. In order to get the army across the River of Golden Sands – which crashes along the Yunnan–Szechuan border – before enemy bombers could discover it, Lin Piao was sent with one division to make a feint at the provincial capital, Yunnanfu, and draw enemy armies and bombers after him. . . .

'On the way to Yunnanfu, Lin Piao's division captured an enemy caravan of military and medical supplies on its way to Kweichow. When his division came within sight of the gates of Yunnanfu, Chiang Kai-shek and his wife, who had flown there from Kweichow together with other Kuomintang figures, hurriedly left again.'[17]

While Lin Piao was making as loud a noise as possible on the road to Kunming, where the warlord Lung Yun (Dragon Cloud) frantically prepared for an attack, and whence Chiang and his wife, in Snow's description, 'hastily repaired down the French railway toward Indochina',[18] Liu Po-cheng, the field chief-of-staff, led vanguard forces directly to the Chinsha River via Yaunmow. It was touch-and-go whether the 45,000-strong Communist force could get across.

When the Kuomintang realized that the drive on Kunming was a mere diversion and that the bulk of the Communists had moved north-west to the Chinsha River, there was some relief among its leaders. It seemed obvious that the Red Army was heading for Leng-kai (or Lungchieh), one of the few navigable stretches of the river. The drama of the next few days is best captured by Edgar Snow :

'Through the wild mountainous country of Yunnan, the Yangtze River flows deeply and swiftly between immense gorges, great peaks in places rising in defiles of a mile or more, with steep walls of rock lifting almost perpendicularly on either side. The few crossings had all been occupied long ago by government troops. Chiang was well pleased. He now ordered all boats drawn to the north bank of the river and burned. Then he started his own troops, and Lung Yun's in an enveloping movement around the Red Army, hoping to finish it off forever on the banks of this historic and treacherous stream.

'Seemingly unaware of their fate, the Reds continued to march rapidly westward in three columns toward Lengkai. The boats had been burned there, and Nanking pilots reported that a Red van-guard had begun building a bamboo bridge. Chiang became more confident; this bridge-building would take weeks. But one even-ing, quite unobtrusively, a Red battalion suddenly reversed its direction. On a phenomenal forced march it covered eighty-five miles in one night and day, and in late afternoon descended upon the only other possible ferry crossing in the vicintiy, at Chou P'ing Fort. Dressed in captured Nanking uniforms, the battalion entered the town at dusk without arousing comment, and quietly disarmed the garrison.' [11]

Liu Po-cheng, the Chief-of-Staff himself, explains the incident :
'Chiang Kai-shek's planes flew over the area every day trying to

detect our movement. It was a race against time. The Red Army, marching by night, approached the Chinsha River by three routes: the First Army Group was to seize the Lungchieh Ferry, the Third Army Group the Hungmen Ferry, the Cadres' Regiment the Chiaoche Ferry, while the Fifth Army Group was again to provide cover to the other units by serving as rearguard.

'The Cadres' Regiment stole across the Chinsha River and sprang an attack on the enemy, destroying a whole platoon. The regiment immediately took control of both ends of the Chiaoche Ferry and seized seven ferry boats. The main force of the regiment sped on to the plateau thirty li away, traversing the yawning valley on the north bank of the river and routing the enemy reinforcements from Szechuan. The river was very swift-flowing at the Hungmen Ferry and very wide at the Lungchieh Ferry, where enemy planes flying at low altitudes could harass the crossing. Therefore, the Fifth and Third Army Groups moved to the Chiaoche Ferry to cross the river under the protecting fire of a division of the Fifth Army Group.

'Three days later, about six regiments of the enemy's "dare-to-die" 13th Division reached the Chiaoche Ferry in pursuit of the Red Army. But they were beaten back in a surprise attack by the Fifth Army Group, and were forced to retreat along the Chinsha River in utter confusion. Chiang Kai-shek discovered the change in the Red Army's tactics and called a meeting in Kweiyang at which our tactics were studied and plans made to try and outwit us, and so save his forces from annihilation by the Red Army. The enemy decided on a tactic of "long pursuit, well-planned attack". Now far away from its parent body and stunned by events, the Kuomintang's 13th Division dared not take action and dug itself in Tuanchieh. By the aid of the seven ferry boats captured from the enemy our army crossed the Chinsha River at the Chiaoche Ferry in nine days and nine nights. When large reinforcements of the enemy arrived on the tenth day, the Red Army was already far ahead, and all the ferry boats were destroyed.

'Thus the Red Army extricated itself from the several hundred thousand Kuomintang troops hot on its heels or trying to intercept and encircle it.' [20]

Chapter 13

The River of Golden Sand

LET the story of the actual capture of the Chou P'ing Fort crossing be told by Captain Hsiao Ying-tang, who commanded the 5th Company of the 2nd Battalion of the Red Cadres Regiment:

'Of the three columns advancing westward [from Kweichow to Yunnan], our Red Cadres Regiment was the central one, whose duty it was to protect the Party and government leaders.

'The Cadres Regiment consisted of two infantry battalions and a Special Course Battalion, in addition to a Senior Cadres Group. The members of the regiment, except for those of the Senior Cadres Group, were all officers of company or platoon ranks – vigorous young men with rich fighting experience. I was in command of the 5th Company of the 2nd Battalion from 1932 till we entered northern Shensi at the end of the Long March.

'Yunnan in April was hot enough to make people feel sticky. Even if one were to put on a single tunic, he would sweat profusely. In the wet paddy fields tufts of young shoots nodded in the wind, as though welcoming us. The hills on both sides were heavily timbered and blanketed with grass and flowers. Bees hummed among the honey-laden blossoms and butterflies fluttered from flower to flower. The scene in spring was enchanting. But we were not destined to enjoy it. We could not linger, for more than a hundred thousand Kuomintang troops were after us.

'One night we billeted in a village. At midnight, I went out on a round of inspection. As I passed the courtyard where the Party and government leaders had been put up, I saw the light of a lamp within. Which one of our leaders was still not abed at this time of night? I was exchanging a word with the sentry when a man came out from the room. When he came near, I realized that it was Comrade Chou En-lai. I stood at attention in the darkness. "Vice-Chairman, you haven't gone to bed yet?" I asked.

' "No. Ah! Is it you? Have you finished inspecting? Come in and have a chat."

'The house, formerly the property of a landlord, was of better quality. In the room in which the Vice-Chairman lived were a handful of quaint-looking chairs and a table to match. On the table stood an oil lamp and a few pieces of writing material. There was also a paper packet. A large map hung on the wall. The Vice-Chairman was studying the route of advance. In the dim reflection of the oil lamp, his face looked yellow and thin, and his eyes were not as brilliant as usual.

'When we were seated, he asked: "How many men are there in your 5th Company?"

' "We suffered some casualties during the battle in Tsunyi and Tucheng. We are now one hundred and twenty strong," I replied.

'He proceeded to inquire about the conditions of our company during the march; about the weapons and equipment; about the morale of the rank and file. To each of his questions I made reply.

'The Vice-Chairman thought for a moment, and then said, smiling: "Your company fought well in Tsunyi and Tucheng. You must maintain this glory in future."

'He opened the packet of biscuits on the table and invited me to eat. It was his midnight ration prepared by his orderly.

' "You yourself had better eat, Vice-Chairman," I said. "I've eaten too much during the evening meal, I still feel full."

'He shoved the packet before me and pressed me to eat. So I had to pick up a half piece, and chewing, waited for further queries. But he raised no more questions. Finally he said: "All right! It's rather late now. Go and have a rest."

'Coming out of the Vice-Chairman's room, I felt puzzled. The Vice-Chairman had inquired about the company in detail. Did he mean it as a general investigation or was he looking for a company to which he would entrust an important mission? My heart beat rapidly. I regretted I had not been bold enough to ask for information.

'The troops did not march the next day. The men availed themselves of the opportunity to clean up or supplement themselves with rations. Some were husking rice, patching up clothes, polishing their rifles or sharpening their bayonets. I and some others were sitting under the eaves of the house, making straw sandals and listening to the mixed chattering.

' "The enemy are hard upon us, but here we have come to stay. Isn't it strange!"

' "What is so strange about it? Either we are waiting for the enemy to come up to fight, or an important mission calls for preparation."

' "What important mission? Is it the march against Kunming or the crossing of the Golden Sand River?" someone put in.

'That question brought silence. Everybody looked at me.

' "Who knows? The leading comrades have given no direction," I said.

'By afternoon, preparations were nearly complete. Clothes were washed and darned, ration bags refilled, and rifles and bayonets shining. The men kept asking me why we were not leaving. I was very anxious myself, and their question made me feel the more restless. I went out to hunt for news.

'The village was fair in size, with more than 200 households. It was quiet and tranquil, with cottages and hedges surrounded by green paddy fields. The people lived not at all badly, much better off than those in Kweichow. Judging from their costumes, there were quite a number of minority people here. But in every family, the young people had fled, leaving only the old folk and the children. Doubtless the Kuomintang had spread all sorts of lying rumours – they always did when they were licked.

'Before a deserted primary school I picked up a map of Yunnan among a heap of paper fragments eddying in the wind. We had relied on the leadership and the guides to give the directions. Now a map, though simple, would give a lot of help. From the map it was clear we must cross the Golden Sand River if we were to march north to resist the Japanese. The Golden Sand River, which the enemy would guard jealously, confronted us with yet another obstacle. If we were to cross in force, a grim battle would ensue.

'Coming back I passed the house where the Party and government leaders lived. People were hurrying in and out. It seemed a meeting was being held. Though I knew some of them, I did not feel it appropriate to raise a question. I went to the other companies but they were just as puzzled as I. It seemed a new, important question was presenting itself.

'By the forenoon of the third day, the pursuing enemy, it was said, was pressing in and was beginning to surround us. Still no order for action. Every fighter was feeling increasingly uneasy. At noon, I saw the regimental messenger come towards our company headquarters.

' "Does the regimental commander call for us?" I hurried to ask.

' "How did you know?" replied the messenger.

'At once I knew it was true. Overjoyed, I ran towards regimental headquarters, pulling with me Political Instructor Li.

'The house was crowded with people. Apart from Regimental Commander Chen Keng and Political Commissar Sung Jen-chiung, there were also responsible comrades from the Central Authority, some of whom I recognized. The air was heavy with the smell of dried tobacco leaves. A meeting was in progress. Seeing us enter, the regimental commander said: "The Central Authority has decided that our force cross the Golden Sand River, and has given our regiment the task of capturing the ferry. We in turn have decided to send the Second Battalion as the advance contingent and the Fifth Company as the vanguard. Your mission is: Capture the ferry at all costs and as quickly as possible; cover the succeeding troops in crossing the river. Start as soon as you are ready!" He pointed at a comrade in black uniform. "This is Comrade Li, who is to lead the task group sent by the Central Authority to help you fulfil the mission. He will be in general charge."

'We shook hands with Comrade Li, had a few words with him about the time to start, and returned to company headquarters.

'The troops were mobilized and, after eating a full meal, set out with equipment along a short-cut to the Golden Sand River. I and Deputy Battalion Commander Huo Hai-yuan walked behind the vanguard platoon; the political instructor and the task group brought up the rear. The cadres, after scoring two splendid victories in Tsunyi and Tucheng, were in high spirits. Two days' rest had freshened them up. As the vanguard company of the advance contingent, they were greatly exhilarated and marched briskly. Though the path was rugged and was undiscernible in some parts, and despite the blazing sun which caused them to sweat profusely, they walked a dozen *li* without a break. Nobody complained; not a single one fell behind. They marched the whole night through. At daybreak, after ten minutes' rest, during which they gobbled the cold rice they had brought with them and drank a few mouthfuls of cold water, they continued on their way. They marched more than seventy *li*.*

'After scaling a mountain, the troops took a breather at a point some sixty *li* from the Golden Sand River. During the break, Comrade Li and we studied how to capture the ferry. It was decided to wipe out the enemy guards on this side of the river first, and capture the boats for a forced crossing; then we would put the enemy on the opposite shore out of action, and protect the ferry so that the main force which followed might cross.

'At sunset we approached the river bank. In the distance towered a pitch-black mass: we couldn't tell the trees from the mountain slope. Before the mountains lay the Golden Sand River like a long grey sheet. Between the mountains and the river glittered points of light, like the eyes of the enemy peeping at us. Who knows whether the enemy has discovered us? Maybe they are already waiting for us. But never mind, we are bound to have it out. Now we are nearing the bank. I passed back the order: "The Golden River is reached, make ready for action!"

'In the darkness the leader of the First Platoon ran up, panting, and reported the situation. The enemy, it was found, had learned of the Red Army entering Yunnan. Fearing that we might force a crossing of the Golden Sand River, they had in the last few days stationed troops on a line stretching for hundreds of *li* on the opposite shore, keeping under control all the ferries, seizing all the boats and sending them to the opposite shore and breaking all communication. They kept sending plain-clothes scouts across the river to hunt for information. Today those agents had probably gone to blackmail the local people again, leaving the boats that sent them across waiting by the riverside. When our scouts went down there, a boatman, thinking their men had returned, said drowsily: "So you've come back." "We have," replied our

---

*About twenty-three miles, there being approximately three *li* to the mile.

scouts, quick at seizing the chance, and with a few sprints were at the boatmen and the boats became our booty.

'When the platoon leader had finished, I hurried to the bank and, after confronting the scared boatmen, tried to elicit from them what information they had regarding the situation on the opposite shore. The boatmen spoke stutteringly, supplementing each other. The situation thus gathered was like this: On the opposite shore was a small town where there was a taxation office in which were stationed thirty or so policemen. That morning a company of regular troops had arrived. They were quartered at the right wing of the town. In the centre of the town, by the riverside, was a stone jetty. It had always been picketed by a policeman, but since the situation had become more tense, the enemy had put one more man on the beat. Though the enemy was afraid the Red Army might cross the river, they thought this was not the main ferry. Nor did they believe the Red Army would come so soon. So their defence there was rather slack.

'After consulting with the deputy battalion commander, I decided on crossing at once. The political instructor questioned the boatmen, promising them rewards. These people had been roughly handled by the enemy. Now, when they saw they could gain something, they were all eagerness: "At your service, sir! At your service!"

'I ordered the 1st and 2nd Platoons to cross with me, leaving behind the deputy battalion commander, the political instructor and the task group. The Third Platoon was to patrol the riverside and shoot to support us if anything should happen to the boats crossing.

'The 3rd Platoon deployed on the beach, training their rifles on the lamp-lit town. After I had told them what we should do after landing or if some emergency should arise, I and the men of the 1st and 2nd Platoons quietly boarded the two boats, which pulled out from the shore.

'It was a windy night. Over the 300-metre-wide river, the boats were tossed by the waves on the quick-moving waters. Some of the men gave a hand to the boatmen at the oars. The rest crowded together clasping their rifles to prevent them from being wet by the spray.

'Nearer and nearer we drew to the shore. The outline of the

town was now visible and the lights became brighter. Shadows could be seen moving about and shouts were audible. A fierce battle was impending. My heart tightened. Grabbing my Mauser I looked intently at the approaching town.

'As the boat drew up along the bank, I pushed lightly the two sitting next to me who quickly jumped ashore and mounted the stone steps holding their rifles.

' "Hey! You, why have you come back so late?" said a cracked voice in a Yunnan accent.

'The two made no immediate response. Then we heard one say quietly: "Don't move!"

'As soon as I heard that, I led the others up the steps, and before they knew a thing, the two enemy sentries were captives.

'The depositions of the captives were more or less like the boatmen's. I ordered the 1st Platoon to go up the street and attack the Kuomintang regular troops and the 2nd Platoon to attack the police. I stayed on the jetty. They were to report back to me.

'The boats were sent for reinforcements.

'According to plan, I made the messenger gather some rushes and burn them by the riverside as a signal that our company had succeeded in crossing.

'The fire lit up quickly, lending a glow to the shimmering waters. Now that the signal was given, it all depended on the smooth progress of the action of the platoons. While I was thus thinking, a few shots rang out on the street, then a few more, then silence. What did it mean? I was getting fidgety when the messengers of the 1st and 2nd Platoons came running back.

'The situation, it appeared, had developed thus: When the 1st Platoon reached enemy company headquarters, the sentry shouted "Who goes there!" "Your own people, the police," answered the captives, as directed. Before the sentry could throw out more questions, the advance squad rushed up and grabbed him. After a brief interrogation, the platoon entered the courtyard and ran towards separate rooms. Kicking open doors, they shouted, "Hand over your weapons and you live!"

'The enemy soldiers looked up, stupefied. Then, slowly, they raised their hands and said in puzzled tones: "We just arrived today. Maybe there is a misunderstanding!"

' "Rest assured," said our men. "There isn't any misunderstanding. We are the Red Army; we have come for you all right!"

'The enemy soldiers looked at one another with bewilderment and walked amid the menacing bayonets to the courtyard to assemble. Only the enemy company commander and some officers who were in a separate small room escaped after firing a few shots. It being dark and the road unfamiliar to us, we did not pursue them.

'The 2nd Platoon had the same experience as the 1st. They disguised themselves as tax-payers and entered the taxation offices. The policemen were caught like fish in a net; not even the captain escaped.

'All was now plain sailing. Excitedly, I put my Mauser back into its holster and ordered the messenger to light a bonfire on the shore as a second signal.

'The jetty having been captured, I walked leisurely towards the town. As I put my feet down the slab-paved street and saw the black mass of houses, a sense of exhaustion came over me and I would fain at that moment have found a place to eat and sleep my fill. I was on the point of consulting with the political instructor when the deputy battalion commander came along.

' "In order to consolidate the defence of the ferry and extend our control," he said, "the regimental commander orders you to advance with your men fifty *li* along the mountain path leading to Huili to keep a look-out."

'The troops quickly assembled on the street. Everyone insisted that he could stay the distance. Yet I knew that they were really hungry and that there was not an ounce of strength left in them. And no wonder! For they had marched more than 200 *li* without a real rest, with nothing but a few mouthfuls of cold rice and gruel to sustain them. But there was no time to cook a meal, and it was unlikely that there would be an eating house around. We walked on. Then I noticed a signboard hanging in front of a shop. I went closer to scrutinize it. It proved to be a pastry shop. "All right," I thought, "pastry would be better than nothing."

'We pushed open the door and entered. It was pitch-dark. We shouted for the shop-owner. There was no answer; probably he had fled when he heard the shots. A lamp was lit. We found a lot of pastry set on the racks. The men licked their chops, picking [the pastry] up again and again to smell.

' "There's no alternative," I thought, "we will have to make the deal ourselves."

'We collected all the pastry – thirty catties all told, and distributed them among the men, averaging about three ounces each. Some popped them into their mouths and ate them up in a twinkling.

' "Aiya! far too little. I don't even know how it tasted!" they complained, wiping their mouths.

' "Don't grumble. If we had not been the vanguard company, could you ever have eaten even this much?" someone remonstrated.

'After the "meal", the quartermaster wrote a slip and left a packet of a dozen or so silver dollars on the counter. Then we blew out the lamp, shut the door and continued our march.

'Coming out of the town, we walked about seventeen li along a stony path which led towards a gully on the left. Here we reached a comparatively flat spot and decided to make camp. The men gathered firewood and fetched water. After the jobs of cooking the rice and boiling the water were assigned, they all went to sleep, sprawling on the ground with rifles clasped in their arms.

'Some time passed when I was jerked to consciousness. I opened my eyes to find the deputy battalion commander standing before me.

' "Get up quickly, Company Commander Hsiao! Continue to advance!" he said in urgent tones.

'I sat up in surprise. "Is anything the matter?" I asked.

'The deputy battalion commander pointed at the shadow of a tall mountain in the distance. "Proceed along this road for forty li and you will reach the top of the mountain," he said. "If the enemy occupies it, from such a vantage position they would seriously threaten us. The order of the regimental commander is that we must occupy it before dawn so as to push further ahead and consolidate the defence of the ferry."

' "Our regiment and the Party and government leaders should have crossed in a day's time. Why should we prolong the defence of the ferry?" I asked doubtfully.

'The deputy battalion commander gave a smile. "It sounds

quite simple to you," said he, "but the main force is coming along this route."

' "What! Are the I and III Corps all coming this way?" I asked.

' "That's so!" the deputy battalion commander nodded.

'Now everything was clear. The hasty meeting of the leaders before the march, the worries of Vice-Chairman Chou En-lai and his inquiry about our company – all these were not only for the central contingent, but the movement of the whole force. Now luckily the ferry was under our control. I seemed to see in my mind's eye our fraternal troops crossing the river in an unending stream. "This route has been opened by the Cadres Regiment," they would be saying to one another. Thus thinking, I was excited. Then I felt the heavy responsibility of the vanguard company. I got together the platoon leaders at once, bade them eat quickly and make ready to start.

'Wakened from their dreams and hearing that they were to set out at once, the men grumbled: "We have taken control of the ferry and crossed the river. What is the hurry now!" "It is so dark! You can't see the path ahead. It would be much better to set out after it is light." "Why hurry! There is no enemy, no fighting."

'However, when the political instructor made them see the significance of occupying the mountain top and consolidating the defence of the ferry and gave them to understand that they were the forward unit of the whole army, their attitude changed at once.

' "Come on, we will do the forty *li* and make camp on the mountain top!" shouted a throaty voice.

'This started off the entire group.

' "Occupy the mountain top, cover the crossing of the army!"

' "Fight our way to the mountain top, welcome our elder brothers!"

'Then they went to hurry the cooks to prepare the meal so that they could eat and go. Nobody wanted to stay any longer.

'As day dawned, the company reached the summit of the mountain in time, though everybody was dead tired. The top of the mountain was a piece of relatively level ground. In the distance stretched unendingly a chain of small hills, and towards this mass of hills extended the meandering path that led towards Huili. We decided to occupy two hills flanking the path some distance away as our position. These two hills commanded the path leading from Huili towards the ferry.

'As we were advancing towards the hills, the vanguard squad gave the alarm. Twenty minutes after a skirmish, the enemy came in swarms.

'It was indeed a timely lesson. Had we camped in the gully last night, we would have had to pay a heavy price in an upward assault.

'The enemy, not knowing the situation, dared not attack. We too kept quiet. So we stood facing each other. By four p.m. the heavy machine-gun company of the Special Course Battalion and the 4th Company came up. Walking in front were Regimental Commander Chen and Political Commissar Sung. They looked very happy. "You are very competent indeed!" were the first words they addressed us. While I reported on the position of the enemy, I observed with the commanders their position.

'Shortly afterwards, the regimental commander called a meeting of the officers of our company, the 4th Company and the heavy machine-gun company to assign their tasks. Our company was to attack the enemy to the right of the road from the top of the hill on the right; the 4th Company was to attack the enemy to the left of the road from the hill-top on the left; while the heavy machine-gun company would cover our men from the two hill-tops. After the enemy was defeated, pursuit should be given and should be kept up till further orders were given.

'Under the unified command of the regimental commander, the heavy machine-guns spoke up and the bugle sounded. I led the charge. The enemy collapsed. Terrified, they ran helter-skelter, scattering throughout the mountains and fields. We pursued them for twenty *li*. Some were killed in action, some pretended dead on the ground, and some fell off from the steep slopes to their death. As we were chasing the enemy to the back of a village, a mounted messenger brought the order from the regimental commander: "Stop pursuing the enemy. Make camp on the spot and keep a look-out."

'I brought the troops to the slope at the back of the village to camp. We were now utterly exhausted. Some just dropped on the ground and did not stir, not even claiming food and water. Others, having sat, could not summon up enough energy to rise.

'Just before dusk, people suddenly began to shout and run towards the hillside. I looked and saw a large number of troops passing by the foot of the hill. The advance unit was nearing the village, while the rear stretched beyond vision. The men had heard the messenger say that this was the III Army Corps, so they forgot their fatigue and sleepiness and ran up and shouted greetings, little caring that their comrades could not hear them.' [1]

Mao's own bodyguard and batman, Chen Chang-feng, also records the crossing of the Chinsha:

'It was on one evening in April 1935, I remember,' he says, 'that we reached the Golden Sand River, we being the Ninth, First, Fifth and Third Red Army Groups, and the Cadres' Regiment – all belonging to the First Front Red Army. The Central Committee staff was also with us. The Golden Sand River was the first big river to face us after the crossing of the Wukiang. It was in spate, with angry dragon-headed waves confronting us. All the leaders were greatly concerned with the problem of crossing, as we had practically no craft at our command. Chairman Mao, of course, was in the thick of these discussions, which went on all night.

'I was his personal bodyguard. Just before dawn I crossed with him. We had hardly landed when he was off to General Liu Po-cheng [the Chief-of-Staff] to plan the next stage of the march. I set about looking for somewhere for him to use as a temporary office and home.

'It didn't look hopeful. The river bank was nothing but bare rocks, with a few holes in the cliffs, dripping with moisture, hardly big enough to be called caves. I sought in vain for planks or even straw to use for a bed. In the end I had to lay out a piece of oiled cloth and put the blanket on that, feeling that that would at least give him something to lie down on – he hadn't rested at all the whole night. Come to that, he had had no rest for the last few days.

'My next task was to lay out his documents – maps and papers.

Usually I did it with his secretary, Comrade Huang, whenever we made camp. We used to rig up some kind of a table or desk. But now there was nothing at all to use even as a makeshift, and Comrade Huang was still on the other side of the river. I couldn't think what to do. I tried pinning one map up on the side of the cave, but it was no good – it was just sand and wouldn't hold the nail, and there wasn't room to spread the documents out. Already I had wasted enough time; I was expecting Chairman Mao back from his conference any minute, and I hadn't even got a drop of boiled water ready. I knew he would need it, after all he had been through. I put aside the problem of the documents and hurried out to see what I could do about the water.

'It was broad daylight when Chairman Mao did come back and sent for me. When I reached the cave I saw that he was standing there, deep in thought.

' "You've come back," I said.

' "M'm . . . everything ready?"

' "I've done what I can," I said, pointing at the "bed". "There are no boards to be found, so I've made this up. Will you lie down for a bit? The water will be boiled any minute."

'I turned to go to see how the water was getting on, but he called me back.

' "Haven't you found me a place to work?" he asked.

' "Comrade Huang hasn't come over yet," I said without thinking. "I couldn't find anything to use as a desk. Why don't you have a bit of a rest and a drop of water first?"

'He took a step towards me, as though he had not heard what I told him, and said, very seriously, but not at all angrily, "The work's the all-important thing at a moment like this. Rest, or food, or drink are trifles. Twenty to thirty thousand of our comrades are still waiting to cross the river there. Thirty thousand lives in peril!"

'I didn't know what to say, but stood there looking at Chairman Mao. I could feel my heart pounding. He came right up to me and patted my shoulder. "Go on," he said, "find me a board or something to use as a desk before you do anything else."

'I pulled myself together and ran off, and by hunting high and low found a small board which must have been used as a door for a cave mouth. Chairman Mao helped set it up, wedging it underneath to make it flat and steady, and spreading out his maps and documents. Then I remembered the water; it must have boiled by now. I got up to go and fetch it, when Chairman Mao spoke to me again.

' "Chen Chang-feng !"

' "Yes?"

' "Come back !"

'I went back right into the cave, stepping carefully over our desk.

' "I'll have to give you some punishment, you know," he said. Although the tone of his voice was mild and there was a kind look in his eyes, I felt the air very tense. I realized how I had failed in my job, and stood looking at him, very miserable.

' "I want you to stay by me and keep awake."

'I felt an uneasy smile come over my face and sat down opposite him.

' "Right," I said.

'He had got telegrams and documents all over the desk. The field telephone which the signal corps had rigged up was going all the time, and he was absolutely immersed in work. He had not allowed a minute for himself. I found it hard to keep the tears back as I realized that I had wasted his time over the desk, and if I had understood my job, I would have had it ready before.

'I was awfully drowsy, and had a habit anyway of dropping off beside him when he was working. I knew what he meant when he said he would "punish" me by asking me to keep awake, although he only said it as a joke. But when I saw how he was working with all his heart and soul, without showing the least sign of wanting to sleep, and even looking at me from time to time with a cheerful smile, I felt terribly uneasy. I got up and went and fetched the water after a bit, and poured some out to cool.

'Time enough to eat two meals passed before Chairman Mao stopped and stood up to stretch himself.

' "You've been with me several years now," he said. "How is it that you still don't understand what comes first? The first thing you have to do is to find somewhere where the work can be done. Food and rest are quite secondary to that. You must realize that

the work is the most important thing under all circumstances."
He stopped a minute and then rubbed his hand over my head.
"You'll have to get a bit of sleep," he said. "You can hardly
keep your eyes open." ' [2]

Another account of the crossing explains that there was only
one boat at the ferry site, and that two more were captured at the
next crossing twenty miles away. 'With the three boats all the
men and horses crossed the river after nine days and nights of
ferrying. When the enemy discovered what had happened they
rushed troops to the river – but the Red Army had already burned
the boats and were marching north.' [3] According to Hsu Meng-
chiu an enemy messenger carrying the order to burn all the boats
was captured and led the Communists to the single boat left at the
ferry, while four other boats were later discovered.[4] Chu Teh told
Agnes Smedley that Liu Po-cheng's vanguards reached Chou Ping
Fort on 4 May, 'disarmed the astounded Szechuan garrison, seized
nine large boats, arms, ammunition, food stores, and the complete
war plans and orders of Chiang Kai-shek'. Li Chang-chuan asserts
that six small boats, all sabotaged, were captured for the crossing.[5]
Snow's account has 'six big boats' working round-the-clock for
nine days to ferry the Red Army without the loss of a single life :

'When Chiang's forces reached the river, two days later, the
rearguard of their enemy called cheerily to them from the north
bank to come on over, the swimming was fine. The government
troops were obliged to make a detour of over 200 li to the nearest
crossing, and the Reds thus shook them from their trail. Infuriated,
the Generalissimo now flew to Szechuan, where he mobilized new
forces in the path of the oncoming horde, hoping to cut them off
at one more strategic river – the great Tatu.' [6]

Lo Ping-hui's rearguard was cut off, however, and crossed
downstream via Tungchuan (or Hweitse) by the stratagem of
capturing the local magistrate's seal and forging an instruction for
the boatmen to assemble a hundred boats for the Communists,
disguised in enemy uniforms.[7]

Looking back on this dramatic escape from yet another Kuomintang trap, one is forced to wonder how a crossing which took so
many days could have been allowed to succeed bloodlessly by the
Kuomintang air force. Jerome Ch'ên, who puts the crossing at

1–9 May, remarks that 'these eight days and eight nights without serious harassment from Lung Yun's troops suggest that Lung [the Yunnan warlord] adopted an equivocal attitude to the Communists and may also explain his position after 1949'.[8] Lung later revolted against Chiang Kai-shek and became Vice-Chairman of the National Defence Council and Vice-Chairman of the Southwest Administrative Committee of the Chinese People's Republic. The Chinsha River crossing may be yet another case where Red survival was owed to a combination of Communist daring and ruggedness on the one hand – and equivocation on the part of the Kuomintang's so-called allies on the other.

But Mao could not yet congratulate himself. A glance at the map will show how sanguine was the idea of the Red Army's challenging the Kuomintang from the mountain fortresses of this part of Szechuan, boxed in by three great rivers – the Chinsha (or Yangtze), the Min and the Tatu. It seemed inconceivable that Chiang could fail to hold this line of defence so generously endowed by nature. The Szechuan trap looked even deadlier than the Yunnan or the Kweichow traps. Could the Communists prove themselves as skilful strategists against nature as they were against the Kuomintang?

Chapter 14

The Land of the Lolos

BEFORE the Communists, now numbering some 60–70,000, could even try to escape from the trap of the Tatu–Min–Yangtze–Chinsha river system they had to vanquish an entirely new kind of enemy. The mountains of Sikang, which they now had to traverse – along the road once used by the army of Kublai Khan – in the early part of May 1935, were inhabited by non-Han, that is to say non-Chinese, tribes of more or less primitive behaviour. Some of them were hostile to all Hans, or Chinese, and all of them were suspicious of outsiders. Few Chinese armies had ever passed through without heavy losses.

The terrain itself was enough of a hazard. The terrible Fire Mountain, where no tree or shrub or plant or blade of grass grew and no drop of water could be found, had to be climbed. Tung Pi-wu, the Party elder with the long drooping moustache, consoled the young teenagers in the column – the 'little devils' – by telling them the ancient legend of Monkey, who had to cross this same Fire Mountain on his way to India to search for Buddhist manuscripts. The mountain was so fiery that all the hair on the Monkey's bottom was burnt off – which is the reason why monkeys have bare bottoms to this day.

'If that is true,' one Red Army little devil retorted, 'why is not your long moustache burnt off?'

But 'Old Tung' tried to encourage them with the moral that if Monkey could survive the Fire Mountain, so could they.[1]

Water was eventually found in the scattered mountain villages, with terraced fields of rice and sugar-cane, near the rivers which the Red Army now followed north towards the Tatu, after a brief Politburo meeting at Hweili. Their rout was by Tehchang and Sichang, on the Anning River, to Mienning and Yuehsi. At

Hweili a skit was staged by the Mengchin Drama Troupe of the Fifth Army called *One Worn-Out Sandal of Straw*. Its author, Huang Chen, poked fun at the Kuomintang forces whose chase of the Communists to the Chinsha banks had yielded only one piece of booty – a discarded Red Army sandal.[2]

But this was the land of the dreaded Lolos, one of the Yi tribes. As one chronicler puts it, 'the land of the Lolos is 110 *li* [say thirty-five miles] from south to north, but no one knows how long it is from west to east because no one has ever traversed it that way'.[3]

There were two kinds of Lolo, according to contemporary Chinese accounts – the 'Black Bones' and the 'White Bones'. The Whites were the slaves of the Blacks, and the Blacks were the nobility. The Whites included some descendants of Han, or Chinese, people. While the Whites could manufacture certain articles and carry on trade, they were always under the total control of the Blacks and were never allowed to marry with their Black masters. The Lolos, though a 'barbarian' race in the Chinese book, were thus clever enough to exploit aliens. They were also brave warriors, as their tenacity in this part of Sikang in spite of repeated Han invasions proved. They were the equivalent of the American Indians in the sagas of the European colonization of the American West.

The Lolos raised grain, but not enough for the whole year round, so that they had to come down into the valleys to rob the Han people whenever they ran out of food. Their armoury included a number of Mausers and rifles as well as knives, spears and axes, and their men were skilled and accurate in their use. Sometimes tribesmen would line the path to watch the Red Army passing by: most of them were barefoot, some had hemp shoes, and they all wore a bewildering assortment of clothes stolen from the Hans.

The Communists took an enlightened attitude towards the minority nationalities which inhabited various parts of China, regarding them, in theory at least, as the equals of the Chinese and as people who had suffered exceptionally from class exploitation. They had already gone through the tribal areas of the Miao and Shan peoples, earlier on the Long March, in Kweichow and

Yunnan, and they had made friends with them, gaining recruits for their ranks. When they came to Mienning, a town of Han people, they found a prison full of manacled Lolo prisoners, and, following their usual practice, they set them free. The townspeople took strong exception to their release, and made repeated objections. The Government officials and gentry of the town had fled before the Red Army and came into Lolo territory where they were ill-treated and robbed. The district chief was killed by the tribesmen and the wife of a section head was stripped naked and sent back to the town.

The Communists then had to climb into the Hsiaohsiang mountains across the territory of the Lolos, who tried to prevent their passage by force. This was where the Taiping rebels of seventy years before had sought to chart a path on the eve of their extermination. Hsu Meng-chiu explains that at Tachou on the border between the Chinese and the Lolo districts, 'the people of the town had run away, and the Lolos had heard the news and were planning to come down to capture them and take all their goods. The people begged the Red Army to defend them against the Lolos. We had no alternative, and we defeated the Lolos.' [4]

But the Reds managed to come to terms with the Lolos. As Hsiao Hua recalled :

'Shortly after we entered the Yi area, we saw thousands of people on the mountain slopes. They were brandishing home-made shotguns, spears and clubs, shouting and running about in the forests, apparently attempting to stop the Red Army. We were compelled to close our ranks and continue our march very cautiously in order to be prepared against a surprise attack.

'When we reached Kumatzu, a place about thirty li inside the Yi area, our way was blocked by a big crowd of people and we were forced to stop. They were shouting words which we could not understand, but their gestures and the excited expressions indicated that if we tried to force our way forward an armed clash was inevitable. At that moment, startling news came from the rear adding tension to the situation. The Engineers' Company marching at the rear of the main force, and lagging about a hundred metres behind, had been attacked by the Yis. Our men were unarmed and all their bridge-building and other equipment had been stolen. The Yis even stripped them of their clothes, but had refrained from hurting them. Eventually the engineers were compelled to withdraw from the Yi area and retreat to their starting point.

'As soon as our advance party stopped, the Yi people began to close in from all directions. We asked the interpreter to explain to them that the Red Army was totally different from the Kuomintang Army, and that its sole purpose was to pass through the Yi area on a northward march. It would neither rob nor kill the Yis, and would not stay even one night in their area. In spite of all these explanations, the Yis waved their hands and weapons and continued to protest, "No passing!" and "Pay us if you want to pass!" We decided to offer them 500 silver dollars so that we might pass peacefully. When they saw the money, all rushed forward to grab it. After we had distributed several thousand dollars they still clamoured for more.

'In the midst of this confusion, we saw a cloud of dust rising before us, at the mouth of the narrow valley. A black mule headed a party of mules and horses galloping towards us. It was mounted by a tall Yi of over fifty years of age. He was lightly tanned and had a linen cape thrown over his back. The noisy crowd calmed down a little as he drew nearer. I was told that the man was the fourth uncle of Hsiao Yeh Tan, chief of the local Yi tribe.

'With this headman before me, I thought, the time has come to discuss the problem and find a proper solution. I told the interpreter to tell him that the commander of the Red Army wished to speak to him. The elderly Yi, uncle of chief Hsiao Yeh Tan, gladly agreed to talk. He jumped off his mule and signalled the crowd to disperse.

'I explained that the Red Army fought for the oppressed, and that our purpose in entering the Yi area was to go north on the Long March and not to harass the local people. Knowing that the Yis had a high regard for brotherhood, I told him that Commander Liu Po-cheng, who was personally leading a big army in a northern expedition, was passing through, and would like to become a sworn brother of the chief of the Yis.

'Listening to my explanation of our reasons for entering the Yi area, Hsiao Yeh Tan's uncle looked rather doubtful. However, his doubts were dispelled as he looked around at the well-disciplined Red Army men and saw no sign of the looting and killing as practised by the Kuomintang "government troops". Reassured, he was all smiles at the thought that the commander of a big army desired to enter into an alliance with the Yi chief, and gave his consent. Both parties believed they would benefit by the alliance. Along the route of the Red Army's advance, at that time, there were two Yi tribes, the Kuchi and the Lohung, who were constantly at war with each other. The chief of the Kuchi tribe, Hsiao Yeh Tan, hoped by alliance with the Red Army to secure help to defeat the Lohung tribe. We, however, aimed only to smooth out the difficulties in the way of our advance. As a token of sincerity, we presented him with a pistol and several rifles, and in return, he gave us his mount, the black mule.

'Thus the negotiations came to a successful finish. When I went to see Commanders Liu Po-cheng and Nieh Jung-chen, I found them worrying about the possibility of conflicts between the Red Army and the Yis. If the advance party failed to reach an agreement with the Yis, it would be impossible for the main force of the Red Army to pass through peacefully. Everyone was endeavouring to devise a plan for this peaceful passage. They were overjoyed when I reported our successful negotiations. Commander Liu Po-cheng immediately mounted his horse and came out to meet Hsiao Yeh Tan. For the sake of uniting with the brother Yi people and of enabling the main force of the Red Army to pass peacefully, he was ready to play the leading role in concluding the alliance.

'As Commander Liu Po-cheng came to the head of the Red Army column on horseback, Hsiao Yeh Tan and other Yi chiefs hurriedly stepped forward to greet him. When I introduced Commander Liu to them, Hsiao Yeh Tan fell to his knees in salutation. Commander Liu alighted from his horse, and amiably helped Hsiao Yeh Tan to his feet again. Then he proceeded to reiterate the Red Army's purpose in entering the Yi area and his willingness to become Hsiao Yeh Tan's sworn brother. . . .

'Preparations for the ceremony of concluding the alliance were very simple. Two bowls of clear water and a huge, majestic-looking cock were secured. The beak of the cock was broken and the fresh blood therefrom sprinkled into the bowls, reddening the water.

'The ceremony was to be held beside a lake in the small mountain valley. The lake water, clear as a mirror, reflected the nearby thick forests. A spring breeze rippled the water, which, beating gently against the rocks on the shore, seemed like the rhythm of a song of praise for the forthcoming memorable event.

'When everything was ready, Commander Liu, Hsiao Yeh Tan and his uncle came to the shore of the lake. The three men knelt side by side on the ground before the bowls of water and chicken blood. . . .

'Commander Liu held high one of the bowls while calling out his oath, "To Heaven above and Earth below . . . I, Liu Po-cheng, swear that I am willing to become a sworn brother of Hsiao Yeh Tan. . . ." As soon as he finished speaking he drank the blood-stained water at one gulp. Hsiao Yeh Tan and his uncle took the other bowl and drained it in a like manner. The ceremony ended. . . .[5]

'As it was already late it was impossible for the Red Army to march through the Yi area before nightfall. The command of the advance party decided to withdraw thirty li from the Yi area and put up for the night at Tachiao in the Han people's area. Hsiao Yeh Tan and his uncle were warmly welcomed to the camping centre of the Red Army as honoured guests. Knowing that the Yis were great drinkers, we bought up all the wine in the nearby village, but even after draining the wine jars, the guests were only slightly drunk.'[6]

According to another account Liu Po-cheng undertook the ceremony of the 'three kneelings and nine prostrations' before gaining an audience with the Lolo Empress, to whom he gave 200 rifles and a thousand silver dollars in return for permission to pass through Lololand. The Red Army was then allowed to pass, but at each step they were expected to buy their needs from the 'barbarians' in cash, not paper money. Hsu Meng-chiu told Nym Wales afterwards: 'These Lolos were first-class confiscators, and we were not too much amused to find someone who could do this much better than ourselves. The whole body of troops was mobilized to hand over gifts to the Lolos to buy our way through, but the tribesmen were never satisfied and took more and more. They looked in the pockets of our soldiers and even pulled off their clothing very rudely. In fact they took away everything portable that the Red Army had to spare. But we had no way to save our lives but to grin and forbear. At all costs, we wanted to be friendly with them, and we had to be extremely careful. They had many taboos, and we had to learn what these were and observe them. We never entered their houses. One of their taboos was that nobody should ever move the iron vessels in which they cook.' [7]

Edgar Snow was told a little more of the arguments which Liu used in his confrontation with Hsiao Yao-da (or Hsiao Yehtan): 'The Lolos, he said, opposed warlords Liu Hsiang and Liu Wen-hui and the Kuomintang; so did the Reds. The Lolos wanted to preserve their independence; Red policies favoured autonomy for all the national minorities of China. The Lolos hated the Chinese because they had been oppressed by them; but there were "White" Chinese and "Red" Chinese, just as there were "White" Lolos and "Black" Lolos, and it was the White Chinese who had always slain and oppressed the Lolos. Should not the Red Chinese and the Black Lolos unite against their common enemies, the White Chinese? The Lolos listened interestedly. Shyly they asked for arms and bullets to guard their independence and help Red Chinese fight the Whites. To their astonishment, the Reds gave them both.

'And so it happened that not only a speedy but a politically useful passage was accomplished. Hundreds of Lolos enlisted with the "Red" Chinese to march to the Tatu River to fight the common enemy. Some of those Lolos were to trek clear to the north-west. Liu Po-cheng drank the blood of a newly killed chicken before the high chieftain of the Lolos, who drank also, and they swore blood brotherhood in the tribal manner. By this vow the Reds declared that whosoever should violate the terms of their alliance would be even as weak and cowardly as the fowl.' [8]

One of the three Lolos, or Yis, recruited to the Red Army (he later became a Colonel) subsequently told his own story of the Communists' arrival in Yuehsi, one of the last towns before the Tatu River, and of some of the incidents that followed:

'In March 1934, we Yis and the poor Han people in Yuehsi

County, unable to stand the cruel rule and exploitation of the reactionary Kuomintang government, rose simultaneously in the three districts of Haitang, Wangchiatang and Paoan, 4,000-strong, we wiped out the three companies of the Kuomintang Twenty-fourth Army and surrounded the county town for three days. Soon after we had broken into the town, the enemy sent up reinforcements from Hsichang. We suffered a setback and had to retreat. We took cover in the forest on a mountain in the eastern part of the country. By April 1935, it was rumoured that the Red Army was coming.

'One report said the Kuomintang troops were scattering, and that the big landlords and wealthy people in the town were also departing in great haste. Some said the Red Army would have it out with the Kuomintang and the landlords and do good things for the poor; but others depicted the Red Army as man-killers and ravishers. Were they actually troops who fought the Kuomintang on behalf of the poor? Or did they behave like the Kuomintang troops? W had no way of knowing. Finally we decided to send three men to investigate.

'Their reports confirmed the withdrawal of the Kuomintang troops, the moving of the rich families and the expected arrival of the Red Army. Local Kuomintang officials were endeavouring to coerce the people into moving, saying that the Red Army and Communists would "communize everything, properties, wives, and all", and forbidding them to ask questions about the Red Army. Not knowing the actual conditions, some people had moved away.

'After all, what actually did we know of the Red Army? All had their guesses. One thing we did know, and that was that the Red Army fought the Kuomintang. If not, why should those brutes and murderers fly in such a hurry? And this being the case, wouldn't it be all right for us to help the Red Army fight the Kuomintang? Reasoning thus, we left the mountain and returned to the country town.

'Yueshi was a scene of misery. Those who had opposed the Kuomintang and landlords had their houses destroyed. The troops had plundered the residents before they fled. Many a house was a mere wreck, with doors ajar. The lonely streets were strewn with fragments of tiles, planks, straw and rags. Afraid of anticipated calamity, people bolted their doors and shut their windows.

'One morning, still searching for information, we were asking in a shop about the Red Army when from the distance came the beating of hoofs. Peeping out, we saw five horses coming, on each a martial-looking young man in a black tunic, an eight-cornered, visored cap studded with a red star on his head, a pair of straw sandals on his feet, a rifle slung across his shoulder and a cartridge belt around his waist.

'As soon as they saw us, they alighted.

' "Friends," they said, all smiles, walking towards us, "whatever you've been told, you need not be frightened of us."

'We were unsure, but, seeing they were very friendly, we went over to meet them.

' "Don't be afraid, fellow-countrymen. We are the Red Army, who work for the good of the minority people and destroy the Kuomintang reactionary troops."

' "The Red Army!" we said with surprise, and at once surrounded the five gentle-looking Red Army men. Hand grasping hand, we scrutinized each other, they looking at our top-knots and cloaks and we at their red stars.

' "We got wind that our fellow-countrymen, especially our Yi brothers here (the first time we heard such endearing salutation), were heavily oppressed by the Kuomintang reactionaries. We are sure you've been frightened by the rumours the enemy spread before they fled. We hope you'll pursue your normal trade. We'll put up here for a few days and we guarantee you won't suffer any loss."

'Smilingly, they shook hands with us and, escorted by a crowd which had gathered at the news, went on to visit families in the town.

'Gradually shops on the streets were opened. The news of the arrival of the Red Army men passed from mouth to mouth.

'In the afternoon, the Red Army, striking up a military tune with great vigour, entered the town, amid the clapping and curious glances of the residents. Some Red fighters wore civilian dress, but they all looked fresh and vigorous, smiling and waving to the people as they walked along. They didn't enter the empty civilian houses but went on till they reached the entrance of the drum tower where they sat down to rest. The people immediately gathered around them. Some fighters began to talk with us; others picked up the children and fondled them. As more and more people came up, forming rank upon rank around the soldiers, a fighter with a Mauser hanging on his hip mounted the platform and addressed the gathering.

' "Fellow-countrymen! We are the Chinese Workers' and Peasants' Red Army led by the Chinese Communist Party. We were like you once, poor people who suffered from the oppression of the reactionary officials, landlords and capitalists. When we could endure no longer such sufferings, we joined the Red Army. Unless we overthrow the Kuomintang reactionaries and liberate the whole of China, nobody will live in peace and happiness. Now the Japanese imperialists are invading our country and the Chiang Kai-shek government will not resist them. To save the nation, we are going north to fight the Japanese. We welcome our brothers from all nationalities who are devoted to the motherland to join the Red Army."

'The crowd stirred. The terms: "Join the army!" "Fight the reactionaries!" and "Fight the Japanese imperialists!" were new to them.

'I felt moved and excited. They had really come to fight the Kuomintang. I was for putting down my name, but on second thoughts, I decided to wait a little longer before making up my mind.

' "Look! the Red Army is opening the prison. Hurry!"

'People began to run towards the county government headquarters, shouting. When I came up, the building was already crowded to overflowing. On the hall and in the courtyard before the prison burned fires on which the fighters, their faces flushed from the blaze, were throwing bundles of reactionary documents. Looking at them, we were very happy. All the time there were shouts of "Long Live the Red Army!"

'Hoisting a tremendous log, a team of stalwart Red Army men stamped towards the tall, sombre iron gate of the prison in front of which they stopped and poised at the ready. Then one of them shouted: "Ready – Go!"

' "Bang!" The log crashed against the gate, which shattered and fell to the ground with a creaking sound.

' "Long live the Red Army! Long live the Red Army!"

'Tense with excitement, I wedged my way through the crowd towards the prison. It was frightfully dark inside. From the gloom came a revolting, stomach-turning smell. The Red fighters, with torches and hammers, went in imperturbably, calling out as they entered: "Fellow-countrymen, how you have suffered! We are the Red Army, we've come to save you.'

'I followed them in. What a heart-rending sight it was! Thin as withered vines, with long dishevelled hair, they lay, stark naked or at best with a piece of rag around their loins, on a mixture of mud, excrement and foul water. They were chained together, handcuffed and fettered. Some were dead. The Red fighters carefully knocked off their chains and carried them out into the fresh air. I and many others helped. Altogether we brought out about two hundred. They were heads of the various tribes of Yuehsi and of Puhsiungngole, Ahou and Kuochi. They had been in prison for as much as a dozen years. Countless numbers had been tortured to death in various ways. And all because of what? Because they did not carry out the Kuomintang policy of "pitting the Yis against the Yis"; because they did not have the heart to kill their brothers from other tribes; because they did not provide young girls for the Kuomintang officials according to the "regulations"; or because they could not afford the endless exorbitant taxes. As a warning to others, the Kuomintang had set up the so-called "shift" system. If the head of a certain tribe was "guilty" of one of the above-mentioned "offences", he would start a long term of imprisonment, in which every successive head of the tribe and his own sons and grandsons would, in turn, be committed. Actually, it was death either way – at the prison or, later, at home from the after-effect of the torture and imprisonment. In this way, certain tribal groups had already become extinct.

'The pitiable sight of those who survived and the dreadful sight of those who had died evoked outbursts of wailing and suppressed sobbing from their family members who were present, then from sympathizers around. I, too, could not suppress my tears. The living and their families gave their thanks to the Red Army; the families of the dead, crying, supplicated them to avenge their loved ones. The Red fighters, with tears in their eyes, soothed them. "Fellow-countrymen, we shall remember your trust and wipe out the Kuomintang to avenge all who have suffered at their blood-stained hands."

'I felt a wave of bitter indignation and cried impulsively: "I'll join you to fight the Kuomintang!"

'The sombre atmosphere was broken by my sudden cry. For a moment everybody looked at me with a blank expression. Then many of them followed my example: "I, too, will join to fight the Kuomintang!" was the cry.

'The Red fighters clapped to welcome us and said that we could register later.

'There came many soldiers carrying medicine cases, food, garments and bolts of cloth, and baskets filled with silver dollars, ingots and coppers. Full of gratitude the crowd watched while the Red Army men helped the victims to put on the clothes, and gave them food. Those who were ill were given medicine and a bolt of cloth and a dozen silver ingots each.

' "Dear fellow-countrymen!" It was the one with the Mauser again. He had a broad face and dark, bushy eyebrows. He was very amiable. The moment I saw him I liked him from the bottom of my heart.

' "All these goods were squeezed by the reactionary Kuomintang officials and landlords from the labouring people; we now distribute them to you to help you to live and develop production. Tomorrow we will open the granary. We hope you will come with bags, and tell those who haven't come today, to come also. It's time all should enjoy themselves."

'An outburst of passionate shouts succeeded his speech. "Thanks for the Red Army!" "Long live the Red Army!"

'Subsequently, I discovered that the speaker was Political Instructor Liu Chih-chun. He led us to company headquarters, which was housed in a wealthy man's courtyard. The political instructor summoned a medium-sized, small-eyed man.

' "These three comrades will be in your squad," he said, referring to us. "Take good care of them, they are Yi comrades." To us he said, "Don't be afraid. It'll be like in your own home." And pointing at the small-eyed man, he said, "This is Comrade Ho Hsiang-jung, your squad leader." Then he walked away with the other new comrades.

' "Comrades, come to welcome the new comrades!" At the announcement of the squad leader, seven or eight young fellows rushed from the courtyard. There was a bustle of water-fetching, tea-pouring and hand-grasping. A comrade entered with a bundle and gave us each a robe (which we cut short for the convenience of marching and fighting) and a pair of straw sandals. "Now I'm a Red fighter, I'll give it hard to the Kuomintang bandits!" I thought.

'Three days later, the troops set out. All the people were present to see us off, their cloaks fluttering all over the fields and hills. They brought pigs' heads, whole sheep, beef and wine and pressed us to accept. The troops declined repeatedly. Didn't our wounded and sick comrades lack meat? I thought. We should accept when these were proffered with genuine sincerity. More people came with presents, particularly old men and women who were in tears. "The Red Army's done so many good things for us during their few days here," they said. "And now they won't drink even a mouthful of wine. That will never do."

'The leadership told them we had to fight battles on our way, and if we had too many things it would inconvenience our movement.

'Actually we were only lightly equipped. I couldn't see why we should hold aloof at the expense of our bellies. However, the people wouldn't let us go. At last we were obliged to sip a mouthful of the wine held up by our well-wishers lining both sides of the road.

'Now a crowd of people, carrying swords, spears and sticks, came and demanded to join us. It took a lot of persuading to settle the matter. As a result our ranks were swelled by four hundred vigorous youngsters. The long line of troops seemed to fade into infinity at the rear.

'Two days later, while approaching Haitang, we were informed that the people there had intercepted and surrounded the fleeing Kuomintang county head and a few leaders of the Kuomintang party branch at Yuehsi, together with two companies of the

Security Forces, and were waiting for us to put an end to them. I remembered I had been given no rifle and reminded the squad leader of this. He said the leadership were afraid that the new comrades might be inconvenienced in the march by the weapons and had decided to let them do without them for the first few days. Upon my repeated pleading, however, I was issued an old piece made in Hanyang Arsenal, together with three cartridges, one of which was dead.

'We were nearing Haitang. The thought of the coming encounter with the enemy excited me, when the squad leader summoned us. He said that since we were new we should first watch how the old comrades fought. I was angry and said: "I've come to fight the Kuomintang, not to watch the fighting!"

'The squad leader tried to persuade me, but I stuck to my point. Finally he said, "Comrade Aerhmuhsia, you are now in the army, not a citizen. You should obey orders." I thought, "That's true, I'm a Red fighter now," and dropped back to the rear, but I must say that I obeyed with no degree of pleasure.

'When we reached Haitang, we saw everywhere our Yi brothers, armed with various sort of weapons, who waved their cloaks to welcome us. The firing was fast and furious. The enemy, under the protection of the earthen walls and fortifications, was putting up a stubborn stand. Just in time I noticed an enemy soldier aiming at our squad leader who was shoving another bullet into the chamber of his rifle. I raised my gun and fired. The enemy dropped dead behind the wall. Startled by the report behind him, the squad leader looked back at me and immediately understood. Without saying a word, he charged forward with others. The county head and four Kuomintang county party leaders were captured. The two companies of the Kuomintang Security Force had fled but were driven back by the Yi people and annihilated.

'The Haitang residents had been forced to leave their homes, which were left open, broken furniture and articles being scattered all over the place. As I kicked at a pile of junk in front of a house, a small, elegant wine-cup rolled out. I put it in my pouch for drinking wine later. As I was walking along, I met the squad leader who was looking for me. As we walked past a wine shop, we saw that some of the jars were broken, wine running all over the place, while the lids of some were missing. The aroma was most tantalizing. Picking up a broken bowl on the counter I dipped and was about to drink when the squad leader checked me. "Comrade Aerhmuhsia," he said, "you are a Red fighter, you must not drink wine which belongs to someone else." I had to give up but I couldn't see why. The squad leader was very stubborn, I thought. The wine was wasted, anyway, and what was the harm if I had a swig?

'The squad leader had a meeting. The leader was telling us what to observe in tomorrow's marching and fighting. He laid special stress on the correct observance of the Party's nationality policy and mass discipline.

' "I must criticize myself," he said, looking contrite. "I've been paying too much attention to fighting these days. I've forgotten to take care of the new comrades, to help and educate them. Today, Comrade Aerhmuhsia ..."

'I lowered my head shamefacedly. Comrades all looked at me.

' "Comrades, don't blame him. It was I and the old comrades who were to blame. We did not give him sufficient help. He didn't know the 'three disciplines and eight points for attention' and the Party's nationality policy."

'The old fighters lowered their heads. Still I didn't see anything amiss. As I moved abruptly the wine-cup rolled out from my pouch.

'All gazed at it. "Where did that cup come from?" everybody seemed to ask.

'Why raise a storm in a teapot, I thought.

' "I just picked it up in a rubbish heap, and if I hadn't done so it would certainly have been trodden on and broken." I spoke what was in my mind.

' "You've soiled the honour of the Red Army !" a rough-looking comrade shouted at me. Other comrades showed regret; still others indignation.

' "Keep cool, comrades." the squad leader shouted, easing the tenseness a little. Turning to me, he said, "Comrade Aerhmuhsia, we Red Army men are whole-heartedly devoted to the people. We will not take anything from them. Today you've acted against our rules of discipline. Although the cup was found in a heap, it nevertheless was the property of the people and should not have found its way into your pouch. See that nothing like this happens again. The Kuomintang bandits specialize in trampling upon the people; we must not act like them. Now take this cup back.' His tone was mild and his small eyes fixed gently on me.

'As I listened to him, the scenes of the Kuomintang bandits killing and burning, and of the Red Army opening the prison and the granary, distributing grain to the Yi and poor Han brothers, came back to my mind. The Red Army wouldn't take even a small cup from the people. It was then I saw clearly that I had done wrong . . .' [9]

These official reminiscences play down the tension between the Red Army and the tribespeople. But Liu Po-cheng, the Kuchis' new blood-brother, had to admit that in spite of (or perhaps because of) this alliance, the Communists could not gain the co-operation of the Kuchis' enemy, the Lohungs. 'We had some trouble,' he observes with mild understatement, 'with the Lohung tribe which constantly attacked us . . .' [10] When it came to their own survival the Chinese Communists had to resort to the classic device of imperialism, namely *divide et impera.*

Chapter 15

The Heroes of the Tatu
River

THE Red Army now faced the savage Tatu River, its most difficult obstacle in the whole epic of the Long March. The Tatu River springs up in the icy plateau of Chinghai and tumbles south, under the name of Tachin (or Takin) River, to converge with the Siaokin River at Tanpa. From here downwards it is named Tatu, flowing into the Min River (at Loshan in Szechuan), which soon afterwards enters the Yangtze. The current is too rapid for navigation, and ferrying across is extremely risky. The water roars like thunder and throws up rainbow mists as it crashes against the cliffs. Where the main roads cross the Tatu there are usually bridges made of iron chains or ropes.

There were many precedents for military defeat at the Tatu. The heroes of *The Three Kingdoms* and other warriors of ancient Chinese history had fallen on its banks, and in these same gorges the last remnants of the Taiping rebel army under Prince Shih Ta-kai had been surrounded and destroyed by the troops of the Manchu Emperor.

At the main crossing at Anshunchang, where the unruly torrent begins its eastward turn towards Loshan, local legend says that the spirits of the Taiping cry out for vengeance on dark nights. When the Red Army arrived there, General Chu Teh, who was with the vanguard division of Lin Piao, retold to his comrades the stories which the Old Weaver used to tell him in his childhood about the army of Shih Ta-kai.

'Yes,' the Old Weaver used to say, 'our army perished at the Tatu River. Prince Shih's troops died by the thousands at the Tatu River, and some in the river because they were starving and preferred death in the river to surrender to the Tartars. They had no food and they ate all the horses and mules. . . . The Tartars . . . bribed the savage Lolos and armed them with foreign guns to attack Shih from the rear and cut off his food supply. . . . They built defences along the Tatu River and Shih Ta-kai could not cross, for we Taipings had only bows and arrows. . . . Shih's soldiers . . . made rafts, and 5,000 boarded them and held their leather shields before them and their spears in their hands. . . . But the foreign cannon blazed, the rafts were destroyed, and the Tatu River was clogged with the bodies of the dead.' [1]

The Old Weaver would close his story with the words: 'On dark nights, when there is no moon, you can still hear the spirits of our Taiping dead wailing at the Tatu River crossing and over the town where they were slaughtered. They will wait until they are avenged. Then their spirit will rest.'

Shih surrendered and suffered a gruesome death. The Viceroy of Szechuan, Lo Ping-chang, recorded in his memoirs:

'On the 13th he came into camp leading his child, four years of age, by the hand, and gave himself up with his chiefs and followers. Shih Ta-kai and three others were conveyed to Chengtu on the 25th and put to death by the slicing process. . . .' [2]

Chu Teh told Agnes Smedley afterwards that 'such would have been the fate of myself and other men of the Red Army had we ever surrendered to Chiang Kai-shek. . . .' But at the time the Red Army arrived, apprehensively, at the same fateful site in May 1935, Chu no doubt left such grim thoughts unspoken. Instead, Smedley records that in the middle of his story-telling a soldier came up and said:

'We bought and slaughtered a hog. I snitched the liver and a few other pieces for you. Suppose we have a meal!'

'Good!' replied Chu Teh with gusto. 'I'm a good cook! Come, you cut up the meat and I'll do the cooking.'

A dozen men followed him into the house where he was quartered, and stood about sniffing the smells of the pork delicacies while Chu went on with his tales of the Taiping. When the dish was ready and they were eating it with relish, General Chu turned to the soldier who had brought the meat and told him:

'If you lay your hands on any tripe, bring it along and I'll cook it to make your mouth water.' [3]

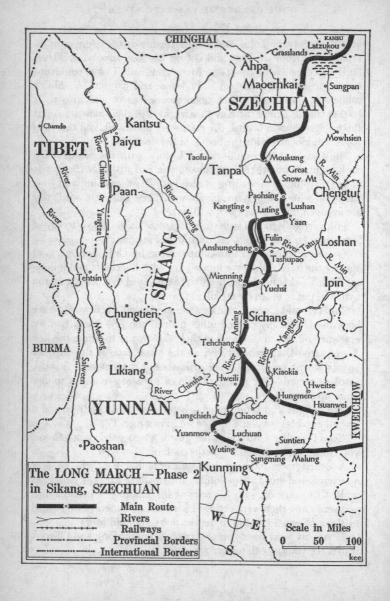

The LONG MARCH — Phase 2
in Sikang, SZECHUAN

	Main Route
	Rivers
	Railways
	Provincial Borders
	International Borders

Scale in Miles

0   50   100

Generalissimo Chiang Kai-shek knew his history, too. He radioed to his allies Liu Hsiang and Liu Wen-lui, the Szechuan warlords, as well as to his own generals in command of the Kuomintang pursuit, a call to repeat the story of the Taiping at the Tatu River.

But one mistake of Shih Ta-kai's was avoided by the Communists. The Taiping leader had halted at the banks of the Tatu to celebrate the birth of his son, a prince. Those days of rest had allowed the Manchu or Tartar forces to concentrate against him on both sides, front and rear. The Red Army was determined not to repeat Prince Shih's mistake, and it made as much speed as possible up the narrow valleys of the Anning River in Sikang.

There were three main crossings of the Tatu which the Communists could attempt. One was the iron chain suspension bridge at Luting, where the historic main road from south-central China to Lhasa, Kashmir, Samarkand and Europe crosses the Tatu River. This is the last feasible crossing upstream. The bridge was built by the Emperor Kang Hsi in 1701, from charcoal-smelted iron, and a stone slab at its head bears the couplet:

> Towering mountains flank the Luting Bridge.
> Their summits rise a thousand *li* to the clouds.

The next point was at Anshunchang, fifty miles [4] downstream from Luting, where the Taipings had met their fate. Here there was a ferry. Finally, another minor road crossed at Fulin-Tashupao, the normal road for travellers from the Tatu River or Chengtu aiming southwards across Sikang to the upper Chinsha and Yunnan, whence the Red Army had come.

A company of Liu Wen-hui's Szechuanese army was in occupation of Fulin on the northern bank of the Tatu. The Red Army high command decided to make a feint here to distract the enemy's attention while the main force attempted the Anshunchang crossing. According to the account of Liu Chung, who commanded the reconnaissance detachment which struck at Fulin, Liu Po-cheng told them on 20 May that Tso Tsuan and Liu Ya-lou would lead a company of the V Army Corps and a reconnaissance battalion over the Hsiaohsiang mountain through the Lolo territory to Tashupao, opposite Fulin.[5] Their job was to demonstrate and pin the enemy down while the main force moved along a less obvious path (the one taken by the Taipings) from Mienning to Anshun-chang.

Lin Piao's I Army Corps provided the vanguard, as usual, and the best eyewitness account is that by Colonel Yang Teh-chih, in command of the 1st Regiment of the 1st Division of the I Army Corps:

'We learned through reconnaissance that the enemy had placed three so-called "backbone regiments" near the Luting Bridge, one regiment on the shore opposite Anshunchang to hold the ferry, and two more regiments thirty *li* downstream.

'After analysing the situation, we decided to cross at Anshun-chang.

'Anshunchang, which was situated on the south bank to the west of the Tatu River, was a small town of about a hundred families. It was guarded by two enemy companies. To make the task more difficult there was only one boat in the whole of that stretch of the river. To cross, the Red Army must first wipe out the enemy on the south bank and seize the boat.

'It was already past ten at night, when we arrived at a large slope, a dozen *li* from Anshunchang, after marching twenty-four hours in the rain [the Kuomintang aeroplane pilots had already lost track of them in the dense foliage of the forest]. On the slope were scattered a few houses. The gurgling of the waters of the Tatu could be heard. Gazing towards Anshunchang we could see a sprinkling of lights to the north of the hill, like stars on a pitch-black wintry night.

'We decided to stop for a time, and wait for further orders. The soldiers were knocked up after marching 140 *li* in twenty-four hours.* The minute they halted they dropped to the ground and fell into a heavy sleep. While the troops were resting, I sought out the local people for more information.

'An order came from command headquarters: Make a surprise attack on the enemy at Anshunchang tonight and seize the boat to cross the river in force!'

Incredibly, one of the three ferry-boats was made fast on the

---

* Almost fifty miles in one day, an extraordinary achievement in that terrain.

south bank, contrary to Chiang Kai-shek's orders. Snow explains this: 'On the opposite shore there was only one regiment of the troops of General Liu Wen-hui, the co-dictator of Szechuan province. Other Szechuan troops, as well as reinforcements from Nanking, were leisurely proceeding towards the Tatu, but the single regiment meanwhile must have seemed enough. A squad should have been ample, with all boats moored to the north. But the commander of that regiment was a native of the district; he knew the country the Reds must pass through, and how long it would take them to penetrate to the river. They would be many days yet, he could have told his men. And his wife, one learned, had been a native of An Jen Ch'ang,* so he must cross to the south bank to visit his relatives and his friends and to feast with them. Thus it happened that the Reds, taking the town by surprise, captured the commander, his boat, and their passage to the north.' [6]

To continue Colonel Yang's narrative: 'After studying the situation, I and the political commissar of the regiment, Comrade Li Lin, made the following decision: the 1st Battalion would go with me to take Anshunchang; the 2nd Battalion would be led by Commissar Li to the shore opposite the enemy fifteen *li* downstream to make a false attack so as to attract the enemy main force; the 3rd Battalion would remain in the original place to protect command headquarters.

'The decision was quickly turned into action. The tired soldiers rose from the muddy ground and continued towards Anshunchang.

'The darkness was by now absolute, and it was drizzling. We groped our way forward. We made about a dozen *li* more and were now near Anshunchang. The three companies of the 1st Battalion separated, and took three different routes which thrust like three daggers at the enemy.

'The enemy at Anshunchang never anticipated that the Red Army would come so quickly. A number of the officers were playing *mahjong* in their quarters.

'Our advance party was noticed by the enemy sentries.

'Which unit are you from?' they asked. (They thought we were their own men.)

---

* Or Anshunchang.

'The roar of the Red Army fighters came like thunder out of the dark sky: 'We are the Red Army! Hand over your weapons and you will be spared!'

'Ping ... ping! The enemy fired in a panic, but too late. Our guns opened up from all directions. Those who resisted had the worst of it; some became our captives; the rest fled. The two enemy companies collapsed in less than half an hour. They had given us a meagre chance to try our strength.

'We took Anshunchang. I was in a small room, worrying myself about the boat. "Who goes there?" I heard someone cry. Then: "Stand still! Hand over your weapons!"

'It was the enemy soldiers in charge of the boat. They had just come from the riverside. Not knowing the real situation, they meekly surrendered their guns. I quickly ordered a messenger to send the captured enemy squad leader to the 1st Battalion and for them to use him in their task of securing the boat.

'It was after much effort that the 1st Battalion succeeded in getting the boat, our only hope of ferrying our men over the river. Most important, there was no boatman; and in any case we were not prepared. So the crossing was put forward to the day following. I hadn't a wink of sleep that night, pacing the small room at the end of the street of Anshunchang, racking my brains over the problems of crossing the river. I was troubled over the immediate failure to cross.

'I opened the window to let the night wind blow in. It was quiet outside, except for a few intermittent shots. The black clouds had dispersed; a pale moon showed. The hills on the opposite shore were barely visible.

'Again and again I asked myself: "How are we going to tackle this broad, turbulent river?"

'I thrust my head out of the window. The night was infinite. Query after query kept cropping up in my mind. When I remembered the words of the divisional commander, I was all the more worried. But what was the use? We could only wait till to-morrow. I drew a deep breath.

'Dawn came at last. The weather was fine, clusters of white cloud floating in the azure sky. The steep cliffs on both banks of the river seemed more forbidding than ever; the waters boiled and raced between them. Through the field-glasses everything on the opposite shore was clearly visible. There, about one li from the ferry, was a tiny hamlet. The houses were in enclosures about half a man's height. The position of the ferry was surrounded by black rocks and fortifications set at uneven spaces. The main force of the enemy battalion might be hidden in the hamlet. Obviously, the enemy intended to make a counter-charge and force the Red Army down the river before they could gain a foothold after crossing.

'How should I cope with the cunning enemy? I decided: "He who strikes the first blow will be the winner!"

'I ordered the artillery battery to place three guns and several heavy machine-guns into advantageous positions. The light machine gunners and the crack shots moved into position under cover by the river bank.

'The network of fire was arranged, but crossing remained the serious question.

'I had turned all the possibilities over in my mind last night. Swimming was impossible. The river was 300 metres wide. If one's strength failed him, he would be swept away by the rapid current.

'We had considered throwing up a bridge. But with the flow at four metres per second,[7] even driving a stake would be very difficult, let alone the piles of a bridge. The only hope was the ferry-boat. So I ordered the commander of the 1st Battalion to find some boatmen.

'After scouring the surrounding valleys the troops at last found a dozen boatmen. They promised to get us across.

'But there was only one boat; so not all could go at once. I made the commander of the 1st Battalion responsible for picking the men who were to go first. When the soldiers learned that a river-crossing team was to be organized, they surrounded the battalion commander and demanded to go in the first trip as the vanguard.

'One hour had passed. The crossing should not be delayed another minute.

' "What shall we do?" the battalion commander asked for my instructions. I looked at the soldiers, happy and worried – happy because they all looked so brave, worried because if this state of things continued it would go badly with us.

' "You shall decide which unit goes;' I told the battalion commander.

'He decided to send a dozen men from the Second Company which now gathered outside the house.

'It was quiet all round but for the rushing and splashing of the waters.

' "Hsiung Shang-lin, Tseng Hui-ming, Liu Chang-fa, Chang Ke-piao . . .' – those whose names were announced relaxed and looked satisfied.

'Sixteen names were called. Looking at these husky fellows, I thought the battalion commander had chosen well.

'Suddenly a fighter broke from the ranks. "I'll go too! I must go!" he cried, running towards the battalion commander. It was the messenger of the 2nd Company.

'The battalion commander looked at him. "Go!" he said, after a while. He was moved by the scene and approved this exception. The messenger brushed away his tears and ran quickly to join the crossing party.

'The eighteen heroes (the battalion commander himself included) were equipped each with a broad sword, a tommy-gun, a pistol, half a dozen grenades and some working tools. They were organized into two parties. The one led by Hsiung Shang-lin, commander of the 2nd Company, was to cross first.

'The waters of the Tatu rushed and roared. I scanned the enemy on the opposite shore through my field-glasses. They seemed very quiet.

'The solemn moment had come. Hsiung Shang-lin and his men – eight in all – jumped on to the boat.

' "Comrades! The lives of the one hundred thousand Red Army men depend on you. Cross resolutely and wipe out the enemy!"

'Amid cheering the boat left the south bank.

'The enemy, obviously getting impatient, fired at the boat.

' "Give it to them!"

'Our artillery opened up. Chao Chang-cheng, our magic runner, swung his gun into position. "Bang! Bang!" The enemy's fortifications were sent flying into the sky. Our machine-guns and rifles also spoke. The sharp-shooters, more tense than their fellow fighters crossing, fired away feverishly. Shells showered on the enemy fortifications; machine-gun fire swept the opposite shore. The boatmen dug their blades into the water with zest.

'The boat progressed, tossing on the surging waters. Bullets landed around it, sending up spray. The eyes of everybody ashore were glued on the courageous team.

'Suddenly, a shell dropped beside the boat, creating a wave which shook the craft violently.

' "Ah, it's the end!" My heart was in my mouth. The boat rose and fell with the wave, then resumed its normal course.

'On it went, nearer and nearer the opposite shore. Now it was only five or six metres from it. The soldiers stood at the bow, ready to jump.

'Suddenly a grenade and a land mine were rolled from the top of the hill, exploding with a loud report halfway down, sending up a pall of white smoke. It seemed the enemy was really going to make a charge. I looked through my field-glasses and, just as I had expected, the enemy soldiers were sallying out from the hamlet. There were at least 200 of them against our few. Our crossing party would be fighting against overwhelming odds with the river at their back. My heart tightened.

' "Fire!" I ordered the gunners.

'Followed two deafening reports. The mortar shells directed by Chao Chang-cheng exploded right among the enemy. The heavy machine-guns rat-rattled.

' "Come on! Give it to them hard!"

'Shouts arose from the slope. The enemy scattered in a fluster, running for their lives.

' "Fire, fire!" I ordered.

'We pumped another shower of metal at them. Our heroes who had landed dashed forward, firing with their light and heavy weapons. The enemy retreated. Our men occupied the defence works at the ferry. But the enemy was still around.

'The boat came back quickly. The eight other men, led by the battalion commander, went on board.

' "Advance with the greatest possible speed, support the comrades who have landed!" I heard the battalion commander say to his men.

'The boat pushed away and made quickly for the opposite shore.

The enemy on the hill, trying to organize its entire fire to destroy our second landing party, fired desperately towards the middle of the river.

'The little boat dashed through wave after wave and dodged shower after shower of bullets.

'As it got near the shore, it was enshrouded by the hail of machine gun bullets. I looked through my field-glasses. A soldier was holding his arm.

' "How is he?" I had little time to think. The boat shot forward scores of metres. Bang! It struck a big boulder and ran aground.

' "Too bad!" I looked towards the river. The boatmen were clutching at the rock. The water, splashing and foaming beneath the little craft, seemed on the point of capsizing it. If it was swept down till it reached the rapids then it would surely be wrecked.

'I was so tense my heart seemed to be bursting.

'Four boatmen jumped from the boat. Wading in the water, with great effort they pulled. The four other boatmen in the boat poled strongly. It was free. Slowly it moved forward. Bullets whizzed around it. Minute by minute passed; in half an hour it made only half the distance. A whole hour passed before it reached the shore. I took a deep breath of relief.

'There ensued a duel of artillery fire between us and the enemy on the hill. The enemy threw a shower of hand mines and began to charge at the call of the bugle.

'I ordered the gunners to keep the enemy in check. "Continue firing!"

'Shell and machine-gun bullets kept raining on the opposite shore. The sharp-shooters fired, taking careful aim at the enemy. The enemy soldiers finally fled.

'The two groups of landing heroes joined forces – eighteen of them – rushing towards the enemy, hurling their grenades, firing their tommy-guns and brandishing their swords. Utterly routed, the enemy ran desperately towards the rear of the hill. The north bank came under the complete control of our landing party.

'After a while the boat returned to the south bank. This time I brought with me a number of heavy machine-gunners to consolidate the defence of the position.

'It was getting dark. More and more Red Army men crossed

safely. Pursuing the enemy, we captured two more boats on the lower reaches which sped up our crossing. By the forenoon of the next day, the whole regiment was on the opposite bank.' [8]

For three days and three nights – 26, 27 and 28 May, by most accounts – the three ferry-boats of Anshunchang worked back and forth carrying almost a division of the Red Army to the north bank. But the River Tatu flowed faster and more furiously as the spring thaw brought the headwaters down from the Chinghai mountains. On the third day it took four hours to get each boat-load (of up to eighty men) from one bank to the other, and at that rate the Red Army would take weeks to get all its men, animals and supplies across. The Kuomintang air force had found the spot and was already bombing the ferry crossing. Enemy troops were racing up from the south-east, others from the north. The Red I Army Corps had now crowded into Anshunchang, and behind it the flanking columns, transport units and rearguard were pressing forward. What should be done?

Chapter 16

The Bridge of Iron Chains

A HURRIED conference was called at Anshunchang, attended by Chu Teh, Mao Tse-tung, Chou En-lai, Peng Teh-huai and Lin Piao.[1] They decided to march to the Luting Bridge, the last hope for crossing the Tatu into north China. If they failed, they would have to retrace their steps back through Lololand and Yunnan, a hopeless detour. Failure at Luting, to all intents and purposes, would mean the end of the Long March.

The main force pushed upstream along the western bank with Lin Piao in command of the vanguard, while the 1st Division of the 1st Army Corps which had already crossed to the other side, under the command of Army Chief-of-Staff Liu Po-cheng and Political Commissar Nieh Jung-chen, marched in parallel up the eastern bank of the Tatu River.

'Sometimes,' writes Edgar Snow, 'the gorges between them closed so narrowly that the two lines of Reds could shout to each other across the stream; sometimes that gulf between them measured their fear that the Tatu might separate them forever, and they stepped more swiftly. As they wound in long dragon files along the cliffs at night their 10,000 torches sent arrows of light slanting down the dark face of the imprisoning river. Day and night these vanguards moved at double-quick, pausing only for brief ten-minute rests and meals, when the soldiers listened to lectures by their weary political workers, who over and over again explained the importance of this one action, exhorting each to give his last breath, his last urgent strength, for victory in the test ahead of them. There could be no slackening of pace, no half-heartedness, no fatigue.' [2]

Yang Cheng-wu was the Political Commissar of the regiment that was given the task of taking the bridge. (He later rose to become Acting Chief of Staff to the People's Liberation Army during the Cultural Revolution of the late 1960s.) Let him tell his own story:

'Early in the morning of the 23rd [3] I set out with our regiment from Anschunchang, heading along the west bank towards the bridge, about 320 *li* away. We were given three days in which to reach it. The road twisted like a sheep's gut along the side of the mountains, and was full of ups and downs. To the left was the side of the mountain, rising sharply vertical, as if cut by a knife, straight up into the clouds. On the higher slopes was snow that never melted all year round. It dazzled the eyes and gave off a frigid chill. To the right, dozens of yards below, were the white-capped waves of the rushing river. One mis-step and you were a goner. But no one worried about the danger. There was only one thought in everyone's mind: Hurry on, take the Luting Bridge.

'After we had marched about thirty *li*, enemy troops on the opposite side of the river began firing at us. To avoid needless losses, we made a detour of a dozen *li* through the mountains. This consumed a bit of time.

'After covering about sixty *li*, we found ourselves confronted with a large mountain. Our vanguard ran into a company of the enemy and pounced on them like tigers. There was a brief fierce clash and the enemy unit was smashed.

'The mountain was about a dozen *li* high. On the other side was a stream, not wide but very deep. The enemy had destroyed a bridge that had been there, and fording was impossible. We felled some trees and soon were across.

'Cheered by our first victory, we marched with a spring in our step. Scattered firing broke out ahead. Suddenly, one of our scouts came flying back to report: "There's a mountain pass ahead of us on the left. It's being held from above by an enemy unit about the size of a battalion. They're blocking our advance."

'At once, together with the regimental C.O., I led a few men forward at the double to scout out the terrain. The mountains ahead rose in sheer cliffs. There was only a narrow path between them, climbing so sharply it was like a ladder to heaven. Your cap fell off when you tried to look all the way to the top. Forts had been built both on the mountain summits and at the head of the pass.

'The river was on our right, so we couldn't circle around from that direction. The heights directly ahead looked impregnable. On the left was a sharp cliff sparsely covered with shrubs and brambles; from the top of the cliff, the tall mountain continued to rise steeply.

'After careful scouting, we decided to send a party up from the left to circle around, attack the enemy from the rear, and take the pass from behind. While one company was around from the left flank, our 3rd Battalion pretended to make a direct assault. The enemy put on a tremendous show with their machine-guns, sealing the mouth of the pass so tight that even a bee couldn't have flown through.

'In less than an hour we heard shots from the enemy's rear. 3rd Battalion then attacked in earnest, and the enemy were driven out of their fortifications. We pursued them relentlessly, destroying three companies at the foot of the cliff. We captured one battalion and one company commander and over 200 prisoners.

'The next day we received an order reading as follows: "Our Left Route Army has been given until the 25th to take the Luting Bridge. You must march at the utmost speed and act in the shortest possible time to accomplish this glorious mission. We are confident you can do it. Are preparing to congratulate you on your victory." Below was the forceful signature of General Lin Piao.

'When we finished reading the order, Commander Wang and I looked at each other, then said together: "A glorious but very tough mission!"

'The 25th! The 25th was the following day, and we were still 240 li from the Luting Bridge. We would have to cover two days' march in one. No one had thought our time schedule would be changed so quickly and made so urgent. 240 li* in one day is a tremendous march, and we had to do it on foot, every step of the way! What's more, we'd have to fight our way through strong enemy resistance.

---

* About eighty miles. Another version puts the distance required to be covered in this twenty-four-hour period at 190 li, or sixty-three miles (Chu Li-fu, *Erh-wan Wu-chien Li Chang-cheng-chi*, p. 39).

'But orders were orders. It was a glorious task and we certainly had to carry it out. We couldn't delay a minute, not a single second. Time was everything now. Originally there were two enemy regiments holding the bridge. But we had seen with our own eyes two more brigades on the other side of the river hurrying to reinforce them.

'Part of the bridge's forces were left to block our 1st Red Division crossing over at Anshunchang, but the main body was racing us to the bridge. If we got there first, there was hope of victory. Otherwise it would be very difficult, if not impossible, for the Red Army to cross at Luting.

'We couldn't stop. Time was too precious. As we marched we held a meeting of military and political officers to discuss what we should do. First we issued a number of rallying cries: "The 4th Red Regiment has a glorious battle record. We must complete our mission and preserve our glory!" "Emulate the 1st Red Regiment, which captured Anshunchang. Compete with them and take the Luting Bridge!" "Our mission is glorious but very difficult. We can pass the test!" We set six the following morning as the deadline for reaching our objective. After the meeting, the officers went back to their units to rally their men.

'Just about the time this was completed, Wild Tiger Mountain was sighted ahead.

'To cross Wild Tiger Mountain you have to go up some forty *li*, then come down the same distance. It is a dangerous climb, with the Tatu River on the right, high cliffs on the left, and the path just a narrow twisting trail. People say it's the neck of the road between Anschunchang and the Luting Bridge, and that's no exaggeration in the least.

'An enemy battalion held the path where it cuts through the summit. It was the height of the foggy season; you couldn't see five paces beyond your nose. They spotted us as we neared the summit, but because of the fog they couldn't see us clearly. They could only fire wildly in our direction. Taking advantage of this help from nature, we ordered our men to hold their fire. When we got close enough, we charged with hand grenades and bayonets. You could hear them bursting in the fog, and the exultant cries of our men. Terrified, the enemy turned and fled. Our vanguard battalion pursued them all the way down the other side of the mountain, capturing prisoners and considerable booty – including not only rifle bullets, but white flour ! As the chase reached the village of Mohsimien, the battalion ran into an enemy battalion and a regimental headquarters unit which were quartered there. Our victorious spearhead plunged in, and again the enemy scattered. We then occupied Mohsimien.

'The wretched enemy had destroyed a bridge over the stream to the east of the village, putting a new obstacle in the way of our march. After spending two hours repairing the bridge, we continued our advance, covering fifty *li* without a stop. We arrived at a little hamlet of ten or so families by the edge of the Tatu at about seven in the evening. We were still 110 *li* from Luting.

'Troubles never come singly, and no one can control the weather. Suddenly there was a tremendous downpour, with thunder and lightning. The sky was so black you couldn't see the fingers of your own hand. Our men hadn't eaten all day; they were suffering from hunger. Marching at night in the slippery mud, the pack animals with our food and supplies couldn't keep up. As we came down Wild Tiger Mountain we had seen the enemy on the other side of the river still racing with us neck and neck. If they beat us to the bridge, everything would be finished. We simply had to find a solution and at once.

'The more difficult our problems became, the more we had to intensify our political work among the men. We put out a call to all our Communists, Youth Leaguers, and other enthusiasts; we stated plainly the hardships that lay ahead, but insisted that we must be at Luting by six the next morning. An order was issued for every man to cut himself a staff. Anyone who couldn't march could walk leaning on the staff. Those who couldn't walk with the aid of staffs could crawl – but they still had to reach our objective on time ! We couldn't stop to cook. Everyone was directed to eat his rice ration raw – and wash it down with unboiled water.

'The call, spreading through the ranks like wildfire, roused the men's fighting spirit. From the look of them, not even a mountain of knives could have held them back. But how could we march 110 *li* through slippery mud in pitch-darkness? That question weighed on my heart like a thousand-catty stone.

'Suddenly a few points of light appeared in a dip in the mountains on the opposite side of the river, changing in an instant into a long string of torches. Enemy troops were making a forced march by torchlight. That gave us an idea. We'll do the same, I thought, and conferred immediately with our regiment commander, our chief-of-staff and our Party secretary. But the problem was this: The enemy were only across the river. Suppose they signal us, and ask that we identify ourselves? If they find out who we are and engage us in combat, how will we reach the bridge in time?

' "When things are toughest, strike out boldly." We decided to adopt the designations of the three enemy battalions we had beaten yesterday and today. Buying all the reed fences from the folks in the hamlet, we tied the reeds together to make torches and issued one to each man. On the march, one torch was lit by each squad – the torches were not to be wasted. Our aim was to cover at least nine *li* per hour. We directed our bugler to be prepared to give the responses we had learned from the captured enemy materials. Liu Wen-hui's troops were all Szechuanese; we picked out a few Szechuan comrades from our own ranks and some Szechuan men from among the prisoners so that they could shout back replies to any questions.

'For the sake of speed, we left all our animals, baggage and heavy weapons – including my horse and the mount of the regimental C.O. – in the care of a platoon led by two officers, with instructions that they follow behind as best they could.

'I had a leg wound at the time which had not yet healed. It caused me some inconvenience on the march. The comrades – especially the regimental C.O. – urged me to continue on horseback. But at a time when all officers should set an example, how could I ride? I issued a challenge: "We'll all march together, comrades. Let's see who walks the fastest. Let's see who gets to the Luting Bridge first !"

'Delighted, the men held their torches high and pressed forward.

'Our torches and those of the enemy column, facing us on the opposite bank, crimsoned the waters of the Tatu. From a distance the lines of torches looked like two writhing fiery dragons. Above the sound of the waves we heard the sharp notes of an enemy bugle, followed by the weaker cry, "Which unit are you?" The enemy was making contact with us.

'Our bugler blew the call required by enemy regulations as a response, and our Szechuan comrades and prisoners shouted an answer back in chorus. The stupid pigs on the other side never guessed that marching parallel with them was the gallant Red Army that day and night they dreamed of eradicating. They marched along with us for nearly thirty li. At about midnight, the rain grew heavier, and the torches on the opposite bank disappeared. We figured that they must have found the going too hard and made camp. The news spread quickly through the regiment. Our comrades were overjoyed. This is our chance, they said. March on! . . . In single file, we pushed ahead for all we were worth.

'The rain pelted mercilessly; torrents rushed down the mountain gullies into the river. The twisting path along the side of the mountain had been difficult enough before; now the water made it slick as oil. Our walking staffs proved of little use. One slip and you landed on your head. It was a case of every three steps a skid, every five steps a fall. We rolled rather than marched forward.

'Even under those conditions, men kept dozing off. A soldier would slowly come to a halt and the comrade behind would push him and yell, "Keep going! They're way ahead of you!" Only then would he suddenly waken and hurry to catch up. Finally, the men simply unwrapped their puttees and tied themselves together in a long chain, each pulling the other along.

'After proceeding at a forced march all night, at a little after six the following morning, we succeeded in reaching the Luting Bridge and capturing its western end and western approaches. In twenty-four hours, besides fighting and repairing wrecked bridges, we had marched 240 li. Truly an exploit of winged feet!

'We occupied several buildings at the western end of the bridge, and there the men dried out their clothes, cooked some food, and rested. Regimental Commander Wang and I went out with the battalion and company officers took over the terrain.

'The Luting Bridge was located in a dangerous setting indeed. Even we who had braved the greatest difficulties couldn't help being taken aback. Below, the reddish waters, cascading down from the mountain gorges of the river's upper reaches, pounded against the ugly boulders rising from the river bed and tossed white froth high into the air. The roar of the rushing torrent was deafening. Not even a fish could hold its own against that water. Fording or crossing in boats was out of question. The bridge was the only way to get to the other side.

'We examined it. It was made not of stone or of wood but of iron chains – thirteen in number, each big link as thick as a rice bowl. Two chains on each side served as railings; nine formed the surface walk. Originally, planks had been laid across the nine chains, and the whole bridge, suspended between two cliffs, swayed like a cradle with the motions of the person walking upon it. Now the planks were gone, having been taken by the enemy into Luting City. All that remained were the black hanging chains. At the head of the bridge two lines of a poem were inscribed on a stone slab:

> Towering mountains flank the Luting Bridge,
> Their summits rise a thousand *li* into the clouds.

'Across the river on the eastern side was the city of Luting, half of it along the shore, half of it against the slope of a mountain. Surrounded by a wall seven and a half metres high, the city was directly beyond the eastern end of the bridge. After you crossed the bridge you had to enter the city's West Gate. There was no other road. Luting was garrisoned by two enemy regiments; they had built strong fortifications along the mountain slope. Machine-gun emplacements close to the bridge kept us under continual fire, and mortar shells rained down on us.

'Confident that their position was impregnable, the enemy sneered and yelled at us: "Let's see you fly over! We'll give up our arms!"

'Our soldiers shouted back: "We don't want your arms. It's your bridge we're after!"

'We set a battalion in position to seal off with rifle and machine-gun fire any enemy reinforcements which might try to reach the eastern end of the bridge from the south. Just as on our side, there was only a narrow path between the mountainside and the river along which they could come. Then we went among our companies to begin our battle rallies. Enthusiasm ran high. Each company submitted a list of names of men volunteering as an assault squad, each demanding that the men of their unit be given the task of taking the bridge.

'At noon we called a meeting of all the officers in the regiment to decide on the composition of the assault squad. No sooner had we started our discussion than enemy mortar shells blew a big hole in the roof of the building in which we were gathered. Not one of us moved, but every pair of eyes stared angrily at the east bank.

' "The enemy is urging us on," I said. "We must drive across the bridge immediately. Now let's decide which company shall be responsible for driving the opening wedge."

'Liao Ta-chu, the commander of 2nd Company, jumped to his feet. Usually a taciturn man, he now forced himself to speak, though his dark sun-burnt face blushed to the ears with the effort. His short wiry frame trembled with excitement as he said:

' "1st Company was commended as a Model Company when we forded the Wukian River. We'd like to emulate them and win the title of Heroes Company in taking the Luting Bridge."

' "You've got to give the assault mission to 3rd Company," the excitable commander of that company interrupted, spluttering like a machine-gun. "3rd Company has done well in every battle. We can guarantee to take the bridge." Standing as solid as an iron pagoda, he added plaintively, "If you don't give the assault mission to 3rd Company, I won't be able to go back and face my men."

'A heated debate followed, no company willing to yield to any other. It was up to the leaders to decide. Regimental Commander Wang and I talked it over; then he stood up and announced that 2nd Company would lead the assault. I then rose and said:

' "If it's fighting you want, there's plenty more to come. You'll each get your chance. At Wukiang River, 1st Company led off; this time we'll let 2nd Company start. The assault squad will be formed of twenty-two men – Communists and other bold young fellows – from 2nd Company, and will be led by Commander Liao. It seems like a good arrangement to me. What do the rest of you think?"

'The response was a burst of applause from all present. Only the commander of 3rd Company continued to sulk. "3rd Company's job isn't easy either," I assured him. "You have to go over directly behind 2nd Company and lay planks across those chains, so the rest of the men can charge into the city." Only then did his face break into a smile.

'Finally I instructed the company commanders to issue to each man one catty of the salt pork we had captured from some of the local tyrants. The men fought better on a full stomach. After the meeting, I asked the regimental Party secretary to help the assault squad of 2nd Company get ready.

'We began our attack at four in the afternoon. The regimental C.O. and I directed it from the west end of the bridge. All the buglers of the regiment blew the charge call in unison, and we opened up with every weapon we had against the enemy on the opposite bank. The firing, the shouts of the men, reverberated through the valley. Carrying tommy-guns, big knives strapped across their backs, twelve grenades apiece tucked into their belts, twenty-two heroes, led by Commander Liao, climbed across the swaying bridge chains, in the teeth of intense enemy fire. Behind them came the officers and men of 3rd Company, each carrying a plank in addition to full battle gear; they fought and laid planks at the same time.

'Just as the assault squad reached the opposite side, huge flames sprang into the sky outside Luting City's West Gate. The enemy was trying to block us by fire, to consume us in its flames. The blaze, reddening half the sky, licked fiercely around the east end of the bridge.

'The whole outcome of the attack hung by a hair. Confronted by the fire at the city gate our assault squad hesitated. The men standing with me and the regimental C.O. shouted across the river: "Go on, comrades, charge! Victory depends on you! Never mind the fire, charge! The enemy is cracking."

'Emboldened by our cries, the twenty-two men, at the sound of a clarion bugle call, plunged boldly into the flames. Commander Liao's cap caught fire. He threw it away and fought on. The hair and eyebrows of the men were singed, but, streaming smoke and flame, they continued charging behind Liao, smashing their way into the city. In the street fighting that followed, the enemy brought their full weight to bear, determined to wipe our assault squad out. The twenty-two fought until all their bullets and grenades were gone. The situation was critical. It seemed to be all up with them.

'But just then 3rd Company came charging to their rescue. Next, Regimental Commander Wang and I sped across the bridge with our second contingent and also entered the city.

'In two hours' time, we destroyed half of the enemy's two regiments. The remainder broke and scattered. By dusk we had completely occupied the city of Luting and were in firm control of the bridge.

'Our main task now was to guard against an enemy counterattack and hold on to the bridge at all costs. We knew there were a couple of enemy regiments near Tachienlu, so we sent one battalion in that direction to stand as an outpost guard. We sent another battalion south along the river to hold off the two enemy brigades we had seen hurrying towards the bridge the day before. Around ten in the evening we heard the battalion's forward point open fire. Assuming they had made contact with the enemy, we prepared for a bitter battle. Our battalion took the position, then sent out an assault squad which brought back a wounded prisoner. He turned out to be a comrade of the 3rd Regiment of our 1st Red Division. Only then did we know that the 1st Division had already arrived. We had been tensed for a cruel struggle, but now everyone relaxed and celebrated joyfully.

'The 1st Red Division had caught up with the enemy brigades sixty li from Luting. Afraid of being caught in an attack from both south and north, the brigades fled in panic towards Hualingping.

'We at once dispatched men to meet Army Chief-of-Staff Liu Po-cheng and General Nieh Jung-chen, who were following behind, and lead them into the city. It was a very happy reunion.

'Although it was two in the morning, the two commanders insisted on inspecting the bridge. Carrying a lantern, I accompanied them across. General Liu examined every detail carefully, as if he were trying to memorize the entire bridge. On the way back, he stopped in the middle and leaned over to look at the turbulent waters of the Tatu. Tapping his foot against the planking, he murmured, "We've spent plenty of blood and energy to get you, Luting Bridge, but we've done it !"

'Among the captured enemy documents, we found an urgent directive issued by General Liu Wen-hui. It read : "Chu Teh and Mao Tse-tung are going to become the second Shih Ta-kai. Ahead of them is the Tatu River, behind is the Golden Sand River. They're caught like fish in a bottle. Now is the time to annihilate the Red bandits."

'Liu Wen-hui even offered a reward for the capture of our military leaders. "The enemy rates us very highly," our Army Chief-of-Staff remarked drily. "You see, they've put a 100,000 silver dollar price tag on me ! . . ."

'The following day, General Lin Piao marched up with our main force. His warm congratulations were a great encouragement to us. Then Chairman Mao, Commander-in-Chief Chu, Vice-Chairman Chou and the staff of other organizations arrived too. Thousands of troops strode across the Luting Bridge. We had conquered the seething barrier of the Tatu River.

'The twenty-two heroes who had first smashed across were highly commended by the Military Committee. Their fearless exploits are a glorious page in the annals of our military history.' [4]

Other accounts of the capture of the Luting Bridge vary slightly. The pictures show clearly that there are thirteen chains – nine underfoot and two at each side to protect the crosser. Yet Snow writes of sixteen chains,[5] Chu Teh told Agnes Smedley there were twenty,[6] Chu Li-fu and Hsu Meng-chiu state twelve [7] and Tsai Shun-li talks of nine.[8] Smedley says the bridge was captured on 30 May, and she implies that Lin Piao was with the 1st Division on the left bank rather than with the main force on the right.

More importantly, the eye-witness story of Colonel Yang implies that *all* the planks had been removed, and other 'official' versions state this as a fact.[9] In fact, only about half or two-thirds of them had been taken away from the west side. 'The bridge should, of course, have been destroyed,' comments Snow, 'but the Szechuanese were sentimental about their few bridges; it was not easy to rebuild them, and they were costly. Of Liu Ting * it was said that "the wealth of eighteen provinces contributed to build it". And who would have thought the Reds would insanely try to cross on the chains alone?" [10] The fact that the part of the bridge nearest to the enemy was still covered with timber explains, firstly, why so many of the Communists at the front were able to survive enemy bullets (the flooring giving them some protection as they neared the other side) and, secondly, how the fire at the eastern end caused so much trouble – it was the remaining planks which the enemy set light to, but too late ! Hsu Meng-chiu claims that it was the terminal building at the far end of the bridge which was set on fire, and that the twenty Red heroes went into it to fetch the planks to replace them on the bridge, but this sounds less convincing.[11]

Smedley's description of the final scene is the best : 'Platoon Commander Ma Ta-chiu stepped out, grasped one of the chains, and began swinging, hand over hand, towards the north † bank. The platoon political director followed, and after him the men. As they swung along, Red Army machine guns laid down a protecting screen of fire and the Engineering Corps began bringing up tree trunks and laying the bridge flooring.

'The army watched breathlessly as the men swung along the bridge chains. Ma Ta-chiu was the first to be shot into the wild torrent below. Then another man and another. The others pushed along, but just before they reached the flooring at the north bridge-head they saw enemy soldiers dumping cans of kerosene on the planks and setting them on fire. Watching the sheet of flame spread, some men hesitated, but the platoon political leader at last sprang down on the flooring before the flames reached his feet, calling to the others to follow. They came and crouched on the planks releasing their hand grenades and unbuckling their swords.

'They ran through the flames and threw their hand grenades in the midst of the enemy. More and more men followed, the flames lapping at their clothing. Behind them sounded the roar of their

---

* Luting : the original name was Liu Ting Chiao, 'The Bridge Made Fast by Liu'.

† The north-east or left bank.

comrades, and, beneath the roar, the heavy THUD, THUD, THUD of the last tree trunks falling into place. The bridge became a mass of running men with rifles ready, tramping out the flames as they ran. The enemy retreated to their second line of defences. . . .' [12]

The losses were minimal. One source puts the dead at seventeen, with 'many scorched and wounded, and a few severely burned', another at under fifty, of whom twelve were blown by the wind into the river below.[13]

Agnes Smedley reports that 'a staff officer who was with Chu and Mao while the bridge was being crossed told me that Chu made no sound, no sign, but stood like a man turned to stone. He knew that the fate of the Red Army was being decided at that moment. . . .' [14]

Yet a single stick of dynamite at the moorings would have condemned the Communists to destruction.

Chapter 17

The Great Snow Mountain

THE Red Army was now less than 100 miles away from its comrades of the Fourth Front Army under Chang Kuo-tao and Hsu Hsiang-chien in north-eastern Szechuan. But it took seven weeks before the reunion could be accomplished. In between the two forces lay the awesome Great Snow Mountain range, which was to take a further toll of the Long Marchers.

The Communists were still attacked from the air from time to time. Mao Tse-tung's batman recalls an incident on the march from Hualingping to Shuitseti soon after the Tatu crossing:

'It was the usual early start. Chairman Mao was held up by some business or another and went with the medical corps instead of the Central Committee staff. The squad leader of the bodyguards and I went with him. We were crossing an open valley, a dozen *li* long, when we were suddenly dive-bombed by three enemy planes. The bombs fell really near and we rushed to shield Chairman Mao. He was up at once, though, bending over the squad leader, who had been hit. He lay there, clutching his abdomen, quite silent. Chairman Mao touched him gently, and turned to the medical corps officer.

' "Can you do anything?" he asked urgently. My squad leader struggled to wave help aside.

' "No!" he said, "go on."

'He could hardly speak. He was terribly pale, as though all the blood was draining away from him. Chairman Mao sat down by him and lifted his head.

' "You'll be all right, Comrade Hu Chang-pao," he said gently. "Just keep quiet, and we'll carry you to Shuitseti, where we can get a doctor who'll see to you."

'My squad leader moved his head as it lay on Chairman Mao's arm.

' "I can't let you carry me," he said. "Don't trouble yourself. I can feel I'm bleeding inside. It doesn't matter about me, I'm quite content. But will you tell my parents? They live in Kian, in Kiangsi. I'm only sorry that I can't go on with you to Shensi, and see our base there."

'He stopped and breathed hard for a minute. Then he looked at me.

' "Chen Chang-feng," he said, "take good care of our Chairman Mao and the other leaders."

'His voice died away, and we couldn't hear what else he said. He tried to speak again; we could see his lips move. Suddenly, with a great effort, he spoke loudly.

' "Victory to the Revolution !" he cried.

'His head fell over and his eyes fixed and closed.

' "Squad leader, squad leader," I cried, but he was dead.

'Chairman Mao slid his arm out from under him and stood up.

' "Give me the quilt," he said.

'I gave him a quilt from the bedding-roll, and Chairman Mao laid it over the body.' [1]

Seven distinct ranges of high mountain had to be negotiated on the path to Kansu province, of which the Great Snow Mountain – Chiachinshan – was only the first. Paotung Kang Mountain, the Chung Lai range, the Dream Pen Mountain and the Big Drum Mountain also lay ahead.

There was a preliminary scuffle with Tibetan warriors before the ascent of Great Snow Mountain began. 'A regiment of Tibetan braves,' Agnes Smedley relates, 'came down from Tachienliu to reinforce the Szechwan troops. The Tibetans were clad in sheepskin coats and their Chinese officers in fur-lined uniforms. The officers had brought their concubines along – baby-faced women hung with jade and swathed in beautiful white fur, and, like their masters, riding fine horses. Since the Red Army needed fur garments, it did not take them long to strip the Tibetan regiment, including the baby-faced concubines. They also took the horses, and the boxes of silver which the officers were carting with them.' [2]

The Communist troops were given a week's rest after their forced marching in Sikang, and another ten days' preparation for surmounting the glaciers and snow ahead. Every man had to carry enough food and fuel to last ten days, and to go as warmly clothed as possible. They were never to march for more than six or seven hours a day. They had to be ready to build shelters and to use white camouflage when necessary. Rivers would have to be crossed with captured boats, or else the men would have to be prepared to build their own of wood or leather. The officers inspected their men closely, looking at their shoes, lifting packs to test the weight and inquiring into their health. Medical units were told to march in the rear and care for the old, the exhausted and the sick who fell behind.[3]

Chu Teh issued orders-of-the-day, on 'paper which told an eloquent story of the backward, primitive life in the vast Chinese–Tibetan borderland. Some were written on the reverse side of old military maps roughly torn into squares; some on cheap, soft paper of many gaudy colours which Chinese use for New Year celebrations; others on coarse, thick Tibetan paper decorated with Tibetan designs or on pages torn from military account books. And some on great square sheets of coarse paper from which previous Tibetan printing had been roughly washed off with water or chemicals.' [4]

The Red Army ascended to 16,000 feet on the Great Snow Mountain, and from the crest its soldiers could gaze through the rarefied air over a sea of snow peaks in far-off Tibet. It was June, but many of the poorly-clad, thin-blooded southerners in the ranks, unused to high altitude, died of exposure. On the Paotung Kang Mountain the Communists had literally to build their own road from bamboos laid over 'a tortuous treacle of waist-deep mud'. Mao Tse-tung told Edgar Snow that on this peak, 'one army corps lost two-thirds of its transport animals. Hundreds fell down and never got up.' [5]

Lin Piao, with a weak heart, had to rest on the Great Snow Mountain, according to Robert Payne, and endure the full face of a storm, and one report has him fainting several times.[6] Hsu Meng-chiu, who became the official 'historian' of the Long March, had both his legs frozen on this mountain, and later had to have them amputated.[7] Mao himself had to be carried on a stretcher, ill with malaria again, at this stage.[8]

One survivor said afterwards: 'Chiachinshan is blanketed in eternal snow. There are great glaciers in its chasms and everything is white and silent. We were heavily burdened because each man had to carry enough food and fuel to last ten days. Our food was anything we could buy – chiefly corn, though we had a little buckwheat and some peppers. We carried our food in long cloth pouches over our shoulders. General Chu carried his food like everyone else. He had a horse but he gave it to sick or wounded men to ride.

'We would not have suffered so much, or had such heavy losses in life, if we had been able to buy rice. The change from rice to a corn diet gave our men diarrhoea and other stomach disorders. The corn passed straight through them – they couldn't digest it at all. Another torment was lice. Wherever we slept in the huts of the people, the lice seemed to come up out of the earthen floor to settle on us. Everybody had lice, everybody hunted lice.' [9]

Tung Pi-Wu – the 'old Tung' who had encouraged the 'little devils' in Sikang with his story of Monkey – described the crossing to Agnes Smedley:

'We started out at early dawn. There was no path at all, but peasants said that tribesmen came over the mountains on raids, and we could cross if they could. So we started straight up the mountain, heading for a pass near the summit. Heavy fogs swirled about us, there was a high wind, and halfway up it began to rain. As we climbed higher and higher we were caught in a terrible hailstorm and the air became so thin that we could hardly breathe at all. Speech was completely impossible and the cold so dreadful that our breath froze and our hands and lips turned blue. Men and animals staggered and fell into chasms and disappeared forever. Those who sat down to rest or to relieve themselves froze to death on the spot. Exhausted political workers encouraged men by sign and touch to continue moving, indicating that the pass was just ahead.

'By nightfall we had crossed, at an altitude of 16,000 feet, and that night we bivouacked in a valley where there was no sign of human life. While most of us were stretched out exhausted, General Chu came around to make his usual inspection. He was very weary, for he had walked with the troops. Yet nothing ever prevented him from making his rounds. He gave me half of a little dried beef which he had in his pocket. He encouraged everyone and said we had crossed the worst peak and it was only a few more days to Moukung.

'To avoid enemy bombers, we arose at midnight and began climbing the next peak. It rained, then snowed, and the fierce wind whipped our bodies, and more men died of cold and exhaustion.

'The last peak in the range, which we estimated to be eighty *li* (twenty-seven miles) from base to summit, was terrible. Hundreds of our men died there. They would sit down to rest or relieve themselves, and never get up. All along the route we kept reaching down to pull men to their feet only to find that they were already dead.' [10]

The most detailed reminiscence of this, the cruellest hazard of the Long March, was penned by Colonel Chang Kuo-hua, the orderly to the head of the Supply Section of the Third Red Army Corps. Already ill when he crossed the Tatu, Colonel Chang worsened during the days immediately prior to the assault on Great Snow Mountain with bad vomiting and diarrhoea. He ate nothing for several days. But he insisted on not being left behind, and set out with a stick: a comrade carried his rifle. He tells the story:

'Early next morning, the bugle sounded. The troops began to advance towards the mountain. Clinging to their sticks, the men climbed steadily up the narrow, twisting goat track. Soon the sun rose. Looking up from the base, we could see the summit of the mountain glittering and the troops advancing like a dragon wriggling heavenward. We started, the weather was cool and the ground relatively flat and I had a comparatively easy time of it. As time went on, however, it grew worse with me. After covering a certain distance, I had to purge, and then I had to have a rest. Gradually I dropped behind. Clenching my teeth, I clambered up. When I reached a great pine tree, I felt my head spinning and could not move another inch. So I sat down to rest. Li Chiu-sheng, the young carrier, two chests suspended from his shoulder pole, came swinging past me. We used to make fun of each other. Seeing me in such a state, he called out: "How now, Chang Kuo-hua! Let us have a competition. Step on it! To the other side of the mountain and meet the comrades of the Fourth Front Army!"

'I felt greatly troubled. Who didn't want to go! But damn my legs! At this very moment they just wouldn't move. "Come on, get up," I prompted myself. "Just go slowly. Almost all comrades of our unit have gone ahead."

'I pressed at the stick with great effort and stood up, only to sink down immediately. Looking up, I saw I had made only a trifling progress on the steep slope. Alas, would this state continue? I was in a dilemma when the groom, Old Wang, came up leading a dark brown mule. At a glance I knew it belonged to my chief.

' "Get up on it! This section of the road is reasonably level," said Old Wang.

'I hesitated and made no answer. Frankly, how I longed to get a lift on a mule. But how could I ride? I had nothing on me. The Supply Section head must be very tired carrying my rifle. Instead of taking care of him, I had let him take care of me. I looked at the mule, then at Old Wang, and for a long moment could not utter a word.

'Old Wang seemed to have guessed what was on my mind. "Hey, you!" he urged. "I have brought the mule at the order of the Supply Section head. Mount quickly. You'll be all right after we've scaled this mountain. The Fourth Front Army is waiting for us on the other side and there'll probably be a base hospital there."

'My tears flowed. Old Wang helped me mount the mule and I continued to advance uphill.

'The higher we went, the narrower the path became. The slope was getting steeper, the air thinner. It was very dangerous to ride, so I dismounted and, grasping the tail of the mule, continued to struggle upwards. On this path rising through the sombre, virgin forest, were several other comrades who like me, were ill. They climbed, gritting their teeth, following closely the footsteps of the comrade in front.

'At eleven a.m. we had, after much difficulty, reached to within six *li* of the summit when the bugle sounded for a rest. All sat down on the side of the path. Some ran down to the gully to drink water. Others took out their rations and began to eat. We would give the final battle to the snow mountain after we had eaten.

'Though this section was not long, every step demanded the strength of my whole body. I purged less frequently, but I felt awfully weak, as if I had not eaten for a long, long time. The air suddenly became thinner when we were some two hundred metres from the summit. Breathing became more difficult. With head spinning and eyes blurred, I could hardly stand, let alone go forward. "Now I am done for," I said to myself. But immediately thought: "Am I going to be defeated when the summit is in sight? I must not fall, for that would be the end of everything."

'I controlled myself with the utmost effort. I was struggling desperately when, luckily, comrades from the signal squad came up and gave me a hand. Just at this moment there was a thud from behind, followed by an outcry. I looked back. A carrier had fallen to the track, pole and all. Steadying my gaze, I saw that it was the young comrade Li Chiu-sheng who, so short a time before, had challenged me to a competition. Tears stood in the eyes of my comrades around. I was racked with grief. We had lost another close comrade-in-arms.

'The Supply Section head, hearing what happened, quickly hurried back and, with tear-filled eyes, buried Li Chiu-sheng's body. The two chests left by Li Chiu-sheng suspended from his shoulder pole, he came toward me, took me by my arm and walked with me.

'Without warning there came a blast of wind. The sun was quickly shrouded by a heavy black cloud, and soon the whole sky darkened. Rain, intermixed with hail, came pattering down. The storm gathered force, and hailstones, the size of potatoes, beat down on us. The men covered their heads with basins, or shrouded them in quilts. I struggled with all my might to fold up two sheepskins. One I gave to my chief; the other I wrapped over my head.

'Eventually the storm passed. Strewn on the track were ice and snow which were soon trodden into a lane as deep as a man's height as the troops proceeded. On both sides of this lane lay numerous dear comrades who, for the future of the people of the motherland, had struggled until they breathed their last. They sleep everlasting on this snow mountain. "The nation's heroes are immortal."

'My chief, pole on his shoulder, leading me by the hand, continued to advance towards the last stretch.

' "It is no easy task to carry on the revolution," he kept saying to me. "And aren't those comrades who now lie on the roadside heroes who sacrificed themselves for it?"

'As he talked, I saw his eyes redden. A few hot tears fell on my hand.

' "We are still alive," he went on, "we mustn't slacken our effort. We must take up the cause of the martyrs and continue to struggle."

'Hearing his words I was too moved for speech. Though I had not eaten for days and was racked by illness, I was a Communist. I was still quite young. But so long as I had one breath left in me, I would exert my last ounce of strength to scale the mountain. Gritting my teeth, I climbed and climbed and at last was at the summit.

'The Supply Section head gave a happy laugh. "Ha-ha! No matter how high the Chiachin Mountain, it could never restrain the firm will of our heroes. Now, Chang Kuo-hua, you have triumphed; you have made it!"

'Of course, now that I had reached the mountain top, I was overjoyed. But I was absolutely exhausted. Everywhere were snow and hailstones. There was a structure as high as a table, piled with stones. Here, I thought, I would rest. I was on the point of sitting down when I found myself being pushed, and I ran staggering downhill for thirty or forty paces. When I halted I looked around; it was my chief who had pushed me.

' "Now you can sit down and rest," he said with a smile. "But I could not let you rest at the summit."

'So saying, he trudged off to take care of other comrades.

'I looked at his retreating figure with gratitude. Then I leaned against a rock to rest. Shoving a handful of snow into my mouth, gradually I felt better. The mountain was wrapped in mist. The sun shone brightly at the summit. I rose, and supporting myself on my stick, walked slowly downhill, leaving the lofty snow mountain behind me.' [11]

Mao wrote a poem a few months later which captured some of
the memories of these grim mountains of the Kunlun range:

> Towering aloft
>   above the earth,
> Great Kunlun,
>   you have witnessed
>   all that was fairest
>   in the human world.
> As they fly across the sky
>   the three million dragons
>   of white jade
> Freeze you with piercing cold.
>
> In the days of summer
>   your melting torrents
> Fill streams and rivers
>   till they overflow,
> Changing men
>   into fish and turtles.
> What man can pass judgement
>   on all the good and evil
> You have done
>   these thousand autumns?
>
> But today
>   I say to you, Kunlun,
> You don't need your great height,
>   you don't need all that snow!
> If I could lean on the sky
>   I would draw my sword
> And cut you in three pieces.
> One I would send to Europe,
> One to America,
> And one we would keep in China.
> Thus would a great peace
>   reign through the world,
> For all the world
>   would share your warmth and cold.[12]

In these high mountain districts the Communists continued to encounter minority nationalities and to suffer at their hands. Tung Pi-wu – 'Old Tung' – told Agnes Smedley that after passing over the great mountains:

'When we finally reached a valley and found a cluster of tribal houses, we gathered around and rejoiced at the mere sight of human habitation. The tribespeople had fled because we were Chinese, and centuries of cruel oppression had engendered in them fear and hatred of every Chinese. We had a number of Lolo tribesmen with us, but they also could not understand the tribal language in these areas.

'I lost track of time, but I think it was middle or late June when we finally reached a broad valley dotted with many tribal villages of huts or black yurts made of yak wool. Here were great fields of barley, two breeds of wheat, millet and peas, and herds of pigs, yak, sheep and goats. We established such friendly relations as we could with the tribespeople and bought food from them. We paid for our food with national currency.

'By that time we had so many sick and exhausted men that our main forces decided to rest for a week while Peng Teh-huai led eleven regiments ahead to establish contact with our Fourth Front Red Army in the Moukung, Lianghokou, Lifan and Maohsien districts. The Fourth Front Red Army had occupied these areas for a number of months, but there were still many mountains and rivers to cross before we reached it. The mountains were not so terrible as those behind us, but the whole territory ahead was peopled with fierce Fan tribes who fought every step of our advance.' [13]

General Chu Teh ordered the Red Army to be 'kind and courteous to the tribespeople'. But this was a difficult discipline to follow when the route was dotted with corpses of Communist soldiers who had straggled behind, exhausted from the march and the fighting, and been murdered by tribesmen. Agnes Smedley asked Chou how he dealt with such a situation. His laconic reply was:

'When attacked, we drove the tribal warriors away, but we tried not to kill.' [14]

One of the soldiers in the Red Army vanguard, this time com-

manded by Peng Teh-huai, described how the Fan tribesmen tried
to thwart their reunion with the Fourth Front Army:

'For four days we fought Fan tribesmen in the Black Water
River region and finally reached a shabby little village called
Weiku. The people had evacuated and destroyed the rope suspension bridge over the river. They took up positions on high,
precipitous cliffs directly behind Weiku and rolled huge boulders
down the mountainside against us. Peng had to send troops to
drive them away.

'Everywhere from the cliffs and mountains we heard the tribal
horns calling men to battle: WUNG-G-G-! WUNG-G-G-G-G
WUNG-G-G-G-G-G-G-G!

'Our troops had begun building a pontoon bridge when we saw
a column of armed men coming down from the hills on the far
shore, running and shouting, but the roar of the river was so great
that we could not hear them. One of them wrapped a message
around a stone and hurled it across to us. It read:

' "We're Fourth Front Red Army troops. Forty li up the river at
Inien is a rope suspension bridge where you can cross."

'On the way to Inien we passed through empty tribal villages
where the Fan tribesmen again hurled boulders down from overhanging cliffs. The river at Inien was wider than at Weiku and
the rope suspension bridge had been destroyed. Again we saw
marching men, and when they reached the bank a Fan guide who
was with them threw a message across the river to us. It was from
Hsu Hsiang-chien.

'We all marched back to Weiku where our engineers constructed a pontoon bridge and we crossed the Black Water River
and united with our comrades. We embraced, we sang and
wept.' 15

Chapter 18

Chilly Reunion

THE ordinary soldier may have been delighted by the reunion at Moukung, but the two rival leaders and their respective lieutenants must have had the gravest misgivings. Chang Kuo-tao represented at this moment Mao Tse-tung's strongest challenger for the leadership of the Chinese Communist Party. The two men, both participants in the C.C.P.'s First Inaugural Congress and both, therefore, to be counted among the Party's 'founding fathers', had first met seventeen years before at Peita – Peking University. Chang was a radical undergraduate, Mao a library assistant. They met again in Shanghai at the First Party Congress in 1921, and in Canton at the Third Party Congress in 1923. It was on this latter occasion that the first known conflict between them is recorded. Chang Kuo-tao criticized the Chen Tu-hsiu leadership at that Congress, largely on account of its handling of the trade union question. Mao voted for Chen, his old mentor, and against Chang.

Chang had plunged into proletarian work, and organized the Peking–Wuhan railway workers' strike in 1923. The potential difference in views between Mao and himself can be guessed from a typical passage from an article by Chang Kuo-tao at that time: 'The peasants take no interest in politics. . . . All they care about is having a true Son of Heaven to rule them and a peaceful bumper year.'[1] It is 'almost certain', in one historian's view,[2] that Mao and Chang met again at the Fifth Congress in 1927, but that must have been the last confrontation before this highly-charged encounter in the unlikely foothills of Tibet.

After the setbacks of 1927 Chang went to the U.S.S.R. with the other Party leaders, and at the Sixth Congress in Moscow in 1928 he spoke against the Li Li-san–Chou En-lai coalition as well as against the unfortunate Chu Chiu-pai. He came back to China in 1931 and the Party Central Committee assigned him to the Oyuwan soviet area, the stronghold in the Hupeh–Honan–Anhwei border districts which had been established by Hsu Hsiang-chien's First Red Army in 1929, with a claimed population by then of two million. Chang's task was to form a branch of the Central Bureau of Soviet Areas. He continued to fill important Party posts, was elected to the Central Executive Committee of the All-China Central Soviet Government (with headquarters at Juiching in Kiangsi) and served as one of the two Vice-Chairmen under Mao's chairmanship. But he remained physically at the Oyuwan base as the political counterpart of Hsu Hsiang-chien – whose army had been renamed as the Fourth Front Army. His relation to Hsu corresponded with Mao's relation to Chu Teh.

In 1932 the Fourth Front Army began seriously to threaten the strategic city of Wuhan, attempting to cut China's only north–south railway link and to blockade the Yangtze River. The Kuomintang sent a strong force to repel this threat, and although it was defeated at the night battle of the Liu Lin River the casualties were so high and the remaining strength of the enemy so overwhelming that the Fourth decided to pull out. It had probably lost almost two-thirds of its peak force of 100,000. At a meeting in Hsinchi some spoke for staying to have it out decisively with the enemy, but the final order was to evacuate the Oyuwan soviet, to march west to find a more secure base territory, and to leave Hsu Hai-tung behind to lead a rearguard of local Communist guerrilla units.[3] Foreshadowing what happened to the First Front Army two years later, the Fourth in October 1932 had to break out of a Kuomintang encirclement, escape enemy bombers and nurse its civilians and its wounded through a harassing retreat. Its strength at this moment was officially claimed to be 50,000, but Chang Kuo-tao himself later estimated that only 16,000 men set out on the escape to the west.[4]

At Tsayang the Kuomintang trapped the Fourth Army on the bank of the Han River, but the Communists managed to escape by night to the north after a battle in which the enemy came within fifty yards of the Red Army HQ. 2,000 Red soldiers died in this engagement, and another thousand wounded had to be left behind. The leaders decided to aim for northern Hupeh by way of south-west Honan and the Shensi border region. The chief concern of the local militia in the districts they now went through was bandits, and the Red Army was able to come to terms with the militia commanders by promising not to stay more than one night, to pay cash for all food consumed or goods damaged, and not to fight.

Another Kuomintang trap at Menchuan Gate was evaded by the capture of three enemy spies who led the Communists to the only escape route, a small mountain track leading to the Shansi border. The Fourth Army had to ascend the track in single file.

It was now late autumn and the weather was turning. The Fourth soldiers were still in light summer uniform and food was short. Chang and Hsu decided to go on to northern Szechuan, where the Kuomintang forces would not dare to pursue because of the poor relations between the Central Government in Nanking and the Szechuan provincial warlords. They jettisoned some of their weapons to free thirty horses which could then take some of the hundred wounded on this last stage to Szechuan, and the rest of the wounded were carried by their fit comrades.

The Fourth thus arrived at Tungchiang in Szechuan early in 1933 with only 9,000 men, having lost in its eighty-day march about two-fifths of its soldiers and weapons. A new soviet base was formed there, with a local government to organize land distribution, taxation and various social reforms for a population of about one million. A *modus vivendi* was negotiated with the Szechuanese provincial forces in the area. Chang tried to convince Tien Tsung-yao, the most belligerent local warlord, that the Communists would stay only temporarily in Szechuan and would go back to fight Chiang Kai-shek in central China in the spring. Tien attacked the Fourth Army all the same, but was defeated.

The C.C.P. Central Committee did not view the Fourth Army's withdrawal from the Oyuwan base with favour. They branded it as 'rightist escapism' and sent messages reproving its leaders. Chang explains that 'because we did not dare to rely on our secret code, we seldom communicated with the Central Committee by radio'. In Honan province the Fourth Army received an order to stop retreating to the west, but only on arrival in Szechuan did

Chang send a telegram to say that the Fourth Army was now prepared to set up a soviet base. The C.C.P. asked for more details.

The Fourth Army radioed its local government programme to the Central Committee and received for its pains a lengthy exhortation to go all out for confiscation of land and redistribution to poor peasants instead of merely abolishing taxes and reducing rents to help the latter, and also to refrain from setting up a people's government in case this encouraged others to retreat to the western interior. In other words, the leaders in Shanghai or Juichin disapproved of policy towards landlords and were still resentful of his abandonment of the Oyuwan base. They openly threatened Chang with dismissal: 'They issued us a serious warning,' as Chang himself puts it, 'that I would be trusted as the fully-authorized representative of the Central Committee to direct all Party, government and military operations if our wrong policies were corrected, but that otherwise the Central Committee would consider the necessity of changing the leadership. This order, though not entirely unexpected, greatly surprised and excited us.'

Chang explained the situation to his colleagues at Tungchiang, arguing that the immediate task was to defeat Tien Tsung-yao's armies which were threatening the Communists and were three times their number. They would have to be lured into the soviet area in the time-honoured guerrilla style, to be destroyed part by part. Chang ridiculed the Central Committee's haggling over the use of the term 'soviet' and asked why on earth they should not set up a Szechuan People's Government? He apparently swayed the majority of his colleagues to disregard the Central Committee, and by then those who had doubted the whole strategy of marching west had lost some of their misgivings in the course of having to work hard to get the new base going. The immediate challenge of Szechuan kept second thoughts and dwelling on past mistakes to a minimum.

But eventually the pressure of the Szechuan provincial armies, stiffened after the beginning of 1935 by the Kuomintang military mission from Nanking, dislodged Chang Kuo-tao and the Fourth Front Army from its new base in the Pachung region, as has already been described. In April it crossed the Chialing River at Tsanghsi and zigzagged along the northern border of Szechuan to reach Moukung in June, only weeks before the First Front Army arrived there.

The Central Committee, whose centre of gravity was now with the First Front Army on the Long March, was presented with a further grievance against Chang in that, having already fled too precipitately from the valuable Oyuwan base, he proceeded to pull out from the north Szechuan soviet at the very moment when it might have become the centre for a combined Communist force, including the First Army, to take Szechuan province entirely over. Furthermore, the Fourth's retreat to Sungpan left the First Front Army open to the unfettered and undistracted attentions of the enemy. Mao Tse-tung's condemnation, delivered in 1945 when his victory over his rivals for the Party leadership was consummated, was that, 'As for the Chang Kuo-tao line, which once dominated the Hupeh–Honan–Anhwei and the Szechuan–Shenshi areas, it was not only a "Left" line of the general type but was also characterized by a particularly serious form of warlordism and by flightism in the face of enemy attacks.' Chang Kuo-tao afterwards claimed that he deliberately left the base and crossed the Chialing River in April in order to distract the Kuomintang from following the First Front Army into Sikang, but this does not carry much conviction. Another source says the Tsunyi Politburo conference telegraphed the Fourth Army to move west across the Chialing to help its plans.[5]

On 20 July the main forces of the First Army marched into the village of Erhokou (or Lianghokou), near Moukung, and united with their comrades of the Fourth. It was pouring with rain, but posters and banners had been put up all over the village, and a speakers' platform had been prepared. Chu Teh and Mao Tse-tung began a series of exhaustive talks with the officers of the Fourth, including its Commander, Hsu Hsiang-chien. Then they came out in the heavy rain, to greet the arrival of Chang Kuo-tao himself. One of the Long Marchers afterwards gave this description of the meeting:

'The Fourth Front Red Army had about 50,000 men. They were big, brave fellows from Szechuan, Honan, and Hupeh. They were poor peasants or former slaves, and anything could have been done with them. They had fought with great heroism and they had suffered. Chang Kuo-tao had taken good care of them physically – they were well fed and warmly clothed – but he had done nothing to educate them generally or politically. Chang had been appointed political commissar of this army by the Central Committee of our party. His duty was clear: to develop the troops politically to prevent the army from becoming an instrument of any ambitious military leader.

'Chang Kuo-tao had transformed the Fourth Front Army into his own personal instrument. He had – following a good old Kuomintang custom – built up a powerful clique of officers as his personal followers. He had organized the army on the Kuomintang pattern and even introduced the same officer rank. He had established special privileges for himself and his clique – the best clothing and food, for example – and kept thirty horses for himself and his bodyguard.

'Of course Mao and Chu and a few other commanders in the Central Red Army each had a horse. Mao had to ride because he was sick, and he had one bodyguard. Chu Teh also had one bodyguard. Except when he inspected army units, Chu Teh gave his horse to others to ride. We often protested because he had to direct the whole army during the Long March, but he said nature had given him a particularly strong body and that other men needed his horse.

'Chang Kuo-tao had contempt for the whole Central Red Army because we were so ragged and battered and were now numerically weaker than his army. Before leaving Kiangsi, we had fought a million enemy troops for months. Our men went on the Long March directly from the battlefield. In the nine months of fighting and marching across the plains, rivers, and mountains, we had suffered heavy losses. We had left most of our sick and wounded with the peasants; we had also left companies along the way to develop partisan warfare, so that we had only 45,000 men left when we reached Moukung.

'We had approached Moukung as men approach an oasis in a desert. Because of this we were appalled at the attitude of Chang Kuo-tao and his officer clique. They acted like rich men meeting poor relatives.

'Chang Kuo-tao's arrogant attitude was clear from the very

beginning. When we held our unification meeting at Erhokou, he came riding in with his mounted bodyguard of thirty men, like an actor coming onto the stage. Chu and Mao rushed forward to meet him, and he waited for them to approach him. He didn't even meet them halfway. General Chu's speech to the assembled troops praised Chang Kuo-tao's long revolutionary record, but when Chang spoke he introduced Chu Teh to his army merely as "a man who has struggled with us for eight years".

'Our party alone could determine the policies and programme, strategy and tactics, of all the Red Armies. They had been decided on the Long March to north China. The guiding Politburo had called a conference at Erhokou, following the unification meeting, where our continued march northward was to be mapped. Despite all this, in his speech to the assembled troops Chang Kuo-tao announced his own private programme, stating that the vast borderland regions of Sikang and western Szechuan were an ideal place to establish a soviet base and "build a new world".

'We had not made the Long March in order to stick in the high Tibetan–Chinese borderland while the Japanese continued lopping off province after province, and Kuomintang traitors continued surrendering.

'Of course, in every great revolutionary upheaval, all kinds of problems arise and mistakes are made. Problems must be solved and mistakes corrected. The mistakes of the Fourth Front Red Army leadership were therefore discussed frankly at the conference of the Politburo. Chang Kuo-tao, however, was not a man to accept criticism or admit mistakes readily. He was even arrogant enough to point to the good condition of his 50,000 troops and to the losses and poor condition of ours, by which he implied that he was the only man capable of leading the Red Army.' [6]

This account accurately reflects the mood of bitterness in which Mao and Chu approached this fateful encounter. Chang Kuo-tao's own account of the meeting is somewhat different. He describes his journey from Maohsien to Moukung to meet Mao Tse-tung in some detail:

'There were many Tibetan settlements along the route. Rivers and streams flowed swiftly, and the means of communication were bamboo chain bridges, wooden bridges, leather boats and suspension bridges. To the west of Wenchuang lay thick virgin forest where a Szechuanese warlord operated a sawmill. The timbers were cut at will and scattered untidily over the riverbank and the roadside, so that I had to make a detour through a jungle path.

'The Tibetans who believed in Lamaistic Buddhism appeared to be civilized. Their houses were mostly three-storeyed. The ground floors, dark and dirty and stuffy, were used as cattle-yards and they smelt vile. People lived on the first floors in windowless, airless rooms, and up in the second floors were shrines with Buddha figures and scriptures, tidy and clean. The Tibetans had plenty of green grain, cheese and clothing in their living rooms, but articles of iron were scarce and were regarded as highly precious.

'Sometimes a church would be seen, often run by foreign priests. Near Lifan there was a huge stone church which was considered the biggest building in the region, and its vicar was a foreigner who had lived there for a long time. When our Thirtieth Army halted there, he left and avoided meeting us. The church owned an apiary, some land and a handsome mill. There were big heaps of grain and a collection of farm tools inside the church, and the foreign priest had boxes of oranges from California and apples and wine.

'There were even some Japanese here, running photographic studios and trading in opium and morphia.

'But I did not linger on the road. I was in a hurry to reach Moukung. With Huang Chao and ten cavalry guards I plunged through thick forest, scaled high mountains and cliffs for three days to reach Fupien, a small town of about thirty families some thirty miles north of Mao Tse-tung's and Chu Teh's temporary headquarters at Moukung.

'At about five o'clock one June afternoon Mao Tse-tung was at the head of a party of forty or fifty men, including Politburo members and senior Party workers and Red Army officers, to welcome us on the roadside a mile out of Fupien. On seeing them I alighted from my horse and rushed to embrace them and shake them by the hand. The reunion after such long suffering made our hearts bubble with excitement.

'Mao Tse-tung stood on a platform and made a warm speech of congratulation and welcome. I replied, paying tribute to the

Chinese Communist Party and expressing great concern for the First Front Army after its struggle against so many difficulties.

'Then we walked, Mao Tse-tung and I and the others, shoulder-to-shoulder towards Fupien, talking and laughing and exchanging stories . . .'[7]

According to Chang, Peng Teh-huai's III Army Corps of the First Front Army, Tung Chen-tang's V Army Corps and Lo Ping-hui's XII Army Corps were then stationed at Chokochi to the north of Fupien, while Lin Piao's I Army Corps was at Moukung. The Fourth Front Army took over the responsibility of keeping guard, with its Thirtieth Army to the south of Moukung to check the pursuing troops from Yaan, its Ninth and Thirty-first Armies engaging the enemy in northern and north-eastern Szechuan, and its Fourth Army near Sungpan blocking another approaching enemy force.

'On the first night,' Chang Kuo-tao's memoirs continue, 'during dinner, somebody advised me not to talk about the Long March or the Tsunyi Conference. Mao Tse-tung, who as a Hunanese enjoyed the taste of chilli, expounded a theory that chilli-loving people were natural revolutionaries. But Po Ku, a native of Kiangsu where chillis are not taken in food, refuted Mao's theory.

'After dinner, Chu Teh walked back with me and we had a long talk, lasting till dawn, in his quarters. He told me not to attach too much importance to the Tsunyi Conference. It had been held at a time when the Central Committee and the First Front Army were in pressing difficulty. Mao had offered an initiative at a moment of dilemma, and his suggestions for guerrilla strategy were adopted. So he was elected to assume responsibility in the Party and thus resolve the dispute within its leadership. Chu Teh held that the main question ahead was a military one, namely what kind of strategy and field operations should be adopted now that the two armies had joined together. It was not, said Chu, a good occasion to review the Central Committee's work or discuss the prospects of the Chinese Soviet Republic. He evidently intended to hint that I would be wise not to bring up any political questions.'[8] Whatever reservations one might entertain about Chang's belated testimony, this particular passage carries a ring of authenticity.

Chang Kuo-tao regarded himself as having the initiative, in view of the better condition of his own army, and as the C.C.P.'s 'expert' in Szechuan, having for two consecutive years operated a full-scale soviet government there. His Fourth Army now comprised mostly new Szechuanese recruits organized around a hard core of Oyuwan veterans (in contrast to Mao's First Army, which was a veteran and seasoned force well used to operating outside its various provinces of origin). Chang had already created a 'Government of the North-west Confederation' intended to include all the minority nationality areas in this part of China, whereas the Long Marchers under Mao Tse-tung, cheated of their plan to set up soviets in the Kweichow–Yunnan–Szechuan region, saw their destination as northern China where the fight against Japan and the Kuomintang could be resumed.

The official Communist, in other words Maoist, histories put the two rival armies at Moukung as almost equal in strength, with 45,000 to 50,000 men each to total almost 100,000 together. Yet Chang Kuo-tao himself subsequently claimed that the First Front Army had lost 80,000 men since leaving Kiangsi, and could boast only 10,000 at Moukung.[9] His own forces he put at 45,000. If the First had really been outnumbered by more than four to one, then the cards would have been decisively stacked against Mao Tse-tung's leadership. It seems much more likely that the two armies were in fact more or less equal in numbers, and Chang's recent memoir raises the question whether perhaps both armies were smaller than the claimed 45,000 each. 50,000 was an incredibly large number to keep together through the vicissitudes of fighting the aboriginal tribes and scaling the Great Snow Mountain. If 45,000 Long Marchers did cross the River of Golden Sand at Chou Ping Fort in May, as Chou En-lai claimed, a certain proportion of them would have been lost or left behind in the ensuing ten weeks.

And could the Fourth Army, for its part, really have kept more than 35,000 Szechuanese recruits[10] from the Pachung area through all the trials of the flight into the unfriendly mountains of the Tibetan border? One is strongly inclined to suspect that each army, First and Fourth, may have been rather below the claimed level. This is a point to which we shall return when considering the numbers which finally reached Shensi at the end of the Long March.

The reunion duly celebrated with public speeches, feasting and rejoicing, the leaders went into private debate in the form of a 'stormy' Politburo conference at Lianghokou. In Chang Kuo-tao's account,[11] the main participants were Mao Tse-tung, who took the chair, Chu Teh, Chou En-lai, Po Ku, Chang Wen-tien, Liu Po-cheng and Chang himself. Mao began by advocating a joint march to the north to the regions bordering on Mongolia, citing the Comintern telegram received just before the Kiangsi base had been abandoned. He argued that Ninghsia was the richest province in the north-west, that its warlord Ma Hung-kwei could be relatively easily resisted and that the Russians might be able to send help through Outer Mongolia. If even Ninghsia could not be held by the combined First and Fourth Armies, then they could retreat into Mongolia until another chance to lead an uprising in China presented itself.

According to Chang, Mao made no reference at this meeting to the idea of marching north to resist the Japanese invaders of China, nor to that of joining forces with the soviet base operated in Shensi by Liu Chih-tan, Kao Kang and Hsu Hai-tung.

Chang opposed Mao's plan. He argued that the combined Communist armies had three choices, as follows:

(1) *The Chuan–Kan–Kang Plan*, to return to northern Szechuan and southern Kansu and seek to re-enter central China and re-assert Communist influence south of the Yangtze. This terrain was far easier than what lay to the north of Moukung, the local warlords' forces were relatively weak by comparison with the combined First and Fourth Front Armies, and there was plenty of grain. But in the event of any setback the only retreat would be into Tibetan Sikang, where food would be extremely scarce.

(2) *The Mao Plan*, to move north into proximity with Outer Mongolia. The north-west was more open to guerrilla warfare than the central parts of China. But it was also less well-endowed with food and would give the Communists little cover from enemy bombers' attack. Besides, the march to Ninghsia would take the Red Army over most treacherous country, notably the notorious

Grasslands, and it was said that the Kuomintang had thrown a huge force across the northern route – Chang spoke of 100,000.

(3) *The Chang Plan*, to retreat further west towards Sinkiang, whence the Soviet Union would also be able to lend support, via Tienchuan and Tachienlu (or Kangting) and Sikang. (Li Teh says that this had earlier been proposed by Mao, but dropped before Chang's arrival.)

Mao defended his own plan, declaring that to return to Sikang, whose inhabitants could not afford to sustain the Red Army, would be to risk being caught 'like a turtle in a jar', while to march to Sinkiang would be to stray too far from China. No doubt both protagonists realized that Chang might not be able to retain the loyalty of his new Szechuanese recruits if they were ordered north out of range of their native province, whilst Mao might be forced into second place if the next act of the Red Army's saga were to be played out in or near Szechuan, where Chang's authority was already established. Mao later confessed that this confrontation with Chang Kuo-tao was the 'darkest moment of his life', when the break-up of the C.C.P., and even civil war among the Chinese Communists 'hung in the balance'. Chen Tan afterwards said that Chang's mistakes were to defy both the Internationals *and* Mao, and also to press his claims for the Secretary-Generalship of the Party.[12]

Mao's First Front Army colleagues and the rest of the Kiangsi-based Politburo voted for him, and Chang's proposals were rejected. The policy of continuing the march north was confirmed.

Meanwhile Chiang Kai-shek's troops continued to press in towards the Communists from the east and the north. Chang Kuo-tao's argument all along was that Kuomintang strength to the north was too great to contest without considerable danger, and according to the Maoists he refused to allow the Fourth to act as a vanguard to open up the northern route by Sungpan. One of Chu Teh's supporters explained: 'Since the Fourth Front Army was rested and in good condition, General Chu proposed that it open the northern route by taking the Sungpan region, thus seizing positions of great strategic importance. Chang refused outright, saying the enemy defence works were too powerful.'[13]

So a compromise was reached by which the united armies were reorganized into a West Column and an East Column. The former comprised the bulk of the Fourth Front Army (notably the Thirty-first and Thirty-second Armies) together with the First Front Army's IX and V Corps, all under the military command of Chu Teh with Chang as Political Commissar. The East Column contained the bulk of the First Front Army (notably Lin Piao's I and Peng Teh-huai's III Army Corps), complemented by the Thirtieth Army from Hsu Hsiang-chien's command, and Mao was effectively its leader. The two rival armies were thus divided, but Mao's was preponderant in the East Column and Chang's in the West. Each leader, to put it another way, gave hostages to the other. This compromise may have been the suggestion of Chu Teh, or at least the product of his persuasion.[14]

Mao's troops, finding Sungpan under the control of the enemy (in this case Hu Tsung-nan), camped at Chokechi, sent out reconnaissance units ahead and summoned the generals and leading Party officials to debate the next step. According to Chang Kuo-tao's account,[15] there were still differences of opinion over the right of the C.C.P.'s Central Military Council, which of course Mao Tse-tung controlled, to give orders to the Fourth Army and its units. Each rival army tended to scorn the other's achievements and to criticize its organizational methods. Chang's lieutenants put a number of questions to their opposite numbers in the First Front Army. Why was the Central Committee in such a hurry to march north? Why did it want to abandon the Moukung base and throw away all hope of developing the Communist movement in the southern half of China? Po Ku and Chang Wen-tien, according to Chang Kuo-tao, asked their comrades of the Fourth in return why they followed 'such an old opportunist as Chang Kuo-tao' instead of the Central Committee.

Chang Kuo-tao supports the view that Chu Teh played an important conciliatory role at this juncture. Chu, he says, was particularly distressed about the bad relations between the two armies, blaming it partly on the fact that the decision at Lianghokou to march north was taken too hurriedly, before the two armies had arrived at any understanding, and partly on the actions of 'some elements in the Central Committee' who had voiced ill-judged criticism of the Fourth Army and stirred up passions in consequence. Fearing that the impasse would hinder joint military operations, Chu proposed that the Red Army G.H.Q. be strengthened by the appointment of Chang Kuo-tao as Chief Political Commissar of the combined armies, serving alongside Chu Teh who would remain commander-in-chief. Strategy would be first evolved in the G.H.Q., under this plan, and then submitted to the Central Military Council and the Politburo for 'examination and execution'. Chang says that he accepted this new position as Chief Political Commissar, implying that Chu Teh's plan was implemented.

Without more information it is difficult to interpret this move. Was Chu Teh tired of playing second fiddle to Mao Tse-tung in the military as well as the political sphere? Did he hope to gain more room for manoeuvre by bringing Chang Kuo-tao more closely into the highest echelons of military decision-making? Did he dream of playing off the political rivals – Mao and Chang – against one another? Did he secretly prefer Chang's military counsel at this stage, either because of the hazards of the Grasslands and the Kuomintang divisions to the north or because he yearned to stay in his native south-west?

All these questions could very likely be answered in the affirmative, although it is also conceivable that Chu Teh took Mao into his confidence all along, and that Mao hoped to retain effective control through his relationship with Chu, or that Chu genuinely saw himself as the only possible mediator in a power struggle that threatened to defeat the Communists' entire chances of survival. After all, Chu Teh, as the most famous Szechuanese Red General alive, was presumably able to appeal above Chang's head to the native Szechuanese who formed three-quarters of the latter's Fourth Front Army. He was the one man who could plausibly build up a common loyalty among the two rival armies. Some further light on Chu's inner motives and ambitions will be shed by the sequel.

Chang's story is that Mao sabotaged Chu Teh's new organizational structure by continuing, as Chairman of the Military Council, to see all documents, take all the decisions and pass them on to G.H.Q. for implementation. In Chang's view Mao ought under the new scheme to have left the day-to-day running of the army to G.H.Q. and contented himself with merely checking and approving important G.H.Q. decisions. He should on no account have continued issuing direct military orders. Chang does not say that Chu Teh clashed with Mao Tse-tung on this account, but he does state that Liu Po-cheng, Chu Teh's senior lieutenant and fellow-Szechuanese, registered disapproval of Mao's attitude.

When Mao's East Column reached the Tibetan village of Maoerhkai, some seventy miles from Sungpan, it struck camp for three weeks to rest and prepare for the assault on the dreaded swampy Grasslands which provided the Red Army's only northward escape from the enemy. It also had to wait for Peng Teh-huai's vanguard force to report back from its assignment to collect food in the near-by districts and organize the local tribespeople into People's Governments which would be friendly towards the Communists and furnish them with help and supplies. This halt gave them the opportunity to try once again to resolve the tensions of the inner leadership, and another Conference of the Politburo was convened at the end of July.

The meeting was held in the pavilion of a Buddhist lamasery at Shavo, about seven miles from Maoerhkai. Mao Tse-tung, Chu Teh, Chang Kuo-tao, Po Ku and Chang Wen-tien attended, but Chang tells us that Chou En-lai and Wang Chia-hsiang were absent because of illness, that Teng Fa and Kai Feng attended as 'observers' and that Wang Shou-tao acted as recorder.[16]

According to Chang, Mao presented a resolution at this conference which endorsed the Central Committee's political line since the Tsunyi Conference as correct, praised the Red Army for its achievements, and called on all Party members and Red Army soldiers to unite firmly behind the Central Committee's leadership. Chang says that he was the only one present who had not already been given a sight of the text of this resolution. It was proffered, in other words, as a *fait accompli*. He nevertheless spoke against it, declaring that it was just possible that the political line of the Central Committee was misguided, that the Comintern was mistaken and that the Red Army's military operations were misconceived. As circumstances changed, so policies might have to be modified. It was undeniable, after all, that the soviet movement in south-central China had failed, apparently from insufficient popular support, and this needed to be analysed and explained. Surely it would be wise to summon a larger conference of high-ranking cadres who could speak out their minds, expose their grievances and reach a new consensus in the combined armies? While they were about it, why not bring in some new blood to the Central Committee?

Mao rebutted Chang's exposition point by point. The policy regarding the soviet movement had been laid down by the Comintern and approved by the C.C.P. at its last (Sixth) Congress, and it would in the end succeed. The Central Committee was not the plaything of individual units of the Red Army, but was responsible to China as a whole, including not only the First and Fourth Front Armies but also the Second Front Army and the various secret Communist organizations in the 'white areas'. Its political line could not, therefore, be reviewed by the First and the Fourth Armies alone. Finally, in the midst of pressing military operations, it was inappropriate to call a meeting of senior Party workers. In such emergency conditions on the March the authority of the Central Committee had to prevail above all else. Mao thus used against Chang some of the lines of argument he had himself resisted when staking his claim for the leadership at Tsunyi seven months before. Of course his resolution was passed.

Chang Kuo-tao criticizes the Maoerhkai conferees, including himself, for not really going into the political issues at all. The question of combating Japanese aggression was mentioned, but 'no one suggested that the existing policy of soviet bases be transformed into a programme for a national united front. We hardly believed our salvation could be assured by reference to resisting the Japanese.' The official Party record states that the Politburo on 1 August 1935 at Maoerhkai adopted an 'Appeal to Fellow-countrymen Concerning Resistance to Japan and National Salvation,' in which a United Front was advocated. But the best view is that this appeal originated in Moscow and was inserted into the record after the Long Marchers caught up with Comintern developments again.[17]

Next day, in Chang Kuo-tao's account, his supporter Cheng Chang-hao invited Chang Wen-tien for a talk, hoping to persuade him to change his mind. But Chang Wen-tien was offended by a remark of a Fourth Front Army commander who openly expressed impatience with the Central Committee and his lack of confidence in it. Chang Kuo-tao then tried to talk Wang Chia-hsiang into becoming an intermediary in the argument: 'Wang's colon had been pierced by shrapnel from a bomb in Kiangsi. He took opium to gain relief from the pain and had become addicted to it. He assured me that he would try to patch up the quarrel, and asked me not to criticize the political line of the Central Committee for the time being since it might be reviewed in the days ahead. But I did not hear any more of his intervention . . .'

The Kuomintang troops were still pressing up the mountains towards the Red Army's position. Chang says that he took the initiative at the Politburo meeting to suggest that the debate be suspended, the combined armies proceed swiftly to Minhsien and Lengtan in Kansu, and the final decision whether to go north or west from there be postponed. According to him, Mao Tse-tung accepted with alacrity. Be that as it may, the armies did move off after this Maoerhkai conference had failed to resolve the difference between the two political opponents.

But the two columns took different routes and soon found that they were separated by a river which suddenly swelled up into a raging torrent and defied passage.[18] This was the setting for the most baffling mystery of the entire Long March. 'Chang Kuo-tao,' according to one account, 'declared that the river could not be crossed and that the column had no alternative but to turn back into Sikang Province – which was what he intended doing all along! He insisted that Chu Teh and Liu Po-cheng should turn back with him. Both Chu and Liu were Szechuan men whose names were famous throughout west China, and Chang Kuo-tao wanted to use them for his purposes. Chu Teh also had the only radio generator in the army.

'General Chu and Chief of Staff Liu said a crossing of the river could be found and, if that failed, the western column could join the eastern at Maoerhkai and continue the Long March. That same night Chang Kuo-tao brought up special troops of the Fourth

Front Red Army, surrounded General Headquarters, and took Chu Teh and his staff prisoner. Chang ordered Chu Teh to obey two commands:

'The first was that he denounce Mao Tse-tung and cut all relations with him.

'General Chu replied: "You can no more cut me off from Mao than you can cut a man in half."

'Chang's second command was that Chu denounce the party decision to move into north China and begin the anti-Japanese, anti-Chiang war of liberation. General Chu replied:

' "I helped make the decision. I cannot oppose it."

'Chang Kuo-tao said he would give Chu Teh time to think things over, and if he still refused to obey these two orders, he would be shot. Chu replied: "That is within your power. I cannot prevent you. I will not obey your orders!"

'A number of factors prevented Chang Kuo-tao from carrying out his threat. First, there were the Ninth and Fifth Red Army Corps who wanted to take Chu Teh and his staff back to the eastern column. Chang Kuo-tao warned them not to try! Faced with this situation, which would have led to bloody fighting * on the high plateau of Central Asia, Chu Teh and his staff finally turned back with Chang Kuo-tao.' [19]

The official Maoist version of this melodramatic episode is that when the West Column under Chang Kuo-tao and Chu Teh reached Apa (almost on the Chinghai border), Chang rebelled against the Central Committee orders, detained Chu and Liu Po-cheng, took the troops south and 'secretly ordered the two armies of the Fourth Front Army, which had been put under the Right [East] Column, to go south with him and retreat to Tienchuan and Lushan . . .' [20] But Nym Wales was told that Hsu Hsiang-chien's Thirtieth Army, marching through the Grasslands – without the aid of map or compass – walked into a pocket of land

---

* This could have been the 'civil war' of which Mao spoke later to Edgar Snow as the big threat at this time. The inference of this pro-Chu version told to Agnes Smedley is that Chu averted an armed clash between the two Communist armies by agreeing to go with Chang.

which proved to be a *cul-de-sac*, surrounded by impassable swamps. It therefore had to turn back and rejoin Chang's West Column.[21]

Liu Po-cheng's version of the separation is that after the Maoerhkai Politburo meeting:

'It was decided to push north along two routes. The right [east] route was to be taken by an army comprising the First and Third Army Groups of the First Front Army and the Fourth and Thirtieth Armies of the Fourth Front Army. It would be led by the Party's Central Committee and Mao Tse-tung. The left [west] route was to be followed by a combination of the Ninth and Thirty-first Armies of the Fourth Army and the Fifth and Ninth Army Groups of the First Front Army. It would be commanded by Chu Teh and Chang Kuo-tao.

'The right [east] route army waded through the marshlands and drove on towards Pahsi putting one of Hu Tsung-nan's divisions out of action along the Paotso River. The army on the other route set out from Chokechi and moved across the marshlands towards Apa. Upon arrival at Apa, Chang Kuo-tao revealed more evidence of his personal ambitions to split the Party. He cabled the Party's Central Committee, demanding that the whole of the right [east] route army turn southward. The Central Committee sent him several messages trying to correct his mistake of attempting to go south, and pointing out that the only way out was to march north. Later he was even sternly ordered to do so. Chang Kuo-tao, however, defied the Central Committee's instructions and stuck to his erroneous line.' [22]

Chang Kuo-tao's own story, of course, is quite different.[23] He claims that Mao Tse-tung's East Column let the West Column down by rushing ahead through the Grasslands to save its own skin regardless of what happened to its unfortunate colleagues of the Fourth, who through no fault of their own became trapped behind the First. Chang says that his Fourth Front Army, after setting out from Chuachin, north-west of Maoerhkai, to cross the Grasslands and reach Minhsien in Kansu, was brought to a halt by heavy rains flooding the Machu River. This was 'originally a small stream, no more than three feet wide, but now it became swollen to more than ten feet in depth and 300 yards across'. Without boats, and with food running out, the Fourth turned back to Chuachin and sent a radio message to Mao's column ordering it to halt (the H.Q., after all, was with the West Column in the persons of Chu Teh and Liu Po-cheng).

But Mao took the I and III Army Corps on to the north, the route which had been opened up by Hsu Hsiang-chien's success in defeating an enemy force some thirty-five miles north of Sungpan on the very day that the West Column under Chang Kuo-tao had been turned back by the floods. Mao's action was condemned by Chang's men as like the cicada's bursting out of its old skin, sacrificing one part of its body to save the other.

Chang complains that the chance of following Mao to Kansu was lost because of Kuomintang reinforcements which were sent to control the escape routes again after Mao had passed through them. So he swung south to Achu and Chokochi, where a meeting of thirty senior Party and Army men was summoned. According to Chang Kuo-tao the first speaker was Chen Chang-hao of the Fourth Front Army, who denounced Mao Tse-tung's 'sudden and secret' move north as dishonest. Other speakers condemned Mao's action as defeatist, selfish and immoral and declared they had lost confidence in the Central Committee. Chu Teh pleaded despondently, says Chang, for some room for compromise with the Central Committee, but the meeting decided to form a new provisional Central Committee and elected Chang as its Secretary-General. Later Jen Pi-shih of the Second Front Army, who was not present at the parting of the First and Fourth, investigated the evidence and found both sides at fault because of their prejudice against each other.[24]

Did Chu Teh need to have a gun stuck in his back to go south with Chang rather than north with Mao? This is one of the great riddles of the Long March. He himself refused to give a first-hand account of the incident to Agnes Smedley, conveying the impression that he was a prisoner of Chang's for the twelve months that followed. Li Teh asserts that he was 'forced' to stay with the Fourth, the decision being made in the middle of the night. But Dr Stuart Schram is not alone in doubting if that were all to be said. 'Compulsion or pressure there may have been', he concludes, 'but it is highly unlikely that this is the whole story. Regional loyalties were probably also a factor. ... In any case, there seems to be reason to believe that Chu was not entirely in agreement with Mao at this time.' [25]

The story of Chang's and Chu's retreat into Sikang and their eventual return to the Maoist headquarters at Yenan will be traced in a subsequent chapter. Meanwhile the survivors of the East Column under Mao Tse-tung and his Central Committee Comrades now struck through the notorious Grasslands, the last natural obstacle in their path to the north.

Chapter 19

The Grasslands

AN historian of modern China calls the five-day or six-day crossing of the Grasslands of Chinghai by 30,000 Red Army men in late August and early September 1935, 'undoubtedly the most difficult episode in the history of logistics'.[1] This part of the Sungpan plateau lies between 6,000 and 9,000 feet above sea-level, but it is not in itself mountainous. In the summer green grass grows everywhere and makes excellent pasture for the Tibetans' yaks and horses. But it rains for eight or nine months in the year, and the drainage is poor. The land therefore becomes marshy.

'The Grass Lands,' in Agnes Smedley's description, 'is a vast and trackless swamp stretching for hundreds of miles over the high Chinese–Tibetan borderland. As far as the eye can reach, day after day, the Red Army saw nothing but an endless ocean of high wild grass growing in an icy swamp of black muck and water many feet deep. Huge clumps of grass grew on dead clumps beneath them, and so it had been for no man knows how many centuries. No tree or shrub grew here, no bird ventured near, no insect sounded. There was not even a stone. There was nothing, nothing but endless stretches of wild grass swept by torrential rains in summer and fierce winds and snows in winter. Heavy black and grey clouds drifted forever above, turning the earth into a dull, sombre netherworld. . . .

'The Red Army marched along the eastern fringes where the swamp was less deep and where there were often narrow strips of land which tribal horsemen used on rare occasions. Each man carried enough food and firewood to last eight days, and Lin Piao's First Front Red Army, which spearheaded the march, also carried bamboo screens to build shelters for those coming after. The food carried by each man consisted of parched wheat and tea.'[2]

Lin Piao's men were told to furnish a vanguard, and Yang Cheng-wu and Wang Kai-hsiang, the heroes of the Luting Bridge assault, were named to lead it. Colonel Yang, who later became Acting Chief-of-Staff of the People's Liberation Army, records that he went to Maoerhkai to be briefed by the leading members of the Military Council. Mao Tse-tung was located upstairs in his quarters in a wooden Tibetan house where the ground floor was used as a stockyard and the upper storey for living in.

'At this moment,' Mao explained, 'Hu Tsung-nan and his four divisions are at Changla, Lungfukuan and Paotso in the region of Sungpan. Eastern Szechuanese troops are holding the entire eastern bank of the Min River, and one of their companies is occupying Chiakulao on the western bank. The pursuing forces of Liu Wenhui have already arrived at Moukung and are advancing towards Fupein. Hsueh Yueh and Chou Hun-yuan have made a *rendezvous* with their men at Yachou [or Yaan]. If we turn south it means running away, and the end of the revolution. We have no choice but to go forward. Our enemies have assumed that we will move into eastern Szechuan rather than attempt the Grasslands road into Shensi and Kansu. But the enemy does not understand us at all. We purposely choose the path which he least expects us to take.' [3]

Colonel Yang explained in his turn that preparations were well advanced for the campaign except that the men had only two sets of thin clothes each and this would be inadequate for the Grasslands. Local tribespeople had told them that they would freeze to death without woollen socks and sheepskins, but not enough of these could be bought for all the men. 'Try by every possible means,' Mao advised, 'to get more provisions and clothing. What about your guide?' Yang said that an old man of 60 had agreed to guide them, and that he would be carried on a simple wooden carriage by eight soldiers. Mao suggested they put up posts with arrows along the way to guide the units that were to follow, and he concluded by emphasizing the need to show respect towards the tribesmen and to cooperate well with the Fourth Front Army regiment which was to accompany the vanguard.

Colonel Yang then went to see Vice-Chairman Chou En-lai, but the doctor had ordered him not to receive visitors: his wife, Teng

Ying-chao, confided that she was 'deeply concerned about Vice-Chairman Chou because of the lack of proper medicine. . . .'

The cold, the rain and the lack of rest took a heavy toll of Yang's vanguard. In the central part of the Grasslands they could not sleep on the ground because of the water, so they had to stand all night leaning against each other to keep warm : back to back by two's or four's was the order of the night. Many men collapsed or found their legs paralysed. Yang particularly remembered a 'little devil' of seventeen named Cheng Chin-yu, who began to give way on their fourth day in the Grasslands. 'I am a piece of iron politically,' the young man claimed, 'but my legs fail me.' Colonel Yang gave him a horse and extra rations, and they tied him on the horse's back with pillows to cushion him. But he died next day.

The path thus charted, the rest of the Red Army followed. One participant wrote later that the water underfoot 'looked like horse's urine and gave off a vile smell which made people vomit'. As bad luck would have it August was the worst month here for rain and fog. There were mosquitoes the size of horse-leeches and most of the Red Army's medical supplies were exhausted or lost by now, so that the only treatment for infected sores was boiling water – if you were lucky enough to be able to make a fire. Many succumbed to 'black malaria' – 500, by one account. 'Our faces,' recalled Chen Hsien-cheng, 'went as black as a Negro's, and our bodies became weaker and weaker, needing to rest after every few steps.' [4]

One Long Marcher explained : 'The grass grew in long clusters in shallow water. Between one clump and another the water was very deep. The clusters of grass were dead and rotten, with new grass sprouting on the rotten grass. Under the dense green grass was layer upon layer of rotten grass immersed in the water, so that when you stepped on a clump your foothold was shaky and slippery. Between the clumps the soil was exceptionally soft and loose, and if you took a step you would sink down at least eighteen inches. Sometimes there were bottomless pools of mud. If you weren't careful, and took a false step, a man and his horse would sink down : the more they would struggle, the deeper they would go and if no one pulled them out that was the end of them.' [5]

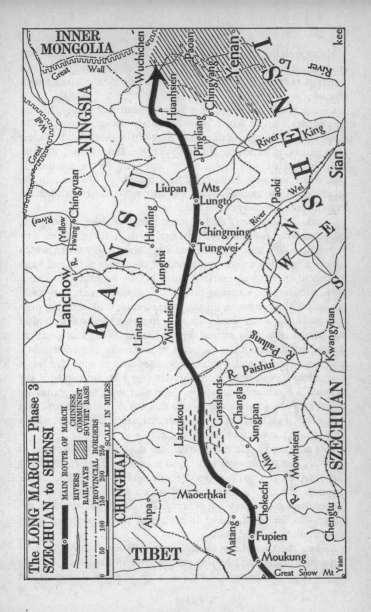

Many recollections of the Grasslands have been published. One of the most interesting is by Major Tan Ching-lin, then a teenage standard bearer in one of the Fourth Front Army units which crossed:

'In the autumn of 1935, the Fourth Front Red Army, having crossed the desolate Great Snow Mountain Range, took a rest of three days at Kangmaoszu on the edge of the marshlands. There, after gathering some pine fungus and cones and roasting some ox and sheep skins for rations, we set out towards the marshes. It took us twenty days to go from Kangmaoszu to Chaliszu on the other side of the swamplands. I was then only sixteen, a standard bearer in the company of the Red Army.

'From Kangmaoszu, the marshes stretched like a great sea, vague, gloomy and illimitable. In sunless days, there was no way to tell the direction. Treacherous bogs were everywhere which sucked a man down once he stepped off the firmer parts, and more quickly if he tried to extricate himself. We could advance only with minute care, stepping on grass-clumps. Even so, one could not help feeling nervous, for the grass mounds sank with the pressure and black water would rise and submerge the foot. Soon after one passed, the grass mound would rise to its original position, leaving not a trace of the footprint. It was really like traversing a treacherous quicksand. Fortunately, the advance unit had left a coarse hair [rope] which led meanderingly to the depth of the morass. We proceeded carefully along this rope, fearing that we might break it, for we knew clearly this was no ordinary rope, but a 'life-line' that was set up by fraternal units at the cost of the lives of many good comrades.

'We advanced along the rope for four days. On the afternoon of the fifth, the troops were resting on a grass bank when suddenly the weather changed. A wild wind sprang up; black clouds shrouded the sky. Then came hail which pelted down, followed immediately by a heavy fall of snow. To counter the attack of the snowstorm, people gathered in groups of several each, covering their heads with lined quilts.

'When the snowstorm abated, knots of people threw off their snow-laden quilts and helped one another to their feet. But the rope was gone. The marshland was a sea of snow. The comrades of our company, led by the commander, formed a single row to search for the rope. They removed the snow on the grass bank, but could find not a shadow of it.

'We could not stay on the bank for long, for it was terribly cold and we had no firewood with which to warm ourselves. Yet, if we continued to advance, we would fall into the bogs. There was no alternative but to return to Kangmaoszu, with the vaguely discernible Weifeng Mountain as our guiding mark, and wait for contact from the advance unit.

'We waited for a couple of days in Kangmaoszu, when the advance unit sent a *tungszu*, a guide as well as a Han interpreter, and we once more set out into the marshes.

'Our unit was deprived of some of its members after the previous trip, and our ration of pine cones and fungus was all consumed. It would be very difficult to find another lot since the hills around Kangmaoszu were now deeply covered with snow. Before setting out again, I distributed the handful of roasted grain (the first time we entered the swamplands, comrades, because I was the youngest among them, had let me share their ration, so I had saved a little of mine) in small quantities among several comrades who washed them down with snow-water. When we entered the marshlands for the second time, for the first couple of days most men drank the bitter black water. The result was that, as they walked, their bellies rumbled, and their legs became heavy and weak. As it would not do to keep on without eating, wild grass and vegetables that had so far been ignored were now plucked and eaten. When no green things were to be found, they would gather dried grass and chew the roots.

'We tried out almost all kinds of wild plants along our way. Later we discovered a sort of prickly, stumpy tree denuded of leaves but with tiny red berries the size of a pea, and with a sour-sweet taste like cherries. This was accounted the best of our discoveries. Whenever this tree appeared in the distance, we would run straight toward it with a sudden flush of vigour. And some comrades, forgetting they were in a swamp, would run headlong into the mire and disappear. Those who reached the tree would begin eating, and when they had their fill, would pluck the rest for the wounded and sick comrades.

'On the sixth day, someone dug out a kind of aqueous plant the size of a green turnip which tasted sweet and crisp. Everybody at once searched for it. It proved poisonous. Those who ate it vomited after half an hour; several died on the spot. Death, however, could not be allowed to delay our progress. Unfastening the quilts of the martyrs and covering their bodies we paid them the deep tribute all Red Army heroes warrant, and continued to push forward.

'However, we took a lesson from this incident. Afterwards, when we found strange plants we tried them carefully before general acceptance.

'Once I was going forward, carrying a red flag, when the grass mound underfoot jerked, and before I had time to draw away my foot, I was in the deadly ooze. "Now I am finished," I thought, "I am not afraid of death, but I must not soil the red flag which is the pride and responsibility of the standard-bearer." Slowly I pulled the flagpole into an erect position and, with one hand clutching at the pole and another pressing on the muddy ground, I attempted to clamber on to solid ground. Beads of sweat stood on my forehead. But the harder I struggled, the deeper I sank. Soon I was waist-deep in mud. At this critical moment, the clerk of the company came up. Taking over the red flag and sticking it on one side, he reached me with one end of his bamboo pole which he bade me grasp. Then he pulled with all his might. But his effort proved futile. On the contrary, the mound on which he stood started rocking . . .

Up came a tall, big fighter. Quickly unfastening his quilt and spreading it on a thick, grassy clump and placing his two rifles on it in a cross, he grabbed hold of the bamboo pole and bade me hang on the other end like grim death. More soldiers came up and they pulled like a tug-of-war team. After what seemed an interminable time, the mire around me was pressed back. Now my body could move freely. The big fellow told me to lie down; then, with a powerful jerk, they brought me right out of the mud.

'It was the first time a comrade had been rescued by this method . . .

'One afternoon, a river about 200 metres wide appeared before us. There were a few leafless trees on each bank. A downpour two days earlier had raised considerably the water level. Now the water raced rapidly towards the south-east.

'The *tungszu* led us to a tree round which was fastened a wire leading towards the opposite shore. At an order of the commander the fighters leaped into the water and with one hand grasping at the wire, the other holding the rifle aloft, they began to wade across. I had made only a dozen metres when the wire, owing to the strain of the men in the pressure of the flow of the river, snapped. I fell with the red flag and was washed downstream. I held to the flag-pole and my body bobbed up and down in the water. I couldn't regain my foothold and I was filling with water. Fortunately, the company commander who was not far from the shore saw me and rode up along the bank towards the red flag. Plunging into the river he made towards me. When he grabbed the flag I rose to the surface and caught hold of the horse's tail with both hands. Soon we reached the shore. The struggle had completely exhausted us and the animal also, and all three lay on the shore, unable to move for a long, long while.

'Later, the battalion commander sent men to connect the wire. Before dusk fell, the whole battalion had successfully crossed the river.

'In the afternoon of the following day, a carp-like, snow-covered hill of medium height appeared in front of us, with clusters of something which, from a distance, looked like snow-capped houses. This led to an argument.

' "There, look at the houses; and the smoke too !"

' "That's no smoke, it's fever mist."

'Who didn't long to see men and smoke and human habitation after the trying experience in the marshland? So the one who spoke first had naturally majority backing. "Maybe the place is really inhabited after all ! Let us put on greater speed."

'As darkness descended, we reached the hill. The illusory houses and smoke faded; what actually met our eyes was a grove of giant pines. "Anyway, we've said good-bye to the marshes !" Everybody felt relieved.

'It was decided to make camp here. Having found a shelter against the wind, we got together some twigs and branches from under the snow and lit a fire. By the sheerest accident the political instructor discovered a few pine cones. With his encouragement, everybody began to ferret for more. Then they sat around the fires, chewing the pine nuts and fungus, their lean, yellowing faces flushed under the glow of the bonfires. The company commander, the clerk, the bugler and I sat together, heating our dilapidated mugs filled with snow-water. Chatting and laughing, we fell asleep by the fire.

'Dawn was heralded by a shrieking north-wester. The fire was dead. The icicles on the branches jerked and clanked and dropped down on us. The company commander had a long struggle before he could get to his feet. He shook me; I had already wakened, but I could not get up, for the ice underneath which had been melted by the warmth of my body during the night had frozen again, so that my feet seemed pinned on the ground. The company commander helped me to loosen up my joints, and it was after much trouble that I was helped to my feet, leaving my bodily seal on the ground. The bugler was shaken again and again but he gave no sign of consciousness. His body was cold and his heart had ceased beating. The company commander pressed his body against his chest, thinking that his warmth might revive him, but it proved useless. I saw the company commander's eyes moisten. Then, silently, he walked towards the other rings.

'Like the company commander, the political instructor and others who succeeded in getting to their feet bustled around, trying to save their comrades-in-arms. A dozen comrades lay in everlasting slumber. Less than a score of comrades now remained of the company which once had more than a hundred persons. The company commander and political instructor had a hard time tearing themselves away from their brothers.

'We descended the mountain. The weather was clearing up; the sun was warm on our bodies. Wisps of smoke rose from our ice-coated clothes as if we had just stepped out of a hot spring.

' "House, look ! House !"

' "It's a lama temple !"

' "Now we are back to the company of men again !"

'No words could describe our excitement when we sighted the Chali Temple in the distance. Everybody rejoiced to have crossed the treacherous snow mountains and laughed death to scorn in the marshland. Our bellies which had so long been tortured by hunger, now grumbled, anticipating a round meal.

'Two or three *li* from the temple, a small river barred our way. With a hurrah, everybody plunged into it, despite the piercing cold of the water, and in a twinkling was on the other shore. High up on the top of the temple, a streaming red flag was greeting us.'[6]

Another reminiscence by an even younger Long Marcher fills out the picture of suffering and danger:

'During the autumn of 1935 I crossed three times with the Fourth Front Red Army the uninhabited area of grassed plain and marshes which covered hundreds of *li*, stretching from Maoerkhai to Shangpaotso. The boundless sea of grass and morass gave me an impression I will never forget. I was then only fourteen.

'The march started at the end of August 1935. The troops flooded towards the flat, green plain. In the rank of the 267th Regiment of the 89th Division was a group of "toddlers" – members of the propaganda group under the regimental political department. They were all teenagers. Of the twenty-odd members the leader, aged twenty, was the oldest. Our sub-group of five was rearranged just before the march. Chao Kang, our leader, was two years my senior and the oldest in the sub-group. He was tall for his years, looking like a grown-up, and was gentle and good towards us. Everybody respected him and liked to talk things over with him. The youngest in our sub-group was Hou Teng-nang who was only twelve. He was short but solid. He ran like a tiger cub but was prone to trip every so often. So I called him "Little Ball", which in time became known throughout the sub-group and which he accepted philosophically.

'We had great ambitions despite our small age. Our leader detailed jobs to everybody a few days before entering the area. He led me and two others to search for food, while "Little Ball" was made to keep watch. Owing to the lying propaganda of the enemy and the recurrence of devastating wars, the Tibetans around the area where we made camp had all fled. There was not enough *chingko* [highland barley] and buckwheat to go round. The grain we could gather for the day was not sufficient to keep us from hunger. But where was the surplus to come from? By the time of departure, there was left only a dozen catties of popped *chingko* and buckwheat for our sub-group, like so many pearls in a bag made of ox-hide.

'The bugle called. The Red fighters began to advance. Our leader personally carried the precious bag. "Nobody's to eat a single grain without the group leader's permission!" he said.

'As for the rest of us, one shouldered a bundle of firewood, one carried a tent made of dilapidated sheets, I had a drum and a gong on my back, and "Little Ball" carried a cracked, soot-blackened basin – excellent for cooking and boiling water. Everybody had on his head a battered, broad-brimmed bamboo hat. We must have looked very funny from afar, wobbling under the sun like a row of mushrooms. The clothes we donned were mostly those confiscated from landlords, and, from the buffeting of wind and rain, were now in a most pitiable state of deterioration. One advantage we had – when we were called to give a performance, we had not to bother about costumes. I wore a landlord's black jacket minus sleeves; our leader was clad in an unseemly flowing robe, and "Little Ball" had on a girl's red blouse patterned with yellow flowers – everybody called him "Sister-in-law!" The long file, with its tattered, kaleidoscope outfit, looked like holiday paraders decorating the silent, uninhabited plain.

'It might well be claimed that we marched on an empty stomach the moment we entered the marshland. For how could five persons trek for seven or eight days on a dozen catties of grain black as charcoal? So work was divided among every member when we made camp. "Little Ball" was to be the "cook", whose job was to make the fire and boil the water. The rest of us dispersed to search for wild vegetables – wild scallion, wild celery, and other plants – all excellent food. But even these were hard to get, for the preceding troops had made a fairly thorough sweep of them, and we had to run a *li* or more to get a handful. We had to watch every step, for the least carelessness would plunge us into the ooze. To prevent this danger, we proceeded grasping each other's hand, or holding a pole crosswise.

'After the wild vegetables were brought back, everybody got busy, washing scalding ... then when the "vegetables" were boiled and had turned yellow, the leader took out the *chingko* and buckwheat from his bag and dropped them in the boiling water, counting every grain as if they were so many silver coins. Then we sat round the fire and ate, talking and laughing.

' "That's *chingko* stewed with beef !"

' "No, it's scallion boiled with *chingko*."

'So, we began to comment about the dish. Finally the leader said : "You are all wrong. It's a fancy cake. See, the *chingko* are the dates and the buckwheat are the lotus seeds. . . ."

' "Fancy cake, indeed !" echoed everybody in great merriment and wolfed the stuff, forgetting the bitter taste of the wild vegetables.

'In the marshland, though it was now mid-August, the weather was subject to change at any hour of the day. A mass of cloud would gather across the sky, and suddenly the blazing sun would disappear and wind and rain would lash down at the vast expanse. Night was more than a bother. The starlit sky was only a transient aspect, and at any moment would come rain, hailstorm or even snow.

'Apart from hunger, we had to give battle to the elements. Hunger and cold and tiredness put the revolutionary will of every Red fighter to a severe test.

'One day as the sun was sinking slowly down the horizon we decided to make camp. The smoke from fires rose into the still air. Having eaten some wild vegetable soup which lifted our spirits a little, we went to find a camping spot. In good time, we found by a winding brook clumps of creeping willows. The leader was greatly delighted. "Look, comrades !" he said. "Tonight we need not sleep squatting. We'll get some twigs, spread the sheets on them and rig up the tent. Won't that be a fine big bed for us all?"

'A sound idea, I thought, and suggested : "Won't it be more comfortable if we put some grass under the sheets?"

' "A multitude always produces a wit," they said.

'In no time we realized our wish. "We sleep in a 'building' tonight," said "Little Ball" humorously.

'So we stretched on our "bed" and slept like a litter of piglings.

'But we were fated not to enjoy this rare comfort long.

'At midnight I woke feeling cold. Sitting up, I could see through the cracks that a thick pall of mist covered the whole sky. It was so thick you could hardly see your hand in front of you. A storm was imminent! Then from afar came the howling of wind, and almost immediately, wind and rain came pouring down on us.

'My four cronies sat up from their sweet sleep. "Bad luck," said our leader, "that it should rain now, of all times!"

'A wild blast tore off the roof of our "building" – the ragged tent. Under such circumstances, we could do nothing but squat back to back, warming ourselves with our mutual bodily warmth. The rain, and hailstones as large as dates, pelted down on us. We were soaked to the skin. The bamboo hats were poor protection from the assault of the hailstones. Our teeth were chattering. We stood up from time to time and stamped our feet, for the alternative was to run the danger of never rising up again.

'The rainstorm kept on in full force until dawn when it gradually eased. We bestirred ourselves, retrieved the tent and arranged the dripping articles. After eating some wild vegetable soup, we set out again. . . .'[7]

Agnes Smedley found this report in the official archives, from a diary kept by Moh Hsu:

'Today I discovered a comrade struggling in the muddy water. His body was crunched together and he was covered with muck. He gripped his rifle fiercely, which looked like a muddy stick. Thinking he had merely fallen down and was trying to get up, I tried to help him stand. After I pulled him up he took two steps, but the entire weight of his body was on me, and he was so heavy that I could neither hold him up nor take a step. Urging him to try and walk alone, I released him. He fell on the path and tried to rise. I tried again to lift him but he was so heavy and I so weak that it was impossible. Then I saw that he was dying. I still had some parched wheat with me and I gave him some but he could not chew, and it was clear that no food could save him. I carefully put the parched wheat back in my pocket, and when he died I arose and passed on and left him lying there. Later, when we reached a resting place I took the wheat from my pocket but I could not chew it. I kept thinking of our dying comrades. I had no choice but to leave him where he fell, and had I not done this I would have fallen behind and lost contact with our army and died. Yet I could not eat that parched wheat.'[8]

This was the worst phase of the Long March as far as food was concerned. The Communists had had to fight the Mantzu tribes-men to get their cattle, and they had also found green Tibetan wheat and enormous beets and turnips * which they were able to harvest. One estimate is that the Red Army had acquired in the comparatively plentiful district of Polotzu, before entering the Grasslands, 'some 600,000 catties of wheat and several hundred sheep and cattle'.[9] 'This is our only foreign debt,' Mao Tse-tung observed with tongue in cheek to Edgar Snow a year later, 'and some day we must pay the Mantzu and the Tibetans for the provisions we were obliged to take from them.' [10] Since there was no firewood in the Grasslands, grain and vegetables had to be eaten raw. They tended to go through the men's stomachs – most of which were in any case used to rice, not wheat – undigested and caused diarrhoea. The southerner Hsu Meng-chiu recalled that 'you cannot eat much wheat or it harms your stomach. I knew two men who died from eating green wheat.' Peng Teh-huai blamed his delicate stomach in later years on the week's forced diet of raw wheat grains and grass which sustained him over the Grasslands.[11] One survivor of the Grasslands recalled that, after they had emerged from the marshes, 'that was when we began eating rats. We cleaned every village of rats. They tasted awful but we ate them.' [12]

When the army did leave the swamp behind it came to tribal settlements which presented other problems. One unit came to a deserted Tibetan village where the houses were made of yak manure, so inflammable that special fire patrols had to be organized:

'Some of the buildings were huge structures of thirty or forty rooms. By then all the provisions of the army had been used up and the men began eating anything they could find: unripened wheat from the fields, grass, wild greens, berries. Some of the rich tribesmen, who had fled before the Hans, had secret storehouses in their great homes. These were built into the walls and completely sealed up. The Red troops discovered them, tore down the walls and distributed the food. Some men boiled cowhides for twenty-four hours and then ate; or they boiled big leather boots and drank the broth.

---

* Big enough to feed fifteen men each, according to Mao Tse-tung.

'Every rich Fan tribal family had a special religious hall in which Buddhist manuscripts and bowls of sacrificial food – nuts, dates, rice and cheese – were kept; and on the altars were figurines of gods and animals painted green or red. One Red Army unit of twelve men was billeted in such a hall for a number of days while the army was cruising far and wide to find and buy wheat.

'One of the men of the unit of twelve returned one evening and noticed that some of the altar figurines had disappeared. When he asked the reason, one of his comrades gave him a bowl of steaming hot wheat porridge with butter floating on top. The fragrance was so delicious that he almost fainted. His comrades had scraped the paint from the figurines and found them to be made of wheat and butter.

' "We were so selfish that we kept the secret," this man said. "At each mealtime we would peel the paint off a few more images and cook them in water with the handful of wheat which was our only army ration. We were so demoralized by hunger that we secretly planned to raid the family altars of other homes. But one day, after treating two famished comrades, our secret came out, and after that our living conditions sank deplorably !" ' [13]

'As we marched on,' wrote Hsiung Huang afterwards, 'someone at the head of the line called out :

' "He who is a lucky man does not need to worry about anything – we've tumbled on something again !"

'He had chanced upon the corpse of a dead horse with some meat still on it. At the mere mention of food, all swarmed to the spot and the carcass was soon stripped clean. I was the last to arrive only to find that hardly anything was left on the skeleton. I refused to be beaten and started to scrape the bones with a pocket knife. I scraped and scraped and finally got about a cupful of meat. It had taken me a long time. Night had come, and my comrades had gone too far for me to catch up with them.

'I groped my way across the grassland, scarcely able to see my hand before my face. I was very worried and feared that I might lose my way or step into a swamp at any moment. I decided to rest under a big tree for the night. I dozed off, pressing the precious meat to my bosom. Suddenly I felt something touching me. Rubbing my eyes, I saw a dark form darting away from me.

My meat had gone. The meat was my life-blood, I could not spare it. I picked up a stone and threw it at the figure which screamed and disappeared in the darkness. Thinking things over I came to the conclusion that the thief was a monkey, and I did not know whether to weep or laugh.'.14

Much depended just before, during and immediately after the Grasslands crossing, on the Communists' relations with the Tibetan tribespeople. A somewhat over-sentimental first-hand report of an earlier encounter by the Fourth Army with Tibetan villagers may help to illuminate some of the problems involved.

'In the spring of 1935,' writes Major Kang Cheng-teh, 'the 91st Division of the Fourth Front Red Army arrived at the Golden Lama Temple in Sikang during the Long March. Divisional head-quarters was stationed in a village by the name of Popa, about ninety li from the temple. I was then working in the propaganda section of the division.

'Popa was the largest mountain village around there, with 900 Tibetan families living in stone houses that looked like square fortifications. The Tibetans had all fled before the troops arrived. We could see red cloth strips hanging at all the doors which were sealed with charms or even locked. The yards were bare of everything, excepting a bit of firewood. To show our respect for minority people, the leadership decided that we should not enter the houses but bivouac outside the village.

'The weather in early spring was still cold enough to make one shiver. More so, sleeping in the open at night, for a fire warmed the front but left the back icy cold. All one could do against the damp ground was to spread some straw over it.

'Food posed a serious problem, for there was not enough even of grass roots and tree bark to suffice for all. The number of the wounded and the sick was mounting every day.

'We decided to rest, recuperate and reorganize here.

'It was said that a melon couldn't be detached from its stem, nor a child from its mother. So how could the Red Army exist apart from the people? But no troops had ever come here before, and the Tibetans were far from knowing that we were troops of the people. When they heard that troops were coming, their headman led them off to the mountains, driving away sheep and cattle. The lamas in the temple also left.

'We must get our strength, the people, to come back. The leadership issued orders that mass discipline should be strictly observed; that the customs and habits of the national minority should be respected; that the red cloth strips and charms on the doors should be left untouched; that the streets should be swept every day; and that we, the propaganda section, should all go out with the interpreters (one or two Hans who knew Tibetan were attached to every company) and try all we could to find the people and persuade them to return.

'We divided our section into several groups. Some inscribed on walls big characters in Tibetan in conspicuous places in the village, slogans of the 'three disciplines and eight points for attention' of the Red Army, and the Party's policy towards national minorities. Some went to the mountains to look for the people. We spent three or four days each trip, passing the nights in the wild mountains, in the forests or on the unbounded grassland. Often we would hear human voices and spot fresh dung of sheep or cattle without seeing a human shadow.

'We had been on the job a dozen days when luck directed us to a stone cave in which the Tibetan headman was hidden. After much explaining and propagandizing we learned that he longed for a horse. That would have been no difficulty at all in the past; but now all horses had been killed for food except the one ridden by the divisional commander. When on our return we mentioned this, he at once ordered his orderly to send the horse over.

'The headman was extremely happy with the gift; yet he did not feel completely assured. He sent some men back with us to have a look at things. When these people saw the slogans at the village entrance, and discovered that the locks, the red cloth strips and the charms over the doors were untouched, that not one of the articles hidden within the seams of the walls was missing, that the streets were swept clean, and that we bivouacked outside the village in the cold, with stewed wild vegetables for food, they were profoundly moved and, palm to palm, saluted to us. Some did not wait but ran straight back to the mountain and related to the headman and their countrymen what they had seen in their village.

'One by one the Tibetans returned from the mountains and the grassland, driving some 37,000 sheep and cattle laden with bags of barley and *chanpa* (a food made of barley flour and butter). With the headman in the lead, they opened the doors of their houses and, despite our protestations, took us into their homes with great fuss and ceremony. Some unearthed bacon which had been buried underground and presented it to us. They also made a gift of 300 sheep and cattle to us.

'Not knowing the customs of the Tibetans, we declined. That made them very unhappy. Seeing they had no salt, nor means to obtain it, each of us shared out a portion of our meagre supply and proffered it to them. They would not accept it. We learned through the interpreter that they were angry with us because, by not accepting their gift, we were treating them like outsiders. We therefore took their food and meat and they in turn accepted our salt and we became like members of one family....' [15]

But not every meeting with the tribespeople went so happily. 'Just before entering the Grassland,' one survivor records, 'we heard shots in our rear. A party of tribal horsemen had fallen upon some of our stragglers and seized their guns.' One of the histories states that 300 men died in combat with minority nationalities while crossing the Grasslands. [16]

'Following our battle,' writes another Long Marcher, 'I was with Chu Teh and a column of men moving along a mountain path. We came to a group of black yurts such as the tribesmen use for dwellings. They had fled, of course, as Han [Chinese] troops approached, taking all food with them. We went into one of the yurts and found fifteen of our men who had gone in advance. They were sitting cross-legged on the earth around a pile of cold ashes. We called out but they did not reply. They sat with heads bowed, like statues. We went up and touched them. They were frozen to death. The tribesmen had taken their guns and packs. In another yurt we found five others, sitting around a pile of cold ashes, each with a shot through the back.' [17]

As Edgar Snow comments: 'The route they chose led through wild country inhabited by the independent Mantzu tribesmen and the nomadic Hsifan, a warring people of eastern Tibet. Passing into the Mantzu and Tibetan territories, the Reds for the first time faced a populace united in its hostility to them, and their sufferings on this part of the trek exceeded anything of the past. They had money but could buy no food. They had guns but their enemies were invisible. As they marched into the thick forests and jungles and across the headwaters of a dozen great rivers, the tribesmen withdrew from the vicinity of the march. They stripped their houses bare, carried off all edibles, drove their cattle and fowl to the plateau, and simply disinhabited the whole area.

'A few hundred yards on either side of the road, however, it was quite unsafe. Many a Red who ventured to forage for a sheep never returned. The mountaineers hid in the thick bush and sniped at the marching "invaders". They climbed the mountains, and when the Reds filed through the deep, narrow rock passages, where sometimes only one or two could move abreast, the Mantzu rolled huge boulders down to crush them and their animals. Here were no chances to explain "Red policy toward national minorities", no opportunities for friendly alliance. The Mantzu Queen had an implacable traditional hatred for Chinese of any variety, and recognized no distinctions between Red and White. She threatened to boil alive anyone who helped the travellers.' [18]

No wonder the Marchers found relief when they returned, after the swamps, to the familiar lands of the Han Chinese. 'I remember,' recalled one, 'when we came out of the Grasslands and broke through enemy lines into Kansu and saw Chinese peasants. They thought we were crazy. We touched their houses and the earth, we embraced them, and we danced and sang and cried.' [19]

No wonder, too, that in spite of the official Communist Party policy of respecting national minorities, a Western visitor ten years afterwards found that there were some high-ranking officers in the People's Liberation Army who openly thought in terms of settling some time the account which the Tibetans owed for their resistance and non-cooperation during the Long March.[20] Some small part of the tragedy of Communist China's role in Tibet during the 1950s and 1960s may be owed to these experiences in 1935 when Tibetan hostility made the difference between death and survival for many comrades of soldiers who survived to take high positions in the Chinese Government and armed forces after 1949.

Chapter 20

Home and Dry in Shensi

ON emerging from the Grasslands the depleted Red Army encountered the 19th Division of Hu Tsung-nan at Paotso, but was able to scatter it without too much difficulty. Now there was one final bottleneck through which it had to pass before it could spill into the soft provinces of northern China, one last trap on which Chiang Kai-shek could count to destroy his most obstinate enemy. This was the only pass leading across the Min Mountains between the headwaters of the Min and the Pailung Rivers. At the Latzu Pass – Latzukou – the only possible road leads between vertical cliffs along which the enemy had constructed bunkers and trenches and installed its guns.

The pass was guarded by a Kuomintang division under Lu Ta-chang. The only entrance to the narrow 1½-mile defile was a single-plank bridge over the waist-high river which ran through it. Enemy defence towers controlled the bridge. But Colonel Yang Cheng-wu, commanding the 4th Regiment of the 2nd Division of the First Red Army (he later rose to be Acting Chief of Staff of the People's Liberation Army in the late 1960s), decided to outflank this concentrated enemy defence by sending climbers up the cliffs on the right bank since these, though as sheer as those on the left, were at least sparsely studded with shrubs. Three companies of Communist climbers set out with plaited puttees for ropes and with grappling irons, and at four in the morning they sent up red and green flares, the signal for the Communist main force to shell the towers defending the bridge and make a fierce frontal assault. The bridge was captured on 18 September 1935 and the Kuomintang expelled.[1]

There were still some hazards after Latzukou. The Pailung River was one. 'The path,' according to one account, 'lies above the river: stones and wooden stakes are placed on a man-made opening through the rocks, then wooden planks are placed on it in imitation of Buddhist bridges ... As for the Pailung River itself, the current is as swift as that of the Tachin and Hsiaochin Rivers of Sikang. The sound of its waves is like thunder and lightning, and the two banks consist of steep overhanging cliffs. The surface of the river varies from several *chang** to several ten *changs* in the broadest places, and is less than one *chang* at the narrowest. If a man or a horse falls into the river there is no possibility of rescue. The path is between ten and twenty *chang* above the surface of the water, and if you should chance to look down at it the experience is truly frightening. The path had been spoiled by the enemy, but the Red Army built a bridge and repaired the road in order to cross the river.' [2]

The Communists had to fight the forces of the local warlords and Moslems as well as of the Kuomintang and suffered several cavalry attacks from the Moslems.

After the Latzu Pass the Communists crossed through the Lunghsi basin and the Liupan Mountains, where Mao Tse-tung's batman almost died:

'Another time, I remember,' says Chen Chang-feng, 'I had got everything ready for Chairman Mao to go to bed – it was in September, when we were nearing Latsekou – and went to find him. He was deep in conference with Lin Piao, Nieh Jung-chen, Liu Ya-lou and Lo Jui-ching bending over maps. I went off quietly.

'Next day we captured Latsekou and pushed on. Mount Liupan lay ahead on our line of march. We were aiming at reaching the village of Hatapu in a day – a distance of about a hundred *li*.

'It was a dark morning, with heavy cloud and a strong wind which brought rain in its wake. By the time we reached the foot of Mount Liupan we were all soaked to the bone.

'Mount Liupan was nothing compared to the Great Snow Mountain Range that we had already crossed, but the ups and downs made the distance very long. We had about sixty *li* of it, very hard going. There was nothing to help get a foothold, no trees after we began getting to the top, only dead grass.

'I had picked up a dose of malaria by this time, and had had

---

* One *chang* equals just over ten feet.

some trouble with my legs in Szechuan – a little time before. The swelling had gone down now, but I still felt rather wobbly. By the time we reached the summit I was so dizzy I felt I couldn't move another foot.

'Chairman Mao noticed this, and asked me what was the matter. I told him that I was afraid I could never cross. As I spoke I crumpled up. Chairman Mao pulled me to my feet. He thought I was having an attack of malaria again, and told another bodyguard to get the medical orderly to give me something for it. But I wasn't having malaria. I was just exhausted from the march.

' "You go on," I said to him. "I'll have a bit of a rest and then catch you up."

' "That won't do," said Chairman Mao. "The air's thin here, and there's all this rain. This is no place to rest. You must pull yourself together and get down this mountain."

'He got ready to carry me himself, with the other bodyguard. I wasn't going to have this, so I tried to start walking again, but my strength failed me and I couldn't move a step, I was so shaky.

' "What's the matter?" asked Chairman Mao. "Cold?"

' "Yes," I said. "I'm chilled right through, I feel all shrivelled up."

' "Come on," said Chairman Mao. "Take my overcoat, and have some hot water. If you get warm again you'll be all right."

'He began to take his coat off, but I pulled at his arm.

' "No, Chairman Mao," I cried, "I won't take your coat. See, I can walk."

'I knew the ordinary uniform he had on underneath would not keep the cold out. He'd been up most of the night, too. I insisted I wouldn't have his coat, and tried to walk, but I was really too weak. I managed a step and then fell down, flat out.

'When I came to, the other bodyguard was in front of me with some hot water, and Chairman Mao's coat was over me. I looked at the wind tearing at his thin uniform, and strength seemed to come over me. He looked at me, with his usual fatherly expression.

' "Better now?" he asked.

' "Yes, I'm fine!" I said, struggling to my feet. "That's a Red fighter!" he said. "Let's go!"

'We were over the mountain by the evening and got to a peasant's hut before we reached Hatapu. As I lay in bed that night my mind went back to the mountain. If Chairman Mao hadn't given me his overcoat, I said to myself, I would be dead up on those heights. Tears came to my eyes as I thought of it.' [3]

Mao Tse-tung himself commemorated the battle at which Mount Liupan was captured with a poem:

> Lofty the sky
>   and pale the clouds –
> We watch the wild geese
>   fly south till they vanish.
> We count the thousand
>   leagues already travelled.
> If we do not reach
>   the Great Wall we are not true men.
>
> High on the crest
>   of Liupan Mountain
> Our banners billow
>   in the west wind.
> Today we hold
>   the long rope in our hands.
> When shall we put bonds
>   upon the grey dragon? [4]

But they did reach the Great Wall and come within sight of mastering the grey dragon of the Kuomintang, for Mount Liupan was the last stage in their Long March.

Towards the end of October 1935 the Long Marchers approached the town of Wuchichen on the upper reaches of the Lo River, inside the northern Shensi soviet area, guided by soldiers from the soviet. They stayed for the first time in caves cut in the side of the loess * hills, and most of them were dismayed as southerners to find that even in this friendly ground there was no rice available

---

* Loess is a yellowish-grey powdery loam or alluvium which covers this stretch of the Yellow River basin and is relatively unproductive: a similar phenomenon at one time covered the Rhine valley and is still to be found in parts of Holland.

– only golden millet. Mao Tse-tung's cook served a leg of mutton ungarnished because he didn't know how to set about cooking millet.[5] While the Red Army settled down in Wuchichen, Mao Tse-tung led a party over to Hsiashihwan, the seat of government of the soviet area and headquarters of the Shensi–Kansu Provincial Party Committee. Mao's batman accompanied him and recorded the scene:

'Large snowflakes were falling when we set out. Although we weren't wearing too many clothes, nobody felt the cold as we trudged over the rough mountain paths. It was dusk when we reached Hsiashihwan. We heard the beating of gongs and drums and the noise of a crowd of people. From a distance we could see a large gathering on a spacious ground at the entrance to the village. The people were waiting to welcome the Chairman. As soon as they caught sight of him, they cheered madly. Amidst a tremendous din of gongs and drums, the crowd rushed up, waving small red and green banners bearing the words :

> Welcome Chairman Mao !
> Welcome the Central Red Army !
> Expand the Shensi–Kansu–Ninghsia Soviet Area !
> Smash the enemy's third encirclement campaign !
> Long live the Chinese Communist Party !

'In his worn overcoat which he had brought along from Kiangsi, and his old cap, the Chairman nodded and waved at the crowd again and again. Then the people cleared a way for a score of leading comrades to come up and shake hands with the Chairman. They included Comrades Liu Chih-tan, Liu Ching-fan [Liu Chih-tan's brother], Ma Ming-fang [Chairman of the Provincial Soviet of Northern Shensi] and Hsu Hai-tung, Commander of the Twenty-fifth Red Army. Standing with Chairman Mao to receive the welcomers were Comrades Liu Shao-chi,* Chou En-lai, Chang

---

* Liu was almost certainly not on the Long March, as has already been argued in an earlier chapter, and his mention here may be a politic fiction in deference to his powerful position in Peking when this account was first published. If so, this only underscores the prestige which attaches to participation in the March. It seems incredible for Liu to have rejoined the Marchers from Peking *before* they linked up with the Shensi soviet authorities.

Wen-tien, Wang Chia-hsiang, Hsu Teh-li, Lin Po-chu, Tung Pi-wu and Hsieh Chueh-tsai. They shook hands all around and introduced one another.' [6]

According to Hsu Hai-tung's and Hsu Meng-chiu's versions, the meeting was on 20 October 1935 at Wuchichen.

'Is this Comrade Hai-tung?' Mao asked. 'Thank you for taking so much trouble to come here to meet us.' [7]

The Long March was over. 'Footsore, weary and at the limit of human endurance' [in Edgar Snow's phrase], 'an army of ragged skeletons, with hundreds of men coughing their lungs out' [in Agnes Smedley's] the main part of the First Front Army and the C.C.P. headquarters had finished their epic trek across China. Even some of the precious sewing machines survived.[8]

The figure sometimes given for the Long Marchers who reached Shensi, in the shadow of the Great Wall, in October 1935, is 20,000, based on the earliest accounts of Smedley [9] and Snow.[10] But this includes the forces already in occupation of the Shensi base whom Chou En-lai estimated at 10,000.[11] The number in Mao's column as it actually entered the Shensi soviet were in fact between 7,000 and 8,000.[12] If one assumes that about one-third of these were recruits taken on during the March, this means that of the 100,000 men who left Kiangsi on 16 October 1935 only about 5,000, and perhaps even fewer, survived the full length of what we usually call the Long March. Only one in twenty came through. But some of the missing 95,000 men had been left along the route to conduct rearguard operations and sow the seeds of guerrilla revolt, while more had been left sick or wounded in the care of peasants and yet others were still with Chang Kuo-tao's column in Sikang.

The Red Army's new home was in districts 'unsurpassed in their poverty and primitiveness in all China proper,' as a scholar describes them. The loess hills of this area of Shensi, Kansu and Ninghsia were the traditional stamping grounds for warlords, secret societies and bandits. In the mid-1920s a nucleus of local radicals, including Kao Kang, had begun to gather around the figure of Liu Chih-tan, a Whampoa Cadet and the Robin Hood of the Chinese north-west. Later these men had helped form a local peasant movement with the help of cadres trained by Mao Tse-tung in the Kuomintang Peasant Training Institute in Kwang-tung: this was the time of the First United Front between the Communists and the Kuomintang.[13]

At the end of 1927 the Communists were 'purged' from the Kuomintang and, although in 1928 a short-lived soviet government had been proclaimed at Hsunyi, it was crushed by General Feng Yu-hsiang's pro-Nanking troops. But the red flag in the Chinese north-west had survived, thanks to two developments: the internal squabbling among the warlords and Kuomintang (the Nanking government fought Feng Yu-hsiang in 1930 and replaced him by Yang Hu-cheng) and the great north-west famine which ravaged the area for three years.

Readers unfamiliar with the China of those days may find it hard to imagine the dimensions of a disaster of this kind. Edgar Snow visited part of the stricken area in 1929, long before he met the Communists, and one or two extracts from his on-the-spot description will provide another part of the essential background against which the Long March and its aftermath must be understood:

'During the great North-west famine, which lasted roughly for three years and affected four huge provinces, I visited some of the drought-stricken areas in Suiyuan, on the edge of Mongolia, in June 1929. How many people starved to death in those years I do not accurately know, and probably no one will ever know; it is forgotten now. A conservative semi-official figure of 3,000,000 is often accepted, but I am not inclined to doubt other estimates ranging as high as 6,000,000.

'This catastrophe passed hardly noticed in the Western world, and even in the coastal cities of China, but a few courageous Chinese and foreigners attached to the American-financed China International Famine Relief Commission – including its secretary, Dwight Edwards; O. J. Todd, the American engineer; and a wonderful American missionary doctor, Robert Ingram – risked their lives in those typhus-infested areas, trying to salvage some of the human wreckage. I spent some days with them, passing through cities of death, across a once-fertile countryside turned into desert wasteland, through a land of naked horror.

'I was twenty-three. I had come to the East looking for the

"glamour of the Orient", searching for adventure. This excursion to Suiyuan had begun as something like that. But here for the first time in my life I came abruptly upon men who were dying because they had nothing to eat. In those hours of nightmare I spent in Suiyuan I saw thousands of men, women, and children starving to death before my eyes.

'Have you ever seen a man – a good honest man who has worked hard, a "law-abiding citizen", doing no serious harm to anyone – when he has had no food for more than a month? It is a most agonizing sight. His dying flesh hangs from him in wrinkled folds; you can clearly see every bone in his body; his eyes stare out unseeing; and even if he is a youth of twenty he moves like an ancient crone, dragging himself from spot to spot. If he has been lucky he has long ago sold his wife and daughters. He has also sold everything he owns – the timber of his house itself, and most of his clothes. Sometimes he has, indeed, even sold the last rag of decency, and he sways there in the scorching sun, his testicles dangling from him like withered olive seeds – the last grim jest to remind you that this was once a man.

'Children are even more pitiable, with their little skeletons bent over and misshapen, their crooked bones, their little arms like twigs, and their purpling bellies, filled with bark and sawdust, protuding like tumours. Women lie slumped in corners, waiting for death, their black blade-like buttocks protruding, their breasts hanging like collapsed sacks. But there are, after all, not many women and girls. Most of them have died or been sold.

'Those were things I myself had seen and would never forget. Millions of people died that way in famine, and thousands more still died in China like that. I had seen fresh corpses on the streets of Saratsi, and in the villages I had seen shallow graves where victims of famine and disease were laid by the dozens. But these were not the most shocking things after all. The shocking thing was that in many of those towns there were still rich men, rice hoarders, wheat hoarders, moneylenders, and landlords, with armed guards to defend them, while they profiteered enormously. The shocking thing was that in the cities – where officials danced or played with sing-song girls – there were grain and food, and had been for months; that in Peking and Tientsin and elsewhere were thousands of tons of wheat and millet, collected (mostly by contributions from abroad) by the Famine Commission, but which could not be shipped to the starving. Why not? Because in the north-west there were some militarists who wanted to hold all of their railroad rolling stock and would release none of it toward the east, while in the east there were other Kuomintang generals, who would send no rolling stock westward – even to starving people – because they feared it would be seized by their rivals . . .

'Yet the great majority of those people who died did so without any act of protest.

' "Why don't they revolt?" I asked myself. "Why don't they march in a great army and attack the scoundrels who can tax them but cannot feed them, who can seize their lands but cannot repair an irrigation canal? Or why don't they sweep into the great cities and plunder the wealth of the rascals who buy their daughters and wives, the men who continue to gorge on thirty-six course banquets while honest men starve? Why not?"

'I was profoundly puzzled by their passivity. For a while I thought nothing would make a Chinese fight.

'I was mistaken. The Chinese peasant was not passive; he was not a coward. He would fight when given a method, an organization, leadership, a workable programme, hope – and arms. The development of "communism" in China had proved that. Against the above background, therefore, it should not surprise us to learn that Communists were popular in the north-west, for conditions there had been no better for the mass of the peasantry than elsewhere in China.' [14]

A League of Nations health expert, Dr A. Stamper, also toured these areas and found that in some countries two-thirds or three-quarters of the inhabitants had starved in the great famine. 'In the famine of 1930,' he observed, 'twenty acres of land could be purchased for three days' food supply. Making use of this opportunity, the wealthy classes of the province * built up large estates, and the number of owner-cultivators diminished.' Shensi farmers had to pay about sixty-five per cent of their income in taxes: 'Not only is taxation thus fantastically heavy, but its assessment ap-

---

* Shensi.

pears to be haphazard and its manner of collection wasteful, brutal, and in many cases corrupt.' [15]

In these circumstances the Communist guerrillas had survived Kuomintang suppression and in the autumn of 1931 they had launched a rising in the Huanglung Mountains of north Shensi. A few months later they had reorganized themselves as the Shensi – Kansu guerrilla fighters of the Twenty-sixth Red Army. They were sharply criticized by the Communist Party Central Committee, however, for departing from the line laid down in Shanghai on military tactics, social and economic policy, leadership structure and class composition of the rebel movement. This tension between the intellectuals at the centre and the fighters in the field was to worsen.[16]

The Shensi–Kansu Border Region had been proclaimed in 1933, but the guerrillas had sustained a military setback that summer and a power struggle developed between the guerrillas and the Shensi Provincial Committee of the C.C.P. Meanwhile the guerrillas, recovering from their defeat, had expanded again in 1934 and the local Kuomintang staged a series of encirclement campaigns to destroy the Communists. The first two, in the winter of 1934–5 and the summer of 1935, were not successful. The soviet area then boasted two armies – the Twenty-sixth and Twenty-seventh – and they controlled twenty-two counties.

But in the late summer and autumn of 1935 three different kinds of reinforcement of the Communist base came to lend drama to the scene – and eventually to transform this poor and struggling Communist base into the Party's headquarters for the next decade.

First of all, a man named Chu Li-chih [17] arrived in Shensi accredited by the C.C.P. Central Committee to give new policy directions. These turned out to follow the pre-Tsunyi line of the Wang Ming, Po Ku and Chou En-lai triumvirate (presumably the messenger had been sent from Kiangsi or even from the itinerant First Front Army during its march to Tsunyi, and had taken several months to break through to the north-west). The Shensi–Kansu soviet was to be extended and co-ordinated with the Szechuan soviet (Chu apparently had not yet learned of its abandonment earlier in the year, when Chang Kuo-tao and Hsu Hsiang-chien's Fourth Front Army had retreated into the moun-

tains abutting on Tibet). The Communists were to prepare themselves to fight against the Japanese, and the slogan was to be that
of 'attacking everywhere and do not allow the enemy to enter a
single foot of soviet territory'. Anything less in touch with the
actual circumstances of the Shensi Communist guerrillas could
hardly be imagined.[18] According to the account told in Shensi
afterwards, Chu retired Liu Chih-tan from his posts and dismissed
a number of other Communist 'rebels'.

Then in September the Twenty-fifth Army of the Fourth Front
Army was led into the Shensi base by Hsu Hai-tung, the General
whom Chang Kuo-tao and Hsu Hsiang-chien had left behind in
Oyuwan to command the rearguard when they began their westward retreat in 1932. Hsu Hai-tung was a native of Hupei who had
been apprenticed in a porcelain factory at the age of eleven and
joined the peasant movement in the south in his late twenties in
1927. After the main force of the Fourth Army had left Oyuwan,
Hsu Hai-tung's troops had conducted guerrilla warfare around
that area for a time but then moved to western Anhwei to become
part of the general forces under the control of the Central Kiangsi
soviet at Juiching. Just before the Long March began, Hsu's
Twenty-fifth Army had been ordered to march north to east Hupei
in order to distract the enemy's attention from the flight of the
main force of the First Red Army from Kiangsi. Cheng Tse-hua
was his Political Commissar. Hsu's orders were to open up new
bases where conditions were favourable, and in pursuit of this
goal he had reached the neighbourhood of Sian in February 1935.
Here he had seen in June a copy of the newspaper *Ta Kung Pao*
from which he had learned for the first time that the First Front
Army and Politburo had struck northwards. He had therefore decided to go to northern Shensi to meet the First Front Army again
in the area of the existing Communist base there.[19]

The three armies thus conjoined in September 1935 in Shensi –
the Twenty-fifth, Twenty-sixth and Twenty-seventh – were
promptly reformed into the XV Army Corps with Hsu Hai-tung
as Commander, Liu Chih-tan as Deputy Commander and Kao
Kang as Political Commissar. Between them they claimed 8,000
men at arms.[20]

Hsu brought into the somewhat introverted political scene at the Shensi base a rather broader view of Party affairs, and also a stiffening of Party orthodoxy. According to Mark Selden's reconstruction, Liu Chih-tan and Kao Kang were actually arrested, Hsu siding with the Provincial Committee against the guerrillas.[21]

It was at this moment that Mao Tse-tung arrived with his bedraggled but triumphant survivors of the Long March. It could be guessed that Mao took up the cudgels for the guerrillas against those who had followed the pre-Tsunyi line of the Po Ku leadership. Furthermore Hsu Hai-tung may, in view of what had happened between Mao Tse-tung and Chang Kuo-tao (Hsu's former superior in Oyuwan) in Szechuan that summer, have become suspect in Mao's eyes.[22]

Initially Mao interceded on the guerrillas' behalf and they were reinstated. Subsequently Liu Chih-tan was killed in action, in Shensi in 1936. Kao Kang remained an uneasy ally of Mao's, though Mao publicly criticized him in 1937 for holding the view that 'guerrilla strategy is the only strategy possible for an oppressed people'.[23] But that was after the Second United Front had opened, and the C.C.P. leadership needed to underline for Kuomintang consumption its (temporary) suspension of the civil war for the larger interest of defeating Japanese aggression. Hsu Hai-tung went on to assume various high – but never crucial – military posts in the Chinese People's Republic.

Mao Tse-tung himself summed up the Long March in a report dated 27 December, two months after his arrival at Shensi:

'The Red Army,' he concluded, 'has failed in one respect, in preserving its original bases, but has achieved victory in another respect, in fulfilling the plan of the Long March. The enemy, on the other hand, has won victory in one respect, in occupying our original bases, but has failed in another respect, in realizing his plan of "encirclement and annihilation" and of "pursuit and annihilation". Only this statement is correct – that we have in fact completed the Long March.'

He went on: 'We say that the Long March is the first of its kind ever recorded in history, that it is a manifesto, an agitation corps, and a seeding-machine. ... For twelve months we were under daily reconnaissance and bombing from the air by scores of planes; we were encircled, pursued, obstructed and intercepted on the ground by a big force of several hundred thousand men; we encountered untold difficulties and great obstacles on the way, but by keeping our two feet going we swept across a distance of more than 20,000 *li* through the length and breadth of eleven provinces. Well, has there ever been in history a long march like ours? No, never.

'The Long March is also a manifesto. It proclaims to the world that the Red Army is an army of heroes and that the imperialists and their jackals, Chiang Kai-shek and his like, are perfect non-entities. It announces the bankruptcy of the encirclement, pursuit, obstruction and interception attempted by the imperialists and Chiang Kai-shek.

'The Long March is also an agitation corps. It declares to the approximately two hundred million people of eleven provinces that only the road of the Red Army leads to their liberation. Without the Long March, how could the broad masses have known so quickly that there are such great ideas in the world as are upheld by the Red Army?

'The Long March is also a seeding-machine. It has sown many seeds in eleven provinces, which will sprout, grow leaves, blossom into flowers, bear fruit and yield a crop in future.

'To sum up, the Long March ended with our victory and the enemy's defeat.' [24]

Brave, fighting words. But the reality was more sombre. When the Long Marchers straggled into Shensi in October 1935 the total membership of the Chinese Communist Party had fallen to less than 40,000, and both the labour movements in the cities and the peasant movements in the villages were for all intents and purposes dead, save in north Shensi itself. The combined forces in the Shensi base now amounted to about 16,000 (Mao's 8,000, Liu's 5,000 and Hsu's 3,000), while another 14,000 or so were still on the run under Ho Lung and Chang Kuo-tao in the far west. A grand total of 30,000 scattered members of the Red Army were thus left, where a year before the roll-call had reached 300,000. [25] If the aim of the Long March had been to conserve personnel at a time of maximum enemy pressure, then it can hardly be called a success.

Anthony Garavente goes even further in suggesting, in one of the few Western evaluations of the Long March so far published, that the Szechuan episode was in fact a military disaster of the first order. The arrival of the First Front Army at Tsunyi at the beginning of 1935 'caused the Szechuan militarists to recognize the danger to the province and stimulated them to take more decisive action', and was thus a stab in the back for the north Szechuan Communists under Chang Kuo-tao and Hsu Hsiang-chien. The First Army spurred Chiang Kai-shek to make Chung-king his headquarters during 1935, 'so that, in effect, the Kiangsi leaders led the Generalissimo to the other Communist lairs'.[26]

But this is too harsh a judgement. If the First Front Army had not aimed for Szechuan, where else could it have gone to avoid destruction at the hands of a stronger and far-better-equipped Kuomintang? The idea of joining up with the Fourth Army in Szechuan at least offered the prospect of a larger combined Communist force whose survival chances were better than two smaller and divided ones. If the First had not threatened Szechuan it is quite possible that Chiang Kai-shek would still, while dealing with the First elsewhere, have insinuated his military mission into Chungking and defeated the Fourth Army in northern Szechuan with all the greater ease for the lack of distracting pressure from the First in the south of the province. In other words, by trying to come together the extinction of both the main Communist armies may well have been prevented. All this is speculation, but to conclude that the First Army's strategy and route sabotaged the Fourth Army is to stretch the evidence.

Perhaps the best summing-up is that of Professor Howard L. Boorman, who writes: 'When Mao Tse-tung and his threadbare band arrived in the loesslands of Shensi, they represented a force, which, even on an optimistic estimate, was only a marginal element in Chinese political life viewed on a national basis. Sustained principally by discipline, hope and political formulae, Mao's group had, however, fortuitously garnered several hidden assets which were later to prove of major significance.

'First, through surviving both the Nationalist encirclement campaigns and the Long March, they had created a legend of indestructability. Second, though their economic programmes in Kiangsi had not been spectacularly successful, Mao and his associates had gained intensive political and military experience, practical lessons which they were to review with great effectiveness during the Japanese war years.

'And, third, though the hinterland of northern Shensi was a remote and retarded area, it did nevertheless provide a geographical base from which the Communists could, when war came, extend their authority and influence right into the heart of the traditionally conservative but highly important north China plain.' [27]

This was an important consideration, and C. P. FitzGerald, the respected Australian National University historian of modern China, argues that as a result of the Long March, 'the centre of revolutionary activity was removed from the south to the north for the first time since the overthrow of the Manchu dynasty'. The addition of northern recruits in the years after 1936 'contributed a greater unity to the revolutionary movement than was ever achieved by the Nationalist [Kuomintang] or Republican Parties, which were always dominated by southern or southeastern cliques'.[28]

Chapter 21

The Stragglers Return

WHEN Chang Kuo-tao broke the uneasy alliance with Mao and
the First Front Army and defied the majority in the Party leadership by turning south from the Grasslands, he led his troops,
together with the two 'hostages' Chu Teh and Liu Po-cheng and
the V and IX Army Corps from the First Army, back to Maoerhkai. Hsu Hsiang-chien's Thirtieth Army, though supposed to be
with Mao Tse-tung's column, found itself in a *cul-de-sac* in the
Grasslands and was therefore obliged to turn back and rejoin
Chang's western column, and the Fourth Army also turned back
on Chang's command, so the Fourth Front Army was re-united
again. It spent the entire ensuing winter of 1935–6 in the in-
hospitable regions of Sikang.

In October, as Mao's men were arriving at the Shenshi soviet,
Chang proclaimed in Kangting a 'Special Independent Government of the Minorities' – and even, as his enemies say, a 'bogus
Central Committee under his own chairmanship'.[1] But early in
the new year Hsueh Yueh – the same Kuomintang general who
had pursued the Long Marchers with such dedication from the
very beginning in Kiangsi – dislodged the Fourth Front Army
from Kangting, and in March Chang led his men from Tanpa to
Kantzu. Here the countryside was too poor to sustain a large
force, but Li Hsien-nien, the Political Commissar of the Thirty-
second Army, succeeded in negotiating a 'trade agreement' with
the local Tibetans and some food supplies were gained as a result.

Chu Teh, says Agnes Smedley, 'never talked to me about the
year he spent in Sikang as the virtual prisoner of Chang Kuo-tao',
All she could discover from conversations with him and his associates afterwards was that he had kept in touch with world news
through his radio; that he had done more writing than usual,

especially about events in Abyssinia and Japan; that he had spun and woven; and that he had advised Chang Kuo-tao on tactics against the Szechuanese warlord generals. The Fourth fought battles at Tienhu and Mingyah against General Yang Sen's forces.[2]

It is, of course, difficult to believe that Chu Teh or Liu Po-cheng could literally have been detained by force for a full year in the conditions prevalent in Sikang. Had they really wanted to, they could surely have escaped, alone or with a small group of men loyal to them or even with the V or IX Army Corps whose affiliation was with the First Front Army. After the First and the Fourth were separated by the Grasslands it was no longer possible to argue that 'civil war' in the Red Army would be the consequence of any breakaway by Chu Teh from Chang's captivity. And the man whose fame for military exploits against heavy odds had spread throughout China was surely not thwarted for twelve full months by a fellow-Communist.

On the contrary, Chu's role in Sikang is at best ambiguous, and until the real story is known it seems safer to assume that he went back to Sikang at least partly voluntarily, preferring the locale of his native Szechuan and the company of his fellow-Szechuanese who predominated in the Fourth Front Army, momentarily swayed by the eloquence of Chang (a man of some political sophistication) and possibly temporarily suffocated by the embrace of a Mao Tse-tung who had spent the eight months since the Tsunyi Conference consolidating his new-found power as Party leader.[3]

In the middle of May 1936 the 32nd Army marched south to defeat two Kuomintang regiments sent against it, and to prepare the way for the arrival in Sikang of yet another large Communist force, namely the Second Front Army of Ho Lung.

Ho Lung was one more of the colourful peasant generals who hitched their star to the Communist wagon. Born in 1896 in Sangchih, Hunan province, Ho was the son of an army officer and he had risen at first in the ranks of the Kuomintang as well as of the Ko Lao Hui, the secret society which had helped the republican revolution of 1911–12 and was to help the Communist revolution of the 1920s and 1930s. In 1926 Ho Lung had enrolled in the Chinese Communist Party while still holding a Kuomintang military command, and in the following year he had played a leading role in the Nanchang Uprising – his career at this time exhibiting a remarkable parallel with that of Chu Teh.[4]

After the C.C.P. setbacks of 1927, Ho Lung had organized resistance to the Kuomintang in his native Hunan. One story tells of his establishing a soviet district there in 1928 with one single knife: he happened to be conferring in a village with his secret society colleagues when the Kuomintang tax collectors arrived. Ho killed them with his knife, disarmed their guards and used the captured revolvers and rifles to arm the district's first peasant army![5] It was said that he used to enlist entire branches of the Ko Lao Hui into the Red Army. 'He is a big man,' says one of his men, 'and strong as a tiger. He never gets tired. They say he carried many of his wounded men on the march. Even when he was a Kuomintang general he lived as simply as his men. He cares nothing about personal possessions – except horses. He loved horses. Once he had a beautiful horse that he liked very much. It was captured by some enemy troops. Ho Lung went to battle to recover that horse. He got it back!'[6] Impetuous and headstrong, Ho was often accompanied on the battlefield by his sister, a woman general with unbound feet, and sometimes by his wife as well.*

While Mao Tse-tung and Chu Teh were organizing their soviet at Kiangsi in the 1929–30 period, Ho Lung had set up a base on the borders of Hunan and western Hupeh. His Second Army had merged with Tuan Teh-chang's Sixth Army to form the II Army Corps, under Ho's command, to defend the new soviet. But in January 1931 his men had been defeated by the Kuomintang and withdrew – with only 5,000 survivors, according to one account[7] – to Paokang in north-west Hupeh. Towards the end of 1932 Ho Lung moved north to the Honan–Shenshi border, but came back to Hunan to operate hit-and-run guerrilla activities in two pockets of territory in the region where the four provinces of Hunan, Hupeh, Szechuan and Kweichow almost meet. Sangchih, Ho Lung's birthplace, was his new headquarters.

---

* Ho Lung was belatedly elected to the C.C.P.'s Central Committee in 1945 and after the Communists' national victory he became a Minister (of Physical Culture) and Vice-Premier as well as member of the Politburo. But he came under left-wing attack during the Cultural Revolution.

Just before the Long March had begun from Kiangsi, the 6th Army Corps led by Hsiao Ke, Jen Pi-shih and Wang Chen, had been ordered on 7 August 1934 to march from the central soviet area to divert the Kuomintang and join Ho Lung's II Army Corps. On the way it had picked up the two foreign missionaries, Alfred Bosshardt and Arnolis Hayman. When these two forces had combined in October at Sangchi they took the name of the Second Front Army.

Hsiao Ke explained that the Second Front Army leaders lived in the Kweichow village of Nanyaochieh for a year, and that he and Ho Lung married two sisters from the Hunan countryside. The enemy sent ninety regiments to fight them for six months but withdrew defeated in August 1935. 'This,' Hsiao proudly claimed, 'was the most important fighting done by the Red Armies during 1935, Chu and Mao being on the Long March and comparatively out of warfare.' In September they made another drive to extend their territory, but on 19 November they were dislodged, soon after Mao had arrived in Shensi, and began a Long March of their own. After circling and feinting in Hunan and Kweichow to acquire funds and throw the Kuomintang off the scent, the Second Front Army passed near Kunming to cross the River of Golden Sand (or Yangtze) on 23 April 1936 and reached Sikang in June, swinging even further westwards by way of Tehtsin to avoid the worst mountain ranges. If this story could be fully told it should be the equal of the Long March itself. According to the account given to Edgar Snow, the Second had left Sangchih with 40,000 men (Smedley was told 35,000) and reached Sikang with 'not more than 20,000, more likely 15,000'. Hsiao Ke said it had 20,000 from the start, and Chang Kuo-tao says it had dropped to 5,000 by Sikang.[8]

When the Second and Fourth met at Kantzu in Sikang in the summer of 1936 their respective leaders dined delightedly not on the local butter and millet but on such delicacies as sea-slugs and shark's fin captured *en route* from the Kuomintang. Once again, as at Moukung a year before, two sets of commanders debated, this time for two weeks, what their next step should be. Ho Lung and his political commissar, Hsiao Ke, 'seriously advised Chang', according to the version of the story related to Smedley, 'to allow Chu to assume command and lead all the Red troops into north

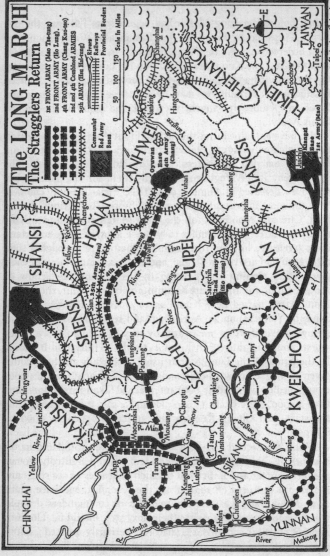

The LONG MARCH
The Stragglers Return

1st FRONT ARMY (Mao Tse-tung)
2nd FRONT ARMY (Ho Lung)
4th FRONT ARMY (Chang Kuo-tao)
2nd and 4th Combined ARMIES
25th ARMY (Hsu Hai-tung)

Rivers
Railways
Provincial Borders

Scale In Miles
0   50   100   150

Communist Red Army Bases

Malcolm Gabriele

China. By then Mao's column had reached north China and had developed a powerful political revolutionary base directly across the route of a possible Japanese advance. By then, also, political conditions throughout the country were better for the revolution and the food situation in Sikang so bad that Chang Kuo-tao agreed. General Chu therefore assumed command and led the Red forces northward to rejoin Mao Tse-tung [on 14 July according to Hsiao Ke]. Chang, however, still retained control of the Fourth Front Red Army, whose troops had still not been educated properly.' [9]

Why did Chang change his mind about marching north? Ho Lung, Hsiao Ke and Jen Pi-shih had not had direct contact with Mao Tse-tung since before the Tsunyi Conference and might well have had reservations about the Politburo reshuffle – just as Chang Kuo-tao had. But Jen Pi-shih was a *protégé* and former pupil of Mao, while Ho Lung and Hsiao Ke may have nursed some feeling for Mao as a fellow-Hunanese. Chang – and possibly Chu Teh as well – could well have argued that the leadership question was still an open one and that Mao's permanence as Politburo Chairman was far from assured.

But such arguments, if they were put forward at the Kantzu discussions, could only have underlined the real fact of the situation, namely that the centre of C.C.P. power and decision-making was in Shensi, not in Sikang. Whatever the outcome of the Party leadership tussle, it would be fought in the north and not in the west. No one likes to be on the edge of the action if he can help it, and Ho Lung, with his colleagues, had presumably intended all along to proceed north to the Shensi soviet. By this time Chu Teh may have sufficiently regretted his lapse of the previous August and grown tired of Chang Kuo-tao's company and of the backwaters of Sikang. Chang had at the most 30,000 men, Ho Lung at most half that number. But the arrival of Ho Lung's Second Army meant that Chang's hold over Chu Teh, if it ever existed, disappeared. Chang could hardly dictate to Ho Lung in these circumstances. And the bleakness of the prospects for food supply must have provided the final factor in Chang Kuo-tao's decision not to remain in a sulky minority of one but to join the march north.

For the third time, then, Chu Teh crossed the Grasslands of Chinghai, but on this occasion it took him forty days. He had negotiated them by July, and by the beginning of October his vanguard made contact with the men of Hsu Hai-tung's advance forces at Talachih in southern Kansu. There is some confusion over the order in which the units were reunited. According to Smedley, Chu Teh and Chang Kuo-tao arrived at Huihsien or Huining on 7 October 1936, Nieh Jung-chen and Tso Chuan led a welcome party of eight divisions from the First Front Army to meet them, and Dr George Hatem, the American doctor (of Syrian origin) who had thrown in his lot with the Red Army in Shensi, accompanied it.

'What a reunion !' the good doctor noted in his diary. 'Men threw their arms around each other, laughing and weeping at the same time, or walking arm-in-arm and pouring out questions about other comrades. Chu Teh was completely swallowed up in the crowd.'

But he observed of Chang : 'Chang Kuo-tao, the political commissar, is fat, tall and smooth. I wonder how he kept so fat while others lost every ounce of excess weight.' [10]

In this version, Ho Lung and Hsiao Ke followed with the Second Front Army some ten days later, arriving at Huihsien on 19 and 20 October 1936 – 'thus bringing the two-year migration to its end,' as Dr Jerome Ch'ên adds.[11] The 40,000 or more winter uniforms brought along for the new arrivals were inadequate, and Chou En-lai estimated that the survivors of the Sikang winter from all three armies – the Fourth, the Second and the two Army Corps of the First – to reach northern Kansu in October 1936 numbered between 40,000 and 50,000.[12]

What had happened was that the marchers from Sikang had divided at Lintan. Chang Kuo-tao and Chu Teh proceeded by a left route by way of Tungwei and Chingming, engaging the enemy forces of Hu Tsung-nan along the route. Meanwhile Ho Lung and Hsiao Ke made a diversionary detour to the right, near the Kansu–Shensi border, to draw the enemy off and, by one account, to act as a buffer between the rival First and Fourth.

But Chang Kuo-tao was not content to camp in Mao Tse-tung's new and enlarged compound. He decided to march on, still set on his old plan to establish a soviet base in the far north-west, in or near Sinkiang, in contact with his Russian friends and patrons. He ordered the V and IX Army Corps as well as Hsu Hsiang-chien's Thirtieth Army to cross the Yellow River at Chingyuan and strike towards Sinkiang. But Hsu was trapped by Kuomintang troops west of Sian; his army was thoroughly mauled and split in two. One column under Li Hsien-nien made towards Sinkiang but was then attacked by Chinese Moslem soldiers. It arrived at Urumchi with only 2,000 survivors. Snow declares that Hsu Hsiang-chien and Chang Kuo-tao were cut off from their men and arrived at Yenan in Shensi with only their personal bodyguards, sick and dispirited. Hsu Hsiang-chien was described by Nym Wales a few months afterwards as nervous, under the care of doctors, and 'the only man I met who seemed neurotic'. He and Li Hsien-nien were the only two senior Fourth Army officers whom Mao did not suspect of taking the Chang Kuo-tao line.[13] The few hundred survivors of this costly and mistaken venture were picked up in lorries by Chen Yun at Hsinghsingsia on the Kansu–Sinkiang border and brought back to the Yenan base in May 1937.[14]

Whatever might have been Chang Kuo-tao's chances of discrediting or even replacing Mao Tse-tung in Shensi in 1936, they were totally destroyed by his loss of both the Fourth Front Army and his military credibility as a result of this Sinkiang fiasco. In January 1937 he was formally tried for his errors before the C.C.P. Central Committee at Yenan, and condemned to study until the mistakes were rectified. Chu Teh was the leading testifier at the trial. But in 1938, after the United Front had been proclaimed, Chang defected to the Kuomintang.[15]

Nobody has recorded what transpired privately between Mao Tse-tung and Chu Teh when they first met at Paoan on 2 December 1936 after their thirteen-month separation.

PART THREE

The Consequences

Chapter 22

From Shensi to Peking

THE Shensi–Kansu soviet base, later named the Shensi–Kansu–Ninghsia Border Region, became in 1935–6 as a result of the Long March the new centre of the Red Army and of the Chinese Communist Party, with about 40,000 regular effective men under arms. Here, beneath the Great Wall of China, the Party took roots that were never again to be entirely pulled up; here it began its gradual but relentless drive to control the whole of China; here it established the basic pattern of administration that was to be followed on a nation-wide scale after 1949; and here Mao steadily consolidated his personal supremacy.

The capital of the Soviet was at first Paoan, or Waiyaopao, and it was here that Edgar Snow arrived as an eager young American journalist in 1936. 'The Reds,' he wrote, 'were putting up some new buildings in Pao An, but accommodations were very primitive while I was there. Mao lived with his wife in a two-room *yao-fang* with bare, poor, map-covered walls. He had known much worse, and as the son of a "rich" peasant in Hunan he had also known better. The Maos' chief luxury (like Chou's) was a mosquito net. Otherwise Mao lived very much like the rank and file of the Red Army. After ten years of leadership of the Reds, after hundreds of confiscations of property of landlords, officials, and tax collectors, he owned only his blankets and a few personal belongings, including two cotton uniforms.' [1]

At the end of the year the Red troops took Yenan from the Kuomintang and made it their new capital: for the next eleven years this was the Chinese Communists' headquarters and the name most readily associated with them at that time all over the world. 'It was certainly,' remarked Field Marshal Lord Montgomery after visiting it a quarter of a century later, 'a good place for a military headquarters.' [2]

The soviet had a population of about one and a half million, of whom ninety per cent were peasants. Its products included cotton, grain, livestock, salt, kerosene, coal and iron, and its economy was run by Lin Tsu-han (Chairman of the soviet Government) and Mao Tse-tung's brother, Mao Tse-min. The land policy, always a crucial indicator in the perpetual Marxist struggle between ideology and practical politics, was moderate. There was no indiscriminate confiscation of plots, but only an enforced reduction in rents, by between twenty-five per cent and forty per cent in 1937 so that they reached a maximum of one-third of the value of the yield. Security of tenure was provided by automatic renewal of tenancies save where the ownership changed hands. The landlords thus became 'rich peasants' and the rural labourers became small tenants.

Agriculture in these circumstances flourished. By 1941 the Border Region, as the soviet was then called, was self-sufficient in food. Yet, after ten years of Communist administration, two-thirds of the population remained illiterate. Yenan, in the word of one historian, was 'sex-less', with simple informal arrangements for marriage and divorce and a sternly puritanical attitude towards such offences as rape or promiscuity. Woman intellectuals dressed like men: 'Why should we look like women?' one explained.[3]

But the Communists were sadly vulnerable to Kuomintang attack, and if it had not been for the intensification of Japanese aggression against China it is almost certain that the Red Army would have been defeated in Shensi by another series of Kuomintang encirclement campaigns. Instead Mao Tse-tung was able to persuade the local warlords that Japan was a worse enemy than Communism, and that a joint front of all patriotic Chinese against the foreign enemy was necessary. He initiated discussions with the Kuomintang with a view to forming a second united front against Japanese aggression. His judgement proved correct: in the 1940s the Communists swept to power in China on a tide that was as much peasant nationalism as class revolt,* and Mao's patriotic

---

* This has been spelled out in a classic of modern sinology, Chalmers A. Johnson's *Peasant Nationalism and Communist Power: The Emergence of Revolutionary China 1937–45* (Stanford University

stand against the Japanese ensured that the intellectuals of the cities also came to admire him more than they did Chiang.

In all of this the Communists at Yenan found an enthusiastic ally in the 'Young Marshal', Chang Hsueh-liang, the leading northern warlord. Chang was technically on the side of the Kuomintang in the Chinese civil war and had fought some fierce battles against the Red Armies. But the Japanese had driven him from his Manchurian homeland and his chief concern was now to repel them and return home again. When news reached the Kuomintang Government in Chungking that the Young Marshal was flirting with Mao Tse-tung's forces in the north, Chiang Kai-shek himself flew up to Sian to investigate and, if necessary, bring his headstrong partner back into line. Instead Chang Hsueh-liang turned the tables on the Generalissimo by kidnapping him and forcing him in December 1936 to agree to an anti-Japanese united front as the price of his release.

Chou En-lai negotiated the precise terms of the new pact, by which the Communists agreed to place their armies under the command of the Kuomintang Military Council. Later the Kuomintang argued that this meant installing its own men in key positions in the Red Armies, but Mao rejected this interpretation and the united front proved, as it had once before, a fragile arrangement. Meanwhile, only a few weeks after the Marco Polo Bridge incident, where an exchange of fire between Japanese and Chinese troops near Peking heralded the final all-out phase of the Sino-Japanese war that was to last from mid-1937 to mid-1945, the Communists went through the outward motions of reconciliation with their old foes.

The main Red Army under Chu Teh and Peng Teh-huai was renamed the Eighth Route Army, with its three divisions commanded by Lin Piao, Ho Lung and Liu Po-cheng. It comprised 45,000 men. now Kuomintang-paid and Kuomintang-equipped, to harass the Japanese without internal distraction (and also to extend its influence while the Kuomintang's hands were tied behind its back). The rest of the Communist guerrillas still surviving in

---

Press, 1962). The formal decision for a united front was made at a Politburo conference at Waiyaopao in December 1935.

central China regrouped in Anhwei as the New Fourth Army under Yeh Ting, with about 15,000 men. They were similarly instructed.

But the Japanese advanced in an irresistible surge, taking most of the important cities and coastal areas by the end of 1938 in spite of Communist–Kuomintang resistance. The Sino–Japanese war then became a stalemate in which the internal differences on the Chinese side came once more to the fore. Early in 1941, after a number of incidents between mutually suspicious Red and Kuomintang forces in central China, Yeh Ting's New Fourth Army was almost wiped out by Chiang's troops. This put an end to what little collaboration there had been between the two organizations. The Nationalists, for their part, alleged that the Communists were 70 per cent concerned with extending the territory under their control, 20 per cent with co-operating with the Kuomintang government and only 10 per cent with fighting Japan.

During these years of stalemate, from 1942 to 1945, Chiang's troops gradually lost morale, softened by inaction, corrupted by smuggling, crushed by natural calamities and intimidated by the Kuomintang Party's political suppression tactics. Chiang, in the words of an American diplomat on the scene, had become a 'hostage of the corrupt forces he manipulates',[4] and a New York Times report of 1944 described his administration as 'bureaucratic, inefficient and corrupt'.[5] The Generalissimo had lost his two trump cards – the vitality of the economy (now distorted by the war and the Japanese blockade) and the efficiency of his army.

Meanwhile the Eighth Route Army grew and grew and grew under cover of the united front. From the original 45,000 stipulated in 1937 it swelled to 156,000 in 1938, to 400,000 by 1940 and 600,000 by 1945. The depleted New Fourth Army was revived under Chen Yi and Liu Shao-chi, whom Mao despatched south to ensure its reconstitution on sound ideological lines.

When Japan surrendered unconditionally in August 1945 after Soviet Russian intervention and the two atomic bombs, Mao flew to Chungking to confront Chiang. With American help, the two rivals were persuaded to sign an armistice agreement on 10 October, but it quickly collapsed in the prevailing atmosphere of mistrust and deliberate sabotage. Even the diplomacy of General

Marshall, the American President's personal conciliator, failed to paper over the cracks. In 1946 the civil war burst out again. By now the Communists, aided by the Japanese surrender, held sway over 315,000 square kilometres embracing nineteen million people. They were self-confident and their military tactics had been tested the hard way.

In the spring of 1947 Chen Yi registered a crushing defeat on the Kuomintang forces in Shantung province, and in the following year the Communists took all the north-eastern cities, having already controlled the north-eastern countryside ever since the Japanese defeat. Mao, who had estimated that another two to three years could be required to rout the Kuomintang, had to revise his timetable. In January 1949 the Red Armies took Peking and Mao wrote a poem:

> Thirty one years have passed
> And I am back in this ancient capital.[6]

In May Shanghai fell and by the autumn Chiang had fled the mainland to the island of Taiwan, where his Kuomintang administration still sits.

On 1 October 1949, Mao proclaimed the People's Republic of China from the Gate of Heavenly Peace, traditional rostrum in Peking for revolution and new dynasties. He thus inaugurated a régime which, though outwardly a coalition of various parties, was entirely controlled by the Chinese Communist Party whose unity he had been so instrumental in forging. It began with a mission to Moscow, where Mao spent several months negotiating aid. For a time it looked as if the Chinese Communists had become tame satellites of the Russian sun, but those who knew better had only to bide their time for a few years.

After a short honeymoon in which the Russian model was followed in everything from industrialization policy to school curricula, and in which the Soviet-trained Liu Shao-chi came into prominence as the skilful Party organizer who also got on well with the Russian leaders, Mao declared his independence in 1957–8 with the Hundred Flowers Campaign (an attempted revolt against the secret-police methods of the Kremlin), the Great Leap Forward (a rebellion against the conventional gradualism of the

Soviet economic advisers) and People's Commune (an explicit abandonment of the Soviet pattern of collectivization).

The Hundred Flowers, which were meant to open up debate within the Communist Party and between it and its critics, were promptly suppressed by Liu Shao-chi and his Party *apparatchiks*. The Great Leap was sabotaged by bad weather and excessive optimism : even Mao had to concede that you cannot double food grain production in a single year. The Communes were discredited by the barely-controlled famine of 1960–61.

The Liu-ists came back in a flurry of reproachful 'I-told-you-so's', and Mao retired sulking to the wings again. Liu was named Chairman of the Republic, and proceeded to settle the country back on a safe, ideologically conventional course. But Mao had inserted one of his chief supporters, Lin Piao of Long March fame, as Minister of Defence, and during the 1960s Lin gradually prepared the army for a break with the insufficiently revolutionary, excessively foreign-influenced and bureaucratic Liu-ists.

At the end of 1965 an obscure controversy over the ideological correctness of certain playwrights sparked off the Great Proletarian Cultural Revolution, in which Mao utilized the army and the younger generation (organized in the Red Guards) to unseat his opponents. Liu Shao-chi was disgraced, along with a good half of the top leadership of the country. But Mao's personal clique of supporters, including Chiang Ching, his wife, and Chen Po-ta, his former secretary, was too little respected to have it all its own way. Though Lin Piao threw the army, and Chou En-lai the government machine, on the side of Mao against Liu, neither ally was wholeheartedly sympathetic with the ultra-radicalism of the Maoist clique. They were more anti-Liu than pro-Mao, more in favour of Mao himself than of the policies and personalities of the Maoist group.

By 1970, therefore, as the People's Republic celebrated its twenty-first anniversary, China's political condition was complex and contradictory. After a high point of central government control in the 1950s, power was once more slipping out to the provinces and regions, and yet China was in many senses more united, more aware of being governed by a group of men with specific social objectives, than ever before. More progress was recorded in those twenty-one years in economic development, public health and education, family reform and social modernization, the cultivation of patriotism and hard work, than in any similar period in Chinese history. Every section and class of the population had become involved in the ferment of change. But the tensions within the highest ranks of the Communist leadership meant that these gains were partly hidden by the confusion and disorder of the Cultural Revolution.

The 1970s were to be the decade in which the Long Marchers would finally and grudgingly hand over to the next generation, and there was no way of telling what kind of leadership the latter would produce – except that it could take for granted, what the pioneer Communists could never assume, a fundamentally united nation, its borders respected by its neighbours and its military strength feared by its rivals. For without actually aggressing or absorbing indisputably foreign soil, the Communist government of Mao Tse-tung had proved – in Tibet in 1950, in Korea in 1951, on the Himalayan border with India in 1962, in Indo-China throughout the 1960s and on the Ussuri River in 1969 – that China at last possessed both the intention and the physical capacity of defending her heritage as fiercely and uncompromisingly as the Western powers had nibbled away at it throughout the preceding 150 years.

The four outstanding features of this remarkable régime – its group discipline, its treasuring of the guerrilla ethic, its sturdy independence of Russian tutelage and the towering authority of Mao – are not likely to be inherited by its successors, and each of them owes something to the epic Long March of 1934–5.

Chapter 23

The First Legacy:
Discipline

EVEN before the Long March the Communist Party had acquired a reputation for cohesiveness and collective self-control unusual in Chinese politics, where personalities and private factions had almost always provided the driving force. For the most part the Communists tried to act as if they trusted each other and were working for the same higher cause. But after the Long March their discipline and group loyalty became a byword both inside and outside China. For most of the time between 1935 and 1970 the leaders maintained an extraordinary degree of outward unity. As Teng Hsiao-ping, the C.C.P. Secretary-General, once declared: 'In our Party, all important matters have been for a long time decided by a Party collective not by any individual. This has been established as a tradition.' [1]

Mao had shown during the Futien mutiny that he was as ruthless as it was necessary to be in an emergency. But his knowledge of men had convinced him that persuasion does a job ten times better than compulsion. Like Xenophon, another leader of a long march, he believed that 'willing obedience always beats forced obedience'. His gift for political manipulation enabled him to maintain a balance between the various groups and cliques in the Party and in the Red Armies, and the outward harmony of the Politburo rested largely on his successful chairmanship of a coalition of factions.

After the Tsunyi Conference of 1935, where his ascendancy was first acknowledged, Mao gradually stripped the security police, under Teng Fa, of their power and kept colleagues in line by private argument and negotiation – in sharp contrast with contemporary developments in the Soviet Union. Instead of being subjected to physical threats, imprisonment and prejudged trials, those who criticized the Party majority decisions were obliged to argue it out in protracted ideological remoulding or political education sessions where every factor in their position, however embarrassingly personal or subjective, was brought out into the open. Mao invariably prevailed at these Party rectification struggles, which began to take formal shape after he had pledged, at the Sixth Plenum of the Central Committee at Yenan in 1938, the bolshevization of the Party through indoctrination, study and intellectual-cum-emotional rectification rather than through the crude purges of Stalinist Russia.

The initial threats to the outward harmony of the Long March leaders came from outsiders, from rival claimants to a seat at the top table who had not participated in the Long March. Wang Ming, who returned from Moscow at the end of 1937, was the first of these. Mao must have spent an anxious few days when Chou En-lai, Po Ku, Hsiang Ying and Yeh Ting – all his peers – went to confer with Wang at Hankow. But the ideas of the Twenty-eight Bolsheviks had already been discredited by the events of 1934, and Wang Ming's challenge to the Mao leadership subsided almost without trace.

The second threat came from Kao Kang, one of the Communist veterans who headed the Shensi soviet before the Long Marchers reached there in 1935. As the man in charge when the Long Marchers arrived, Kao held an initial advantage over them. As late as in 1942, Mao felt it wise or tactful to introduce a political speech with the phrase: 'I came to northern Shensi five or six years ago, yet I cannot compare with comrades like Kao Kang in my knowledge of conditions here or of the people of this region.' [2]

Almost two decades later, in 1955, Kao was expelled from his high positions and committed suicide. It was said that he had created in the Manchurian north-east an 'independent kingdom' of his own, parleying directly with the Soviet Union over Peking's head. Having inherited the top Party position in the north-east after Lin Piao went south to rout the retreating Kuomintang in 1948, Kao became identified as an effective fixer in Soviet relations. He was made Chairman of the State Planning Committee (which was not then under the Cabinet) and presided proudly over the opening of the Russian-aided refurbishment and expansion of

the Anshan Steelmill, centre-piece of the new régime's industrialization programme. He was virtually in complete control of the
first Five-Year Plan, and evidently threw his weight around too
much for the others in the Politburo.

In 1954 Liu Shao-chi spoke publicly about leaders who tried to
create their own kingdoms, and over a period of fourteen months
Kao was gradually stripped of his powers. No doubt this was one
of the factors in the deterioration of Sino–Soviet relations which
set in very soon afterwards.

The next public victim of intra-Party dissension was the general
who had led the III Army Corps, the vanguard of the Long March,
Peng Teh-huai. After the Great Leap Forward had started to
collapse in 1959, and the full measure of the damage which the
excessive ambition and optimism of the Maoists had wrought on
the economy began to stand revealed, Peng rebelled against the
Maoist line. As Minister of Defence he controlled the armed
services, which had been more influenced by Russian advice than
had the Party itself. Peng declared the Great Leap a disaster and
urged a return to the more conventional paths of development on
the Muscovite model. It turned out that Peng, like Kao, had been
unwise enough to lobby for Russian support in his manoeuvres.
In September 1959 he was disgraced:* his letter of confession
contained a plea for rehabilitation by working as a peasant, and
he was given a junior post, ironically, on the Sino–Soviet Friend-
ship State Farm in the north-east.[3]

Until 1966 these were the only public cracks in the façade of
Party unity. Considering the ability and creativeness of such men
as Liu Shao-chi and Chou En-lai, the ambition and organizing
capacity of such generals as Lin Piao, Chu Teh and Chen Yi, this
was no mean feat. Only when the memories of the Long March
had faded with the lapse of thirty years – a whole generation –
did the ranks of the Marchers begin publicly to break. And even
then the first major rebel against the Maoist leadership was
alleged to be a man who had not taken part in the March. Liu
Shao-chi, whom the Cultural Revolution of 1966–9 toppled from

---

* Others who were apparently implicated, or so it appeared at the
time, were Chang Wen-tien, Wang Chia-hsiang, Huang Ko-cheng,
Chen Yun, Lin Po-chu, Yang Cheng-wu, Li Ta and Hsiao Ke.

his previously secure position as Mao's deputy, successor and heir, almost certainly missed the Long March.

It is true that Kuo Hua-lun declares that Liu took part,[4] and Chen Chang-feng, Mao's batman, describes the three heroes – Mao, Chou and Liu – reaching the Shensi soviet together in October 1935. There is even an artist's depiction of the scene, with Liu's pudgy face at Mao's shoulder along with Chou En-lai, Tung Pi-wu and the rest.[5]

But the general belief, shared by Jerome Ch'ên and Edgar Snow, is that Liu was not on the March, being preoccupied with Party work elsewhere, in the big cities and the north of China. He may, of course, have begun the March but left it *en route*. He made a speech at the Second National Soviet Congress in Juiching in January 1934. According to Howard L. Boorman, Liu spent the two years up to October 1934 in the Kiangsi soviet, but was left behind then, 'assigned to political work in the "white areas"'.[6] Later the Central Committee praised his role in this urban work in the Kuomintang-controlled areas, and in December 1935, under the pseudonym Hu Fu, he was organizing student demonstrations against the Japanese in Peking. The German Communist, Hans Heinrich Wetzel, in his biography of Liu, describes him as leaving Kiangsi on the eve of the Long March, disguised as a history professor, to take up Party work in the 'white' or Kuomintang-administered areas of north China.[7] The other records are silent on this question, which is curious and it is better to assume, pending further testimony, that Liu was elsewhere.

In the Yenan period Liu emerged as a key supporter of Mao, often having the first sight of his writings – with the invariable request for criticism. It was Liu who underpinned the Maoist claims for ideological independence from Russian tutelage, and who lobbied strenuously for Mao against Wang Ming. He was the chief manager, as it were, of the 1945 Party Congress which openly adopted Maoism as its bible, and he was the principal spokesman for the notion that under Mao the Party had success-fully sinified Marxism and adapted it creatively to the special conditions of China (and thus of countries similarly placed in Asia and Africa).

Yet Liu was at home in the city rather than the village, and his genius was in urban organization rather than rural education.

Right at the beginning of the Party's career he had roundly declared that the urban workers, the proletariat of China, would have to 'take the peasants by the hand and lead them like children'.[8] It is questionable how far Liu really sympathized with many aspects of Mao's political beliefs, however much he may have admired his leadership of the guerrilla struggle for power. He was essentially an élitist, a Russian-trained Stalinist whose concept of the C.C.P. was different from Mao's vision of a mass line.[9] He may have hitched his wagon to Mao's star, seeing that Mao was being carried on a victorious wind, the better to ensure that policies of his, Liu's, own preference were followed in the Communist-China-to-be. We may never know.

What is certain is that in the days of the People's Republic Liu became the great organizer and Party administrator: unimaginative, shunning the limelight, strangely clumsy in his rare public appearances, he came gradually to stand for the safer, more orthodox, less risky road to socialism. Not for him the romantic voluntarism of the Maoist. And in 1967 he was named, unfairly, as the arch-saboteur of the Communist movement and dismissed from his various positions. There fell with him a number of Long March heroes, notably Teng Hsiao-ping who was, however, temporarily rehabilitated in the early 1970s to become senior Vice-Premier and effective head of government during Chou En-lai's illness. In the course of the contradictory recriminations of the Cultural Revolution such figures as Chen Yi, Ho Lung and even Chu Teh himself were publicly accused of all sorts of crimes and lapses. Some of the allegations went back to the pre-March days, and it was clear that personal jealousy, professional rivalry and political argumentation had been all along as prevalent in the Chinese Politburo as in any other group of intelligent reformers – only hidden from the outside world. The final public rupture in the Politburo spelt the end of the Long Marchers' solidarity, since it centred on the defection of Lin Piao himself, possibly the most able general the Communists produced and personally selected by Mao to be his named successor after the fall of Liu Shao-chi.

That capacity to sink differences, to smile together in public while arguing fiercely in private, was certainly a heritage from those months on the March, and in particular to the harnessing together of the unusual conciliatory gifts of Mao and Chou En-lai. It served the Party in good stead throughout the 1950s and 1960s, and was a major factor in its success, assisting it to maintain the tightest possible control over the Chinese population, the maximum acceptance of its consensus (or majority) decisions, and an international credibility which made China both feared and misunderstood to a degree unique in history.

Indeed the artificial façade of Politburo harmony became disastrously counter-productive – too successful for comfort – when it led Dulles and a whole generation of Western diplomat leaders to assume that the appearance was backed up by reality. If the Americans had witnessed some overt mud-slinging and public give-and-take in Chinese Communist politics they might not have taken the Maoist threat so seriously, and Sino-Western relations might have avoided the utter impasse of the Dulles–Rusk era.

Similarly the professional discipline of the People's Liberation Army, codified in the famous Three Rules of Discipline and the Eight Additional Rules, helped to sharpen the army and the 'veterans' or ex-servicemen who undertook civilian Party or Government roles after the assumption of power in 1949. The memories of the *camaraderie* of the March provided an emotional cement without which both army and Party would have been weaker.

Teng Hsiao-ping, the peppery limping Napoleon of the old Seventh Army, spoke for many March veterans when, as the new Party Secretary-General, he shed a tear at a 1956 Party Congress for the good old days when 'the soldiers carried water for the people, and the army officers covered the soldiers with their blankets'.[10]

Thus the Peking *People's Daily* in May 1963 recorded with pride that the soldiers of the so-called 'Good Eighth Company' who had 'liberated' Shanghai from Kuomintang rule in 1949 had already returned 1,390 lost articles, including 87 fountain-pens, to their rightful owners. This particular unit had, the Party newspaper went on to eulogize, 'triumphantly withstood the test of steel bullets in time of war and of sugar-coated bullets in time of peace'.[11]

When the anarchism of the Red Guards was unleashed by Mao in 1966–7, it was the army which kept it within bounds that at least preserved national unity and the basic apparatus of administration. It could well be that when the story of the Cultural Revolution comes finally to be told, the extra reserves of *esprit de corps* and group solidarity bequeathed to the People's Liberation Army by the Long March may be credited with the fact that the relatively modernized Chinese polity which the Communists had created did not disintegrate when the leaders began to quarrel openly.

Chapter 24

The Second Legacy: The Guerrilla Ethic

BUT the consequences of the shared hardships of the Long March went beyond the methodology and the framework within which the triumphant Communists ruled China after 1949. They are to be found even in the content of the policies pursued by the Government of the People's Republic. If post-March discipline was an important instrument for Communist power and for the minimally successful realization of Communist policies, the guerrilla ethic forged by the March profoundly affected the Party's social goals and the image which it had of the ideal China it proposed to construct.

The fact that the Communist armies won power on the basis of guerrilla warfare, as epitomized in the feats of daring against overwhelming odds on the March, meant that the Maoist leaders after 1949 saw as the supreme virtue the capacity to assert the power of one's will against a seemingly insuperable obstacle. So much so that the ideal was sometimes mistaken for reality, as in 1959 when Mao and his colleagues solemnly praised China's farmers for bringing in a grain harvest twice as big as the previous year's and called on them to notch up another forty per cent gain in the following year.

The Marchers were excellent for restoring China's self-confidence, sapped by a century of misrule and the ease of foreign encroachment, but they were not the best of planners and tended to be lamentable administrators. Chou En-lai was an obvious exception, but he and his 'technocrats' who built up the government structure after 1949 could not command a majority in the senior Party councils.

The primacy of will-power, the breathtaking voluntarism of Maoism, is linked with a deep-seated idealization of simple peasant virtues and a suspicion of all things urban. This is where the romanticism of Mao comes out most characteristically. The People's Commune – an integrated super-cooperative of 50,000 souls combining (unlike the Russian collective farm) all state, judicial, police and economic functions – was elevated to be the model not only for the whole of China, including the cities, but even for the entire world. 'A new social organization has appeared, fresh as the morning sun above the broad horizon of East Asia,' the Central Committee lyricized in 1958.[1]

The suspicion of the city, the dislike of its tendency to erode the honest old peasant values and to breed selfishness, greed and human exploitation, had been a strong feature of Mao and those of his colleagues who had spent the early 1930s building up the rural soviets in China. It was reinforced by the experiences of the March and became an ineradicable feature of Communist policy after 1949. For the Maoist leadership the ideal Chinese would be an all-rounder, a person equally adept at intellectual and manual work, as at home in agriculture as in industry.

When one of the Chinese economic planners told Han Suyin in the 1960s, 'We are not going to build any more cities', he reflected a fundamental policy premise which a different leadership would not have accepted. The idea, Han Suyin explained, was to pursue 'ruralization (even, perhaps one day, the abolition) of the cities as they were created, as strongholds of property and wealth, fortresses against a peasantry in revolt'.[2]

In 1959, intoxicated by the early results of the Communes, the Party attempted to organize the urban proletariat and middle class into similar organizations. 'In the future, the urban People's Communes ... will ... become instruments for the transformation of the old cities and construction of the new, socialist cities,' declared the Central Committee. But the urban Commune could not be foisted on the townspeople and was quickly dropped. In 1967 the Red Guard radicals of Shanghai again declared, in the heat of the excitement surrounding the Cultural Revolution, a Shanghai Commune – but the leadership had eventually to disapprove of it as premature. The Chinese urban classes resisted the Long Marchers' peasant romanticism right to the end.

The average Long Marcher despised desk-work, bureaucracy,

file-passing, and anything which impeded the direct relationship between ruler and ruled. After 1949, while Chou and Liu worked round the clock in their respective Government and Party head-quarters, Mao and his cronies preferred to tour the country inspecting conditions and progress, returning to Peking occasionally to compose a timeless resolution, report or memorandum. If Chou and Liu were the journalists concerned with day-to-day events, Mao was the creative writer striving for perfection and fame after death.

The army had a particularly difficult role in Communist China. It began its peacetime function in 1949 as a force trained on guerrilla lines. Its instinctive skills were those of attrition and of exploiting the enemy's weakness. 'If the enemy advances, we retreat; if the enemy halts, we harass; if the enemy tires, we attack. ...' As Mao put it in one of his standard texts: 'The ability to run away is precisely one of the characteristics of the guerrillas. Running away is the chief means of escaping from the passive state and regaining the initiative.' [3]

But in the final stages of the civil war it was the Kuomintang armies which were running away, to be almost literally pushed into the sea, and the Red generals resorted more to the positional warfare appropriate to a force which by then was equal in numbers with the foe, if not superior. In Korea, the next theatre of war where the Chinese army became involved, the Americans allowed little scope for guerrilla fighting, and Peng Teh-huai, who commanded the Chinese 'volunteers', must have emerged with heightened appreciation of the military hardware (especially aircraft) which only the Russians could supply.

Soon after the People's Republic was proclaimed, the army luxuriated in Russian patronage. Chu Teh sported a fancy uniform, and by 1955 some professional distinctions had been introduced. Ten senior generals were given the title of 'Marshal', decorations were dispensed, salaries (ranging from US $3 a month for privates to $250 for generals) took the place of the former 'free supply' of goods system, conscription was introduced and outward manifestations of rank were formalized. A Soviet-aided nuclear programme was initiated. A decade later the tide turned again. The guerrilla-ists took charge again, and the egalitarianism of the

March was once more the military goal. By then the Russians had reneged on their promise to help China develop nuclear weapons, and the Chinese scientists had developed their own low-budget H-bomb.

The army by then had begun to resist the economic reconstruction work which the Party imposed on it, as well as the everyone-a-soldier campaigns under which the Party sought to develop an amateur part-time militia whose standards the increasingly professionalized army officers could only despise. Peng Teh-huai's removal from the Ministry of Defence and the Party leadership in 1959 was largely bound up with these dissensions within the army. Lin Piao (who was technically commanding the Chinese armed forces during the Korean War but who was almost certainly ill, probably with tuberculosis) was supposed to inculcate more of a guerrilla ethic and a loyalty to Maoism in the armed forces after he succeeded Peng in 1959. But Peng merely reflected a view of affairs deeply held in the senior ranks of the army and there were others, notably Lo Jui-ching, who spoke for it in the 1960s.[4]

These were some of the tensions and contradictions produced by the debate over the relevancy or irrelevancy of the Long March experience to the problems of governing eight hundred million Chinese people and presiding over their modernization. Mao recognized the dilemma himself when he said soon after 1949: 'A serious task of economic construction is ahead of us. Things in which we were well versed will soon be needed no longer, and we shall have to do things in which we are not versed. This is our trouble.'[5]

For a few years he stood back and watched Chou and Liu build up their corps of technocrats and party-men, but finally he could not resist intervening to save something of the pristine purity of the earlier years. The technically trained must not forget the need for the guerrilla ethic – humility, the knack of keeping close to the ordinary man, of remembering the overriding need to restore his self-confidence and overcome his fear of authority. One must be both red *and* expert in Mao's China, in the China where the Long March is not merely recalled but relived.

When one tries to summarize the subtle differences between the various personalities and groups in the Chinese Communist leadership since 1949 it is impossible not to distort. Liu and Chou supported a considerable number of Mao's eccentricities, just as Mao accepted some of what he must inwardly have regarded as Liu's and Chou's unorthodoxies. They all compromised to some extent in the People's Republic.

Besides, their views as to what it was possible to achieve during their ever-lessening lifetimes in the China of their day must certainly have developed and been modified through the years. The good and the bad of the legacy of the Long March was in them all, if to differing degree.

It was Chou En-lai who, only a few months before becoming Prime Minister of the largest nation on earth, was found by his stretcher-bearers (who had to carry him during some of the last phases of the civil war when he was ill and the Kuomintang were on his heels) to have the soles of his feet showing through the holes in his shoes.[6] Men who had been through that kind of adventure for twenty years were not likely entirely to lose their bearings, forget their ideology or mistrust their comrades-in-arms merely because they were suddenly translated to the finery of the Imperial Palaces of the Forbidden City and the gushing attentions of international diplomacy.

But the habit of mind that the perennial encirclements and threats of encirclement by the Kuomintang engendered caused some of them to see the problems of China as a whole in a spirit of siege – with first the Americans, then the Russians in the role of encirclers. Thus the effort to achieve autarchy before it was strictly necessary, the suspicion of Soviet economic aid, the obsessive emphasis on self-reliance. By the same token that the Communists knew the real China better than Chiang Kai-shek did, so they knew far less of the outside world.

The March brought the fundamentally inward-looking element of the Party leadership to the helm: Mao never set foot outside China at all until after the civil war was over, and by his death he had not seen any foreign country other than Russia. It was inevitable, therefore, that the Chinese Communist's foreign alliances would be one of the most difficult things for all sides to handle.

Chapter 25

The Third Legacy: Independence from Russia

ONE of the most important consequences of the successful Long March was the guarantee which it provided that Moscow would have little sway over the Chinese Communists thereafter. The historical background of Sino-Russian competition in central Asia during the eighteenth and nineteenth centuries (which brought them finally to share what is, after all, the longest land border in the world), together with the fact that both countries represent totally different civilizations, ought to have suggested all along that any government in Peking was going to feel wary of any government in Moscow, whatever their respective ideological colouring. But the formation of the Chinese Communist Party was in origin as much a Russian as a Chinese initiative, and its early leaders were heavily indebted – intellectually and politically as well as financially – to the Kremlin. In the 1920s the U.S.S.R. was popular in China, and the Chinese Party felt little inhibition in leaning on its patron.

Mao was the only leader of real stature who remained outside the Soviet net. He never went to Russia until 1949, after the civil war was over, and he was never close to any of the Russian Comintern advisers during the 1920s and 1930s. The Russians were more at home with the already semi-Westernized or Western-leaning city intellectuals than with the ponderous, uncompromisingly Chinese figure of Mao.

And it was Mao who came first to distrust, almost by definition, their advice. Like the others, he praised them fulsomely up to the Shanghai massacre of 1927 and the collapse of the first united front with the Kuomintang. Indeed, Mao had caused some surprise, even unease, among his Chinese comrades by the thoroughness with which he implemented the Russian-inspired alliance

304

with the Kuomintang in the early 1920s. But after 1927 he distrusted their judgement and came more and more to see that they were playing a kind of blind man's buff in a China which they did not understand.

Mao never ceased to eulogize Marx, Engels, Lenin and Stalin, or to acknowledge his deep intellectual debt to the first three and his political debt to the fourth. But how should the one Chinese revolutionary who had come by the late 1920s to see the peasantry as the best standard-bearers of revolt regard a Leninism such as this: 'The city inevitably leads the village. The village inevitably follows the city. The only question is, which of the urban classes will the village follow'? [1] The Russian Marxists were thoroughly urban-oriented, and so were temperamentally out of tune with the realities of the Chinese revolution as they came to be revealed in the 1920s and 1930s.

It was also unavoidable that Russian strategic advice should be somewhat hit-and-miss. The Kremlin was distant from the Chinese scene in both geography and cultural understanding, and yet Stalin tried to direct the Chinese Communist Party, via the Comintern, very closely – often by the use of telegrams. Unfortunately his biggest preoccupation was the suppression of his own opposition in Moscow, and his China policy therefore tended to be decided on the basis of which set of Chinese advisers were for him or against him, rather than which set had the best grasp of the subject. Incomparably astute in Russian intrigue, the Georgian master was sadly wrong in many of his Chinese moves.

The three main indictments of Russian policy in China before the Long March were: first, the pursuance of the united front far beyond the point at which it had become both doomed and dangerous to the Chinese Communists in 1927; [2] second, the irresponsibly adventuristic push of 1930 which led to the defeat at Changsha; and third, the inflexibly inappropriate military tactics which culminated in the loss of the old Chinese soviet bases in the south in 1934.

This latter fault, debated so hotly during the March, was pinned initially on Braun (Li Teh), the Comintern officer who rode on the Long March. Braun afterwards confessed to Edgar Snow: 'Chinese psychology and tradition, and the peculiarities of the Chinese military experience, have to decide the main tactics in a given situation. Chinese comrades know better than we do the correct tactics of revolutionary warfare in their own country.' [3]

But while Mao was in the process of disproving in the field the pre-eminence of Braun's tactics, the politicians in Moscow were preparing to call for Mao's head. Mao had been out of favour with the Politburo before, and at the time the March began in 1934 the Chinese Communist Party was technically still under the leadership of the Twenty-Eight Bolsheviks. Wank Ming himself, the supreme leader of the Party, was in Moscow, where he retained Stalin's favour and confidence almost to the end of the 1930s.

Although Mao was elected Politburo Chairman at the Tsunyi Conference in January 1935, this was not acknowledged in the U.S.S.R. until 1938 – and then only by way of a casual reference in an encyclopaedia article.[4] Mao's position was an awkward one in that he was in technical defiance of the Comintern – and thus of Stalin – through his insubordination to their representative in China, from Tsunyi onwards.[5] Not until the end of 1937 did Wang return from Moscow, and not until a few years later could Mao succeed in finally denouncing him and drumming him out of the Party leadership.

Meanwhile the Maoist group could pretend to Snow in Yenan in 1936 that the man behind the Kiangsi fiasco was Braun.[6] By then the Comintern was itself racked by Stalin's purges and no one quite knew who in Moscow was supporting whom. Later, when good relations with Stalin became more important, the Maoists transferred the blame from Braun to their Chinese opponents, Wang Ming and Po Ku. But the process by which this embarrassing mutiny was accorded *a posteriori* justification was slow and painful. The 1945 speech in which Mao itemized at length the faults of the Wang Ming faction was kept on the secret list for eight years, and the Seventh Party Congress at which he delivered it (thereby consolidating his unchallenged supremacy in the Party) was entirely ignored in the Russian press.[7]

To add to the trouble, Stalin's advice in the post-war phase was as misguided as it had been earlier. He still doubted the Chinese Communists' potential strength, kept his options open in the direction of the Kuomintang and even suggested on the eve of

Mao's final victory in 1949 that the Red Armies stop at the Yangtze and leave southern China to Chiang – a proposition that horrified the Chinese Politburo, for whom the unification of China under a central government, a goal which had eluded every Chinese Republican since the last Emperor was pulled down from his Dragon Throne in 1912, was a matter of the highest priority.

'After the war,' Stalin conceded to Kardelj in 1948, 'we invited the Chinese comrades to come to Moscow and we discussed the situation in China. We told them bluntly that we considered the development of the uprising in China had no prospects, that the Chinese comrades should seek a *modus vivendi* with Chiang Kai-shek, that they should join the Chiang Kai-shek Government and dissolve their army. The Chinese comrades agreed here in Moscow with the views of the Soviet comrades, but went back to China and acted quite otherwise. They mustered their forces, organized their armies and now, as we see, they are beating Chiang Kai-shek's army. Now in the case of China, we admit we were wrong.' [8]

So when the Chinese Party proclaimed the People's Republic from Tienanmen Square in 1949 it was beholden very little to the Soviet Union. Nevertheless Stalin remained the chief executive of the most powerful country in the Communist camp and of the only nation that could claim the status of super-power beside the arch-capitalist and arch-imperialist United States. A marriage of convenience was patched up. But Mao had to wait for months in Moscow in the winter of 1949–50 before he could get the agreements he wanted, and in all respects the Chinese felt disappointed at the niggardliness of Russian assistance. Gradually the relationship deteriorated. Russian financial support for such other Afro-Asian countries as India and Egypt, disagreements over the cold war with the Western capitalist nations, mutual dissatisfaction with the results of Soviet technical aid to China and ideological differences over destalinization, the Communes and the Great Leap Forward (which Suslov, the Russian theoretician, unkindly described as trying to industrialize by 'cavalry charges') – all these over-burdened an alliance which hardly had time to establish itself.[9]

Later the territorial differences came into the open, and the

Sino-Soviet frontier was revealed to the world as the longest and tensest flash-point of the 1970s. Fighting on the Ussuri River near Vladivostok in 1969 and armed clashes in the late 1960s on the Sinkiang–Kazakhstan border led some Western commentators to the assumption that war was inevitable: Harrison Salisbury, the veteran *New York Times* correspondent, wrote a book called *The Coming War Between Russia and China*.

Time will tell whether these prognostications are sound. It is doubtful that either set of leaders, in Moscow or Peking, would fall victim to the kind of hysteria which alone could prompt an all-out struggle. The two countries have much to lose and nothing to gain from a fight which neither could win, and it is more likely that they will indulge in sabre-rattling for a considerable time without going over the brink.

But whatever happens, the Long March has ensured that the Chinese have less respect for the Russians, and the Russians less liking for the Chinese, than might have been the case if a different kind of Chinese Communist leadership had come to power – or even if Chiang Kai-shek (whose son and political heir, Chiang Ching-kuo, was trained in Moscow and married a Russian wife) had won the civil war.

The split between the two giant Communist Parties at the beginning of the 1960s had incalculable consequences. It decisively weakened the appeal of Marxism in the world at large, unleashing an undignified competition for influence over the international Communist movement in which the ideals of socialism took second place to the demands of Russian and Chinese chauvinism. It transformed the relatively monolithic nature of the Soviet camp, accelerated the diffusion of power among the smaller countries of the bloc, and brought the Russians closer to the West than they had been since Tsarist days.

It dramatized more than anything else, more even than the United Nations Conference on Trade and Development (UNCTAD), the fact that the most significant division of mankind was not ideological (Communist *versus* capitalist) but cultural-racial-economic (the European-white-industrialized *versus* the Afro-Asian-coloured-underdeveloped). The North-South poverty gap replaced the East-West political confrontation as the big issue of the twentieth century, and the Long March must claim its share of the responsibility for the events which led to this new world polarization's coming as soon as it did.

Chapter 26

The Fourth Legacy: Supremacy of Mao

IT is not at all true to say, as we have seen, that Mao was un-challenged as supreme leader of the Chinese Communist Party by the time his exhausted columns reached Shensi province in the autumn of 1935. There were two senior Party figures over whom he had not been able to impose his authority: Chang Kuo-tao, who had refused to submit to Mao's leadership at Moukung and Maoerkhai that summer, and Wang Ming, who remained scorn-fully in the wings in Moscow throughout the Long March. Chang had been, like Mao, a founder-member of the Party, and Wang was Mao's immediate predecessor as the senior man in the Polit-buro and had never acknowledged the change-over.

There were also a number of other Party figures who had not been participants in the process by which Mao became, during the Long March, accepted by his comrades physically present as leader for the time being, and who would not necessarily endorse his claims. These included Hsiang Ying, Liu Chih-tan, Kao Kang, Hsiao Ke, Jen Pi-shih, Hsu Hai-tung and Ho Lung.

Nor could Mao even be sure that his other peers in the move-ment who had supported him during the March – notably Chou En-lai and Liu Shao-chi – would continue to do so in the different conditions of Yenan. The rigours and the dangers of the March demanded unquestioning discipline and loyalty to the one man whose tactical sense was obviously right. But once the Red Armies were safe again, there was room for manoeuvre, opportunity to debate policy anew.

A clue to Mao Tse-tung's own recognition of his precariousness in the C.C.P. chair at this time came to light in 1969 when Edgar Snow published his revised edition of *Red Star over China*. It in-cluded a remark made to him by Mao Tse-tung at Paoan on 25

July 1936 – nine months after the end of the Long March but three months before the Second and Fourth Front Armies reached Shensi – which Snow had omitted from the first edition because it seemed at the time of little interest.

'Another reason,' Mao had declared, 'for its [the Party's] invincibility lies in the extraordinary ability and courage and loyalty of the human material, the revolutionary cadres. Comrades Chu Teh, Wang Ming, Lo Fu, Chou En-lai, Po Ku, Wang Chia-hsiang, Peng Teh-huai, Lo Mai, Teng Fa, Hsiang Ying, Hsu Hai-tung, Chen Yun, Lin Piao, Chang Kuo-tao, Hsu Hsiang-chien, Chen Chang-hao, Ho Lung, Hsiao Ke – all these, working together for a single purpose, have made the Red Army and the soviet movement. And these and others yet to come will lead us to ultimate victory.' [1]

The inference is that Mao Tse-tung needed in the summer of 1936 to underline, for foreign consumption, the harmony within the C.C.P. leadership to such an extent that he was ready to praise such patent adversaries as Chang Kuo-tao and Wang Ming. Perhaps his strongest motive was to give pause and thought to the Kremlin. But the list is also interesting, as Snow points out, for its omissions – notably those of Liu Shao-chi, Liu Po-cheng, Chen Yi, Liu Chih-tan and Kao Kang.

There is another view of the nature of the change in leadership after Tsunyi which says that the Party merely elevated the post of Chairman over that of Secretary-General – hitherto the senior post. Edgar Snow argues thus in his new edition of *Red Star over China*. Jerome Ch'ên points out that Mao's failure to hold the post of Secretary-General reflects his lack of a Party power base, and this may have caused him instinctively to distrust the men holding that position. Furthermore all the successive Secretaries-General (Chen Tu-hsiu, Chu Chiu-pai, Hsiang Chung-fa, Wang Ming, Po Ku, Chang Wen-tien, Liu Shao-chi and Teng Hsiao-ping) have been foreign-trained, and thus represent another sphere of activity – foreign relations – in which Mao has not excelled.[2]

Chang Kuo-tao took himself out of the running in the Polit-buro stakes, as we have seen, by having ignominiously to swallow his pride and return north with Ho Lung and Chu Teh, and by then proceeding to lose his army in an ill-planned expedition to

Sinkiang. He ceased to be a threat to Mao from the time of his trial in 1937. After the civil war he settled in Hong Kong, where he gave some interviews to Western scholars and wrote his memoirs. Ultimately he emigrated to Canada.[3]

Mao at this time was bursting with the self-confidence that the success of the March understandably generated. A penetrating glimpse into his mind is given by the poem 'Snow' which he probably wrote in 1936:

> The northern scene:
> A thousand leagues locked in ice,
> A myriad leagues of fluttering snow.
> On either side of the Great Wall
> Only one vastness to be seen.
> Up and down this broad river
> Torrents flatten and stiffen.
> The mountains are dancing silver serpents
> And hills, like waxen elephants, plod on the plain,
> Challenging heaven with their heights.
> A sunny day is needed
> For seeing them, with added elegance,
> In red and white.
>
> Such is the beauty of these mountains and rivers
> That has been admired by unnumbered heroes –
> The great emperors of Chin and Han
> Lacking literary brilliance,
> Those of Tang and Sung
> Having but few romantic inclinations,
> And the prodigious Genghis Khan
> Knowing only how to bend his bow
>   and shoot at vultures.
> All are past and gone !
> For men of vision
> We must seek among the present generation.[4]

But Wang Ming was a more difficult customer because of his strong Russian connections. He returned to China in 1937 with all the prestige of being Stalin's adviser on colonial affairs and a member of the Comintern's Executive Committee. From the end of

1937 to the 'Congress of Victors' in 1945 Mao strove to eliminate Wang's threat to his leadership. The big issue of the day was the strategy for the second united front. Wang urged a full-scale alliance with the Kuomintang in order to improve the semi-legal status of the Chinese Communist Party and to gain renewed access to the all-important Chinese proletariat, potential leaders of the revolution.

His position, bluntly, was that the Chinese Communists should thank Comrade Mao heartily for saving the day and preserving the main Red Army force from impossible dangers – but now that it was all over they should get their sights back on the really urgent task of organizing the urban revolutionaries, work which should be left to the 'real' Communists as distinct from the peasant romantics of the Mao group.

Mao retorted that this would be to repeat the old mistakes of ten years before. The basic conflict in China was between peasants and landlords, not between factory workers and industrialists: China was not a capitalist society at all but one still shrouded in feudalism and colonialism. The revolution should be squarely based on peasant grievances and on anti-Japanese patriotism. The united front should go only as far as was necessary to permit the Chinese Communist Party to pursue these aims. To go further in the interests of an overestimation of the value of the urban poor, against all the warnings of the past, would be an act of capitulation to the Kuomintang.

Luckily for Mao his two colleagues who had approved his assumption of the chairmanhip at Tsunyi, Chou and Liu, supported him in this debate also. Possibly they were motivated by the surpassing need for reconciliation of the kind at which Mao was adept, in contrast with the horrific prospect of the Twenty-eight Bolsheviks' recreating in China the bloody Stalinist purges of which they had mastered the techniques. The Chinese comrades had had a taste of these in the months in Kiangsi immediately before the Long March, as practised by Po Ku, then Chinese Communist Party Secretary, and Chou himself had reportedly been involved in one gruesome retaliation for a Party colleague's be-trayal [5] – something which lost support for the Communists.

No doubt Mao also worked on their sense of national pride,

which could be made to see Wang's overt dependence on Russian patrons as demeaning and unnecessarily servile. Mao was doubly fortunate in that the internal schisms in the Comintern at this time prevented that organization from effectively backing up Wang in his mission to China. The European comrades were otherwise engaged.

There is one document, purportedly captured from the Communists by the Kuomintang, in which Chou is described in 1938 as wavering between the C.C.P. and the Kuomintang.[6] Mao, it was said, did not want to provoke the domestic and international repercussions of another split in the Party so soon after Chang Kuo-tao's defection to the enemy, and so he was acting towards Chou with restraint. An open rupture between the two men was, however, in the mind of this commentator, 'eventually inevitable'. But Chou took care to keep any doubts to himself. 'All those who, in the past,' he told a reception committee on his return to Yenan from Shanghai talks with the Kuomintang in August 1943, 'doubted Comrade Mao Tse-tung's leadership or his thoughts are now proved completely wrong.'[7]

Another view is that Wang Ming's return rekindled the dissensions among the Internationals, who until then had met weekly at Chang Wen-tien's house in Yenan with a minimum of harmony. According to Chen Jan and Tu Chen-nung, Wang brought three messages from Stalin; that Mao's ignorance of Marxism-Leninism should be remedied by tuition from the Russian-educated Chinese comrades, that Chang Kuo-tao's disgrace had been overdone, and that Chang Wen-tien was unsuited for the C.C.P. Secretary-Generalship on account of his associations with former Trotskyites in Moscow. This third message naturally aroused the suspicion that Wang coveted the Secretary-Generalship himself. Mao was thus able to play the Internationals against each other.[8]

Mao thus succeeded in getting the Central Committee to endorse his own interpretation of the complex history of the Party debates since the Shanghai massacre of 1927. It did this after an exhaustive series of Party rectification campaigns in which the issues were thrashed out over and over again until everyone professed to accept the logic of Mao's exposition. It was better than assassinations, political executions and physical torture – and it did leave everyone much clearer about the issues involved. It was at this time that the foundation was laid for the cult of Mao and of his Thoughts which was to reach such heights of absurdity in the Cultural Revolution of the late 1960s. This was achieved by a group of young propagandists recruited by Mao, and he relied on it for his supremacy over those who were better organizers than he.

Finally, in 1945 Mao was ready for a full-scale Party Congress (the first since 1928) at which his victory was affirmed, his leadership enshrined and his theoretical writings recognized as original and creative contributions to the science of Marxism-Leninism. Liu Shao-chi announced to the world that the Chinese Communist Party had become a proletarian party of an entirely new type, and the Party's new Constitution explicitly took Maoism as its guiding ideology.

Wang Ming had already been reduced to relatively subordinate Party functions, and the Seventh Chinese Communist Party Congress of 1945 removed his last frail hopes of power. When Edgar Snow met him at Yenan in 1939, he was 'astonished by Wang's youthful appearance (he was then only thirty-two) charmed by his urbanity, and struck by marks of his sedentary life – he was a round little man, a head shorter than Mao – as well as by the mild contempt with which he was referred to by veterans of the Long March. Clearly,' Snow goes on, 'Wang constituted no further threat to Mao, but perhaps the latter welcomed – *pour encourager les autres* – Wang's earnest and open espousal of his cause in order to expose and thoroughly eradicate any remaining tendencies in the Party to exploit borrowed Russian prestige in competing for internal power.'

Wang Ming returned to the Soviet Union, not to be heard of again until the Cultural Revolution of 1966–9 (when there appeared to be at least one lobby in Moscow ready to offer him as an alternative leader for China, hopeless though that must seem to anyone aware of his history).[9]

One other famous name is worth recalling at this juncture. Li Li-San, another of the Party pioneers who had helped Chou to found the original Young Chinese Communist group in Paris in 1921, and the man who took supreme command of the Party in 1929–30, also retired to the U.S.S.R. and then returned to China. But he made his peace with the Maoists, never again sought the highest positions, and instead was satisfied with rather unglamorous specialist functions in the early years of the People's Republic. He was for a time Minister of Labour and remained on the Party's Central Committee.

Finally, it has to be observed that some of Mao's lesser rivals proved surprisingly accident-prone in the crucial four or five years after the Long March. Both Hsiang Ying and Liu Chih-tan were killed in battle in 1941 and 1936 respectively, and a tragic aeroplane crash in April 1946 took the lives of Po Ku, Teng Fa, Yeh Ting and Wang Jo-fei.

But once in power in Peking after 1949, Mao found that the accommodations which Chou and Liu and others had been willing to make with him in the interests of winning power for the revolutionary cause could no longer be taken for granted. Now that the Kuomintang was not on their heels, the Chinese Communists could devote their full energies to national reconstruction and the introduction of socialism – and found that they were not by any means of one mind on these matters.

Kao Kang and Peng Teh-huai, who were both foolish enough to cultivate independent relations with the Kremlin and think they could get away with it, were not by then serious contenders for the chairmanship, and were fairly easily dealt with. But the constant erosion of many of Mao's favourite policies by the men through whom he had to see them implemented – Chou En-lai, the head of the government machine, and Liu Shao-chi, the head of the Party bureaucracy – was more difficult to prevent.

To begin with Mao tended to withdraw into the background and let the 'technocrats' run things. It made it easier to get things out of the Russians. It might also have been pushing his luck to have done otherwise. Whether he intended it or not, Mao soon found himself called on to mediate between his jealous lieutenants. Roderick McFarquhar has characterized the debate of the 1950s as between the 'sloganeers' who followed Liu's flag and the 'pragmatists' who followed Chou's, the central issue being the speed of attempted economic advance.[10] Mao came down on Liu's side, and Chou, though skilful at cutting his losses and trimming his sails to new winds, was considerably discomfited during the period of the Great Leap Forward.

But then the power balance in the Politburo changed yet again. The Leap, with all of the Chairman's prestige behind it, collapsed. Nature struck the deadly blow of three successive crop failures, Khrushchev petulantly cut off Russian technical aid and many Chinese Communist Party stalwarts must have wondered if Heaven were not already withdrawing its mandate from Mao after only ten years of rule. Even the sun, Liu ominously remarked to Party confidants, was sometimes eclipsed.

Things were so bad that Liu and Chou, whose temperaments were utterly different, made common cause again – inferentially against Mao's policies, though not his person. Once again, in the early 1960s, the Chairman was on the side-lines. But he had taken out a good insurance against this turn of events in the form of the appointment of Lin Piao, his most fervent acolyte, as Defence Minister. Lin rallied the army and, through the army, the students – and in 1965 Mao struck again, this time reversing his tactics. He backed Chou instead of Liu.

Another way of putting it would be that he made a direct challenge to Liu's power with the all-important army behind him, and that Chou, obliged to show which horse he was backing, chose, as always, the winner. Whichever way it went, Liu was in fact toppled from power and a new coalition emerged in 1967–8 of Mao, Chou and Lin Piao. There were occasions when Chou and Lin seemed to be ganging up to stop the old man's excesses – but neither had the power base to act fully independently.

Then, in 1969–71, came the final, and probably the most resented challenge to the Chairman, from Lin Piao himself. The favourite turned against his patron, evidently finding his policy uncongenial and believing that in an army-controlled China, he, as army leader, could assume the top position in the state. But he overestimated his support from his colleagues in this endeavour, overstepped himself in trying to assassinate Mao, and reportedly died in an air crash in Mongolia while attempting to flee to the Soviet Union.

Mao thus continued to the end the indispensable Chairman, the manipulator of factions, the mediator of feuds, the anticipator of trouble. Always one step ahead of his friends and two steps ahead of his enemies, he showed a political durability unmatched in modern times. For over forty-two years he reigned as the titular and almost unchallenged Chairman, supreme leader and father figure of the Chinese Communist Party. No other statesman of our time has had such luck, and the heroic circumstances in which Mao assumed the Party chair at the beginning of the Long March, along with the bravado and skill with which he forced his personality on his comrades during the balance of that remarkable epic, played a crucial part in the establishment of the Mao legend.

Chapter 27

Conclusion

IT is hard to know which is the more remarkable, the dogged courage of the Long Marchers in the face of natural obstacles and superior enemy forces, or the sheer good luck which time and again saved their adventure from disaster. The persistence and bravery has been described at some length in this book, but the element of chance over which the Communists had no control must not be lost sight of. The really extraordinary thing is that the Communists' secondary enemies – the provincial warlords in alliance with the Kuomintang, and the Japanese – turned out in certain respects to be their best friends.

The Kuomintang itself never lost an opportunity to take a crack at the Red Armies. But from the passivity of the Kwangtungese provincial troops which allowed the First Front Army to break out of the Fifth Encirclement, and Lung Yun's equivocation at the Chinsha River in May, to the langour of the Shensi warlord Yang Hu-cheng (who left the Paoan base alone for a good year after the Long Marchers had reached it, thus giving them the respite they needed), the Kuomintang's so-called allies proved at worst double-dealers, at best frail pillars of the anti-Communist campaign.

Finally, the Japanese invaders, who had saved the Kiangsi soviet from almost certain destruction at the hands of the Kuomintang at the time of the Third Encirclement offensive in 1931, again came to the rescue in 1936–7. If they had not intensified their aggression against China, culminating in the Marco Polo Bridge incident, the northern warlords would more naturally have backed Chiang Kai-shek against Mao Tse-tung than acted as mediators between them in the interests of a united front against Japan. The Japanese occupation of Manchuria gave the Communists their chance to disarm the Kuomintang, to court the warlords, to consolidate their Shensi base and to plan more thoroughly their blueprint for taking over China. One cannot see, looking back over the decades, any other *deus ex machina* which might have saved the Shensi soviet base from collapse at the hands of an ultimate Kuomintang encirclement in 1936 or 1937.

The Long March was, therefore, a case of good fortune and human courage combining under the leadership of a man who could see better than anyone else the way history itself was moving, and was thus able – or so he gave the impression – by a heave of his own single human pair of shoulders, to give it just that decisive little push at the top of the hill which caused it momentarily to run ahead of itself, carrying him and his cause in its wake. There are not many examples in the twentieth century of a single man making this magical contact with the cycles of human history – Lenin in 1917 and Churchill at Dunkirk, certainly; Kennedy during the Cuban crisis, possibly. The Long March under Mao Tse-tung was such an event, and in some respects more hung on it. The Chinese people, after all, comprise a quarter of mankind, and the Communist victory was the force which began to bring China to life after its centuries of sleep and degradation.

The reader has been subjected to many excerpts from Chinese Communist publications, in the belief that their evocation of detail and first-hand reportage outweighs by some modest margin their depressing polemics and crude Party propaganda. If he has survived thus far, he may stomach one last quotation to rub home the role of the Long March in the imaginations of a new generation of Chinese, and one with which we outsiders will have to deal before this century is out. It is a reminiscence by a young Red soldier from the Japanese war of 1937–45:

'At the end of October, we were nearing Weitsun, the principal point of supply of the Japanese in attacking Hsinkou and other districts. One pitch-black night we were groping our way into the village along a small lane at the south entrance. It was my first engagement with the enemy and I felt very tense, not knowing how I ought to act. Squad leader Hu Tung-sheng told me to follow him closely. He was a veteran fighter who had taken part in the Long March and everybody trusted him.

' "Rat-tat-tat !" an enemy machine-gun at the cross-road opened up; bullets whizzed past me. By the flash we could see a corner formed by the wall in front of us. Instead of sheltering himself in this safe nook the squad leader shoved me in it, pressing himself tight against the outer wall alongside me. The enemy machine-gun snapped at us with greater fury, nipping the padding of our sleeves.

'The squad leader kept shooting at the enemy to make them consume more bullets. As day dawned the enemy machine-gun became silent. Suddenly the squad leader turned towards me and said :

' "Little Wang, make ready to charge !"

'Without waiting for my reply he jumped out and dashed forward. I followed him. As we approached the enemy machine-gun I thought I heard him shout :

' "Off with it !" followed immediately by two deafening reports. In a twinkling, amid the pall of smoke, we were at the enemy. Grappling with one of them, the squad leader grabbed hold of the machine-gun, and with a mighty jerk, pulled it over. Then he administered a ferocious kick or two at the fellow, who gave a pained squeal and dropped back motionless. At this instant, there was firing from the left and the squad leader fell, still clutching the machine-gun. Horror-stricken, I hurried to lift him and support him against my body, not knowing what to do. (By now, all our troops had entered the village.) After a while, he raised his head slightly and said,

' "Little Wang, don't be afraid. . . ."

'A faint smile flickered over his face. With his last ounce of strength he fished out an old worn cap and placed it in my hand. He tried to say something but could not summon up sufficient strength to give utterance to it. But I understood what he would have said had he been able.

'Squad leader Hu Tung-sheng was in the habit of telling us the story about the cap.

'He was a newly-enlisted fighter of sixteen during the Long March, with a peasant towel tied round his head. He had a great fancy for the regular cap worn by the older comrades, with its attractive visor and red star. He felt that, being a Red Army man, he was entitled to a cap! So he made a point of pestering the political instructor for one during the Long March. Although rather advanced in age and in bad health, the political instructor had a mild temper. He looked upon the little fighter as a child, and whenever the latter reminded him about a cap, he would laugh and say he would issue one to him later. Actually he could not keep his promise, for they did not have even a spare strip of cloth, least of all a spare cap!

'The troops were continually on the march. Despite the fact that there was a lack of food and health in general was bad, they kept marching. One day, when the troops were about to tackle another snow-capped mountain, Hu Tung-sheng felt he couldn't move a step. Having gone two days without food, he was desperately weak with hunger. His shoes were worn out and his legs swollen. Sitting on the snow and staring at the mountain before him the top of which rose beyond view, he panted and was unable to rise. Thinking it was the end, he burst into tears.

'At this moment the political instructor came. He had aged considerably in the last few days, with sunken features, high cheekbones and stubbly beard. His face was pale and emaciated. As he walked, he panted in a distressing manner. It was obvious that, weak as he had always been, he was now at a very low ebb. But he always looked composed and never complained of being tired. He stopped beside Hu Tung-sheng.

' "Oh, it's you! Why are you crying?"

' "Political Instructor, I'm so hungry and I can't walk."

'Sitting down beside Hu, the political instructor massaged his leg. Then he fished out from his pocket the last piece of boiled ox-hide and offered it to Hu. At first Hu declined, being aware that the political instructor had had nothing himself for the past two days. But the political instructor insisted on his eating it and he was at last obliged to accept it. He felt a tremendous love surge through him.

'Eating the ox-hide, Hu Tung-sheng listened to the political instructor. One must not sit here, the political instructor was saying: if he did, he would die. The revolution was hard, but it was for the happiness of all the Chinese people, so we must make every effort to play our part in it.

'Now Hu Tung-sheng felt warmer and strength came to him. The political instructor pulled him to his feet and helped him along.

'Next day, when it was getting dark, snow came down in big flakes. Hu Tung-sheng was trudging along laboriously pulling out his legs, step by step, from the deep snow. Breathing was difficult. He really wanted to lie down and rest. But he didn't dare, remembering the political instructor's words. Then he saw ahead of him a man lying on the snow. As he came near, he saw it was the political instructor! Greatly upset, Hu Tung-sheng hurried to him. The political instructor had just fallen. He looked as white as the snow and was already at his last gasp. The political instructor recognized Hu and said brokenly:

' "Never mind me . . . go on . . . don't fall out. . . ."

'Hu Tung-sheng crouched silently in front of the political instructor. The latter took off his cap.

' "Tung-sheng . . ." he said softly, "the Red Army cap . . . take it. . . ."

'Noticing the dilapidated shoes on Hu Tung-sheng's feet, he pointed to his own, still in fairly good condition, and said, panting:

' "Shoes . . . mine . . . put them on . . . I am no more."

'The last words struck Tung-sheng like a dagger thrust in his heart. He checked himself with great effort and held back his tears. He could not accept the cap, nor the shoes. How could he take shoes from the feet of his leader and comrade-in-arms – even though he stood in great need of them? Seeing that he would not take the shoes, the political instructor said:

' "Go on . . . go on . . . go on. . . ."

'It was all he was capable of uttering. It sounded like a command. His voice became weaker and weaker, till finally it became inaudible.

'The wind howled madly, the snow thickened. When Hu Tung-sheng woke from his stupor, the political instructor's body was already cold and stiff. Only then did he realize the full significance of the political instructor's words: he must "go on!" He stood up abruptly, broke some branches from a shrub at the side of the path and placed them over the political instructor; then he put the cap on his head, and carefully taking the cloth shoes from the political instructor's feet and putting them on his own, walked on with a determined air, braving the wind and snow. Tears streamed down his face, like flood-waters in a mountain stream.

'For the first time, Hu Tung-sheng put on his Red Army cap – the very cap he had just handed me.

'Squad leader Hu Tung-sheng died quietly after placing the cap in my hands. Although he didn't say much, I knew all he intended to say. More than once, I had seen the cap, and heard its history. How unhappy he had felt when, the Red Army having been reorganized into the Eighth Route Army, the leadership, for the sake of solidarity in resistance to Japanese aggression, had exhorted them to doff the Red Army cap and wear the Kuomintang one. He had obeyed, of course, but for a long time he chafed inwardly. He had wrapped the cap in oiled paper and put it in a bundle which he placed in his pillow. When a battle was on, he kept it on his person. He often took it out and looked at it, and told us what the political instructor had said to him.

'So I knew what the squad leader wanted to say was this: Be with the revolution everlasting. Don't fall out; keep on! Live and die for it, like the old political instructor. Be loyal, as he had been, to the revolution, give all, including one's life if need be, for the revolution.' [1]

The sentimental reader whose eye is moistened by this tale, and the sceptical reader whose nostrils quiver in indignant revulsion at yet another dose of patently contrived political propaganda, are both right. The Long March itself, as an historical event, is such an amalgam of true heroism and false political reconstruction. Historians will continue to argue over their respective proportions. But one thing is certain: the Long March is the main fare on which the national pride and will to improvement of millions of young Chinese are being nourished. Red Army caps are being handed on, figuratively speaking, in all walks of Chinese life and in all spheres of the effort to modernize in which this nation is now engaged. Even outside China, in Singapore and San Francisco, Hong Kong and Soho, the Long March is fixed in the minds of young Chinese as a sort of Pilgrim's Progress, and Chinese teachers use it as a model for idealistic struggle. A splurge of publicity was given in the Chinese press to the 40th anniversary of the Long March in 1975.[2] It has become the subject of a Chinese play and a Western novel.[3]

Of the 800 survivors of the Long March who ran the Chinese Communist Party and the Chinese Army and Government in 1949, there are perhaps only 200–300 alive today – managing factories or communes, at desks or parade-grounds, behind microphones or in front of blackboards. They have established their legend. Now another generation is taking it over. The non-Chinese three-quarters of mankind would do well to know this legend, and to evaluate it with the scepticism that historical truth demands but also with the sympathy that any expression of idealism, however mistakenly one may believe it to be channelled, ought to evoke.

Notes

INTRODUCTION

1. Edgar Snow, *Red Star Over China*, Gollancz, 1969, p. 190. The phrasing was slightly different in the original edition.
2. Viscount Montgomery, *Three Continents*, Collins, 1962, p. 20.
3. Samuel Griffith, *The Chinese People's Liberation Army*, Weidenfeld & Nicolson, 1968, p. 47.
4. As translated by Michael Bullock and Jerome Ch'ên, in Jerome Ch'ên, *Mao and the Chinese Revolution*, Oxford University Press, p. 336.
5. Griffith, op. cit., pp. 55–6.
6. Nym Wales, *Red Dust*, p. 76. Edgar Snow recorded on his second visit to the Shensi soviet: 'To my regret, however, I discovered that the collective history of the Long March, which was being compiled when I left Pao An in 1936, had been abandoned. It was considered "inconsistent with the united front" ' (*The Battle for Asia*, p. 268). Nym Wales comments that when she arrived in Yenan in 1937, 'I discovered that the Communist officials had lost nearly all their records during the Long March, in 1935. I was, during those months, the only person there who was comprehensively gathering historical information. Hsu Meng-chiu, the Communist historian ... was frustrated in his efforts to compile party history, owing to the preoccupation of other officials with affairs of the moment. My position as a foreigner and a guest gave me, then, an advantage over the official keeper of the records in that the individuals with whom I sought interviews felt bound by courtesy to spend some time with me – even the busiest ones' (ibid., p. ix). Edgar Snow has told me that much of his material from participants on the Long March he lent to Ting Ling, the Communist woman writer, who was then planning to write herself on the Long March: she never returned his notes and subsequently fell into disgrace in the 1960s.

7. Jerome Ch'ên, 'Resolutions of the Tsunyi Conference', *China Quarterly*, No. 40, October 1969, pp. 1, 37–8.
8. Robert Payne, *Mao Tse-tung*, Weybright & Talley, New York, 1969, p. 145.
9. ibid., pp. 145 and 223.
10. Howard L. Boorman, *China Quarterly*, No. 16, October 1963, p. 12.
11. Snow, *Red Star Over China*, op. cit., p. 205. But Snow is a little too lyrical in calling the March, in the same passage, 'the emigration of a nation'.

PART ONE *The Context*

Chapter 1. Tradition of Peasant Uprising

1. Lo Erh-kang, *Tai-ping Tien-kuo Shih-kang*, Shanghai, 4th edition, 1938, p. 52 – as cited in McAleavy, *The Modern History of China*, Weidenfeld & Nicolson, 1967, p. 68.
2. See generally Vincent Yu-chung Shih, *The Taiping Ideology*, University of Washington Press, Seattle, 1967.
3. Agnes Smedley, *The Great Road*, Monthly Review Press, New York, 1972.
4. See Victor Purcell, *The Boxer Uprising*, Cambridge University Press, 1962.
5. Ch'ên, *Mao and the Chinese Revolution*, op. cit., p. 8.
6. But later the Communist scholars began to reassess these predecessor movements and down-grade their revolutionary nature – especially the Taipings. See James P. Harrison, 'Communist Interpretations of the Chinese Peasant Wars', *China Quarterly*, No. 24, October 1965, p. 92, or his *The Communists and Chinese Peasant Rebellions*, Atheneum, New York, 1969.
7. Grosset & Dunlap, New York, 1933. Re-published by C. Chivers, 1969.
8. J. L. Buck, *Chinese Farm Economy*, Shanghai, 1930.
9. London, 1932, p. 64.
10. *Report of the Council Committee of Technical Co-operation Between League of Nations and China*, Geneva, 1934, pp. 18 and 20. See the useful discussion in Shanti Swarup, *A Study of the Chinese Communist Movement 1927–1934*, Oxford University Press, 1966, pp. 50–56.
11. Translated from the first Chinese edition of Mao, *Selected Works*, Vol. IV, Peking, p. 190.

12. Benjamin I. Schwartz, *Chinese Communism and the Rise of Mao*, Harper & Row, New York, p. 191.
13. See the discussion in J. E. and S. R. Rue, *Mao Tse-tung in Opposition*, Stanford University Press, 1967, pp. 286–7, and in Arthur Cohen, *The Communism of Mao Tse-tung*, University of Chicago Press, 1964, pp. 38–50.
14. Ch'ên, *Mao and the Chinese Revolution*, op. cit., p. 224.

Chapter 2. The Kuomintang

1. Williams, *A Short History of China*, p. 600.
2. Quoted in Schwartz, op. cit., p. 52.
3. *The Soviet in World Affairs*, Vol. II, London, 1930, p. 653.
4. Robert Payne, *Chiang Kai-shek*, Weybright & Talley, New York, 1969.
5. *Chiang Kai-shek: China's Destiny, and Chinese Economic Theory*, notes and commentary by Philip Jaffe, Dennis Dobson, 1947, p. 322.

Chapter 3. The Chinese Communist Party

1. Schwartz, op. cit., p. 8.
2. Chow Tse-tsung, *The May Fourth Movement*, Stanford University Press, 1960, p. 248.
3. For the controversy over numbers and names see Rue, op. cit., pp. 293–5; and Ch'ên, *Mao and the Chinese Revolution*, op. cit., pp. 361–2.
4. *The Fourth Congress of the Communist International*, op. cit., London, 1922, p. 221.
5. Hua Kang, *Chung-kuo te Ko-ming-shih* (History of the Great Chinese Revolution), Shanghai, 1932, p. 447.
6. Schwartz, op. cit., p. 97.
7. See Smedley, op. cit., pp. 199–200; Rue, op. cit., pp. 67–8; J. Guillermaz, 'The Nanchang Uprising', *China Quarterly*, No. 11, July 1962, p. 161; C. Martin Wilbur, 'The Ashes of Defeat', *China Quarterly*, No. 18, April 1964, p. 3; and Roy Hofheinz, Jr, 'The Autumn Harvest Insurrection', *China Quarterly*, No. 32, October 1967, p. 37.
8. Smedley, op. cit., p. 209; Ch'ên, *Mao and the Chinese Revolution*, op. cit., p. 132; Chu Li-fu, *Erh-wan Wu-chien Li Chang-cheng chi*, pp. 3–4; Snow, *Red Star Over China*, op. cit., pp. 165–6.
9. Hsiao Tso-liang, 'Chinese Communism and the Canton Soviet of 1927', *China Quarterly*, No. 30, April 1967, p. 49.
10. *Byulleten 'Oppozitzii'*, 1930, No. 15–16, pp. 2–3.

11. Shinkichi Eto, 'Hai-lu-feng – the First Chinese Soviet Government', *China Quarterly*, No. 8, October 1961, p. 161; and No. 9, January 1962, p. 149.
12. 'Mu-chien Cheng-chih Hsing-shih yu Chun-chung Kung-tso' (Present Political Conditions and Mass Activities), p. 42, as translated and cited in Schwartz, op. cit., p. 128.
13. *Ti-liu-tzu Ta-hui-hou ti Cheng-chih Kung-tso* (Political Activities After the Sixth Congress), p. 52, as translated and cited in Schwartz, op. cit., p. 137.
14. Smedley, op. cit., p. 274. See generally James P. Harrison, 'The Li Li-san Line and the C.C.P. in 1930', *China Quarterly*, No. 14, April 1963, p. 178 and No. 15, July 1963, p. 140.
15. Tang Shin-she, 'Comrade Mao Tse-tung', *Inprecorr*, Vol. X, No. 14, 20 March 1930.
16. Leon Trotsky, *Problems of the Chinese Revolution*, Pioneer Publishers, New York, 1932, p. 302; also Stalin, *Works*, Vol. 12, p. 258.
17. *A Documentary History of Chinese Communism*, p. 185.
18. Smedley, op. cit., p. 277.
19. 'Attack on Nanchang', as translated by Michael Bullock and Jerome Ch'ên in Ch'ên, *Mao and the Chinese Revolution*, op. cit., p. 329.
20. Li Ang, in Chou En-lai, *Mu-chien Chung-kuo Tang Ti Tsu-chih Wen-ti* (Organizational Problems of the Chinese Communist Party), Shanghai, 1929, p. 15 (as translated and cited in Schwartz, op. cit., p. 149).
21. *Mao Tse-tung Hsuan-chi*, Peking, 1961, Vol. 1, p. 150.
22. Swarup, op. cit., pp. 163, 238–9.
23. Rue, op. cit., pp. 244–6.

Chapter 4. Mao and Chu, The March Commanders

1. The account that follows is drawn principally from Ch'ên, *Mao and the Chinese Revolution*, op. cit.; Stuart Schram, *Mao Tse-tung*, Penguin, 1970; and Snow, *Red Star Over China*, op. cit., pp. 130–81.
2. Snow, *Red Star Over China*, op. cit., pp. 148–9.
3. ibid., p. 152.
4. Reminiscence of Professor Pai Yu (Schram, op. cit., p. 64).
5. Schram, *The Political Thought of Mao Tse-tung*, Penguin, 1969, p. 143.
6. Rue, op. cit., pp. 37–9.
7. Schram, *Mao Tse-tung*, op. cit., p. 72.
8. ibid., p. 80.

9. Schram, *The Political Thought of Mao Tse-tung*, op. cit., pp. 178–80.

10. Schwartz, op. cit., p. 74; Howard L. Boorman, 'Mao Tse-tung: The Lacquered Image', *China Quarterly*, No. 16, October 1963, p. 17.

11. Rue, op. cit., p. 37.

12. Snow, *Red Star Over China*, op. cit., p. 90.

13. Payne, *Mao Tse-tung*, op. cit., p. 217.

14. Agnes Smedley, *Battle Hymn of China*, Gollancz, 1944, p. 122.

15. Snow, *Red Star Over China*, op. cit., p. 96. The first incident has excited some indignation among Mao-ologists: see Jerome Ch'ên's reproach for Robert Payne's version of it in Ch'ên, *Mao and the Chinese Revolution*, op. cit., p. 211.

16. Payne, *Mao Tse-tung*, op. cit., p. 278.

17. Schram, *Mao Tse-tung*, op. cit., pp. 232–3.

18. Gunther Stein, *The Challenge of Red China*, Pilot Press, 1945, p. 83.

19. Chai Tso-chun, *Tsai Mao-chu-hsi Shen-pien* (With Chairman Mao), Wuhan, 1959, pp. 10–17, as translated and cited in Ch'ên, op. cit., p. 209.

20. Snow, *Red Star Over China*, op. cit., p. 94.

21. Ch'ên, *Mao and the Chinese Revolution*, op. cit., p. 315.

22. Schram, *Mao Tse-tung*, op. cit. (first edition, 1966), pp. 267 and 295.

23. Snow, *Red Star Over China*, op. cit., p. 147.

24. Snow, *Red Star Over China*, op. cit. (first edition, Gollancz, 1937), p. 153. The latter remark was omitted in the second edition (p. 155).

25. Translated by Bullock and Ch'ên, Ch'ên, *Mao and the Chinese Revolution*, op. cit., p. 347.

26. Schram, *Mao Tse-tung*, op. cit., p. 191, says Yang was executed in 1930, and Ch'ên, *Mao and the Chinese Revolution*, op. cit., p. 150, says Mao married Ho in 1928.

27. See the report in Paul Johnson's 'London Diary', *New Statesman*, 20 January 1967; also Chu Hao-jan, 'Mao's Wife – Chiang Ching', *China Quarterly*, No. 31, July 1967, p. 149.

28. Schram, *Mao Tse-tung*, op. cit., p. 49.

29. See Rue, op. cit., passim.

30. Payne, *Mao Tse-tung*, op. cit., pp. 269–70.

31. Ch'ên, *Mao and the Chinese Revolution*, op. cit., pp. 212–13; Boorman, op. cit., p. 29.

32. Most of the following account is from Smedley, *The Great Road*, op. cit.; and Chang Han-ching, *Hsi Chan-chang ti Chu-chiang Chu Te*.

33. ibid, p. 138.
34. Snow, *Red Star Over China*, op. cit., p. 335.
35. Smedley, *Battle Hymn of China*, op. cit., p. 150.
36. Smedley's account of Chu's story is the only evidence for this meeting, but Rue, op. cit., pp. 67–8, accepts it as most plausible.
37. Martin C. Wilbur has suggested that Chu's role in the Nanchang Uprising – known mainly by his own account – may have been exaggerated. 'The Ashes of Defeat', *China Quarterly*, No. 18, April 1964, p. 6.
38. Smedley, *Battle Hymn of China*, op. cit., pp. 226–7.
39. Payne, *Mao Tse-tung*, op. cit., p. 117.
40. Snow, *Red Star Over China*, op. cit, p. 337.
41. Smedley, *Battle Hymn of China*, op. cit., p. 226.
42. Hsiao Jen-ho, 'Chu Teh, from Student to General', *Ming Pao Monthly*, Vol. 4, No. 3, Hong Kong, March 1969, pp. 29–34.
43. J. Chester Cheng, *Asian Survey*, June 1964, referring to the *Kung-tso Tung-hsun* or P.L.A. Bulletin of Activities. But this identification is challenged by John Gittings, *China Quarterly*, No. 27, July 1966, p. 175.
44. See the Red Guard publication, 'The Ambitious Warlord Chu Teh', in *Chan-pao* (Battle) of 24 February 1967, reproduced in *Ming Pao Monthly* (Hong Kong), Vol. 2, No. 6, June 1967, pp. 32–5.
45. Anthony Garavente, 'The Long March', *China Quarterly*, No. 22, April 1965, p. 122.
46. Jerome Ch'ên, *China Quarterly*, No. 40, October 1969, pp. 36–7.
47. According to Chen Jan: see Warren Kuo, 'The Soviet Movement of the Chinese Communist Party', Part II, *Issues and Studies* (Taipei), Vol. II, No. 5, February 1966. pp. 40–41.
48. According to Kung Chu, *The Red Army and I*, Hong Kong, 1954, p. 226. See also Chu Wen-lin, 'Lin Piao – Mao Tse-tung's Close Comrade-in-Arms', *Issues and Studies* (Taipei), Vol. III, No. 4, January 1967, p. 7.
49. Warren Kuo, 'The Underground Struggle Between the Kuomintang and the C.C.P.', Part III, *Issues and Studies* (Taipei), Vol. III, No. 5, February 1967, p. 36.
50. In a talk at the General Work Conference of 24 October 1966, as reported in *Mao Tse-tung Ssu-hsiang Wan-sui* of April 1967 and quoted in Jerome Ch'ên (ed.), *Mao*, Prentice-Hall, N.J., 1969, p. 95. Chou also voted against expulsion, according to Mao.

Chapter 5. Chingkangshan and the Kiangsi Soviet

1. See Rue, op. cit., p. 83. Another source says Mao arrived with only 400 men: Warren Kuo, *Issues and Studies* (Taipei), Vol. II, No. 4, January 1966, p. 46 Much of this chapter is based on Rue's reconstructions.

2. See Schram, *Mao Tse-tung*, pp. 115–17 and Stuart R. Schram, 'Mao Tse-tung and Secret Societies', *China Quarterly*, No. 27, July 1966, p. 1.

3. See Rue, op. cit., p. 81.

4. *Selected Works of Mao Tse-tung*, Vol. IV, p. 156.

5. Rue, op. cit., pp. 93–4.

6. Wang Shou-tao, in Wales, op. cit., pp. 78–9.

7. Smedley, *The Great Road*, op. cit., p. 235.

8. ibid., p. 262.

9. Payne, *Mao Tse-tung*, op. cit., p. 116.

10. Rue, op. cit., pp. 231–5; Ch'ên, *Mao and the Chinese Revolution*, op. cit, pp. 164–5.

11. Documents in the Chen Cheng Collection cited in Wu Tien-wei, 'The Kiangsi Soviet Period', *Journal of Asian Studies*, Vol. XXIX, No. 2, February 1970, p. 398; *China News Analysis*, Hong Kong, No. 217, 21 February 1958.

12. Kai-yu Hsu, *Chou En-lai*, pp. 102–3. Most of the information and quotations relating to Chou in the text are taken from Hsu, especially pp. 2 and 8.

13. Trygve Lötveit, *Chinese Communism 1931–1934*, Scandinavian Institute of Asian Studies, Copenhagen, 1973, p. 72.

14. Edgar Snow, *The Other Side of the River*, Gollancz, 1963, p. 298.

15. Hsu, op. cit., p. 229.

16. Helen Foster Snow, *Women in Red China*, Monton, The Hague, 1967, p. 250.

17. Rue, op. cit., p. 45, declares that: 'Chou argued against Mao's theories of guerrilla warfare until at least 1938, and probably was not completely won over until the first Party rectification movement in 1942–43.'

18. Testimony of Chen Jan: see *Issues and Studies* (Taipei), Vol. III, No. 8, May 1967, p. 50.

19. *Selected Works of Mao Tse-tung*, Vol. I, pp. 214–15 (text of 'Strategy in China's Revolutionary War' of December 1936).

20. *Mao Tse-tung Ssu-hsiang Wan-sui*, April 1967, cited in Ch'ên (ed.), *Mao*, op cit., p. 95.

21. 'The Organization Problem of the C.C.P. at Present' (Chou's

elaboration of a Central Committee resolution 9 January 1932), as translated in Hsu, op. cit., p. 107, from a document in the Hoover Collection. For another, hostile summary of the differences between Mao and Chou at this period, see Warren Kuo, 'The Anti-Mao Struggle during the Government 4th Encircling Offensive', *Issues and Studies* (Taipei), Vol. III, No. 8, May 1967, at pp. 45–6.

22. Liu Po-cheng, 'On the Time Factor of Strategy and Tactics and the Question of our Red Army's Negligence in Current Strategy and Tactics', *The Revolution and War*, No. 1, 1 August 1932.

23. Though he may have passed through Juiching en route: Rue, op. cit., p. 246.

24. Snow, *Red Star Over China*, op. cit., p. 389 (first edition), p. 479 (second edition).

25. Ch'ên, op. cit., pp. 177–8; Warren Kuo, 'The Struggle Against the Lo Ming Line in the C.C.P.', *Issues and Studies* (Taipei), Vol. III, Nos. 10 and 11, July and August 1967, pp. 31 and 37.

Chapter 6. The Decision to March

1. Ku Wu-chung, a Red Commander who was captured, said that salt in the Red areas cost 'more than a dollar an ounce' (*North China Herald*, 17 October 1934, p. 114). Kiangsi always relies on Coastal Kiangsu, via the Yangtze, for its salt. See generally Anthony Garavente, 'The Long March', *China Quarterly*, No. 22, April 1965, p. 94.

2. Speech at the National Political Work Conference, *Hung-hsing*, No. 28, 18 February 1934, p. 80, as cited in *China Quarterly*, No. 40, October 1969, p. 24. The Communists used ladder-charges against the blockhouses, and also built their own: Shi Buzhi, *Chingkangshan ti Fenghuo*, pp. 120–26. See generally F. F. Liu, *A Military History of Modern China*, Princeton University Press, 1956, pp. 97–8.

3. Kung Chu, op. cit, p. 397.

4. Kuan-yu Chung-yang Shih-hsing Wei-yuan-hui Pao-kao te Chueh-i (Resolution of the Report of the Central Executive Committee), pp. 126–7, in Chung-hua Su-wei-ai Kung-ho-kuo ti Erh-tzu Chuan-kuo Tai-piao Ta-hui Wen-hsien (Documents of the Second National Congress of the Chinese Soviet Republic), March 1934 – 008.6102P/5044/0246, reel 16, in the microfilm of the Chen Cheng collection, as translated and cited by Lötveit, op. cit.

5. Edgar Snow, *Random Notes on Red China*, Harvard University Press, 1957, p. 60. See also the Tsunyi Resolutions in Chapter 11 below.

6. 'The Fukien Rebellion and the C.C.P.: A Case of Maoist Revisionism', *China Quarterly*, No. 37, January 1969, p. 31.
7. Lötveit, op. cit.
3. Kung Chu, op. cit., p. 397.
8. The Second All-China Soviet Congress is described in Rue, op. cit., pp. 261–3, and in Lötveit, op. cit. See also two unpublished theses: D. K. Waller's 'The First and Second National Congresses of the Chinese Soviet Republic, 1931 and 1934' (School of Oriental and African Studies, London) and Chi-hsi Hu's 'La Lutte pour le Pouvoir dans la République Soviétique Chinoise de Jiangxi, 1931–34' (Centre de Documentation sur Chine Contemporaine, Paris).
9. Kung Chu, op. cit., pp. 395–400; confirmed by Chang Kuo-tao in an interview with H. R. Lieberman in Hong Kong in 1952 (recorded at Stanford University).
10. Snow, *Red Star Over China*, op. cit., p. 437. Li Teh flew back to Europe from Yenan in 1939, and in 1964, after the Sino-Soviet split, wrote an anti-Maoist article in *Neues Deutschland* (East Berlin) on 27 May identifying himself as Otto Braun.
11. *Hung-hsing*, No. 47, 10 June 1934, p. 3, as translated by Jerome Ch'ên, *China Quarterly*, No. 40, October 1969, p. 27; *Issues and Studies* (Taipei), Vol. 4, No. 4, January 1968, p. 42.
12. Schram, *Mao Tse-tung*, op. cit., p. 162.
13. See Miao Min, *Fang Chih-min, Revolutionary Fighter*, Foreign Languages Press, Peking, 1962, pp. 103–5 et seq.; Garavente, op. cit., p. 102; Snow, *Red Star Over China*, op. cit., p. 467; Ch'ên, *Mao and the Chinese Revolution*, op. cit., pp. 182–3; and Chu Li-fu, *Erh-wan Wu-chien Li Chang-cheng Chi*, op. cit., pp. 20–21.
14. Lien Chen, *Tsung Tung-nan Tao Hsi-pei*, p. 3. There is one view that the break-out was agreed in principle as early as the Second Soviet Congress in January 1934, and there is evidence of some preparations being made from February onwards: see Garavente, op. cit., p. 99. A German ex-Communist says that Liu Shao-chi was the first to propose in January a shift to Shensi, near Soviet Mongolia, and that Mao supported him: Hans Heinrich Wetzel, *Liu Shao Chi, Le Moine Rouge*, Denoel, Paris, 1961, pp. 163–4.
15. Fu Lien-chang, 'Mao Chu-hsi Tsai Yu-tu', *Hung-chi Piao-piao*, January 1959, pp. 6–7.
16. *History of the Twentieth Century*, B.P.C. Publishing, 1969, p. 1,356.
17. See the Tsunyi Resolutions in Chapter 10 below.
18. *China Quarterly*, No. 40, October 1969, p. 16.
19. Payne, *Mao Tse-tung*, op. cit., p. 148.

20. André Malraux, *Antimemoirs*, trans. Terence Kilmartin, Hamish Hamilton, 1968, p. 533.

21. Payne, *Mao Tse-tung*, op. cit., p. 164; see also the Tsunyi Resolutions in Chapter 10 below.

PART TWO. *The March*

Chapter 7. Daily Life on the March

1. Smedley, *The Great Road*, op. cit., p. 309. See also Snow, *Red Star Over China*, op. cit., p. 189; and T. A. Hsia, 'Chu Chiu-pai's Autobiographical Writings: The Making and Destruction of a "Tender-Hearted" Communist', *China Quarterly*, No. 25, January 1966, p. 176.

2. Edgar Snow, *The Battle for Asia*, Random House, 1941, pp. 131–3. Hsiang Ying is here – and on three occasions in *Red Star Over China*, and also by Payne – referred to as Han Ying. He was killed in battle in 1941.

3. Snow, *The Battle for Asia*, op. cit., p. 487, says Mao Tse-tan but Ch'ên (*Mao and the Chinese Revolution*, op. cit., p. 184) says Mao Tse-min. See his genealogy of the Mao family in *Mao Papers*.

4. *Hsing-huo liao-yuan* (A Single Spark Can Light A Prairie Fire), Hong Kong, 1960, pp. 3–4; Carl K. Wei in *Issues and Studies*, Taipei, Vol. 5, No. 4, p. 36; Chang Nan-sheng in *Peking Review* No. 47, 21 November 1975, p. 15.

5. Griffith, op. cit., pp. 330–31; and Adam Hopkins, 'The Missionary's Ordeal', *Sunday Times*, 4 January 1970 – the reminiscence of Alfred Bosshardt.

6. Griffith, op. cit.

7. ibid., p. 80.

8. Smedley, *The Great Road*, op. cit., p. 310.

9. *Sunday Times*, 4 January 1970; Snow, *The Battle for Asia*, op. cit., p. 362.

10. Wales, op. cit., p. 217; Smedley, *The Great Road*, op. cit., p. 329; and Ch'ên, *Mao and the Chinese Revolution*, op. cit., pp. 150 and 197.

11. Wales, op. cit., p. 173; Li Tien-min, *Chou En-lai*, Taipei, 1970, pp. 189–90.

12. Chen Chang-feng, 'With Chairman Mao on the Long March', in *Stories of the Long March*, Peking, 1959, p. 5.

13. Smedley, *The Great Road*, op. cit., p. 310.

14. Chen Chang-feng, op. cit., pp. 8, 10, 22 and 39.

15. Payne, *Mao Tse-tung*, op. cit., p. 152, says three of Mao's babies were left, Snow, *Red Star Over China*, op. cit., p. 468, two. Wang Cheng's remark (he says only ten women marched) is in Wales, op. cit., p. 101.

16. Ch'ên, *Mao and the Chinese Revolution*, op. cit., pp. 184 and 198.

17. *Sunday Times*, 4 January 1970.

18. Payne, *Mao Tse-tung*, op. cit., p. 152.

19. Ch'ên, *Mao and the Chinese Revolution*, op. cit., p. 198.

20. 'A Red Woman Fighter – Kang Ke-ching', *Ming Pao Monthly*, Hong Kong, Vol. IV, No. 3, March 1969, p. 40; Wales, op. cit., p. 217.

21. Helen Foster Snow, *Women in Modern China*, op. cit., p. 243; Snow, *Red Star Over China*, op. cit., p. 500; ibid. (first edition only), p. 376; Chu Li-fu, op. cit., pp. 48–9 (where Chu names thirty of the women Marchers); and Ch'ên, *Mao and the Chinese Revolution*, op. cit., p. 190. Kang Ke-ching refers to Hsu Hsiang-chien's organizing 800 women in Szechuan.

22. Shi Buzhi, *Chingkangshan de Fenghuo*, pp. 82–5.

23. Snow, *Red Star Over China*, op. cit., pp. 323–7.

24. ibid., p. 84; Chang Nan-sheng in *Peking Review*, No. 47, 21 November 1975, p. 16.

25. *Ti-erh-tzu Kuo-nei Ko-ming Chan-cheng Shih-chi Shih-shih Lun-tsung*, Shanghai, 1938, pp. 54–65.

26. Snow, *Red Star Over China*, op. cit., p. 84.

27. *Sunday Times*, 4 January 1970.

28. Smedley, *The Great Road*, op. cit., p. 312.

29. Snow, *Red Star Over China*, op. cit., p. 91; Payne, *Mao Tse-tung*, op. cit., p. 162; Cheng Wan-li, *Pa lu-chun Ti Chan-tou-li*, p. 35.

30. Chen Chang-feng, op. cit., p. 60.

31. *Sunday Times*, 4 January 1970.

32. Snow, *Red Star Over China*, op. cit., pp. 204–5; see also Li Chang-chuan in *Ti-erh-tzu Kuo-nei Ko-ming Chan-cheng Shih-chi Shi-shih Lun-tsung*, p. 90.

33. See Dr Fu's reminiscences in Wales, op. cit., pp. 171–3; and Lo Ping-hui's at p. 130, ibid.

34. Smedley, *The Great Road*, op. cit., pp. 310–11.

35. Snow, *Red Star Over China*, op. cit., p. 201.

Chapter 8. Breaking out of the Circle

1. This is Payne's translation, which reads better than that in Chen Chang-feng, op. cit., p. 22.

2. *North China Herald*, 14 November 1934, p. 247.

3. Shi Buzhi, *Chingkangshan ti Fenghuo*, pp. 120–26.

4. *China Quarterly*, No. 40, October 1969, p. 31.

5. These details, and similar topographical ones in the ensuing pages, are chiefly based on Li Chang-chuan, 'Recollections of the 25,000-li Long March', *Ti-erh-tzu Kuo-nei Ko-ming Chan-cheng Shih-chi Shih-shih Lun-tsung*, pp. 91–2; Chu Li-fu, *Erh-wan Wu-chien Li Chang-cheng Chi*, pp. 21–36 and 54–63; and Anthony Garavente, 'The Long March', *China Quarterly*, No. 22, April 1965, p. 89 (and sources cited there, including Lien Chen, *Tsung Tung-nan Tao Hsipei*, although I suspect Garavente places too much reliance on these memoirs of a Kuomintang doctor captured by the Communists a few weeks before the Long March).

6. Smedley, *The Great Road*, op. cit., pp. 311–12. One such force to be left behind was the 34th Division which was cut off when the enemy destroyed the pontoon floating bridge over the Hsiang-chiang River in South Hunan: see Hsu Meng-chiu in Wales, op. cit., p. 65.

7. E.g. Chang Chen – see *China Quarterly*, No. 40, October 1969, p. 31.

8. See e.g. Jurgen Domes, *Vertagte Revolution: Die Politik der Kuomintang in China, 1923–37*, Gruyter, Berlin, 1970.

9. Lien Chen, op. cit., p. 5. Lo Ping-hui of the Red Army vigorously denied this later, telling Nym Wales: 'It is simply nonsense to say, as you say some foreign journalists do, that he [Chiang Kai-shek] tried to divert us into certain provinces.' But Lo went on to concede that 'it is true that we weakened the provincial forces and that he could get control of the provinces by following in our rear and reaping the benefits . . .' (Wales, op. cit., p. 129).

10. Griffith, op. cit., pp. 330–31.

11. 'Resolutions of the Tsunyi Conference', *China Quarterly*, No. 40, October 1969, pp. 32–3.

12. Liu Po-cheng, 'Looking Back on the Long March', *The Long March, Eyewitness Accounts*, p. 207 (supported by Li Tien-yu's article 'Stop the Enemy Forces at the Hsiangkian River' in the same book, p. 5); Wales, op. cit, p. 65; Ch'ên, *Mao and the Chinese Revolution*, op. cit., p. 189. Huang and Whitson estimate that 25,000 men deserted before crossing the Hsiang River during 26 to 28 November.

13. Hsueh Yueh, *Chiao-fei chih-shih*, Part II, p. 3.

14. Garavente, op. cit., p. 106; Braun, 'Von Schanghai bis Jänen', *Horizont* (East Berlin), No. 31, 1969.

15. *China Quarterly*, No. 40, October 1969, p. 12.

Chapter 9. The Kweichow Campaigns

1. Liu Po-cheng, 'Looking Back on the Long March,' *The Long March, Eyewitness Accounts*, p. 208; also in *Peking Review*, No. 45, 7 November 1975, p. 12.

2. Robert W. McColl, 'The Oyuwan Soviet Area, 1927–1932', *The Journal of Asian Studies*, Vol. XXVI, No. 1, November 1967, p. 54, and sources cited in his footnote 29; Chang Kuo-tao, 'My Reminiscences,' *Ming Pao Monthly* (Hong Kong), Vol. IV, Nos. 8, 9 and 10, pp. 76–9, 72–7 and 95–9 (also in *The Rise of the Chinese Communist Party 1928–1938*, Vol. 2 of the Autobiography of Chang Kuo-tao, Chapter 4).

3. Smedley, *The Great Road*, op. cit., pp. 313–14.

4. Liu Ya-lou, in *Stories of the Long March*, p. 11; see also Warren Kuo in *Issues and Studies* (Taipei), Vol. 4, No. 4, January 1968, pp. 43–4.

5. See Chapter XI below; also Garavente, *China Quarterly*, No. 22, April 1965, p. 106. Braun puts the blame squarely on Mao (*Horizont*, No. 31, 1969).

6. Wales, op. cit., pp. 127–8.

7. The following account of the crossing of the Wu River is derived from Pao Tsun, *Hung-chun Chang-cheng ti Ku-shih*, pp. 6–8; Chu Li-fu, *Erh-wan Wu-chien Li Chang-cheng Chi*, p. 24; Chang Chun-ju (ed.), *Chang-cheng Ku-shih*, pp. 1–5; Liu Ya-lou, 'The Fight for The Wukiang Crossing', in *Stories of the Long March*, pp. 11–22 and *The Long March, Eyewitness Accounts*, pp. 11–21; and Li Chang-chuan, 'Recollections of the 25,000-li Long March' in *Ti-erh-tzu Kuo-nei Ko-ming Chan-cheng Shih-chi Shih-shih Lun-tsung*, p. 95. Since this is the first engagement on the Long March to be described in detail, it may be worth underlining how difficult the details are. Chang, for example, attributes the battle to the Fourth Army Corps rather than the First. The Wu River is variously given as 300 and 250 metres wide, with a flow of 2 or 1.8 metres per second. The precise dates are not agreed. Liu places the length of downstream drift of the successful first raft on the second night at 1,100 yards, Chang at almost two miles. Chang gives the Captain Mao detachment two carbines, Liu only one. The striking of the match is interpreted differently by Chang. The exact strength of the enemy and of its reinforcement is disputed. As for the number of swimmers on the first night, Chang says ten, Chu and Liu (also Hsin Ko, *Erh-wan-wu-chien Li Chang-cheng* eighteen, Pao twenty and Li twenty-two. Many of these

discrepancies are insignificant, but I list them here in full to illustrate the pitfalls of the attempt to describe such incidents truthfully. If we had some enemy accounts as well, the contradictions would be even worse. Having said this, I shall draw attention in the pages that follow only to the most significant conflicts in the evidence.

8. Wang Chi-cheng, 'How We Stormed Tsunyi', in *Stories of the Long March*, p. 23.

9. I.e. European foreigners, presumably Russian Communists.

10. *Stories of the Long March*, pp. 28–33. A slightly different English version of the same original Chinese account is in *The Long March, Eyewitness Accounts*, pp. 22–8.

Chapter 10. Second Thoughts at Tsunyi

1. Various dates are given: Chu Li-fu, *Ehr-wan Wu-chien Li Chang-cheng Chi*, p. 24, gives 13 January; so does Li Chang-chuan, *Ti-erh-tzu Kuo-nei Ko-ming Chan-cheng Shih-chi Shih-shih Lun-tsung*, pp. 91–2. The Chu Li-fu and Yu Ku itineraries both give 13 January, but after an unexplained five-day wait at the Liyu dam. Chang Chun-ju (ed.), *Chang-cheng Ku-shih*, p. 5, gives 3 January, while Wang Chi-cheng (*Stories of the Long March*, p. 33) states 5 January. Jerome Ch'ên (*China Quarterly*, No. 40, October 1969, p. 18) argues that the date supplied by the Kuomintang General Hsueh Yueh from his contemporary diary, 7 January, sounds the likeliest (*Chiao-fei Chi-shih*, Part 3, pp. 3 and 7). But most official accounts of the Politburo Conference in Tsunyi place it on 6 to 8 January (*Ta Kung Pao*, Peking, 26 February 1966; *People's Daily*, Peking, 11 January 1967).

2. Smedley, *The Great Road*, op. cit., p. 315.

3. Liu Po-cheng, *Hsing-huo Liao-yuan*, p. 5; Hsueh Yueh, op. cit., pp. 7 and 9. The Communists returned later to Tsunyi, but stayed there twelve days on the first occasion (Hsu Meng-chiu says only a week: Wales, op. cit., p. 66).

4. Hu Chiao-mu, *Thirty Years of the Chinese Communist Party*, Lawrence and Wishart, 1951, p. 35.

5. Most of these details, and the text of the Resolutions, are drawn from Jerome Ch'ên, 'Resolutions of the Tsunyi Conference', *China Quarterly*, No. 40, October 1969, p. 1. Braun (*Horizont*, No. 31, 1969) insists that no written version of the Resolutions was circulated at the Conference itself, and that the version published later was 'edited'.

6. Chi-hsi Hu, e Nua Fu, The Fifth Encirclement Campaign and the

Tsunyi Conference', *China Quarterly*, No. 43, July 1970, p. 31.

7. Snow, *Red Star Over China*, op. cit., p. 115; Warren Kuo, 'The Tsunyi Conference', *Issues and Studies* (Taipei), Vol. 4, No. 5, February 1968; Dieter Heinzig, *China Quarterly*, No. 42, April 1970, p. 131; and Chi-hsi Hu, op. cit.

Chapter 11. The Politburo Reshuffle

1. Wetzel, *Liu Shao, Le Moine Rouge*, Denoël, Paris, 1961, p. 166.

2. *Chugoku Kyosanto-shih*, Tokyo, 1961, Vol. IV, pp. 260–61. As in the preceding chapter, I am indebted for this and many subsequent references relating to the Tsunyi Conference to Jerome Ch'ên, 'Resolutions of the Tsunyi Conference', *China Quarterly* No. 40, October 1969, p. 1; Dieter Heinzig, *China Quarterly*, No. 42, April 1970, p. 131; Warren Kuo, 'The Tsunyi Conference', *Issues and Studies* (Taipei), Vol. 4, Nos. 4 and 5, January and February 1968; Carl K. Wei, 'The Truth about the C.C.P. Tsunyi Conference', *Issues and Studies* (Taipei), Vol. 5, No: 4, January 1969, p. 29 and No. 5, February 1969, p. 20; and Chi-hsi Hu, 'Hua Fu, The Fifth Encirclement Campaign and the Tsunyi Conference', *China Quarterly*, No. 43, July 1970, p. 31.

3. But Snow has recently claimed that Wu Liang-ping was loyal to Mao before the March, and Dr Jerome Ch'ên omits him from his exhaustive list of the Twenty-eight Bolsheviks (see footnote 15 below). Warren Kuo declares (op. cit., No. 4, p. 36) that Liang Po-tai was absent from Tsunyi, in the 'white' areas.

4. *Peking Hung-wei-ping*, No. 2, 1967 (*Survey of China Mainland Magazines*, US Consulate-General, Hong Kong, No. 590) gives eighteen; Kuo Hua-lun and Wei Ke-wei, *Fei-ching Yueh-pao* (Communist Affairs Monthly), Taipei, Vol. X, No. 7, 31 August 1967, and Vol. XI, No. 8, 8 September 1968, give nineteen; Braun says thirty-five to forty (*China Quarterly*, No. 42, April 1970, p. 132) and remarks that 'certainly two-thirds, probably three-quarters' of the Tsunyi conferees were neither Politburo nor even Central Committee members.

5. Ch'ên, 'Resolutions of the Tsunyi Conference', op. cit., p. 19; *Hung-wei Chan-pao*, April 13, 1967, translated in *Survey of the China Mainland Press*, No. 4007 (see Roderick MacFarquhar's note in *China Quarterly*, No. 41, January 1970, p. 113); and Dieter Heinzig, op. cit.

6. Teng's presence and role at Tsunyi became a matter of dispute when he was disgraced in the Cultural Revolution, and he was accused of subsequently adding a nineteenth portrait to the gal-

lery of eighteen participants in the historic conference room, now preserved as a museum in Tsunyi: see *Survey of China Mainland Magazines*, Hong Kong, No. 590, pp. 14–16.

7. Rue, op. cit., p. 270, suggests Chen Yun as an International, but Jerome Ch'ên disagrees and Snow, *Red Star Over China*, op. cit., pp. 458 and 502, regards him as a Maoist, adding that he did participate at Tsunyi. He went to Moscow, disguised as a merchant, via Hong Kong, to report on the Tsunyi deliberations.

8. Chang Kuo-tao tells us that Kai Feng, like Teng Fa and Wang Shou-tao, attended the Maoerhkai Politburo conference seven months later, so their presence at Tsunyi seems a good inference; *Ming Pao Monthly*, Hong Kong, Vol. V, No. 3, March 1970, pp. 78–83, *The Rise of the Chinese Communist Party, 1928–1938*, Vol. 2, p. 412.

9. Warren Kuo, op. cit.

10. *China Quarterly*, No. 40, October 1969, pp. 37–8.

11. Ch'ên, *Mao*, op. cit., p. 15.

12. Snow, *Red Star Over China*, op. cit., p. 514; and Warren Kuo, 'The Conference at Lochuan', *Issues and Studies*, Taipei, Vol. V, No. 1, October 1968, p. 35. Braun states that Mao was given the new post at Tsunyi of Party Chairman, Heinzig, op. cit., p. 132.

13. Wang Chien-min, *Chung-kuo Kung-chan-tang Shih-kao*, Part III, p. 727.

14. 30 April 1968, cited by Carl K. Wei and possibly written by Wang Ming.

15. Snow, *Red Star Over China*, op. cit., pp. 428–9; Rue, op. cit., p. 270. Dr Jerome Ch'ên has compiled, from various sources, the following complete list of the Returned Students or Twenty-Eight Bolsheviks: Chang Chin-chiu, Chang Wen-tien (or Lo Fu), Chen Chang-hao, Chen Shao-yu (or Wang Ming), Chen Yuan-tao, Chin Pang-hsien (or Po Ku), Chu O-ken, Chu Tzu-chun, Ho Tzu-shu, Hsia Hsi, Kuo Miao-ken, Li Chu-sheng, Meng Ching-shu, Shen Tse-min, Sheng Chung-liang (who in 1970 was alive and well in Lawrence, Kansas), Sun Chi-min, Wang Chia-hsiang, Wang Hsiu, Wang Pao-li, Wang Sheng-jung, Wang Sheng-ti, Wang Yun-cheng, Tu Ting, Tu Tso-hsiang, Yang Shang-kun, Yin Chien, Yuan Chia-yung, and Yun Yu-jung. It will be noted that Wu Liang-ping, Liang Po-tai and Hsu Meng-chiu do not appear on this list.

16. Snow, *Red Star Over China*, op. cit., p. 508.

17. Swarup, op. cit., pp. 131–6, 245 and 252–6.

18. *Chung-kung Chung-yao Jen-wu*, Peking, 1949, p. 11; Swarup, op. cit., pp. 255–6.

19. Swarup, op. cit., p. 252.
20. *Mao Tse-tung Ssu-hsiang Wan-sui*, April 1967, pp. 44–5, as translated in Ch'en, *Mao*, op. cit., pp. 95–6.
21. *Wo-men ti I-chien-su* (Statement of our views), Shanghai, 1929, p. 23.
22. See Rue, op. cit., p. 269, and Hatano Kanichi, 'Shu Onrai Den' ('Biography of Chou En-lai), *Kaizo*, Vol. XIX, No. 7, 1937, p. 89. But Hsiao Chin-kuang was one of those purged (inferentially by Chou, because of their loyalty to Mao) during the Lo Ming affair, at least according to one source; *Issues and Studies*, Taipei, Vol. III, No. 10, July 1967, p. 47.
23. Rue, op. cit., p. 270.
24. Chen Jan, *Issues and Studies*, Taipei, Vol. III, No. 10, July 1967, p. 47.
25. ibid.
26. See Rue, op. cit., p. 270, and Heinzig in *China Quarterly*, No. 42, April 1970, p. 132; Li Tien-min, *Chou En-lai*, p. 186. A Red Guard publication later criticized Peng for 'colluding with Liu Shao-chi, Chang Wen-tien, Huang Ke-cheng and Yang Shang-kun' to question Mao's leadership after Tsunyi (*Ching-kangshan and Kuantung Weni Chanpao*, Canton, 5 September 1967, translated in *Survey of China Mainland Press*, Hong Kong, No. 4047, p. 9).
27. Snow, *Red Star Over China*, op. cit., p. 514 (my italics); Heinzig, op. cit., p. 133.
28. Ch'ên, *Mao and the Chinese Revolution*, op. cit, p. 189; Chi-hsi Hu, op. cit.
29. Snow, *The Battle for Asia*, op. cit., pp. 283 and 287.
30. Hsiao San, *Chang-cheng (The Long March)*, quoted in Nashimoto Yuhei, *Shu Onrai* (Chou En-lai), Keisoshobo, Tokyo, 1967, pp. 148–51.
31. *China Quarterly*, No. 40, October 1969, pp. 20–21.
32. Wales, op. cit, p. 67.
33. *Chung-kung Chung-yao Jen-wu*, Peking, 1949, p. 11.
34. Swarup, op. cit., p. 257.
35. *Mao Tse-tung Ssu-hsiang Wan-sui*, April 1967, pp. 44–5 (quoted in Ch'en, ed., *Mao*, op. cit., pp. 95–6).
36. Op. cit., p. 272. Hsu Meng-chiu recorded afterwards that the chief strategists after Tsunyi were Mao, Chou En-lai, Wang Chia-hsiang and Liu Po-cheng (Wales, op. cit., p. 67), significantly omitting Chu Teh.
37. *Hung-hsing*, No. 29, 18 February 1934, p. 4.
38. *Red China*, No. 288, 30 August 1934.

39. *Hung-hsing*, No. 62, 30 August 1934, p. 1.
40. Rue, op. cit., pp. 272–3.

Chapter 12. A Feint in Yunnan

1. Snow, *Red Star Over China*, op. cit., pp. 191 and 432; and Snow, *Random Notes on Red China*, op. cit., p. 100.
2. Sheng Li-yu, *Chung-kuo Jen-min Chieh-fang-chun San-shih-nien Shih-hua*, Tienstien 1959, p. 23; Liu Po-cheng, *The Long March, Eyewitness Accounts*, op. cit., p. 207.
3. Snow, *Red Star Over China*, op. cit., p. 192, and Smedley, *The Great Road*, op. cit., p. 315, both say 20,000, but Lien Chen, *Tsung Tung-nan Tao Hsi-pei*, Ming Yueh, 1938, p. 22, says 4,000 to 5,000, and Hsu Meng-chiu in Wales, *op. cit.*, p. 67, says 4,000. Huang and Whitson say 10,000.
4. Paul K. Whang, 'Szechuan – Hotbed of Civil Wars', *China Weekly Review*, 22 October 1932, p. 344. The discussion in the text at this point owes much to Garavente, *China Quarterly*, No. 22, April 1965, pp. 107–13.
5. Snow, *Red Star Over China*, op. cit., pp. 234–5; and Snow, *Random Notes on Red China*, op. cit., p. 61.
6. Chu Li-fu, op. cit., p. 25.
7. ibid.
8. ibid.
9. ibid., Part IV, Chapter 6.
10. Li Chang-chuan, *Ti-erh-tzu Kuo-nei Ko-ming Chan-cheng Shih-chi Shih-shih Lun-tsung*, pp. 91–2.
11. *China Reconstructs*, October 1965, p. 15.
12. As translated in Ch'ên, *Mao and the Chinese Revolution*, op. cit., p. 334. Ch'en dates the poem in January 1935, when the Loushan Pass was first taken, but Tsai Shun-li's memoir connects the poem with the second battle of Loushan Pass in February (*China Reconstructs*, October 1965, p. 15).
13. Tsai Shun-li, op. cit., p. 16; Shih Feng, 'Red Army's Four Operations Across the Chihshui River', in *Study and Criticism*, No. 1, Shanghai, January 1975; also Chun Ta in *Peking Review*, No. 49, 5 December 1975, p. 14.
14. Li Chang-chuan, op. cit., pp. 95–7.
15. Smedley, *The Great Road*, op. cit., p. 316. The newspaper report was by the Reuters correspondent Thomas Chow and was dated 9 April 1935.
16. Smedley, *The Great Road*, op. cit., p. 314.
17. ibid., p. 317.

18. Snow, *Red Star Over China*, op. cit., p. 192.
19. ibid., pp. 192–3.
20. *The Long March, Eyewitness Accounts*, pp. 214–15; also *Peking Review*, No. 45, 7 November 1975, p. 14.

Chapter 13. *The River of Golden Sand*

1. 'Crossing the Golden Sand River', *Stories of the Long March*, pp. 35–50. A slightly different English version of the same account is found in *The Long March, Eyewitness Accounts*, pp. 47–60.
2. *Stories of the Long March*, pp. 1–4.
3. Pao Tsun, *Hung-chun, Chang-cheng ti Ku-shih*, Shanghai, 1956, pp. 11–12. See also Liu Po-cheng's description in *The Long March, Eyewitness Accounts*, op. cit., pp. 214–15.
4. Wales, op. cit., p. 69.
5. Smedley, *The Great Road*, op. cit., p. 317; Li Chang-chuan, op. cit., p. 97.
6. Snow, *Red Star Over China*, op. cit., p. 193.
7. Wales, op. cit., pp. 69 and 129.
8. Ch'ên, *Mao and the Chinese Revolution*, op. cit., p. 191. Hsu Meng-chiu's date for the crossing is 15 May (Wales, op. cit., p. 70).

Chapter 14. *The Land of the Lolos*

1. Smedley, *The Great Road*, op. cit., p. 318.
2. Chang Nan-shang, *Peking Review*, No. 47, 21 November 1975, p. 19.
3. Chu Li-fu, op. cit., p. 28. The passage that follows owes much to Chu's account.
4. ibid., pp. 27–8; Hsu Meng-chiu in Wales, op. cit., pp. 65 and 70.
5. See the accounts of this also in Pao Tsun, op. cit., p. 13; and Smedley, *The Great Road*, op. cit., pp. 318–19.
6. Hsiao Hua, 'Crossing the Greater Liangshan Mountains', *The Long March, Eyewitness Accounts*, op. cit., pp. 76–80.
7. Chu, op. cit., p. 28; Wales, op. cit., p. 71.
8. Snow, *Red Star Over China*, op. cit., p. 195.
9. Lt.-Col. Aerhmuhsia, 'The Yis Meet the Red Army', *Stories of the Long March*, op. cit., pp. 105–18 (a slightly different English translation of the same original is in *The Long March, Eyewitness Accounts*, pp. 61–73). Nym Wales says that one of the Lolo recruits whom she saw in Yenan two years later had blue eyes (op. cit., p. 230).
10. Liu Po-cheng, 'Looking Back on the Long March', *The Long March, Eyewitness Accounts*, op. cit., p. 215.

Chapter 15. The Heroes of the Tatu River

1. Smedley, *The Great Road*, op. cit., p. 25.
2. ibid., p. 29.
3. ibid., p. 320.
4. As the crow flies: Snow, *Red Star Over China*, op. cit., p. 197, says 400 li or 130 miles, and Smedley, *The Great Road*, op. cit., p. 320, gives 140 miles. Other sources give 300 or 320 li.
5. *Hsing-huo Liao-yuan*, p. 139.
6. Snow, op. cit., p. 196. Sun Chi-hsien, another senior officer with the vanguard, gives a slightly less dramatic account in his article 'The Forced Crossing of the Tatu River', *The Long March, Eyewitness Accounts*, op. cit., pp. 86–7, suggesting that the version told to Snow may have grown in the telling. See also Wales, op. cit., pp. 71–2.
7. Chu Li-fu, op. cit., p. 29, says 40 metres a second – clearly an error!
8. General Yang Teh-chih, 'Heroes of the Tatu River', *Stories of the Long March*, op. cit., pp. 51–60; see also the more detailed reminiscence of Sun Chi-hsien, op. cit.

Chapter 16. The Bridge of Iron Chains

1. Snow, *Red Star Over China*, op. cit., p. 197.
2. ibid.
3. Chu Li-fu's account says that this was a four-day march from Anshunchang, beginning on 27 May and ending on 30 May. *Erhwan Wu-chien Li Chang-cheng Chi*, op. cit., p. 30. He says the vanguard went via Haierhwa to camp at Tienwan on the first night. Next day it climbed Menghu ridge and camped at Mohsimien after covering 120 li. On the third day it passed through Chu Nipa and camped at Shangtienpa. On the final day it reached Luting via the Hsiatien dam.
4. Yang Cheng-wu, 'The Fight At Luting Bridge', *Stories of the Long March*, pp. 61–76 (a variant translation is 'Lightning Attack on the Luting Bridge', *The Long March, Eyewitness Accounts*, op. cit., pp. 96–109).
5. ibid., p. 198.
6. Smedley, *The Great Road*, op. cit., p. 321.
7. ibid., p. 44; Wales, op. cit., p. 72.
8. *China Reconstructs*, October 1935, p. 19.
9. Tsai Shun-li, op. cit., Hsu Meng-chiu in Wales, op. cit.
10. Snow, *Red Star Over China*, op. cit., p. 198.
11. Wales, op. cit.

12. Smedley, *The Great Road*, op. cit., p. 321. Tsai Shun-li (op. cit.) -says the assault leader was Company Commander Liao Ta-chu but he also says this hero's cap caught fire when the bridgehead was set on fire so he could not have fallen from the bridge before the kerosene phase.

13. ibid., p. 322; Payne, *Mao Tse-tung*, p. 159.

14. Smedley, op. cit., p. 321.

Chapter 17. The Great Snow Mountain

1. Chen Chang-feng, 'With Chairman Mao on the Long March,' *Stories of the Long March*, op. cit., pp. 7–8.

2. Smedley, *The Great Road*, op. cit., p. 323.

3. ibid., pp. 323–5.

4. ibid., p. 324.

5. Snow, *Red Star Over China*, op. cit., p. 200.

6. Payne, *Mao Tse-tung*, op. cit., p. 160; Warren Kuo, in *Issues and Studies* (Taipei), Vol. 4, No. 6, March 1968, p. 43.

7. Wales, op. cit., p. 65.

8. Payne, *Mao Tse-tung*, op. cit., p. 160; Ch'ên, *Mao and the Chinese Revolution*, op. cit., p. 192.

9. Smedley, *The Great Road*, op. cit., p. 325.

10. ibid., pp. 325–6.

11. 'Across the Snow Mountain', *Stories of the Long March*, op. cit., pp. 79–84.

12. As translated in Ch'ên, *Mao and the Chinese Revolution*, op. cit., pp. 338–9.

13. Smedley, *The Great Road*, op. cit., pp. 326–7.

14. ibid., p. 328.

15. ibid., p. 327.

Chapter 18. Chilly Reunion

1. *Hsiang-tao* (Guide Weekly), No. 12, December 1922.

2. Ch'ên, *Mao and the Chinese Revolution*, op. cit., p. 192.

3. This and many other details of the march of the Fourth Front Army are taken from Chang Kuo-tao's reminiscences published in the *Ming Pao Monthly* (Hong Kong), Vol. IV, Nos. 8, 9, 10, 11 and 12, August, September, October, November and December 1969, pp. 76–9, 72–7, 95–9, 96–9 and 79–85 respectively, also in Chang Kuo-tao, *The Rise of the Chinese Communist Party*, Vol. 2, op. cit., Chapter 5. Hsu Hsiang-chien's memoir glosses over these events of 1932 and manages to suggest that the evacuation was by choice (Wales, op. cit., pp. 157–8).

4. Chang Kuo-tao, *The Rise*, op. cit., p. 304, Snow, *Red Star Over China*, op. cit., p. 432, says between 50,000 and 60,000. See also Robert W. McColl, 'The Oyuwan Soviet Area, 1927–1932', *Journal of Asian Studies*, Vol. XXVII, No. 1, November 1967, p. 41.

5. 'Resolution on Certain Questions in the History of our Party (20 April 1945)', *Selected Works of Mao Tse-tung*, Vol. III, pp. 191–2; 'Chang Kuo-tao's Reminiscences', *Ming Pao Monthly*, Hong Kong, Vol. V, No. 1, January 1970, pp. 78–9; Warren Kuo, *Issues and Studies*, Vol. 4, No. 6, March 1968, p. 40.

6. Smedley, *The Great Road*, op. cit., pp. 328–30.

7. *Ming Pao Monthly*, Hong Kong, Vol. V, No. 1, January 1970, pp. 80–83; also Chang Kuo-tao, op. cit., pp. 374–7.

8. *Ming Pao Monthly*, Hong Kong, op. cit., and Chang Kuo-tao, op. cit., pp. 378–81.

9. *Ming Pao Monthly*, Hong Kong, op. cit., Chang Kuo-tao, op. cit., pp. 379 and 382, and see also *Issues and Studies*, Taipei, Vol. 4, No. 6, p. 43. Griffith, op. cit., pp. 53–4, estimates that 25,000 of the First Front Army at Moukung had left Kiangsi, 20,000 having joined en route. See also Huang and Whitson.

10. Snow was told the Fourth had recruited about 50,000 (*Red Star Over China*, op. cit., p. 432). Hsu Hsiang-chien told Nym Wales in 1937 that they had 50,000 under arms in the Szechuan soviet and that recruits swelled the numbers to 80,000 at the time it was abandoned (Wales, op. cit., pp. 159–60).

11. Chang's account of the Moukung or Lianghokou Conference is taken from *Ming Pao Monthly* (Hong Kong), Vol. V, Nos. 1 and 2, January and February 1970, pp. 81–2 and 85–6; and Chang Kuo-tao, op. cit., pp. 383–92. The adjective 'stormy' is from Smedley, *The Great Road*, op. cit., p. 330.

12. Snow, *Red Star Over China*, op. cit., p. 432; Warren Kuo, in *Issues and Studies*, Vol. 4, No. 6, March 1968, p. 44.

13. Smedley, *The Great Road*, op. cit., p. 330.

14. Ch'ên, *Mao and the Chinese Revolution*, op. cit., p. 193.

15. *Ming Pao Monthly*, Hong Hong, Vol. V, No. 3, March 1970, pp. 78–83.

16. *Ming Pao Monthly*, Hong Kong, op. cit., and Chang Kuo-tao, op. cit., p. 19. However, another writer was told by Chang that Chou supported Mao at Maoerhkai: Li Tien-min, *Chou En-lai*, op. cit., pp. 192 and 196.

17. Gregor Benton, 'The Second "Wang Ming Line", 1935–38', *China Quarterly*, No. 61, March 1975, p. 61 and pp. 62–5.

18. Snow, *Random Notes on Red China*, op. cit., pp. 61–2 and 74–5.

19. Smedley, *The Great Road*, op. cit., p. 331 (the story of one of the political workers).

20. *Stories of the Long March*, op. cit., p. vii.

21. Wales, op. cit., p. 74. Kang Ke-ching called Huang Ho (ibid., p. 217).

22. *The Long March, Eyewitness Accounts*, op. cit., pp. 218–19.

23. 'Chang Kuo-tao's Reminiscences', *Ming Pao Monthly*, Hong Kong, Vol. V, No. 4, April 1970, pp. 93–6.

24. *Ming Pao Monthly*, Hong Kong, Vol. V, No. 5, May 1970, p. 91; also *The Rise of the Chinese Communist Party*, Vol. 2, pp. 454–5. Jen's list of 'judgements' on the Chang-Mao dispute as given by Chang here ring true.

25. Schram, *Mao Tse-tung*, op. cit., p. 172.

Chapter 19. The Grasslands

1. Ch'ên, *Mao and the Chinese Revolution*, op. cit., p. 194.

2. Smedley, *The Great Road*, op. cit., p. 337.

3. Yang Cheng-wu, 'Crossing the Grasslands under the Instructions of Chairman Mao', *A Single Spark Can Light A Prairie Fire*, pp. 170–76.

4. Chen Hsien-cheng, 'Crossing the Grasslands with a Cup of Green Grain', *People's Daily*, Peking, 3 March 1961; Payne, *Mao Tse-tung*, op. cit., p. 161; and Chu Li-fu, op. cit., p. 35.

5. Li Chang-chuan, op. cit., pp. 99–100.

6. Tan Ching-lin, 'Victors of the Marshes', *Stories of the Long March*, op. cit., pp. 91–8.

7. Liao Hsing-wen, 'A Small Red Army Man in the Long March', *Stories of the Long March*, op. cit., pp. 99–103.

8. Smedley, *The Great Road*, op. cit., p. 338.

9. Chu Li-fu, op. cit., p. 34.

10. Snow, *Red Star Over China*, op. cit., pp. 203–4.

11. Wales, op. cit., p. 73; Snow, *Red Star Over China*, op. cit., p. 264.

12. Smedley, *The Great Road*, op. cit., p. 337.

13. ibid., pp. 339–40.

14. Hsiung Huang, *The Long March, Eyewitness Accounts*, op. cit., pp. 144–5.

15. Kang Cheng-teh, 'Heart for Heart', *Stories of the Long March*, op. cit., pp. 119–22.

16. Smedley, *The Great Road*, op. cit., pp. 337–8; Hsin Ko, *Erh-wan-wu-chien Li Chang-cheng* (but he gives the dates wrongly so may be unreliable on casualty figures).

17. Smedley, *The Great Road*, op. cit., p. 336.

18. Snow, *Red Star Over China*, op. cit., p. 203. Chang Kuo-tao (*Ming Pao Monthly*, Hong Kong, Vol. V, No. 5, May 1970, p. 86) remarks that the Tibetan forces opposing the Red Armies were 'British-trained'.
19. Smedley, *The Great Road*, op. cit., p. 337.
20. Robert Ekvall, *Current Scene*, Hong Kong, 15 January 1965.

Chapter 20. Home and Dry in Shensi

1. Yang Cheng-wu, 'The Battle of Latzukou', *China Reconstructs*, July 1965, pp. 33–7; see also Hu Ping-yun, 'How We Captured the Pass at Latsekou', in *The Long March, Eyewitness Accounts*, pp. 117–23; and J. Chester Cheng, 'The Mystery of the Battle of La-tzu-k'ou in the Long March', *Journal of Asian Studies*, Vol. 31, No. 3, May 1972, p. 593.
2. Li Chang-chuan, op. cit., pp. 100–101.
3. Chen Chang-feng, *Stories of the Long March*, op. cit., pp. 8–10.
4. As translated by Jerome Ch'ên and Michael Bullock in Ch'ên, *Mao and the Chinese Revolution*, op. cit., p. 337.
5. Chen Chang-feng, *On the Long March with Chairman Mao*, Peking, 1959, pp. 66–7.
6. ibid., pp. 69–70. Chu Li-fu gives the date of reaching Wuchichen as 22 October 1935.
7. *A Single Spark Can Light A Prairie Fire*, op. cit., p. 233; Wales op. cit., p. 75.
8. Snow, *Red Star Over China*, op. cit., p. 204; Smedley, *The Great Road*, op. cit., p. 340; Hsu Meng-chiu in Wales, op. cit., p. 76.
9. Smedley, *The Great Road*, op. cit., p. 341
10. Snow, *Red Star Over China*, op. cit., p. 204.
11. ibid., p. 432.
12. Ch'ên, op. cit., p. 199; Snow, op. cit, p. 434. Hostile sources put the figure at only 2,000: see Carl K. Wei in *Issues and Studies*, Taipei, Vol. 5, No. 5, p. 29. Chang Kuo-tao claimed that Mao led about 7,500 men of the First and Third Armies, plus four re-placement regiments from the Fourth Front Army, from Maoerh-kai, to reach Shensi with 'fewer than four thousand men left in the First and Third Armies' (*The Rise of the Chinese Communist Party*, Vol. 2, p. 445).
13. Mark Selden, 'The Guerrilla Movement in North-west China: The Origins of the Shensi-Kansu-Ninghsia Border Region', *China Quarterly*, Nos. 28, October 1966, and 29, January 1967, pp. 62 and 61.
14. Snow, *Red Star Over China*, op. cit., pp. 214–16.

15. *The North-western Provinces and Their Possibilities of Development*, published privately by the National Economic Council, Nanking, July 1934.

16. This and succeeding paragraphs are drawn largely from Mark Selden's work already cited. See also Warren Kuo, 'The United Front', *Issues and Studies*, Taipei, Vol. 4, Nos. 8 and 9, May and June 1968.

17. This appears to be the man referred to in Edgar Snow's account as Chang Ching-fu or Cheng Mu-tao: Snow, *Red Star Over China*, op. cit., p. 212.

18. Selden, *China Quarterly*, No. 29, January 1967, p. 73.

19. Hsu Hai-tung, 'Shen-pei Hui-shih' (Junction in Shensi), *Red Memoirs*, Vol. III, pp. 174–86; *Who's Who in Communist China*, p. 236.

20. Hsu Hai-tung, op. cit., and Selden, op. cit., pp. 74–5. But Snow, *Red Star Over China* (pp. 432–3), states that Hsu Hai-tung left Anhwei with 8,000 and arrived in Shensi with 3,000, to add to Li Chih-tan's 10,000 – giving a combined total as of September 1935 in Shensi of 13,000. Other sources put Liu's strength at this time at 5,000.

21. Selden, op. cit., p. 75.

22. See especially Selden, op. cit., p. 77. Mao's intercession for the Shensi 'rebels' gained one of the few kind words for him from Chang Kuo-tao, *Ming Pao Monthly*, Hong Kong, Vol. V, No. 5, May 1970, p. 90.

23. *Guerrilla Warfare*, as cited in Griffith (trans.) *Mao Tse-tung on Guerrilla Warfare*, Praeger, New York, 1961, p. 55.

24. *Selected Works of Mao Tse-tung*, Vol. I, pp. 161–2.

25. See Ch'ên, *Mao and the Chinese Revolution*, op. cit., p. 199. New recruits enlisted in Shensi, Shansi, Kansu and Ninghsia during 1935–6 probably added together 15,000 regular Red Soldiers to the total: Snow, *Red Star Over China*, op. cit., p. 433.

26. 'The Long March', *China Quarterly*, No. 22, April 1965, p. 123.

27. Howard L. Boorman, 'Mao Tse-tung: The Lacquered Image', *China Quarterly*, No. 16, October 1963, p. 23.

28. C. P. FitzGerald, 'The Long March', *History of the 20th Century*, B.P.C. Publishing, 1969, Vol. 4, Chapter 49, p. 1351.

Chapter 21. The Stragglers Return

1. Liu Po-cheng, 'Looking Back on the Long March', *The Long March, Eyewitness Accounts*, op. cit., p. 221. In one account, Li Hsien-nien and seven other Fourth Army commanders were 'elected' to

the 'Politburo' at the insistence of Chang and Chen Chang-ho at Lianghoko in West Szechuan on 23 June 1936 (*Issues and Studies*, Taipei, Vol. 6, No. 4, January 1970, p. 89).

2. Smedley, *The Great Road*, op. cit., pp. 332 and 334. Hsu Hsiang-chien was equally reticent about Sikang: Wales, op. cit., p. 160.

3. See Garavente, *China Quarterly*, No. 22, April 1965, p. 122; also Warren Kuo, 'The Zig-Zag Flight of Red Army Troops', *Issues and Studies*, Taipei, Vol. 4, No. 10, July 1968.

4. Another account says that Ho Lung joined the C.C.P. during the Nanchang Uprising: see Chou I-chun's testimony in *China Quarterly*, No. 18, April 1964, p. 24.

5. Snow, *Red Star Over China*, op. cit., p. 79.

6. ibid., p. 80.

7. Warren Kuo, 'The Anti-Mao Struggle During the Government 4th Encircling Offensive', *Issues and Studies*, Taipei, May 1967, p. 39.

8. Hsiao Ke's memoir in Wales, op. cit., pp. 139–40; Snow, *Red Star Over China*, op. cit., p. 432; Smedley, *The Great Road*, op. cit., p. 331. Warren Kuo (*Issues and Studies*, Taipei, Vol. 4, No. 4, January 1968, pp. 42–3) declares that Ho Lung's 5,000, supplemented by Hsiao Ke's 1,000 and a further 4,000 local recruits made a joint army of 10,000 at Sangchih. See Chang Kuo-tao, *The Rise of the Chinese Communist Party*, Vol. 2, op. cit., p. 453.

9. Smedley, *The Great Road*, op. cit., pp. 331–2.

10. Quoted in Smedley, *The Great Road*, op. cit., p. 344.

11. Ch'ên, *Mao and the Chinese Revolution*, op. cit., p. 196.

12. See Snow, *Red Star Over China*, op. cit., p. 433. Braun says no more than 6,000 of the Second and Fourth survived, and Wang Shih et al. (p. 58 of English translation) say less than 30,000 of all the armies survived the Long March.

13. Wales, op. cit., p. 148; *Issues and Studies*, Taipei, Vol. 6, No. 4, January 1970, p. 89. The latter account speaks of the 700 survivors of the 30th Army under Li Hsien-nien being received by the Russians at Hami in Sinkiang. Braun's assertion (*Horizont*, No. 33, 1969) that Mao ordered the Fourth into Sinkiang seems absurd.

14. Snow, *Red Star Over China*, op. cit., p. 434; Ch'ên, *Mao and the Chinese Revolution*, op. cit., p. 197.

15. Meng Po-chen, *Return to Humanism*, Hong Kong, pp. 164–7; Warren Kuo, 'The Incidents Concerning Chen Tu-hsiu and Chang Kuo-tao', Part II, *Issues and Studies*, Taipei, Vol. 5, No. 5, February 1969, p. 32.

PART THREE. *The Conquerors*

Chapter 22. From Shensi to Peking

1. Snow, *Red Star Over China*, op. cit., p. 93.
2. Montgomery, op. cit., p. 47.
3. The material and quotations in this paragraph are from Ch'en, *Mao and the Chinese Revolution*, op. cit., pp. 203–7.
4. *The U.S. Diplomatic Papers 1943 – China*, Washington, Department of State, 1957, p. 399.
5. 31 October 1944, by Raymond Atkinson.
6. Ch'ên, *Mao and the Chinese Revolution*, op. cit., p. 343.

Chapter 23. The First Legacy: Discipline

1. Report to the Eighth Congress of the C.C.P., 16 September 1956.
2. Speech of 1 February 1942: Boyd Compton, *Mao's China: Party Reform Documents 1942–44*, University of Washington Press, Seattle, 1952, p. 25.
3. David A. Charles, 'The Dismissal of Marshal Peng Teh-huai', *China Quarterly*, No. 8, October 1961, p. 63.
4. 'Tsunyi Hui-i' (The Tsunyi Conference), *Fei-ching yueh-pao* (Communist Affairs Monthly), Taipei, Issue X, No. 7, 31 August 1967. Kuo was told by Chen Jan (alias Kuo Chien), a participant in the Long March, that Liu attended the Tsunyi Conference in January 1935. But see *China Quarterly*, No. 40, October 1969, p. 19.
5. Chen Chang-feng, op. cit., p. 70.
6. Boorman, 'Liu Shao-chi. A Political Profile', *China Quarterly*, No. 10, April 1962, p. 8. See also Lötveit, *The Central Chinese Soviet Area*, *The Biographical Dictionary of Republican China* (ed. Boorman, Columbia University Press, New York, 1968, Vol. 2. p. 407) states that Liu began the March but 'later left them' for the 'white' areas.
7. Wetzel, op. cit., p. 166.
8. May 1926, cited in Schram, *Mao Tse-tung*, op. cit., p. 91.
9. Ch'ên, *Mao*, op. cit., p. 26.
10. Cited in *China News Analysis*, No. 151, 5 October 1956.
11. 8 May 1963, cited in *Far Eastern Economic Review*, 1 August 1963, pp. 285–7.

Chapter 24. The Second Legacy: The Guerrilla Ethic

1. Wuhan Resolution of 10 December 1958.
2. Han Suyin, *China In The Year 2001*, Watts, 1967, p. 48.
3. *Selected Works of Mao Tse-tung*, Vol. I, p. 120; Vol. II, p. 128.
4. Ellis Joffe, 'The Conflict Between Old and New in the Chinese Army', *China Quarterly*, No. 18, April 1964, p. 118; John Gittings, *The Role of the Chinese Army*, Oxford University Press, 1967.
5. Quoted in the *People's Daily*, Peking, 11 February 1963.
6. Ch'ên, *Mao and the Chinese Revolution*, op. cit., p. 284.

Chapter 25. The Third Legacy: Independence from Russia

1. Lenin, *The Year 1919*, in *Works*, XVI, p. 442 (quoted in Trotsky, *The Third International After Lenin*, New York, 1936, p. 226).
2. But the multiplicity of differing Chinese Communist voices must take some of the blame: see Robert C. North and Xenia J. Eudin, *M. N. Roy's Mission to China*, University of California Press, Berkeley, 1963. See generally Conrad Brandt, *Stalin's Failure in China, 1924–1927*, Harvard University Press, Cambridge, 1958; and Robert C. North, *Moscow and Chinese Communists*, Stanford University Press, 1953.
3. Snow, *Red Star Over China*, op. cit. (first edition), p. 391. The passage appears to have been omitted from the second edition.
4. Charles B. McLane, *Soviet Policy and the Chinese Communists, 1931–1946*, Columbia University Press, New York, 1958, p. 34.
5. Rue, *Mao Tse-tung in Opposition*, op. cit., p. 271.
6. Snow, *Red Star Over China*, op. cit. (first edition), pp. 389–92.
7. McLane, op. cit., p. 176.
8. V. Dedijer, *Tito Speaks*, Weidenfeld & Nicolson, 1953, p. 331.
9. Donald S. Zagoria, *The Sino-Soviet Conflict, 1956–61*, Oxford University Press, 1962; David Floyd, *Mao Against Khrushchev, A Short History of the Sino-Soviet Conflict*, Praeger, New York, 1964.

Chapter 26. The Fourth Legacy: Supremacy of Mao

1. Snow, *Red Star Over China*, op. cit., p. 449.
2. Snow, *Red Star Over China*, op. cit., p. 514; Ch'ên (ed.), *Mao*, op. cit., pp. 15–16.
3. Chang's memoirs were first published in the *Ming Pao Monthly* of Hong Kong in serial form, beginning in 1969, then in *The Rise of the Chinese Communist Party 1921–1927* and *1928–38*, University Press of Kansas, 1971 and 1972.
4. As translated by Michael Bullock and Jerome Ch'ên in Ch'ên,

Mao, op. cit., p. 340. Ch'ên feels the poem was written later, in 1944–5, but I prefer Schram's view that the official attribution of 1936 be accepted (Schram, Mao Tse-tung, op. cit., p. 179).

5. Kai-yu Hsu, Chou En-lai, op. cit., pp. 94–7.
6. Liu Ning, General Report on the Current Situation of the C.C.P., 1938, as cited in Li Tien-min, 'Chou En-lai – A Profile', Issues and Studies, Taipei, Vol. I, No. 9, June 1965, p. 46, and in the same author's Chou En-lai, Institute of International Relations, Taipei, 1970, pp. 224–5. It has been noted that Chou's role in Party affairs between 1932 and 1949 has been ignored in official Party publications and histories since 1949, and that he was absent from most of the rectification meetings in Yenan in the early 1940s because he was representing the Communists at Chungking, headquarters of the united front.
7. Yenan Liberation Daily, 6 August 1943.
8. Warren Kuo, 'The Conflict Between Chen Shao-yu and Mao Tse-tung', Issues and Studies, Taipei, Vol. 5, No. 2, November 1968, p. 35 and No. 3, December 1968, p. 40.
9. Snow, Red Star Over China, op. cit., p. 505; Yin Ching-yao, 'Wang Ming Openly Attacks Mao', Issues and Studies, Taipei, Vol. V, No. 10, July 1969, p. 46.
10. 'Communist China's Intra-Party Dispute', Pacific Affairs, Vol. XXXI, No. 4, December 1958, p. 323.

Chapter 27. Conclusion

1. Wang Teh-ching, 'The Red Army Man's Cap', Stories of the Long March, pp. 85–90.
2. See in particular China Reconstructs, Vol. XXV, No. 1, January 1976 and Peking Review, No. 43, 24 October 1975; also Chang Ching-li, 'An Examination of the Implications of Chinese Communist Celebration of the Long March', in Issues and Studies, Taipei, Vol. XII, No. 1, January 1976, p. 69.
3. Across Rivers and Mountains, by Chen Chi-tung, himself a Long Marcher (see illustrated outline in China Reconstructs, Vol. XXV, No. 1, January 1976, p. 41). The novel is Alexander Cordell, The Dream and the Destiny, Hodder and Stoughton, 1975.

Short Bibliography

Bosshardt, Rudolf A., *The Restraining Hand: Captivity for Christ in China* (London, Hodder & Stoughton, 1936).

Braun, Otto, 'Von Schanghai bis Jänen', *Horizont* (East Berlin), Nos. 30–33, 1969.

Chai Tso-chun, *Tsai Mao-chu-hsi Shen-pien* (With Chairman Mao) (Wuhan, 1959).

Chang Ai-ping, *Tsung Tsunyi tao Tatuho* (From Tsunyi to the Tatu River) (Hong Kong, 1960).

Chang Chun-ju (ed.), *Chang-cheng Ku-shih* (Stories of the Long March) (Hong Kong, Lien Ho, 1954).

Chang Han-ching, *Hsi Chan-chang ti Chu-chiang Chu Te* (Accounts of Chu Te) (Shanghai, 1938).

Chang Kuo-tao, *The Rise of the Chinese Communist Party, 1921–1927 and 1928–1938* (2 vols), Lawrence, University of Kansas Press, 1971 and 1972.

Chen Chang-feng, *On The Long March With Chairman Mao* (Peking, Foreign Languages Press, 1959).

Ch'ên, Jerome (ed.), *Mao* (Great Lives Observed Series) (Englewood Cliffs, N.J., Prentice-Hall, 1969).

Ch'ên, Jerome, *Mao Papers, Anthology and Bibliography* (Oxford University Press, 1970).

Cheng Wan-li, *Pa-lu-chun ti Chan-tou-li* (The Combat Power of the 8th Route Army) (Shanghai, 1938).

Chow Tse-tsung, *The May Fourth Movement* (Cambridge, Harvard University Press, 1960).

Chu Li-fu, *Erh-wan Wu-chien Li Chang-cheng Chi* (The Long March) (Shanghai, 1937).

Garavente, Anthony, 'The Long March', *China Quarterly*, No. 22, April 1965.

Griffith, Samuel B., II, *The Chinese People's Liberation Army* (Weidenfeld & Nicolson, 1968).

Hsiao Tso-liang, *Power Relations Within the Chinese Communist*

Movement: A Study of Documents 1930–1934 (Seattle, University of Washington Press, 1961).

Hsin Ko, *Erh-wan-wu-chien Li Chang-cheng* (Short Account of the Long March) (Tientsin, 1950).

Hsu, Kai-yu, *Chou En-lai: China's Grey Eminence* (New York, Doubleday, 1968).

Hu Chiao-mu, *Chung-kuo Kung chan-tang ti San-shih-eien* (Thirty Years of the Chinese Communist Party) (Peking and London, 1951).

Hu Hua, *Chung-kuo Hsin-min-chu Chu-i Ko-ming-shih* (History of the Revolution of People's Democracy in China 1919–45) (Tientsin, 1950).

Huang Chen-hsai and William Whitson *Communist China's High Command* (New York, Praeger, 1971).

Kung Chu, *Wo Yu Hung-chun* (The Red Army and I) (Hong Kong, Southwinds, 1954).

Kuo, Warren, *Analytical History of the Chinese Communist Party*, 3 vols (Taipei, Institute of International Relations, 1969).

Li Tien-min, *Chou En-lai* (Taipei, Institute of International Relations, 1970).

Lien Chen, *Tsung Tung-nan Tao Hsi-pei* (From the Southeast to the Northwest) (Ming Yueh, 1938).

Liu, F. F., *A Military History of Modern China* (Princeton, Princeton University Press, 1956).

Liu Po-cheng *et al.*, *Hsing-hao Liao-yuan* (A Single Spark Can Light a Prairie Fire) (Hong Kong, San Lien, 1960).

Lötveit, Trygve, *Chinese Communism 1931–1934* (Copenhagen, Scandinavian Institute of Asian Studies, 1973).

McAleavy, Henry, *The Modern History of China* (New York, Praeger, 1967).

McLane, Charles B., *Soviet Policy and the Chinese Communists, 1931–1946* (New York, Columbia University Press, 1958).

Meng Po-chen, *Return to Humanism* (Hong Kong, 1953).

North, Robert C., *Moscow and Chinese Communists* (Stanford, Stanford University Press, 2nd ed., 1963).

Okamoto Ryuzo, *Long March* (Japan, Kobundo, 1965) (in Japanese).

Pao Tsun, *Hung-chun Chang-cheng ti Ku-shih* (The Story of the Long March) (Shanghai, Jen-min Chu-pan-she, 1956).

Payne, Robert, *Mao Tse-tung* (New York, Weybright & Talley, 1969).

Rue, John E., *Mao Tse-tung in Opposition, 1927–1935* (Stanford, Stanford University Press, 1966).

Schram, Stuart, *Mao Tse-tung* (Allen Lane The Penguin Press, 1967).

Schwartz, Benjamin I., *Chinese Communism and the Rise of Mao* (Cambridge, Harvard University Press, 1951).

Selected Works of Mao Tse-tung, Vols. 1, 2 & 3 (Peking, Foreign Language Press, 1965), Vol. 4 (1967).

Sheng Li-yu, *Chung-kuo Jen-min Chieh-fang-chun San-shih-nien Shih-hua* (Thirty Years of the Chinese People's Liberation Army) (Tient-sin, 1959).

Shi Buzhi, *Chingkangshan de Fenghuo* (Hong Long, Ng Hing Kee, 1964): pseudonym for Kung Chu, q.v.

Smedley, Agnes, *Battle Hymn of China* (Gollancz, 1944).

Smedley, Agnes, *The Great Road, The Life and Times of Chu Teh* (New York, Monthly Review Press, 1956).

Snow, Edgar, *Random Notes on Red China* (Cambridge, Harvard University Press, 1957).

Snow, Edgar, *Red Star Over China* (Gollancz, 1937 and 1968).

Snow, Edgar, *The Battle For Asia* (New York, Random House, 1941).

Snow, Helen Foster, *Women in Modern China* (The Hague, Mouton, 1967).

Stein, Gunther, *The Challenge of Red China* (London, 1945).

Stories of the Long March (Peking, Foreign Languages Press, 1958).

Swarup, Shanti, *A Study of the Chinese Communist Movement, 1927–1934* (Oxford, Clarendon Press, 1966).

The Long March, Eyewitness Accounts (Peking, Foreign Languages Press, 1963).

Ti-erh-tzu Kuo-nei Ko-ming Chan-cheng Shih-chi Shih-shih Lun-tsung (Articles on the History of the Revolution) (Peking, 1956).

Tsao Po-i, *The Rise and Fall of the Chinese Soviet in Kiangsi 1931–4* (Taipei, National Chengchi University, 1969).

Wales, Nym, *Red Dust: Autobiographies of Chinese Communists (as told to Nym Wales)* (Stanford University Press, 1952).

Wang-Shih, Wang Chiao, Ma Chi-ping and Chang Ling, *A Brief History of the Chinese Communist Party* (Shanghai, People's Publishing House, 1958 – mimeograph translation by U.S. Joint Publications Research Service, Washington, D.C. 1961).

Wang Yung-hsing, *Chingkangshan Toucheng Ku-shih* (Accounts of the Revolutionary Base at Chingkangsham) (Peking, 1957).

Yeh Huo-sheng, *Hsien-tai Chung-kuo Ko-ming Shih-hua* (Manual of Chinese Revolutionary History) (Peking, 1951).

Appendix A

The Command line-up at the start of the Long March

CENTRAL REVOLUTIONARY MILITARY COUNCIL

Chairman: Chu Teh
Vice-Chairmen: Chou En-lai, Wang Chia-hsiang
Commander-in-Chief: Chu Teh
Chief of General Staff: Liu Po-cheng
Director of the Political Department: Wang Chia-hsiang
(succeeded by Li Fu-chun when Wang wounded)

	Central Column	Cadre Corps	I Army Corps	III Army Corps	V Army Corps	IX Army Corps
Commander	Chou En-lai	Chen Kung	Lin Piao	Peng Teh-huai	Tung Cheng-tang	Lo Ping-hui
Political Commissar	Lo Mai	Sung Jen-chiung	Nieh Jung-chen	Yang Shang-kun	Tsai Shu-fan	Ho Chuang-kuang
Chief-of-Staff	Chang Yun-yi	Pi Shih-ti	Tso Chuan	Teng Ping[2]	Chen Po-chun	Chang Tsung-sun
Commissioner of Political Protection Bureau	Teng Fa[1]		Lo Jui-ching	Yuan Kuo-ping[3]	Li Cho-jan	Wang Shou-tao
Director of Central Personnel Corps for Local Work			Wu Liang-ping	Kuo Chien[4]	Teng Cheng-hsun	Feng Hsueh-feng
Director of Political Department			Lo Jung-huan	Chang Ching		

1. Teng Fa was the Chief of the Political Protection Bureau.
2. Teng Ping was killed at Tsunyi and succeeded by Yeh Chien-ying.
3. Yuan was succeeded, according to Chen Jan (per Warren Kuo), by Liu Shao-chi as Director of the Political Department of the III Army Corps, but this is impossible to believe.
4. Kuo Chien is the man whose *alias* is Chen Jan and who became the chief informant for Warren Kuo's accounts of the Long March in *Issues and Studies* (Taipei).
5. There was also the VIII Army Corps, commanded by Chou Kun with Ho Ke-chuan as Political Commissar.

SOURCE: Warren Kuo, 'The Tsunyi Conference', *Issues and Studies* (Taipei), Vol. 4, No. 14, January 1968, pp. 37–9.

Appendix B

The Daily Itinerary of the Long March

ROUTE OF THE VANGUARD I ARMY CORPS OF
THE FIRST FRONT ARMY
(*Daily Mileage in parentheses*)

This itinerary is for the I Army Corps only, and not the main body of the First Front Army; it differs in detail, though not in broad outline, from the latter's route where the vanguard carried out evasive, distractionary or reconnaissance actions. The miles are converted from *li* by taking three *li* to the mile and rounding off fractions. They add up to a round 6,000 miles (18,088 *li*).

The final syllable of a place name often helps to identify it, and translations of the most common ones in the list are as follows:

cheng city	*ling* (mountain) range	*shui* river
chiao bridge	*miao* temple	*ssu* temple
ho river	*pa* dam	*tang* pond
hsien county	*pao* fortress	*tien* palace
kang ridge	*pin* (river) bank	*to* or *tu* ferry
kiang river	*pu* hollow	*wan* bay
kou or *kuan* pass	*shan* mountain	*yu* ruins

Some – but not all – of the names will be found in the maps.

Sources: (1) Yu Ku, 'The Itinerary of the Long March of the Red Army', *I-ching*, Shanghai, 20 July 1937, pp. 40–4: (2) Chu Li-fu, *Erh-wan Wu-chien Li Chang-cheng Chi* (The Long March), also published in Shanghai in 1937, pp. 54–63.

October 1934

16 Tunglowan – Shanwangpa (10). 17 Shanwangpa – Tzushan – Hsiayu (23). 18 Hsiayu – Tangtsun – Hsinshe (23). 19 Hsinshe (0). 20 Hsinshe – Shuangwan (20). 21 Shuangwan – Yenhsiang – Hsintien (20). 22 Hsintien – Shihpei – Taping (30). 23 Taping – Hsiashan – Shihtsaiyu (30). 25 Shihtsaiyu – Laochiehtzuyu (30). 26 Laochiehtzuyu – Nienching – Sanchiangkou (30). 27. Sanchiangkou – Hsiaohsi – Nantsun (30). 28

Nantsun – Pingtouyao – Yianyu (30). 29–30 Yianyu (0). 31 Yianyu – Niupikeng – Niehtu (30).

November 1934

1 Niehtu – Chiuniukuang – Lipiling (30). 2 Lipiling – Leiling – Chenshe (27). 3 Chenshe – Pachiutien – Sanchiangkou (30). 4 Sanchiangkou – Yangkuyao – Chengkou (7). 5 Chengkou – Hsintien (20). 6 Hsintien – Santsaichi – Makeng (27). 7 Makeng – Yaoshan – Shanghsikeng (30). 8 Shanghsikeng (0). 9 Shanghsikeng – Tawangshan – Taochukeng (23). 10 Taochukeng – Kuanchiachiao – Pengkuling (23). 11 Pengkuling – Shitzupachi – Sanchiehyu (20). 12 Sanchiehyu – Tangtsun – Pingtien (23). 13 Pingtien – Huachuhsia – Paishito (17). 14 Paishito (0). 15 Paishito – Yichang – Meitien (20). 16 Meitien – Chiangshui – Linwu (30). 17 Linwu (0). 18 Linwu – Tienshuipu – Yangkulingyao (20). 19 Yangkulingyao – Taipingyu – Chuchiayu (27). 20 Chuchiayu (0). 21 Chuchiayu – Tzutangyu – Tientangyu (27). 22 Tientangyu – Paishuitang (10). 23 Paishuitang – Hsiangtzuyuan – Taochou (30). 24 Taochou – Wuliliu – Chiangchialing (20). 25 Chiangchialing – Yungankuan – Hsiangkou (13). 26 Hsiangkou – Wenshih (7). 27 Wenshih (0). 28 Wenshih – Anshanpa – Shihtangyu (23). 29 Shihtangyu – Taipingyu – Shaoshui (20). 30 Shaoshui (0).

December 1934

1 Shaoshui – Meitzuling – Tawan (13). 2 Tawan – Chingmingkuan – Yuchaping (23). 3 Yuchaping – Ssushihtien (20). 4 Ssushihtien – Paimaokuan – Chantou (13). 5 Chantou – Paimaokuan – Henglukou (23). 6 Henglukou – Chayuan (13). 7 Chayuan (0). 8 Chayuan –Wutang – Paichuping (22). 9 Paichuping – Kuangnanchen – Pingteng (23). 10 Pingteng –Pingshi – Liuyen (23). 11 Liuyen – Shuangchiang – Chintien (27). 12 Chintien – Changku – Hsintu (23). 13 Hsintu – Hsinchang – Pingchaso (20). 14 Pingchaso – Liping – Kutun (23). 15 Kutun – Aoyuchu – Papiao (25). 16–17 Papiao (0). 18 Papiao – Potung – Hokou (22). 19 Hokou – Nanpang – Liuchai (22). 20 Liuchai – Nanshao (27). 21 Nanshao – Chienho (17). 22 Chienho – Chungtou – Shangketung (22). 23 Shangketung – Nienyapu – Pienchai (22). 24 Pienchai (0). 25 Pienchai – Pingchai – Wengkulung (22). 26 Wengkulung – Paihsi – Shihping (22). 27–28 Shihping (0). 29 Shihping – Sunchiapu – Laotangchai (25). 30 Laotangchai – Yuching (17). 31 Yuching (0).

January 1935

1 Yuching – Tutiyao – Lunghsi (23). 2 Lunghsi – Liangfengshao – Chingkangyuan (17). 3 Chingkangyuan (0). 4 Chingkangyuan – Wu-

kiangho – Yuchingszu (20). 5 Yuchingszu – Shuanghsiangpu (20). 6 Shuanghsiangpu – Hsinlungchang – Huangchiapa (20). 7 Huangchiapa – Meitan –Chiatzuchang (23). 8 Chiatzuchang – Liyupa (22). 9–12 Liyupa (0). 13 Liyupa – Tsunyi – Ssuchuchan (25). 14 Ssuchuchan – Loushankuan – Tungtzuchen (20). 15 Tungtzuchen – Shihniulan – Shihmenching (22). 16 Shihmenching – Hsinchan – Erhlitzu (22). 17 Erhlitzu – Chingshuihsi – Sungkan (10). 18–20 Sungkan (0). 21 Sungkan – Chientouo – Shihhao (23). 22 Shihhao – Machiapa – Wenshui (20). 23 Wenshui – Liangtsun – Tushuchan (25). 24 Tushuchan – Fengtsun – Shihcheng (27). 25 Shihcheng – Yuanhou (10). 26 Yuanhou – Fenglinyao – Patan (17). 27 Patan – Fenglinyao – Yuanhou (17). 28 Yuanhou (0). 29 Youanhou – Laoyakou – Malupa (27). 30 Malupa – Tientzupa – Lungchaopa (23). Lungchaopa – Chenchiayen – Hsianglanpa (23).

February 1935

1 Hsianglanpa – Tachai (12). 2 Tachai – Yungning (20). 3 Youngning – Chinochih (23). 4 Chinochih – Tapa (20). 5 Tapa – Wutsun (8). 6 Wutsun – Tanchang – Chienwuchen (30). 7 Chienwuchen – Loyangho – Lohai (17). 8 Lohai – Mahotang – Sankoutang (20). 9 Sankoutang – Kuanhsiung (23). 10 Kuanhsiung (0). 11 Kuanhsiung – Hsihoya – Chahsi (20). 12 Chahsi – Taipingshang (20). 13 Taipingshang – Fenshuiling – Panyaho (22). 14 Panyaho – Chienyangkou – Yingpanshan (23). 15 Yingpanshan – Mahsienpao – Shuangtsun (22). 16 Shuangtsun – Shahungkou – Muchiaotun (22). 17 Muchiaotun – Chiunglungchang – Chenlungshan (23). 18 Chenlungshan – Shihhsiakou – Tsoumapa (20). 19 Tsoumapa – Taipingtu – Mayikou (22). 20 Mayikou (0). 21 Mayikou – Fengtsaipa – Tunghuangtien (23). 22 Tunghuangtien – Tushupa – Tashuichiao (20). 23 Tashuichiao – Tingkuchiao – Shuanglungchang (23). 24 Shuanglungchang – Chiutzupa – Hotsun (23). 25 Hotsun – Chiupa – Litzupa (20). 26 Litzupa – Tungtzuchen – Hsiashenmiao (22). 27 – Hsiashenmiao – Szuchuchan – Tsunyi (33). 28 Tsunyi – Liangshuiching (17).

March 1935

1 Liangshuiching – Lomingchen – Chintaokeng (23). 2 Chintaokeng – Paliushui – Tsunyi (22). 3–4 Tsunyi (0). 5 Tsunyi – Paliushui – Tsaihsi (23). 6 Tsaihsi – Tipa (7). 7–8 Tipa (0). 9 Tipa – Tzufeng – Changkanshan (22). 10 Changkanshan – Pingchiachai (10). 11 Pingchiachai (0). 12 Pingchiachai – Shihkeng – Tienpa (17). 13 Tienpa – Chingpa – Yunganshan (20). 14 Yunganshan – Mingkuangszu (17). 15 Mingkuangszu – Kuanyintang – Wengshihpa (13). 16 Wengshihpa – Kuanyintang –

Maotai (17). 17 Maotai – Tsaotzupa (20). 18 Tsaotzupa – Sanyuan-chang – Sanmupa (17). 19 Sanmupa –Tatsai – Yucha (20). 20 Yucha (0). 21 Yucha – Shihhsiakou – Yenfangkou (27). 22 Yenfangyou – Lichia-miao – Anchingshan (23). 23 Anchingshan – Chouchiachang – Huo-shihkang (30). 24 Huoshihkang – Hsintien – Ssufangtu (27). 25 Ssufangtu – Kuanyinszu – Paitien (23). 26 Paitien – Kanhsi – Hoti (23). 27 Hoti – Huamatien – Tipa (20). 28 Tipa (0) 29 Tipa – Wantzuchang – Shatu (17). 30 Shatu – Yuanshan – Wukiangho (20). 31 Wukiangho – Niuchang – Wangchiaping (17).

April 1935

1 Wangchiaping – Hsiaolungwo (13). 2 Hsiaolungwo – Laoyaho (13). 3 Laoyaho – Paimatung – Tiwopa (27). 4 Tiwopa – Machang – Yang-chang (23). 5 Yangchang – Linpokang – Kaochai (12). 6 Kaochai – Kangchai (10). 7 Kangchai – Laopahsiang (23). 8 Laopahsiang – Kuan-yinshan – Shaokuantien (30). 9 Shaokuantien – Huntzuchang – Chi-changpu (27). 10 Chichangpu – Shangmassu – Tingfanchen (27). 11 Tingfanchen – Kusung – Yangmaochang (20). 12 Yangmaochang – Kechin – Supeichiao (20). 13 Supeichiao – Pache (17). 14 Pache – Chu-chang (23). 15 Chuchang – Tzuyunhsien – Laya (23). 16 Laya – Paho-yang – Yangchia (27). 17 Yangchia – Pankiang – Lachih (27). 18 Lachih – Kaochai – Talan (23). 19 Talan – Peihsiang (27). 20 Peihsiang – Tunchiao – Yangshihtun (23). 21 Yangshihtun – Hsiapa – Kuan-yinshan (30). 22 Kuanyinshan – Chuchang (27). 23 Chuchang – Huangniho – Paiyunching (27). 24 Paiyunching – Hsiaoyangchang – Kuantang (20). 25 Kuantang – Yingshang – Hsiliushui (7). 26 Hsili-ushui – Chutzuchieh (27). 27 Chutzuchieh –Mahungchung – Chitou-tsun (28). 28 Chitoutsun – Malungchen – Tsaohsiehchiao (28). 29 Tsaohsiehchiao – Yilungchen – Sungming (27). 30 Sungming – Chi-chia – Lengshuikou (23).

May 1935

1 Lengshuikou – Chima (47). 2 Chima – Huachiao (33). 3 Huachiao – Maanshan – Wutuho (30). 4 Wutuho – Hsiachili (27). 5 Hsiachili – Talapo (7). 6 Talapo – Lungchieh – Makou (37). 7 Makou – Pingti – Shatan (33). 8 Shatan – Chungwushan – Chinshakiangpin (33). 9 Chinshakiangpin – Tungan (17). 10 Tungan – Wangchengyao – Kuan-yinchiao (27). 11 Kuanyinchiao – Tachiao (13). 12–13 Tachiao (0). 14 Tachiao – Fenshuiling – Yunmawan (20). 15 Yunmawan – Chin-chuanchiao (33). 16 Chinchuanchiao – Anshouho – Tehchang (33). 17 Tehchang – Chiakoutang – Wangshuitang (27). 18. Wangshuitang – Chennanszu (27). 19 Chennanszu – Lichou – Tukuanchung (23). 20

Tukuanchung – Hsilung – Luku (27). 21 Luku – Mafangkou – Mienning (23). 22 Mienning (0). 23 Mienning – Tachiao – Towu (28). 24 Towu – Hsiaoputzu (27). 25 Hsiaoputzu – Hsinchang – Anshunchang (20). 26 Anshunchang (0). 27 Anshunchang – Haierhwa – Tienwan (27). 28 Tienwan – Menghukang – Mohsimien (10). 29 Mohsimien – Chunipa – Shangtienpa (33). 30 Shangtienpa – Hsiatienpa – Lutingchiao (20). 31 Lutingchiao – Lungpafu – Pushuiching (27).

June 1935

1 Pushuiching – Taokou – Santaochiao (17). 2 Santaochiao – Nitou – Huchuangchieh (20). 3 Huchuangchieh – Kanchushan – Tachiao (23). 4 Tachiao – Hsinmiaotzu – Shihping (20). 5 Shihping – Hsiaohotzu – Chenchiapa (20). 6 Chenchiapa – Tashenhsi – Liuchiakou (13). 7 Liuchiakou – Shihyang (8). 8. Shihyang – Shihpataota – Lushanhsien (40). 9 Lushanhsien – Hunchiapa (8). 10 Hunchiapa – Shuanghochang – Hsiaokuantzu (23). 11 Hsiaokuantzu – Paohsinghsien (20). 12 Paohsinghsien – Tachihkou – Fengtungya (27). 13 Fengtungya – Tachiaochi (27). 14 Tachiaochi – Chiachinshan – Tawei (40). 15 Tawei – Kuanchai (15). 16 Kuanchai – Moukung (15). 17 Moukung – Liangshuiching – Pachiao (20). 18–22 Pachiao (0). 23 Pachiao – Fupien (17). 24 Fupien – Lianghokou (23). 25 Lianghokou (0). 26 Lianghokou – Huangtsaoping (10). 27 Huangtsaoping – Mengpishan – Chokochi (33). 28 Chokochi (0). 29 Chokochi – Mamuchiao – Somo (27). 30 Somo – Matang (23).

July 1935

1 Matang – Kangmiaossu (19). 2 Kangmiaossu – Tapanling – Chaitou (27). 3 Chaitou – Tsangte (23). 4–5 Tsangte (0). 6 Tsangte – Takuling – Taku (23). 7 Taku – Tolokang (33). 8 Tolokang – Tachulin (33). 9 Tachulin – Limassu (30). 10 Limassu – Maoerhkai (3). 11–28 Maoerhkai (0). 29 Maoerhkai – Changfang – Latzuling (15). 30 Latzuling – Changfang – Maoerhkai (18). 31 Maoerhkai (0).

August 1935

1 Maoerhkai – Kaying (23). 2 Kaying – Chaliko – Hsiaolamassu (23). 3 Hsiaolamassu – Polotzu (13). 4–6 Polotzu (0). 7 Polotzu – Heishuiho (10). 8–17 Heishuiho (0). 18 Heishuiho – Chaliko – Hsiaolamassu (23). 19 Hsiaolamassu – Kaying (23). 20 Kaying – Maoerhkai (23). 21–22 Maoerhkai (0). 23 Maoerhkai – Chihsingchiao – Latzutang (23). 24 Latzutang – grasslands – Fenshuiling (23). 25 Fenshuiling – grasslands – Houho (27). 26 Houho – grasslands – Tatsaoti (23). 27 Tatsaoti

– grasslands – Hsiaoshenlin (23). 28 Hsiaoshenlin – Panyu – Pahsi (17).
29 Pahsi – Ahsi (7). 30–31 Ahsi (0).

September 1935.

1 Ahsi (0). 2 Ahsi – Maolung (20). 3–4 Maolung (0). 5 Maolung –
Kuangli – Ochieh (30). 6–11 Ochieh (0). 12 Ochieh – Chiaochissu (17).
13 Chiaochissu – Manti (20). 14 Manti – Watsangssu (23). 15 Watsangssu – Shihmen – Moya (13). 16 Moya – Heila (23). 17 Heila –
Latzukou (30). 18 Latzukou – Talashan – Hsuanwo (40). 19 Hsuanwo –
Luyuanli (12). 20 Luyuanli – Hayuanpu (12). 21–22 Hayuanpu (0).
23 Hayuanpu – Luching (80). 24 Luching – Hsinssu (33). 25 Hsinssu –
Yuanyangchu (17). 26 Yuanyangchu – Panglochen (30). 27–28 Panglochen (0). 29 Panglochen – Tungwei (30). 30 Tungwei (0).

October 1935

1 Tungwei (0). 2 Tungwei – Wangchiaho – Ssutzuchuan (20). 3 Ssutzuchuan – Hungssuerh – Hungchiatachuang (23). 4 Hungchiata-
chung – Kaochiapu (10). 5 Kaochiapu – Hsienshengmiao – Changchiachi (33). 6 Changchiachi – Huangfutzufu – Changyipu (23). 7
Changyipu – Chingshihchu – Naichiaho (23). 8 Naichiaho – Paiyang-
chen – Puchihyao (23). 9 Puchihyao – Chenchiawan (30). 10 Chenchiawan – Sancha (30). 11 Sancha – Heichiayuan – Suchiawan (17). 12
Suchiawan – Maochiachuan (33). 13 Maochiachuan – Chenchiawan
(23). 14 Chenchiawan – Miaochiaho – Hungtechen (30). 15 Hungtechen – Tsaochiawan – Kungchiawan (15). 16 Kungchiawan – Miaochiaho – Mukuachen (20). 17 Mukuachen – Chouchiahsiaochung –
Tsochiayaoshan (20). 18 Tsochiayaoshan – Tienpeihou – Tiehpienchen
(20). 19 Tiehpienchen – Mahsingchuang – Wuchichen (20). 20
Wuchichen (0). 21 Wuchichen – Tuchiataotzu – Tangerhwan (13).

Appendix C

Dramatis Personae

THE principal enemy of the Chinese Communists on the Long March was Chiang Kai-shek, President and Generalissimo of the Republic of China, and leader of the ruling Kuomintang or Nationalist Party (in succession to Sun Yat-sen, its founder), with his headquarters at Nanking.

The most important Kuomintang Generals who fought the Red Army on the March were Chen Chi-tang, Chiang Ting-wen, Chou Hun-yuan, Ho Chien, Ho Kuo-kuang, Hsueh Yueh, Hu Tsung-nan, Kuo Chu-tung and Liu Chien-hsu.

The leading provincial warlords and their generals who engaged the Communists during the March were Wu Chi-wei in Kwangsi province; Hou Chih-tan, Yu Kuo-tsai and Wang Chia-lieh in Kweichow; Yang Hu-cheng in Shensi; Liu Hsiang, Liu Wen-hui and Tien Tsung-yao in Szechuan; and Lung Yun in Yunnan.

The Westerners who appeared early on the scene in the Communist base at Yenan after the Long March, and who recorded information on it, would provide in themselves a fascinating study. Edgar Snow (1905–72), a Missouri-born American journalist who had been reporting from China for the *Chicago Tribune, New York Herald Tribune, Daily Herald* and other journals since the early 1930s, was the first to reach Mao Tse-tung's headquarters in Shensi in the summer of 1936 and wrote *Red Star Over China* on the basis of that four-month visit.

His wife, Helen Foster Snow (who wrote under the pen-name Nym Wales) followed him in 1937 and wrote *Red Dust* and *Women in Modern China* partly from material gained from that experience. Snow and Wales were both idealistic young Americans, Chinese-speaking and in full sympathy with the frustrations of their Chinese peers. Later they divorced: Snow revisited China in 1960 and 1964-5 and 1970-71, while Wales has retired in the U.S.A.

Agnes Smedley (1893–1950) was also born in Missouri, but came to China by way of a youthful interest in Indian nationalism and corresponded for the *Frankfurter Zeitung* in the period 1928–33. In 1937 she visited Yenan and undertook a biography of Chu Teh (*The Great Road*).

A list, in alphabetical order, of the Communists who played the leading roles in the Long March now follows.

Braun, Otto: see Li Teh.

Chang Kuo-tao (1897–   ): born in Kiangsi of landlord family; active in May Fourth Movement; delegate to the First National Congress of the C.C.P.; leader of the Fourth Front Army during its march from the Oyuwan base area; challenged Mao's leadership at the Moukung and Maoerhkai conference; and defected to the K.M.T. in 1938. Retired to Canada.

Chang Wen-tien (1898–   ): alias Lo Fu; born in Shanghai of prosperous peasant family; well-known writer and translator who joined the C.C.P. in 1925; one of the Russian-trained 'Twenty-eight Bolsheviks'; General Secretary of the C.C.P. from Tsunyi until 1943; ambassador to Moscow 1951–5 and continued to hold important posts afterwards even though his Russian-trained associates were denounced.

Chen Shao-yu (1904–74), alias Wang Ming: born in Anhwei of prosperous peasant family; joined the C.C.P. in 1925; leader of the Twenty-eight Bolsheviks; General Secretary of the C.C.P. 1931–2; C.C.P. Comintern representative in Russia 1932–7; returned to China in 1937 but was repeatedly criticized by Mao's faction for his policies in the early 1930s; received no real responsibilities after 1949 and has since returned to Russia.

Chen Yun (1900–   ): born in Shanghai; little formal schooling; joined the C.C.P. around 1924; elected to the Central Committee in Kiangsi in 1934; apparently supported Mao at Tsunyi but went to Russia in 1935; returned to China in 1938; after 1949 was Vice-President of the Central Committee and held high economic planning posts in the government.

Chin Pang-hsien (1907–46), alias Po Ku: born in Chekiang of magistrate family; joined the C.C.P. in 1925; one of the Twenty-eight Bolsheviks; General Secretary of the C.C.P. from 1932 until the Tsunyi conference; later edited the official C.C.P. newspaper in Yenan; killed in a plane crash during the civil war.

Chou En-lai (1898–1976): born in Chekiang of gentry family; studied in Japan and France; deputy director of the Whampoa Academy's political department; held high party and military posts in Kiangsi; became General Political Director of the Red Army after the Tsunyi Conference; became China's first Prime Minister and Foreign Minister after 1949 and remained the country's leading spokesman on foreign affairs.

Chu Teh (1886–1976): born in Szechuan of poor peasant family; travelled and worked in Europe in the early 1920s; participated in the Nanchang uprising; founded the Kiangsi soviet with Mao; Commander-in-Chief of the First Front Army during the Long March; participated in Chang Kuo-tao's Sikang expedition after the Maoerhkai conference; Vice-Chairman of the People's Republic 1950–59 and then chairman of the standing committee of the National People's Congress.

Ho Lung (1896–   ): born in Hunan of poor peasant family; received little formal education but became one of the Red Army's most famous generals as commander of the Second Front Army in the Hupeh–Hunan base area; accompanied Chang Kuo-tao to Sikang after Maoerhkai conference but held high civil and military posts after 1949.

Hsiang Ying (1897–1947): born in Hupeh, orphaned at an early age; became a skilful labour organizer and was one of Mao's two Vice-Chairmen in the Central Soviet Government; did not participate in the March but afterwards became political commissar of the famous New Fourth Army during the post-March struggle with the K.M.T.; killed fighting K.M.T. units in Anhwei.

Hsiao Ke (1909–   ): born of Hunanese mandarin family; participated in the Northern Expedition with Chiang Kai-shek; joined the C.C.P. in 1927; led the VI Army Corps before the March and then joined forces with Ho Lung to form the Second Front Army; held important civil and military posts after 1949.

Hsu Hsiang-chien (1902–   ): born in Shansi; studied at Whampoa and joined the C.C.P. around 1927; did organizational work in Hupeh and eventually became commander of the Fourth Front Army with Chang Kuo-tao; went to Sikang with Chang when his troops were cut off from Mao's column; held top military posts after 1949 and was made a Marshal of China in 1955.

Hsu Meng-chiu: 'official historian' of the Long March; lost both legs as a result of exposure during the March.

Kao Kang (1902–54): born in Shensi of landlord family; joined the C.C.P. in 1926; became Liu Chih-tan's political commissar in the Twenty-sixth Red Army in Shensi; helped Liu create the Shensi–Kansu soviet in 1935; held high party posts in Yenan after the March and was highest-ranking party official in north-east China 1949–53; subsequently transferred to Peking and denounced for trying to set up an 'independent kingdom' in the north-east; committed suicide in 1954.

Li Teh, alias Otto Braun: German Comintern military adviser to C.C.P. in Kiangsi; only European to complete the Long March; denounced by Mao at Tsunyi for tactical errors, returned to Russia 1937; wrote memoirs in East Germany 1968.

Lin Piao (1907–71): born in Hupeh of peasant family; brilliant military tactician; studied at the Whampoa Academy; arrived in Kiangsi with Chu Teh's forces; commanded the I Army Corps on the Long March and was personally loyal to Mao; became Minister of Defence in 1959. The 1969 C.C.P. Congress in effect designated him as Mao's successor. However, he led an abortive rebellion against Mao's policies and was killed in an air crash in Mongolia in 1971 while fleeing to the Soviet Union.

Liu Chih-tan (1903–36): born of Shensi landowning family; joined the C.C.P. in 1925; studied at Whampoa; joined forces with Kao Kang to create the Twenty-sixth Red Army in 1932; helped Kao create the North Shensi base which became the final destination of the March; killed during a Red Army campaign in Shensi.

Liu Po-cheng (1892–   ): born in Szechuan; military education; joined the C.C.P. in 1926; one of the most outstanding Red Army commanders, he led some of the vanguard units on the Long March; went to Sikang with Chang Kuo-tao and arrived in Yenan in 1936; headed the training department of the People's Liberation Army 1954–7 and was made a Marshal of the People's Republic in 1955.

Liu Shao-chi (1900–1974): born of Hunanese peasant family; joined the C.C.P. in Moscow; elected to C.C.P.'s Central Committee in 1927 and became the leading theorist on party organization; participated in part of the Long March; became Chairman of the Chinese People's Republic in 1959 and was the second-ranking party member after Mao until 1966 when he became the main target of the Cultural Revolution and was disgraced.

Lo Fu: see Chang Wen-tien.

Lo Ping-hui (19??–43): commander of the IX Army Corps during the Long March; killed in action.

Mao Tse-tung (1893–1976): born in Hunan of peasant family; mixed classical and modern education; participated in the C.C.P.'s First Congress 1921; directed the K.M.T.'s Peasant Department before the K.M.T.–C.C.P. split in 1927; founded the Kiangsi soviet with Chu Teh; established his leading position in the party at Tsunyi during the Long March and became undisputed leader of the Communist movement after Chang Kuo-tao's challenge failed; Chairman of the C.C.P. and leader of China since 1949.

Nieh Jung-chen (1899–): born in Szechuan of poor peasant family; studied in France and then Russia; joined the C.C.P. in 1923; Army at Whampoa; became Political Commissar of the I Army Corps in 1932 and held that post throughout the March; became a Marshal of the People's Republic in 1955 and has led many Chinese diplomatic visits abroad.

Peng Teh-huai (1899–): born in Hunan of rich peasant family; joined the C.C.P. in 1928; commanded the III Army Corps of the First Front Army during the March; was a supporter of Mao and one of the most important commanders during the civil war; Minister of Defence 1954–9; dismissed and disgraced then for anti-Maoist and pro-Russian activity.

Po Ku: see Chin Pang-hsien.

Tso Chuan: chief of staff of the I Army Corps on the Long March; killed in action in 1940s.

Tung Pi-wu (1886–1975): born in Hupeh; studied in Japan; one of the founders of the C.C.P.; Principal of the Central Party School in Kiangsi and participated in the March; became a member of the Central Committee and the Politburo; President of the Supreme People's Court 1954–9; Vice-Chairman of the People's Republic since 1949.

Wang Chia-hsiang (1904–): born in Anhwei; graduated from Shanghai University and became one of the Twenty-eight Bolsheviks; member of the Central Committee in 1931 and Director of the Red Army's General Political Department in 1933; participated in the March and continued to hold high party posts afterwards; was Chinese ambassador to Moscow 1949–51 but denounced during the Cultural Revolution.

Wang Ming: see Chen Shao-yu.

Wang Shou-tao (1907–): born in Hunan of poor peasant family; joined the C.C.P. in 1925; worked for the party in Hunan, Shanghai and Kiangsi; during the March was Director of the Political Department of the IX Army Corps; was an alternate member of the Central Committee 1945–56; held various government posts after 1949.

Yang Cheng-wu (1904–): born in Fukien; joined the Red Army during an uprising in southern Hunan in 1927; became Political Commissar of a regiment of the I Army Corps in 1932 and was in the vanguard of the March; member of the National Defence Council 1954–68 and member of the Central Committee 1956–68;

became acting Chief of Staff of the Army during the Cultural Revolution but was later disgraced.

Yeh Chien-ying (1899–   ): born in Kwangtung; became an instructor at Whampoa and joined the C.C.P. in 1924; was Principal of the Red Army College during the March and a supporter of Mao; became President of the P.L.A. Military Academy in 1958; held high party posts during and after the Cultural Revolution; Defence Minister under Chairman Hua Kuo-feng in 1976–7.

Index

MORE ABOUT PENGUINS
AND PELICANS

Penguinews, which appears every month, contains details of all the new books issued by Penguins as they are published. From time to time it is supplemented by *Penguins in Print*, which is our complete list of almost 5,000 titles.

A specimen copy of *Penguinews* will be sent to you free on request. Please write to Dept EP, Penguin Books Ltd, Harmondsworth, Middlesex, for your copy.

In the U.S.A.: For a complete list of books available from Penguins in the United States write to Dept CS, Penguin Books, 625 Madison Avenue, New York, New York 10022.

In Canada: For a complete list of books available from Penguins in Canada write to Penguin Books Canada Ltd, 2801 John Street, Markham, Ontario L3R 1B4.

EDGAR SNOW

RED CHINA TODAY
The Other Side of the River

In *Red China Today*, Edgar Snow returns to the country he described in *Red Star Over China*, and in a detailed and absorbing survey shows it developing under Communist rule through 'enormous difficulties' towards nuclear power.

For this new Pelican edition the author has substantially revised his 'vast, panoramic survey', which 'has the advantage of a long perspective and of a true knowledge of conditions in China in the past. His book can be recommended as much the most honest and sympathetically written account of what change in China means in actual relief of human suffering and not just in the material sense, but in relief from the misrule which China has suffered as far back as living memory goes. His book ranges far and wide in time and space, often recalling the past and analysing the present, interspersed with racy descriptions' – *The Times Literary Supplement*

SOME BOOKS ON CHINA PUBLISHED IN PENGUINS